DESIGNING
& BUILDING YOUR
OWN HOUSE YOUR
OWN WAY

DESIGNING & BUILDING YOUR OWN HOUSE YOUR OWN WAY

written and illustrated with line drawings by

SAM CLARK

photographs by Thorsten Horton

Houghton Mifflin Company · Boston

*To the New Hamburger Cabinetworks,
Cambridge, Massachusetts, the New Hamburger
Community, Plainfield, Vermont, and
to Amy and Michele*

Library of Congress Cataloging in Publication Data
Clark, Sam.
Designing & building your own house your own way.
Bibliography: p.
Includes index.
1. House construction—Amateurs' manuals.
2. Wooden-frame houses—Design and construction—
Amateurs' manuals.   I. Title.
TH4815.C55   690'.8   78-17228
ISBN 0-395-25486-8
ISBN 0-395-26685-8 (pbk.)

Printed in the United States of America

M 15 14 13 12 11 10 9 8 7

Contents

Introduction   vii

PART ONE   DESIGN   1
1. Choosing a House Site   2
2. Preliminary Design Work   6
3. How to Make Scale Drawings   14
4. Scale Floor Plans   18
5. Elevations and Sections   24

PART TWO   BUILDING BASICS   31
6. The Structure of a House   32
7. Wood   43
8. Heat   51
9. Summer Cooling   55
10. Plumbing and Water Systems   57
11. Post and Beam Construction   67

PART THREE   CONSTRUCTION
             METHODS   73
Introduction   74
12. Foundations   76
13. Floors   94
14. Walls   105
15. Roofs   114
16. Roofing and Flashing   129
17. Windows, Doors, and Shutters   137
18. Siding   154
19. Insulation and Vapor Barrier   162
20. Finish Work   166
21. Stairs   180

PART FOUR   ESTIMATING   189
22. Estimating   190

PART FIVE   ON THE JOB   195
23. Scaffolding   196
24. Using Tools   198

APPENDICES   209
A. Strength of Timbers   210
B. F and E Values for
   Timber Calculations   216
C. Joist, Rafter, Header, Sill,
   and Column Size Tables   221
D. Sun Paths   227
E. Computing Heat Loss   230
F. Sound Isolation   237
G. Wood Preserving   241
H. Bearing Capacities of Soils
   and Bedrock   243
I. Frost Lines   244
J. Snow Loads   246
K. Weights of Various Materials   247
L. Nails and Screws   248

BIBLIOGRAPHY   251

INDEX   255

Acknowledgments

This book is a compilation of knowledge from many different people. Some of the people who contributed directly by reading and criticizing parts of the manuscript are Jules and Helen Rabin, Henry Stone, Larry Duberstein, Bob Oston, Kim Kirchwey, Peter Barrer, Thorsten Horton, Peter Polhemus, Paul Pressman, Carole Neville, Bob Goodman, Margo Jones, Bill Commerford, David Palmer, and David Stein.

The manuscript was typed by Elizabeth Fenton. Jerry Berndt helped with emergency darkroom work. Jim Rader edited the technical material in the appendices.

For permission to photograph their houses, thanks to Norman Bloom, Barry and Lorrie Goldensohn, Julie Graham, Sandy Lillydahl, Polly Rich, Jules and Helen Rabin, Buddy and Barbara Clark, Dave and Pam van de Sande, Pat and Sue Biggam, and the New Hamburger Community.

Anita McClellan of Houghton Mifflin shepherded the project from the beginning with wonderful skill and energy. I should also like to thank Jeff Smith for his copy editing, Joseph F. Weiler for his book design, Louise Noble for her jacket design, Judy Ellis for her proofreading, and Nancy Donovan for the index.

Finally, I would like to thank Dan Breslaw, my friend and co-worker, who spent months working with me on every phase of the manuscript, helping me clarify my thoughts and organize the material. His support, enthusiasm, and advice were invaluable.

Sam Clark

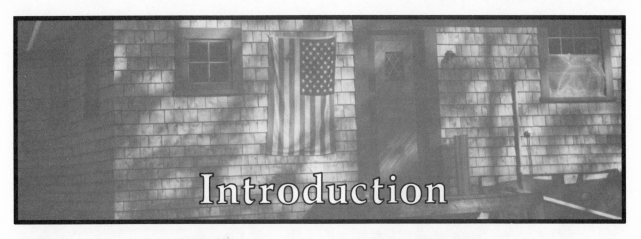

Introduction

This book is about building your own house your own way — not the house I think you need, or that the building industry thinks you need, but what you actually need and can build with your skills, your time, and your money. Throughout this introduction are photographs of houses people have built with varying degrees of help from experienced builders. Most of the houses were designed by their owners. Some of these owner-builders had done small carpentry projects before or had helped friends build houses, but, with one or two exceptions, none were in the building trades, and many were completely inexperienced. I put these photos here to show that inexperienced people can and do build good houses.

PERSONAL HOUSES

The houses in the photographs, and I suspect other owner-built houses you might have seen, don't look like the houses architects design or contractors build from standard plans. They are personal houses, designed to suit the specific needs and tastes of the people who made them.

There are features common to many owner-built houses that set these buildings apart. One is that owner-built houses are often built with different materials than those contractors use. Conventional houses are built with a standard set of products manufactured by large national or international corporations and sold through lumber yards. Lumber will be imported from the forests

House #1. This house was built in four months by a couple working with two and sometimes three part-time paid carpenters. The plumbing and brick fireplace were done by professionals. Outside and most inside finish work was done by the owners gradually over the next two years. Cost: about $16,000.

House #1. Interior view.

of the Pacific Coast, even for a house in Maine, which has huge forests of its own.

Owner-builders use a lot of these products, many of which are very good. But they also use native materials, such as lumber from local sawmills or recycled materials such as old windows and doors, used plumbing fixtures, and lumber from demolished buildings. Also owner-builders sometimes make items such as doors, windows, and cabinets that conventionally are bought ready-made.

Owner-built houses also differ in *design* from conventional houses, chiefly because amateur builders are free to design their houses any way that will work. The layout, roof shape, textures, window shapes, and other details have a very broad range, matched in variety only in the most expensive houses. This variety comes partly from differences in peoples' tastes. It also results from the way owner-builders design their houses, which is very different from the way professionals design.

An architect designing a house for you tries to anticipate rationally what will happen in the house, how it should fit in the land and how peo-

ple will use it. Architects have a whole collection of techniques — particularly drawing techniques — for developing their interpretation. The process is necessarily an abstract exercise, limited by the architect's ability and desire to understand the owner and by business considerations.

A contractor-built house — particularly an economical one — will usually be a standard building designed without reference to the people who use it or the site where it sits. The materials will be those the contractor is most familiar with and which can be installed with minimum labor cost. The design is imposed on the house largely by business considerations and will be an average design for the average customer.

As an owner-builder and designer, you will borrow what techniques and design ideas you can from professionals. But you have other resources too. For one, your knowledge of your own needs is intimate and specific. What's the best place for a kitchen? How many stories should there be? Where should the windows go? You can answer such questions in a way no architect can, and you can include these answers in your design.

When you are building at your site every day,

House #2. Built by three inexperienced people in nine months, with daily advice from an experienced builder. Cost: about $11,000.

and thinking about your new house, you can use a design tool few architects use — improvisation. Many ideas for design improvements will come to you while building. These may be small changes, such as moving a window, or more important ones. You might find, for example, that the extra bedroom should be a detached structure or that the scrubby opening behind the site is actually a beautiful garden in disguise and should be the focus of your house rather than the cold north side with the dramatic view. An architect cannot make such adjustments, because he or she will not be there enough to experience the need for them. A contractor might be there but will be prevented from practicing this kind of creative thinking by the rigid contract's specifications.

Improvisation becomes an even more powerful design tool if you build your house a little at a time. A couple I know built a shed near their proposed building site to live in for the winter until they could begin the real house. That winter they learned that the shed was on the spot best sheltered from the winter winds and was more cozy and attractive than they'd realized. They forgot about their old site and added to the shed. The add-on method works out esthetically too. A house built gradually can have a whole different feel, a fitness and comfortableness in the land hard

to create intellectually on paper. Some old New England farms with attached barns and added-on sheds are examples of good design evolving this way organically over time.

I am not saying everyone should design his or her own house or that a house an architect designs is in any way worse. Often an architect-designed house will be better designed in certain ways. I am saying the two kinds of design methods lead to different kinds of houses, and you may prefer the kind of house you design yourself.

ECONOMY

The other feature that sets owner-built houses apart is that they cost much less. A professionally built house in America in 1977 usually costs $35 or $40 per square foot of floor space. Even a small house can cost $30,000 or $40,000. You can build your own house for about $10 per square foot in materials. Even if you hire people to help you with a lot of the work, you can still build for $15 to $20 per square foot of space. Further, you can eliminate financing costs, which are huge in the long run, by building a small house with savings and gradually adding to it.

The economy occurs partly because you are doing much of the work, since labor is normally about half the cost of a house. You also save con-

House #3. Built by two amateur builders in six months. Cost: about $650.

House #4. Built in five months by a paid crew averaging five in number, one or two of whom were experienced. Cost: about $35,000.

House #5. Built by two people in nine months, with help on roof framing from professional carpenters. Cost: about $17,000.

tractors' and architects' fees, which can account for as much as a quarter of conventional building costs. You also save money by using native or recycled materials. A more subtle economy comes from the fact the house you design can save space by being designed specifically for you. You may not want or need everything that is standard equipment in contracted houses. For example, you might be able to do without a garage or second bathroom or even a living room, if you do most of your entertaining and visiting in the kitchen.

RELATIONSHIPS

Another important difference between a contracted house and one you build yourself is in the relationships between people doing the work. When a contractor builds a house, everybody's role is legally defined and restricted. The architect designs, the contractor supervises, the carpenter builds, the plumber plumbs, and you pay. Each person's area of choice and responsibility is narrow.

With an owner-built house, you have a much broader responsibility. What goes right is to your credit, and what goes wrong is your fault. You must work out gradually who decides what, who does what, and who takes which responsibility. This is very exciting, but not always easy. Since people care so much, conflicts may arise. There can be fights about the design. There can be conflicts when people don't know how to work well together. It may seem odd that people would argue during such an adventure. But two or more people working together on the same house for months on end creates a very close relationship and there will be highs and lows.

REWARDS

Perhaps what most separates building your own house from having one built for you is what you get out of it, the rewards that make the emotional effort worth it. There is the reward of cre-

House #6. A pole house built in three months by two people with occasional professional help. The front wing is a later addition. Cost: about $4500.

ating your house just as you want it, seeing it take shape. There is the reward of physical strengths and new practical skills. More important — at least to me — is the reward of new understanding coming from having built or helped build every part of your house. Having hefted a beam, you know its strength in a way you could not had you merely specified it. Having shingled a wall or hung a door, you will have learned with your two hands why these jobs are done the way they are. This is different from simply knowing in theory that shingles shed water and doors swing on butt hinges. You gain a more detailed and tactile kind of knowledge that will enrich your experience of your own and every house. In other times and places, people had this intimate way of knowing their physical surroundings. We don't. But building a house gives us access to one of the remaining sources of this experience.

RISKS

The fashion in building books is to tell people, by way of encouragement, that building a house is easy. But look at what building a house really means. You are learning and practicing several new skills, each of which people normally spend several years learning. How could this be easy? I have been building about ten years, and I still find it a challenge. Maybe this challenge is what attracts people to doing it for themselves.

If you talk to people who have built houses, you will quickly discover what some of the common risks are. The costs can be more than expected, which will be a serious problem for most people. This can happen because you forget certain materials' costs, because estimates from contractors are wrong, or because you have unanticipated expenses, such as a road or a deep well. Estimating is hard for the professional, so it is no surprise that amateurs have trouble with it.

Also the house can take more time to build than you think it will. This can be particularly serious when you have planned to move in at a certain time and the house is not nearly ready. It

House #6. Interior view.

House #7. Built by a couple for less than $1000 in the 1940s.

is not uncommon for a house to take two or three times the work people expect. When this happens, it is quite a shock.

Another risk is that you will make some irremediable error. My first project as an amateur builder was a house for myself on a site with no readily available water, on a road impassable because of snow in winter and mud in spring. The power line had to come across a neighbor's land, and we had no right of way. The black flies were very bad since the site was overgrown because of

a nearby swamp and because there was rarely a good breeze except in the dead of winter. The house was oriented away from the sun; its windows were too small and faced the wrong way. The roof was shaped to trap rather than shed water.

Making and correcting mistakes is a part of building, even for experts. The mistakes we made were typical of new builders, though the number we achieved was rather spectacular. Errors in construction are usually not too hard to fix. In our

House #7.

House #7. Living room.

case, we enlarged and added windows, added a room facing the sun, cut trees, gradually correcting the house. Real site problems are harder to correct. It can be very expensive to add water, wind, sunlight, or electricity when little are provided by nature or circumstance. One of your most important planning projects will be to make sure the site you choose does not have too many serious problems.

STRATEGIES FOR SUCCESS

Books that make house-building seem easy do amateurs a disservice. The fact is, though the individual tasks of building are easily learned, an entire house is a major project, intrinsically risky for anyone with limited time and money. I want to emphasize not that building is easy but that the difficulties and challenges can be met. You can be in control of the project, instead of the other way around. But to take control you have to go about it realistically. My experience is that building lives up to people's fantasies only when they are hard-headed about it.

House #8. Built by two people over four summers for approximately $6000.

The key, I think, is to follow three strategies. First, use all the resources you can to overcome your inexperience. Two main resources are books and people. The bibliography in this book should be useful. Some of the books help you understand construction techniques. Some focus on design. Some are about the engineering of special systems, such as solar heat. If you're doing your own wiring or masonry, there are books on these subjects too. Don't try to read everything. Find what you want without wading through a lot of irrelevant information.

People are another main resource. Carpenters, designers, farmers, suppliers, and other owner-builders will often be happy to give you information or assistance while you are designing and later when you build. Be looking for such friendly sources of aid so that when you come to a problem, you will know whom to go to for help. How much help you need will depend on how experienced you are. If you have done a significant amount of building, you may only need occasional advice.

If you are really new to building, I suggest you find someone to work with you regularly, beginning when you look at building sites. If money is short, you may only be able to afford somebody to give periodic advice. If possible, hire someone to work with you part or full-time, to help with design and estimating and teach you building skills. You can learn these skills on your own, but an experienced person can show you better and faster ways to work.

Find a person with both design and building experience if possible. An architect with little carpentry experience may lack a sense of what's best for an amateur builder with limited funds. A carpenter with little design experience might show you the usual way when there might be a better way for you. Find someone interested in your building problems, sympathetic to your approach, and easy to get along with. Not every skilled person will be a good teacher for you.

The second essential strategy (and a major emphasis of this book) is to do a lot of advance planning. Planning is a way to learn about build-

House #9. Framed by a paid crew of four in four months and finished by four family members over the next six months. Designed by architect Bob Goodman of Wood Structures, Inc. Cost: about $22,000.

ing and design without learning by mistake. Select your site carefully. Spend a lot of time on design. Check out local laws. Estimate costs. Price materials. Such activities can be done long in advance of actual building. They provide a way of making good decisions and help you think things through. I know many people will find listing and drawing boring when they really want to be building, but planning in advance frees you to concentrate on building later. Paradoxically, careful planning is not restrictive or limiting. When you have methodically thought your way to one solution, it is easier to improvise other equally good ones later. Thorough planning during the winter makes for a more relaxed building experience during the summer.

The third essential strategy is to build a little house at first, and add to it later. If you learn one thing from this book, it should be this: Start small, and you can be sure to get the job done in time. Two rooms completed are of much more use to you than five unlivable rooms. Nothing is more depressing than working all summer on a house

and having nowhere to live in winter because you miscalculated what you could accomplish before the first snowfall.

Starting small allows you to take maximum advantage of the one design tool you have that the professional lacks — your ability to improvise and learn from experience living on the land. Living in your beginning house, you can plan its evolution in the best way. A small beginning house makes it easier to learn basic building skills too. Your mistakes here won't have too broad an effect, and you can approach later additions with confidence and good basic skills. Not everyone will be able to take the add-on approach. If you must build your whole house at once, careful planning becomes even more important.

WHAT'S IN THIS BOOK

This book grows out of my experience, first as an owner-builder, and later as a professional carpenter often working with owner-builders. It elaborates in detail on the somewhat cautious and methodical philosophy I've been expressing in the

House #9. Kitchen.

last few pages. The book provides a method for designing, planning, and building a house for people who want to be in control of the process as much as they can be.

I have tried to make the book comprehensive, and I think you will find it so. I have emphasized the information owner-builders actually look for. I have also emphasized hard-to-find information, because to me nothing is more frustrating than needing the answer to some simple building question and searching dozens of books in vain.

I do not tell you which designs are good or what your house should be like. But I do show in detail how to develop your own design by asking the right questions, and how to use drawing and other design tools to find the design answers appropriate to your needs and building site. Part II provides you with design principles, and the appendices give the technical information you will need to make your design take shape.

This book emphasizes planning information, which is among the hardest information to find.

In particular I have included chapters on how to estimate costs in time and money and how to buy and prepare materials.

I have also included many tricks, shortcuts, and techniques professionals use to increase efficiency and decrease aggravation. For example, chapter twenty discusses finish-work techniques, chapter twenty-three scaffolding, and chapter twenty-four using tools.

The primary emphasis of the book is on economical and ordinary building methods. Economical methods are presented because most people who build their own house don't have much money. It may be less obvious why I emphasize ordinary methods. Periodically, slightly obscure building systems come into fashion that seem to promise tremendous savings in time, money, or both, or that offer the owner-builder other special advantages. Geodesic domes and rammed-earth walls (walls made from compressed soil) are recent examples. However attractive such systems are, in practice people often get in trouble using them

House #10. Built by two people, with occasional help, in one summer for about $1800.

because the materials and systems are not intuitively obvious, the techniques and tools are obscure, and relevant practical advice is hard to come by when problems arise. Usually the money saved is a minor fraction of the total costs and is counterbalanced by extra work.

The first large carpentry job I did was a geodesic dome attached to a house. The dome manufacturer claimed the dome weighed only 4000 pounds, was stronger than a conventional frame, and could be erected in three days. What I wasn't told — and learned by experience over the next six months — was that everything other than the dome shell itself, such as flooring, partitions, and wall surfaces, would take many times longer than normally because in a dome there is not a single square corner or vertical wall to work from.

This book sometimes wanders far from conventional construction methods, particularly when lower costs and broader choices can be achieved. But almost all the building systems shown use ordinary materials, are intuitively understandable,

are easy to learn, and can be accomplished with ordinary building techniques.

EXPERTISE

No matter how much information you collect, you may hesitate just because you are not an expert, and in our world everything is done by experts. But remember that in former times in our culture building houses was something most people knew how to do, an ordinary task, like changing a flat. This is still true in rural America and in less-affluent cultures all over the world. Many of the owner-built houses of the past still exist and are studied in schools of architecture as models of good design. Building your own small house has always been the proper business of ordinary amateurs, sometimes along with help from more skilled neighbors and friends. It is only recently that we have become alienated from the house-building process and turned it over to full-time contractors and architects. Now is a good time to reclaim this basic life activity.

The owner-built bread oven.

PART ONE
DESIGN

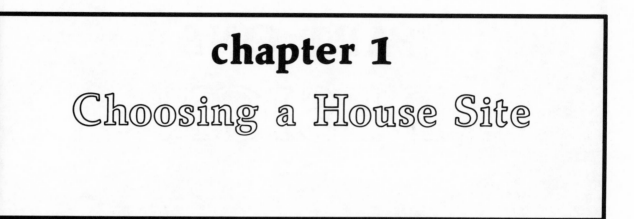

chapter 1
Choosing a House Site

Your site is not only the location of your house, but the source of what makes it livable: water, sunlight, air, wood for heat and lumber, soil for a garden, and other necessities of life. A house is really an outgrowth of the land. A good site will be sunny. It will have good water, preferably nearby and uphill from the house. Electric lines will be close enough so that power can be brought in cheaply. The road will be well maintained and nearby but not so close as to destroy privacy. Perhaps there will be a south-facing slope for a garden and a good wood lot. Such a site helps you build.

A site without these good qualities will cost much more money to build on because the things that are provided free by nature or circumstance on a good site are very expensive when you have to bring them in. It can cost thousands of dollars, for example, to bring water from a remote source or to dig a well. It can cost hundreds of dollars a year extra to heat a house if there is little sunlight. Beyond cost, a house on a poor site will be less of a pleasure to live in. For these reasons, choosing a house site is the most critical decision in the building process.

THINGS TO LOOK FOR IN A POTENTIAL BUILDING SITE

Though no site is perfect, you can do two things to make sure the one you choose will be good. First, evaluate all potential sites systematically, using the procedures given below. Second, when you have found one you like, have someone who knows land and building look at it with you. This is one place where an expert opinion is worth the money because mistakes are costly.

Your evaluation and an expert's take time. And sometimes you must make a decision to buy quickly to keep someone else from buying an obviously good piece of land at a good price. If this happens, you can usually secure the land for a few days for a small, nonreturnable down pay-

ment (often called earnest money) while you inspect the land more thoroughly. You risk losing a few hundred dollars, but you avoid the possibility of losing thousands on an attractive but faulty piece of land.

Water. Availability of water is crucial. You can get your water, without drilling an expensive well, by using a stream or spring. A spring is a place where water surfaces from underground, rather than a place that collects surface run-off. If your land has such a source, you must find out if it can be developed into a good water supply. You can tell a lot by observation. Taste the water. Look around for obvious sources of contamination. Manure, fertilizer, domestic sewage, road salt, animal droppings, and industrial wastes can all contaminate a water supply. Find out where to have water tested, and have a sample from the spring checked. If tests prove that the water is contaminated, find out if the contamination can be eliminated. (If your land has a stream, evaluate it as you would a spring.)

Next, is there enough water? Sometimes your future water supply will be a wet spot in the ground when you first see it. Dig a hole, 2 feet square or so, down past the water level. Take a bucket and quickly remove about 10 gallons from the spring. See how long it takes the spring to refill. If it takes one minute, that's 10 gallons per minute, a large amount of water. If it takes 10 minutes, that's only one gallon per minute. Such a small amount will supply your needs if you can collect it all, although 4 gallons or more per minute is better.

Is the source permanent? Many streams and springs vanish in dry months. The only way to check this is to ask a local expert or look at the source yourself in the dry season.

If you know there is enough good water, next figure out how to bring it to the house. The distance between the source and the house, the depth of the frost line, the relative height of the house and of the source, and the availability of electricity for a pump will all affect the design of a system for a particular water source. Chapter 10 describes different systems for different situations. In addition, get some knowledgeable local advice, because a water system should follow local practices. Study the systems of local farms, because farmers often must construct permanent and reliable systems with limited funds.

If no spring or stream can be developed, you must have a well drilled. Drillers charge around $10 per foot to drill a well, plus $700 to $1000 for the pump and other hardware. You always gamble on the depth at which water will be found; this can be anywhere from 30 to 500 feet. But ask around the neighborhood to get an idea of the depths of typical wells. Find out what drillers charge in your area, and estimate the potential cost.

Electricity.   To find the cost of electric power, measure the approximate distance from the nearest pole to your building site, and then talk to the power company. If the line is to go through the woods above ground, you will have to cut a path for it 30 or more feet wide to keep trees from falling on the line in storms and to facilitate maintenance. While you are at the power company office, ask about a temporary electrical hookup to use while building. Find out when it can be put in, what you must do first, and what it will cost. If your temporary or permanent power must come across a neighbor's land, get a legal right of way before you are committed to that building site. Do not rely on verbal understandings.

Wind.   Ideally, a site will afford you some protection from winter winds while leaving you exposed to cooling summer breezes. Find out as much as you can about wind speed and direction on your site. Usually the prevailing wind will change with the seasons. Call a local radio station to find out typical wind directions in winter and summer, and consult the neighbors. Since your site may vary from the general pattern, put threads or light cloth flags on stakes in one or more spots on your site to observe directly which way the wind blows at different times. Often a site can be improved by cutting trees that obstruct the summer breeze or planting trees to moderate the winter wind.

Access.   If the land you are considering is surrounded by other people's property, make sure you have a legal right of way to it that will meet your needs. But make sure you have physical as well as legal access. Sometimes the best site is in the middle of a piece of land, and you have to build a road to get in. This can be expensive —

especially for a year-round road that must be maintained and plowed. If you need a road built, find out what it will cost.

Find out from neighbors if the public road that leads to your land is passable year-round. If it turns to mud in spring, or is not plowed in winter, find out if the town will maintain and plow it once you move in. In some places towns must upgrade back roads when people build on them.

Sunlight.   When you are looking at building sites, always take a compass. Sunlight comes to you across the southern sky. In winter the sun makes a brief, low trip across the sky from southeast to southwest. In summer it makes a slow, high trip starting in the northeast and ending in the northwest. Appendix D gives the exact range of the sun's path for each latitude. For a house to be light, it must have good southern exposure and some east and west exposure. The southern horizon should not be obstructed too much by woods or nearby hills. A south-facing hill or a level site is ideal from this standpoint. A north-facing hill is poor.

Not everybody will find a perfectly oriented site, and many otherwise excellent sites will have only fair sun exposure. But if sunlight is a priority for you, study the sun orientation of each site carefully. Try to imagine how a house could be built to take advantage of what sunlight there is.

Zoning.   Most places have laws that regulate building. In the Vermont town where I sometimes live, you must build 75 feet from the road and 100 feet from the nearest watercourse. In our zone you must have a lot of five acres, while in other zones you can build on one acre. In the Forestry Zone you can't build at all. In the village itself there are rules that specify how a house must be built, e.g., what kind of plumbing systems can be used. Get copies of zoning laws and building codes from the town clerk. Check the zoning map yourself. Somebody might try to sell you forestry land as a building site or a one-acre lot in a five-acre zone. Also, find out what permits are required.

Drainage.   Good drainage is important if you want your house to be economical to build and maintain. A well-drained site is one that (1) is not subject to flooding in extreme conditions, (2) will not be soggy during the normally wet parts of the year, and (3) has soil that is porous enough to install a well-functioning septic system, if you plan to build one or are required to by local law.

First look at the overall topography at the site. A plain by a river (flood plain) may be subject to floods. If the house site is a valley that collects surface run-off, you may need special drainage to prevent the site from being very wet during the wet season. A depressed area may collect water like a pond and stay wet for months of the year. A flat area, ridge, or gentle grade is most likely to be free of these problems.

If the topography seems good, look at the surface characteristics of the land. If there is a lot of surface erosion, the soil may be too unstable to support the kind of vegetation you want around your house. Do not build in a swampy area either. It can breed bugs, cause your house to settle unevenly, and flood your cellar. A swampy place occurs because the land acts as a basin to trap water, because the ground just below the surface consists of clay or rock, which will not absorb water, or because of springs. Some areas will be dry part of the year, but very wet during the rainy season or during the spring thaw. The presence of cedar trees, ferns, or other swamp vegetation may indicate water problems at other times of the year. This does not mean that any wet place on your land is bad; you need water for plumbing and perhaps for a pond. But the house itself should be on a dry spot.

More and more communities, even in rural areas, are requiring septic systems, which work only in soil that is reasonably well drained. Generally, communities set standards for septic systems and require percolation (perc) tests, which measure the ability of the soil to absorb water. It may be impossible to build on a site if the perc rate is too low. Therefore, if the general topography of a site looks good, your next step is to investigate whether a septic system is feasible by digging some holes in the ground with a posthole digger. These holes will enable you to conduct a makeshift unofficial perc test and also investigate the suitability of the soil for building. Before you do the digging, however, find out what the local regulations are concerning septic systems and what kinds of foundations are permitted. The answers will help you interpret what you find when you dig.

First, imagine where a septic system might be located. This should be an area near the house and even with or below it. The area should be 100 feet away from your water supply and not above it. Local codes will probably require the system to be 100 feet from any stream to avoid pollution. The area should be 500 to 1000 square feet in size, depending on the perc rate and the house size, and fairly level, since a septic system will cost more and work poorly on a steep slope.

When you find a likely spot, dig several holes, 4 to 12 inches in diameter, 2 or 3 feet deep. Dig one of the holes as deep as you can go with the posthole digger. Dig another extra-deep hole in the middle of the spot where you are thinking of building.

The soil that comes out of the holes you dig will tell you what the layers of soil in the ground are like. Feel the soil every few inches with your hand. If you find that it is fine, sticky when wet, and feels like putty, you have found clay, or soil with a high percentage of clay. This can cause several problems. First, clays expand when wet, which can cause the soil to move and basement foundations to crack. Second, clay layers are often impervious to water, so the ground may stay wet and your septic system may not work well. Third, on a sloping site, a clay layer four or more feet down can cause slippage, which occurs when the entire soil surface above the clay slides downhill more or less in one piece.

If you hit bedrock (rather than boulders) you may have other problems. A rock layer can interfere with a septic system. In some towns, you may be required to have six or more feet of soil above the rock to provide 4 feet of soil below the septic system trenches. Rock is impractical to remove for a basement foundation, though a house without a basement can be built easily on rock. When the rock is 4 feet or more down on a sloping site, there can sometimes be slippage just as there can be over a clay layer.

You also have problems if you hit wet soil or if the holes fill up with water. Unless the wetness is caused by recent rains, the ground may drain very poorly or have a high water table. (The water table is the level at which the soil remains saturated with water.) Sometimes local regulations require that the water table be four feet below the septic system (or about seven feet below the surface) in the wet season.

A high water table in any case can cause basement foundations to flood and any type of foundation to settle unevenly or heave up from frost action. If a hole only three or four feet deep hits water you are probably on a bad place to build.

If you find soil below the topsoil that has some proportion of sand or gravel in it, and you do not find clay or water, you probably have a soil that can support the weight of the building and that will be well drained in general.

Continue with your perc test if you haven't hit rock or water by filling the bottom of each hole with about two inches of gravel. Pour at least 12 inches of water into each hole. Add as much water as necessary to maintain the water level for 4 hours, or preferably overnight, particularly in a dry period. The idea is to wet the ground thoroughly, as it would be in a wet season, and then see how well the soil absorbs water. When the soil is saturated, adjust the level to 6 inches above the gravel. Every 30 minutes, measure how much the water level has dropped and fill the hole up to six inches again. Do this for 4 hours. Use the last measurement to calculate the perc rate. With several holes, average the results. Perc rate is expressed in inches per hour. Thus if the water sinks 1 inch in a half-hour, that is 2 inches per hour. One inch per hour is the minimum rate. If the rate is faster, a septic system will cost less and work better.

If your observations show that your potential site may have drainage problems, but you are still interested in building on it, be sure to get advice before you buy the land so you'll know what it will cost to correct the problems. A good source is the United States Soil Conservation Service, or the local Agricultural Extension Service, both of which may have conducted detailed soil surveys of the area. In general, they are experts on local soils. Local designers or builders may also be experienced in solving drainage problems.

Other Resources.   Big softwood trees are good to build with. Big hardwood trees are good for firewood, shade, and perhaps for sale. Old stone walls can be made into fireplaces. Is there a place to build a pond, and water to fill it? And, of course, what does the land look like? A spot may be beautiful, but will it be beautiful after you've built a house on it? Putting a big man-made object in the middle of a beautiful place will often ruin it. Visualize how your house will fit the landscape. Perhaps there will be a dip, corner, or other place where a house will fit without undermining the natural form of the land.

How Much Land?   When looking at a piece of land, don't just think of how big it is or how much it costs per acre. The question should be, how many usable acres are there for the money? How well will the spot suit your specific needs? A hundred acres can cramp you if the only usable place is one acre along the road. Five acres, well placed, can provide privacy and enough land for a small farm. A big forest may have been stripped of all its good wood ten years ago; three acres of good trees may contain more of actual value. A hundred acres of inaccessible backwoods might give less enjoyment than five or ten of varied land. Remember that you don't have to own land to enjoy seeing it or walking through it.

chapter 2
Preliminary Design Work

Having found some land, how do you design a house for it? A common practice is to take an idea of a house seen in a book, in one's travels, or in one's mind's eye, and just put that house on the site chosen. I advocate something different: that you take the information you have about your land, your needs, and your budget, and develop a house design from that. Chapters two through five present a very specific set of steps you can take to do this. If you don't follow every step to the letter, at least consider the questions each one asks. They will make your work simpler and help you avoid major mistakes.

MAKING SITE PLANS

A site plan is a rough map that shows the characteristics of the land and helps you decide exactly where to put your house on it. It is not an accurate map but a schematic sketch. Make one in crayons or markers on a large piece of paper and include such things as:

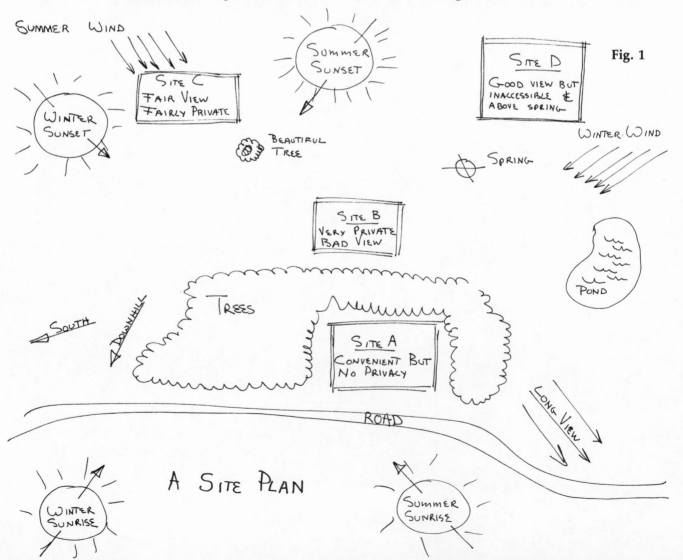

the road
where the water will come from
where the power poles are
possible garden locations
possible sewer locations
woods
direction of slope (fall line)
waterways
driveways
winter sunrise and sunset
summer sunrise and sunset
long views
short views
wind direction, summer and winter
compass points
one or more proposed house sites

Compare the advantages and disadvantages of various locations. In Figure 1 several sites are good, but each has disadvantages, as do most building sites. You must compromise.

Check your prospective site for:

simplicity and cost of a water system
distance to electric power
access
short views
long views
privacy
wind protection in winter
wind exposure in summer
sunlight
drainage
outside space (work or play)
expansibility

LISTING YOUR DESIGN GOALS

Once you have decided on a site, focus on the house itself and how it relates to the site. Begin by listing your design goals and experimenting with the items on your lists. First consider the qualities you might want your house to have:

lots of privacy
skylights
a lot of sun
one (or two) story(ies)
good views
high (or low) ceilings
fireplace
cooking facilities for big groups
expansibility in summer for guests

Your next list should be more specific and include the actual areas you want your house to contain. This should generally not be a list of rooms but of activities and functions:

kids sleeping
adults sleeping
guests sleeping

eating
sitting
studying
reading
home workshop
storing wood
greenhouse
washing
sauna
sewing
sheltering a car
fixing a car
cooking
storing food
root cellar
canning
playing games
roughhousing
playing loud music
being alone
greeting guests
avoiding guests
storing infrequently used possessions

Include everything. This is not the time to be realistic. Activities can be eliminated later if necessary.

Write each activity on small, separate pieces of paper. Shuffle them around in different patterns to see which can be combined. Which functions can occupy the same or nearby space? Which must be isolated? Perhaps you will discover odd combinations that make more sense for you than the usual living room, dining room, kitchen, bedroom, bath arrangement. Perhaps you will want to do your visiting mostly in the kitchen and will not need a separate living room at all. If you need both very quiet and very noisy places, you might be better off with two separate structures. You may want to save money by combining functions:

eat-sit-visit
workshop-noisy games-woodshed-roughhouse
greenhouse-bathroom

Figures 2 and 3 show how to experiment with various options.

Many people do not realize how many choices they have. I am right now designing a house with a family. We're talking about a nucleus of one huge room for eating, visiting, and cooking, with a connected open loft for sleeping. This will be an insulated "warm zone," a concentrated house. In warm weather, when people stretch out and many visitors come, the house will also stretch. Huge barn doors will open up the sides of the house, which will then include large screened-in decks to expand the public area. There will also be non-winterized, easy-to-build, cheap sleeping shelters

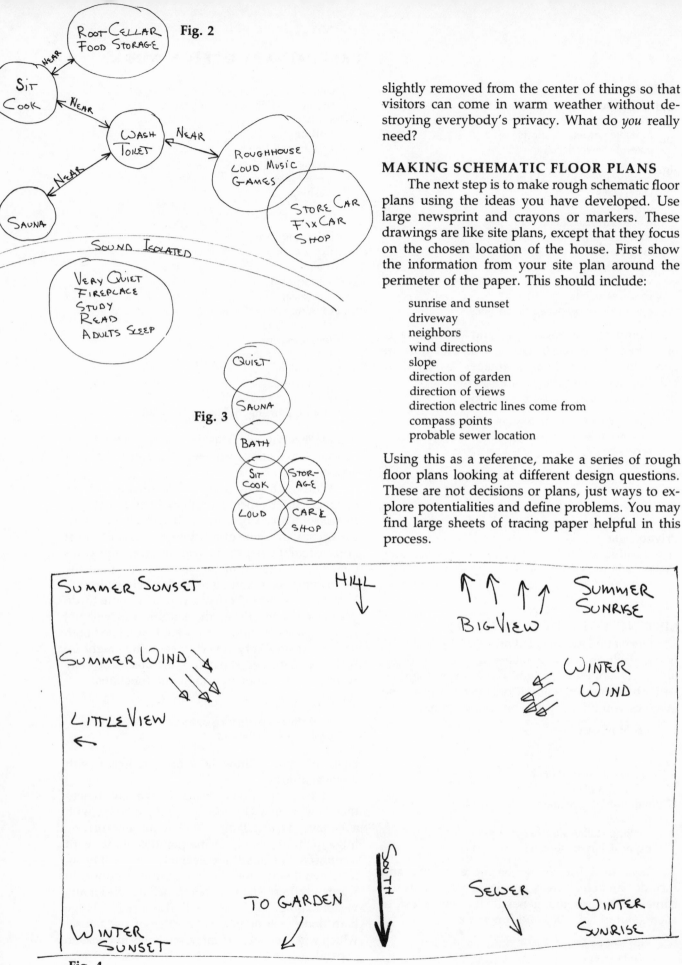

Fig. 2

Root Cellar Food Storage

Sit Cook

Near

Near

Wash Toilet

Near

Roughhouse Loud Music Games

Store Car Fix Car Shop

Near

Sauna

Sound Isolated

Very Quiet Fireplace Study Read Adults Sleep

Fig. 3

Quiet

Sauna

Bath

Sit Cook

Storage

Loud

Care Shop

slightly removed from the center of things so that visitors can come in warm weather without destroying everybody's privacy. What do *you* really need?

MAKING SCHEMATIC FLOOR PLANS

The next step is to make rough schematic floor plans using the ideas you have developed. Use large newsprint and crayons or markers. These drawings are like site plans, except that they focus on the chosen location of the house. First show the information from your site plan around the perimeter of the paper. This should include:

> sunrise and sunset
> driveway
> neighbors
> wind directions
> slope
> direction of garden
> direction of views
> direction electric lines come from
> compass points
> probable sewer location

Using this as a reference, make a series of rough floor plans looking at different design questions. These are not decisions or plans, just ways to explore potentialities and define problems. You may find large sheets of tracing paper helpful in this process.

Summer Sunset

Hill

Big View

Summer Sunrise

Summer Wind

Winter Wind

Little View

South

To Garden

Sewer

Winter Sunrise

Winter Sunset

Fig. 4

Sunlight. Sketch how you want your life on the land to relate to the sun. Do you want the sun to rise into the kitchen, or the bedroom, or set where you can see it while you eat dinner? Arrange areas in the house accordingly (see Appendix D). For maximum sun a house should generally face south.

Fig. 5

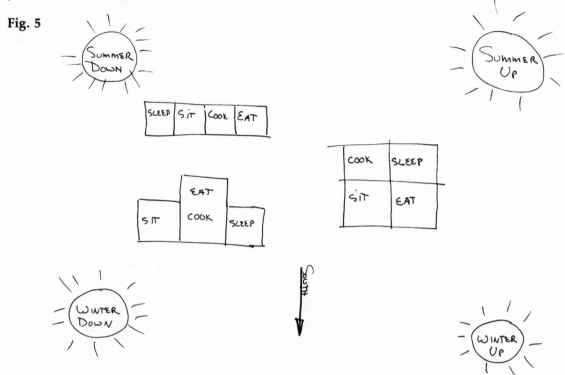

Privacy and proximity. Often the easiest way to create privacy is to separate areas horizontally. Ceilings don't isolate sound very well. Some areas might serve well as transition areas between quiet and loud places.

Fig. 6

Sometimes two buildings is the answer.

Fig. 7

Privacy may also mean separation from the road, or from neighbors, depending on how much privacy you want.

Fig. 8

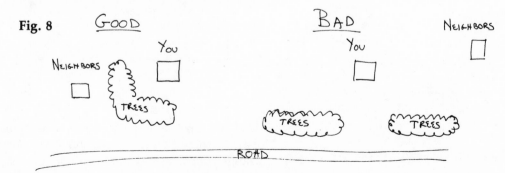

Fig. 9

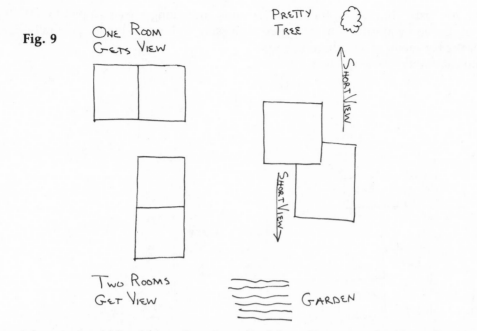

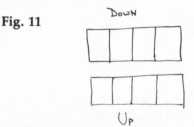

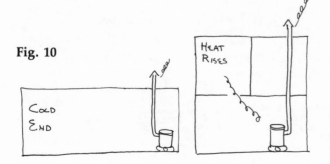

A house should be designed so that people's activities don't conflict, but you also want to have some things close together. Play areas for very small children, for example, should be located where adults can watch the kids. Maybe you want to hear music while cooking, or see who is coming from the kitchen window.

Views.   The view is not just the distant hills. There are medium-range, short, or tiny views that can be just as nice. What would be most interesting to see from where? A particular rock or tree may be the perfect view from a certain bench or stairway. It is better to have a variety of different places to see than to have all windows, floor to ceiling, facing Mount Rushmore (Figure 9).

Number of Stories.   Do you want a one- or a two-story house? One story is more private and easier to build. A two-story house is more work because the further from the ground you get, the more it takes to move workers and materials into place. On the other hand, a two-story house uses fewer materials and heats mord easily, especially if you use wood heat, because the heat from a wood stove moves much more easily up than sideways (Figure 10).

Fig. 10

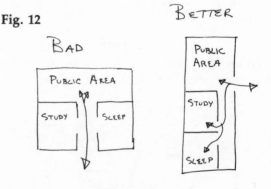

If you are thinking of two stories, your drawings will now come in pairs.

Fig. 11

Traffic Patterns (Circulation).   Architects call the patterns of movement through space *circulation*. You want your house to be designed so that circulation will be efficient, economical of space, and nondisruptive. Make sure that the private parts of the house, such as bedrooms, do not function as hallways to public parts of the house. In fact, it is best if the primary traffic does not even pass near the private areas.

Fig. 12

Public areas will inevitably serve as circulation paths to some extent — and should — but don't arrange your house so that the traffic cuts a specific area in half. It is all right for the traffic to flow through the kitchen, but it should be routed between the cooking and eating areas, rather than right through the middle of one or the other, which would drastically reduce the usable space. Often it is better to create a traffic lane across the corner of a room, or along one wall.

Fig. 13

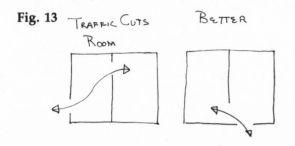

Think about traffic outside too, so you don't carry groceries or firewood halfway around the house before bringing them in.

Fig. 14

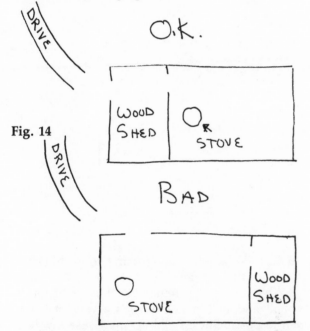

Often a certain part of the house will be given over to circulation. This may be a long hall along one side of the house, a central hallway with the rooms radiating from it, or a hall that winds its way deftly through the house. But just as often it will be simply an area or track defined not by walls, but by doorway locations, furniture position, and the general layout of the house.

A hall or other circulation area can be developed and interesting as well as functional. A hall can be a greenhouse, or have a nice bench to sit and chat on. A stairway can have an odd window to look out of, or be a way to communicate with people, perhaps leading past a sewing area, play yard, or garden.

Fig. 15

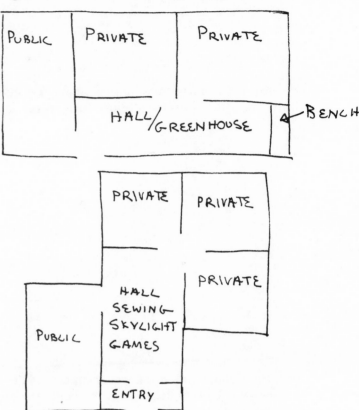

Don't let your circulation plan develop by chance, particularly if your house is big or if many people will use it. Diagram possible plans, rearranging layout, door locations, and other elements until you find an arrangement that seems to work. Some small houses are made even smaller because an unnecessarily large amount of space is given over to traffic movements.

MAKING SCHEMATIC ELEVATIONS AND CROSS SECTIONS

All the drawings you have made so far are plans: they look down on the site. Now make schematic elevation and cross-section drawings, which look at the house from the side. Such sketches can begin with the slope of the land. Then geographical features can be added.

Fig. 16

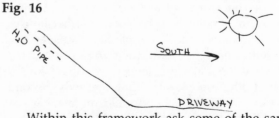

Within this framework ask some of the same questions as in the section on Making Schematic Floor Plans. How will different house shapes use the sun?

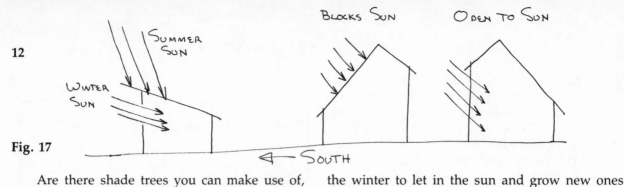

12

Fig. 17

Are there shade trees you can make use of, leafy trees that conveniently lose their leaves in the winter to let in the sun and grow new ones when you need shade?

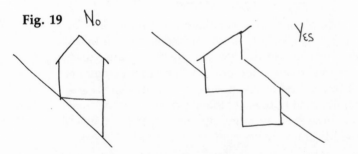

Fig. 18

Think about the general way the house relates to the land. Use the features of the land. Try to come into harmony with it.

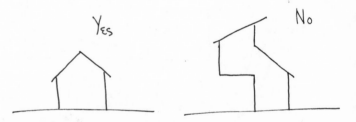

Fig. 19

With these sketches you should be arriving at ideas about the overall shape of your house. It doesn't matter if there are problems. As more thinking and observation of the site go on, some more or less unified idea will suggest itself.

DESIGN STRATEGIES

As you work out a design, keep in mind a few overall strategies. First, observe other houses, especially ones built by people like yourself. Find out what they cost, how they were constructed, and what the major problems were. Become a student of other people's building methods. Second, start on a modest scale and add on later. A season's living on the land will tell you more than fifty pages of drawings. Third, don't let your design ideas become fixed too soon. Keep experimenting. Bring as much information as possible into the process before you commit yourself. Don't build your first design.

While designing, remember that confusion is normal, and in fact helpful. It's a way of being open to possibilities. Building any house involves many, many specific design questions. If these are not included in your thinking early enough, they won't be part of the final solution. Many houses have been built without any regard to the path of the sun. Others have cost twice as much as expected because no attention was paid to cost estimating. Our place in Vermont was built with too little provision for individual privacy. Try to include in your thinking as many factors of this kind as you can. This is the playing-around-with-ideas stage. Consistency — and figuring things out to the eighth-inch — will come later.

MAKING A PRELIMINARY ESTIMATE

You now know a lot about what you want in

a house. But you do not know how much of that you have the capacity to build. This is a good time to determine the scale to think in and build on. If you can afford only three rooms, you should know that so you won't waste time with unrealistic plans you can't execute. Estimating is not easy. In fact, it's harder than building. Things take longer than you think they will, and cost more. The rule is: intentionally overestimate the time and money for any task. Leave yourself room. If you have time and money left over, you can always start something new.

Buildings are measured in square feet of living area. The materials for a good but very economical house cost at current prices about $9* per square foot. Such a figure assumes:

> use of native lumber in general (see chapter seven)
> not too much plywood
> wooden post or concrete pier foundation
> used windows, or windows you build yourself
> wood heat or used space heaters
> no well
> no massive excavation

The following items will send your materials costs up toward $15 per square foot or more:

> central heat
> hardwood floors
> brand-new appliances
> Anderson or other prehung fancy windows
> a well
> fancy lumber

The $9-per-square foot house I am describing is not the house you see on every suburban street. That would cost you more like $40 per square foot if you had it built and $20 per foot to build yourself. The $9-per-foot house will be more like those pictured in the introduction of this book. The economy comes not only from using less expensive and more "raw" materials, but from your ability to plan your house to be economical and your willingness to do without what most people assume to be part of a new house. If you settle for used appliances instead of new ones, you can perhaps save a thousand dollars. If you can do without sliding glass doors, you can save hundreds of dollars. The design priorities that will give you a $9-per-foot house will have to be space, good design, and economy. You must be willing to satisfy your needs the economical way. That way can be

* This figure and the others in this chapter are based on prices listed in 1977, at which time a common 2 × 4 cost .25 or .30 per board foot at lumberyards. To adjust approximately for inflation, find the current 2 × 4 price and increase the figures proportionally.

beautiful, but it may not be in fashion; it will not be what you see in magazines.

If you must build for much less than $9 per square foot, you'll have to use a lot of used or free materials. This might mean tearing down a barn for someone in exchange for the wood in it, or having logs from your own land sawed up for lumber. If your land has good stone, your walls can be built with that. Sod can insulate your roof, and earth your walls. These methods primarily make sense for people with little or no money and a great surplus of time. It takes twice as long to build this way.

In chapter twenty-two you will make a painstaking estimate of your costs. In the meantime, the following chart will help you roughly gauge your total costs:

Rough Estimate of Materials

Item	Cost
Area of house × $9/sq. ft.	
(this means square feet of living space, counting ⅓ of deck area)	
Hardwood floor at $1/sq. ft.	
Central heat by contractor at $1300–$1700 (forced air) $2300 (hot water)	
Well ($10/ft. plus $700 in hardware)	
Basement by contractor at $6–$10/sq. ft.	
Basement by owner at $2/sq. ft.	
Prehung, new windows at $300/room (or $100 each)	
New appliances at $1000	
Long trench for water at .30/ft.	
Fireplace at $1500	
Septic system at $1000	
Plumbing materials $600–$1200	
Electrical materials $350–$500	
Total	$

Total Labor Costs:

Item	Cost
Your living costs while building	
Carpenter, if any, at $6 to $8/hr., or $1000/month	
Plumber, if any, doing all work	$1000
Electrician, if any, doing all work	$300–$500
Total	$

Rough Estimate of Labor. Chapter twenty-two describes a method for approximating how long it will take to build the house you design. For now, since you do not have a design yet, you can assume that it will take about three hours of work per square foot to build your house, if it is fairly simple and the crew consists of both experienced and inexperienced people.

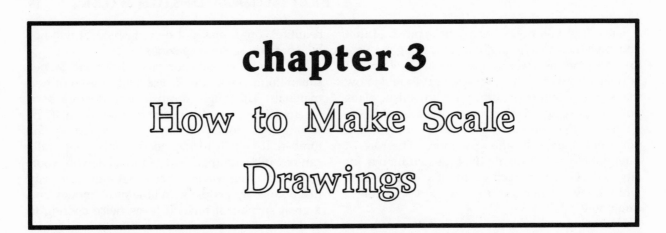

chapter 3
How to Make Scale Drawings

Designing your house will be easier, more thorough, and more under your control if you learn to make and use scale drawings. These drawings will include:

floor plans
elevations (side views) and sections (cross sections)
framing plans, which show parts of the frame of the house
detail drawings, which illustrate construction details not clear from other drawings

You will also need materials lists and cost estimates derived from these drawings.

Making drawings is not just a way to put ideas on paper. It's a way to develop ideas and make them work for you. Basically you make a scale drawing, such as a floor plan, and then systematically ask yourself questions about it. Is the sun orientation good? Is the circulation efficient? Does the layout give enough privacy? Then you revise the drawing — changing dimensions, moving rooms around, moving doors and windows — trying to solve some of the problems. You revise the second version in the same way. This process continues until you have solved as many of the problems as possible, though compromise will always be necessary. When you have finished, your space will be efficient, privacy and communication will be good, views will be visible from the right place, light will come in where it is needed, plumbing will be compact, and so on. If your house has one or two rooms, this drawing process may be quick and easy. But if your house is larger, making drawings will be a major project. This labor may seem excessive when your real interest is not drawing but building, but every hour you spend drawing will save you five hours of building. You can solve problems in advance on paper and avoid big and costly mistakes later. These drawings do not take as long as you might think. With drafting tools and tracing paper you can make a revision in a few minutes, and a dozen revisions can easily be made in a day.

HOW TO MAKE SCALE DRAWINGS

You can make scale drawings using ¼" graph paper, which comes in sheets of various sizes. But this chapter describes how to make drawings with drafting tools. Drafting tools are fairly easy to learn to use. I think making drawings with them is quicker and more versatile. If you decide to use graph paper, you will still find the special ruler

DRAWING BOARD

TAPE HOLDS PAPER DOWN

TRIANGLE SLIDES ON T-SQUARE LIKE THIS

Fig. 20

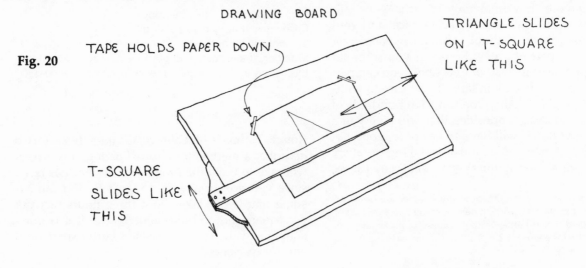

T-SQUARE SLIDES LIKE THIS

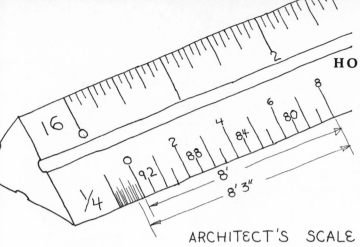

ARCHITECT'S SCALE

Fig. 21

called the *architect's scale* essential.

You will need about $10 worth of drafting tools:

> a piece of plywood for a drawing board
> a T-square
> a 45° triangle
> a 30°-60°-90° triangle
> an architect's scale
> large drawing paper
> tracing paper (same size)
> masking tape
> pencils
> compass
> protractor

Figure 20 shows how these tools are set up. The T-square can be set on the left or right. In either case it slides up and down against the edge of the drawing board and is used like a ruler to guide your pencil making horizontal lines. You can make any number of lines and they all will be parallel.

The triangle rests on top of the T-square and slides side to side to guide you in making vertical lines. Angled lines can be made using the 30°, 60°, or 45° angles on the triangles.

Your drawings need to be exactly in proportion to the building you are planning: they must be in scale. The key to this is the architect's scale, a special ruler that shows dimensions in all the most common scales, such as ¼"=1'. The architect's scale (make sure you do not get an engineer's scale) has eleven different scales on it. Except for the regular ruler scale, there are two on each surface, one starting from each end. If you are using a scale of ¼"=1', you have to use the numbers starting from the end marked ¼.

In Figure 21 the regular ruler scale is at the top, marked 16. The ¼ scale starts at the bottom left with the numbers 0, 2, 4, 6, etc., marking the quarter inches. The high numbers, 92, 88, 84, etc., are the tail end of the ⅛ scale coming down from the other end. The quarter inch to the left of zero is divided into twelve parts, to give you inches when you are using a scale of ¼"=1'. Thus, from 0 to 8 is 8'. From the third tiny line to the left of 0 to 8 is 8'3". Make all your drawings in the same scale so comparing them will be simple.

Figure 22 shows a sketch of a small house and four scale drawings of it. First is a floor plan, with double lines to indicate walls and a single line to

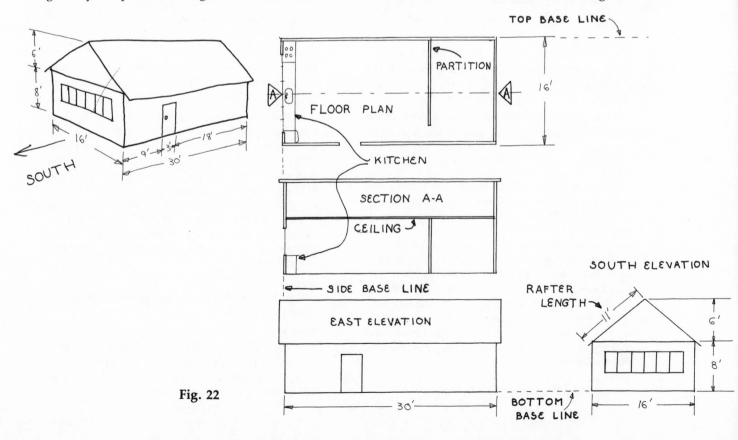

Fig. 22

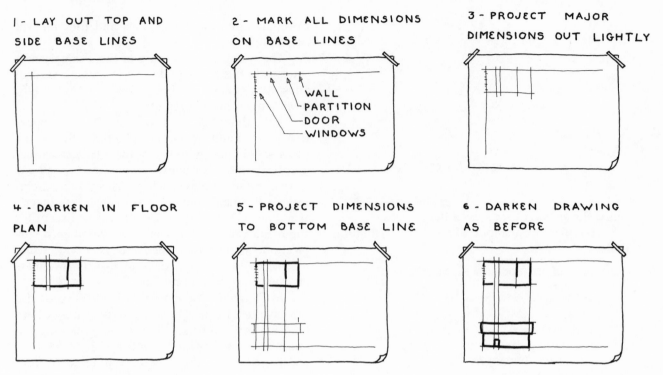

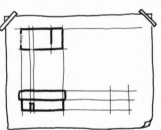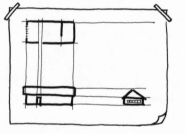

Fig. 23

indicate where the windows are. Beneath it is Section A–A, a cross section of the house through the plane marked A in the plan. At the bottom are two elevations, east and south.

Figure 23 shows a procedure for making these drawings. The same method can be used to draw any building.

Step 1.
Tape the paper down square to the board, and draw the top and a side base line lightly. Everything will be drawn relative to these two lines.

Step 2.
Lay the correct scale on the left-hand base line, with zero at the corner. Mark all the critical east-west dimensions with little light tick marks on the side base line. Tick marks are made not only for the overall size but also for windows, doors, partitions, and other major features. Then put the scale on the top base line, with zero at the corner, and make tick marks for each critical north-south dimension.

Step 3.
Project these lines out with a light line.

Step 4.
With a darker pencil or a stronger stroke, mark in the floor plan with your T-square and triangle.

Step 5.
It is easy to make elevations by projecting from your floor plan in another direction to a new base line. Here I made a bottom base line and transferred the north-south dimensions on the floor plan down to it. The doorway on the elevation is right below the door on the floor plan, and so is everything else. You don't use the architect's scale at all to locate these positions, just the T-square and triangle. Of course the vertical dimensions of the east elevation have to be marked on the side base line using the scale.

Step 6.
When the new elevation is completed, darken it in as you did the floor plan.

Step 7.
You can make another projection from this elevation off to the right to form the basis for the end view of the house. Project the vertical dimensions out to the right with light lines.

Step 8.
Lay out the horizontal dimensions of the end view on the bottom base line, and then complete the drawing like the others.

When you do a lot of drafting, you get so you can lay out several drawings at once. I could have started from the bottom left-hand corner and laid out all four drawings at once, first making the base lines, then all the tick marks, then all the faint lines, and then all the dark lines. Since the drawings are in scale, you can get a lot of information from them by measuring with the architect's scale. For example, in the south elevation the scale can be put right on the roof line to measure the rafter length with enough accuracy for ordering materials. You can also measure hallway widths, headroom over stairs, and other dimensions by putting the scale on the appropriate points.

TRACING

As you are making revisions of your design, you do not have to throw away the old drawings and start over. Instead, mount a piece of tracing paper on the drawing board over the drawing you want to change and quickly reproduce the drawing with new changes.

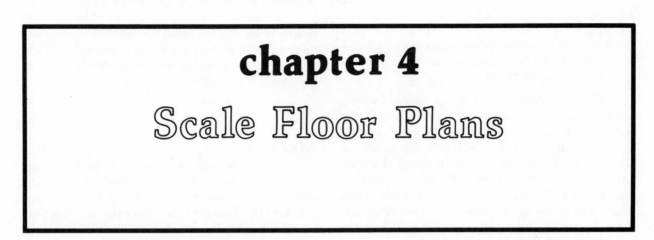

chapter 4
Scale Floor Plans

MAKING A TRIAL FLOOR PLAN

You should only begin scale drawings after you do the preliminary design work in chapter two. Based on this work, you will know quite a few things that will strongly affect your design.

where the road is
where the water comes from
where the electricity comes from
where the views are
the slope of the land
where the sun comes up and goes down
the compass points

You will have made some schematic studies of:

how the house might relate to the sun
what spaces you want in the house
how you might deal with privacy

how you might arrange traffic patterns
what spaces should be separated or nearby each other
what views you want to see from where

You will have thought about possible shapes for the house in relation to the land and made a preliminary estimate of how much space you can build with the time and money you have. Armed with this information, make a trial floor plan in scale. After choosing a particular scale, stick to it. Often ¼″ = 1′ is the most convenient. The first plan can be simply an outline drawing such as Figure 24. The details can go in later.

EVALUATING YOUR TRIAL FLOOR PLAN

Look at your plan with an eye to the following issues, plus others you think of yourself.

Size. Is the house small enough for your budget? Is it big enough for your needs?

Traffic. Is a minimum of space given over to traffic? Is the major traffic directed away from the parts of the house that need to be quiet? Can you easily bring groceries, wood, bicycles, etc., into the house? Are rooms cut up by traffic?

Privacy. Is there enough privacy? Are the private areas sound-isolated by distance, closets, or other types of sound absorption?

Sunlight. You are now ready to determine exactly how the sunlight will fall on the house, as shown in Figure 25. Use Appendix D to find out

Fig. 24

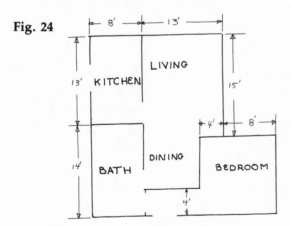

Fig. 25

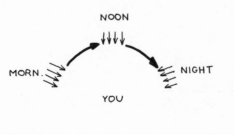

exactly where the sun rises and sets, winter and summer, in your latitude. A diagram of this goes on your drawing together with the compass points.

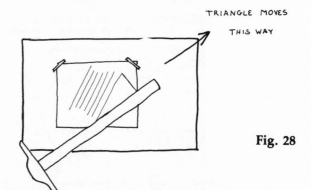

Fig. 28

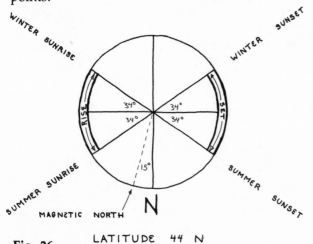

Fig. 26   LATITUDE 44 N

On a copy of your trial floor plan, you can show the maximum sunlight for various conditions. In Figure 27, the parallel lines represent potential sunlight.

Figure 28 shows you how to draw many parallel lines easily.

Views.   Can you see what you want from where you want to see it?

Plumbing Compactness.   One objective in any house design is to keep the plumbing compact to reduce plumbing costs. The kitchen and bathroom pipes should be back to back or one above the other, so they can share the same supply lines, sewer line, and vent.

Storage.   Is there enough space for closets, shelves, cabinets, and other storage?

Simplicity.   Is your design too complex? Jogs in the floor plan, cupolas, skylights, curved walls,

circular staircases, and similar details will extend your building time tremendously. Keep these to a minimum if your time and money are limited. A simple shape is much easier to build.

Your dimensions should also be simple. Lumber comes 8, 10, 12, 14, 16, and sometimes 18 and 20 feet. Plywood comes in 4×8 and 4×10 sheets. Floor dimensions in multiples of 2 feet will result in a minimum of wasted lumber. If your design calls for plywood, your floor dimensions should be multiples of 4 feet. A $16' \times 20'$ plywood floor will be twice as fast to put down as a floor $17' \times 21'$ because the plywood can be installed with no cutting.

REVISING YOUR DESIGN

Your first design will be full of defects, which is to be expected. Revise it until you have a layout that really makes sense. Later you will make a more detailed plan that will include windows, doors, and the contents of the house. This will also be revised. To illustrate how this revision process works, Figure 29 shows a hypothetical first

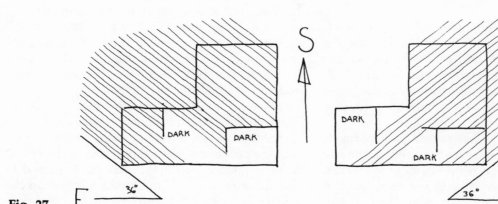

Fig. 27

Fig. 29

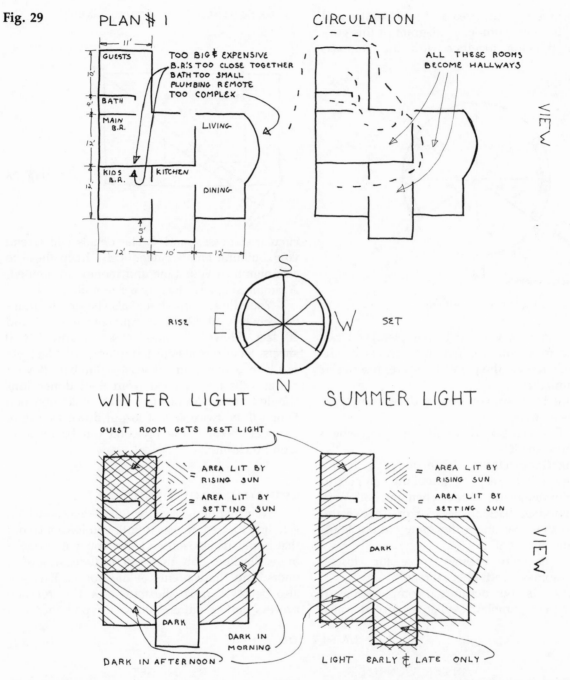

house plan (Plan 1) and points out a few of its many defects.

The design is too complex to be easy to build. The guest room gets the best light and shades the rest of the house. The kitchen in particular is very dark. The kids' room is too close to the main bedroom for privacy. The traffic patterns in the house are very bad. Imagine what would happen every time a child went to the bathroom.

Plan 2 (Figure 30) has several basic changes. The guest room is eliminated to unblock the sun and save money. The main bedroom is smaller. The kitchen is moved over to the south side. A hall is introduced to aid circulation. The bay win-

dow is removed to simplify the work. And a closet has been put in to separate the two bedrooms.

This is an improvement, but there are still serious problems. There is very little storage in the house. The bath has no windows. The kitchen is a tight, cramped space, cut off from the light and cut off from the view to the west.

Plan 3 is an attempt to solve these problems. The bath is moved to the outside wall. The kitchen is opened up to the dining room so the person cooking can see the view. Storage has been added. Most important, the main bedroom is moved to the opposite corner of the house to open up the kitchen to more light, and give the adults more

PLAN #2

NOT ENOUGH STORAGE
CAN'T SEE VIEW FROM KITCHEN
KITCHEN COULD BE SUNNIER
NO WINDOW IN BATH

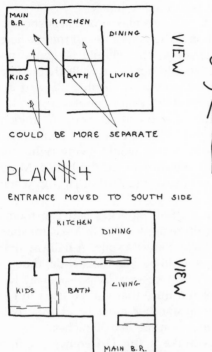

COULD BE MORE SEPARATE

PLAN #3

BETTER, BUT TOO MUCH
HALLWAY

NOTE: ⌐ ⌐ = SLIDING DOORS

Fig. 30

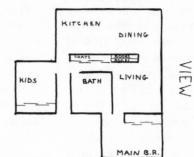

PLAN #4

ENTRANCE MOVED TO SOUTH SIDE

privacy. A lot of time was spent looking for the best arrangement for the hall.

Plan 3 seems fairly good to me. It is a temptation when you find a plan that feels good to stop looking for improvements and consider the job done. When this time comes, quit drawing for the day. Another day you will find new problems and new solutions to them. Something about the design that you can't quite identify will be bothering you, and when you come back you'll know what it is. I was unhappy about the amount of hallway in Plan 3 — all those dark passages in the house. I couldn't figure out a way to avoid them. When I came back to the drawing board the next day, I could see that simply moving the main entrance to the other side of the house eliminated one hallway, enlarged the bathroom, and made room for another set of closets (Plan 4).

You can continue the refining process for a long time. It is worth spending enough time so that the plan feels right to you. No design will meet all criteria; you have to compromise.

TESTING THE DESIGN ON SITE

To see how your plan will fit your site in practice, take the plan to the site. Take along a stepladder, strings, and a compass. Stake out the house location with the proper dimensions and compass orientation. Walking around the layout you can see what short and long views can be seen from what part of the house and how the

house will relate to the sun and all the items shown on your initial site plan. Use the ladder to place yourself at approximate floor level in different rooms, since looking at things from ground level may be misleading. Try to visualize how the house will look on the site. Sometimes the mass of the house itself will damage the site.

MAKING A DETAILED FLOOR PLAN

A floor plan can look perfect when it is a simple line drawing, but it may not work so well when it is full of furniture and when windows, doors, cabinets, and appliances are included. A detailed plan shows how these will fit into your plans. Plan 5 (Figure 31) is a detailed version of our Plan 4, in a larger scale here for the sake of

Fig. 31

PLAN #5

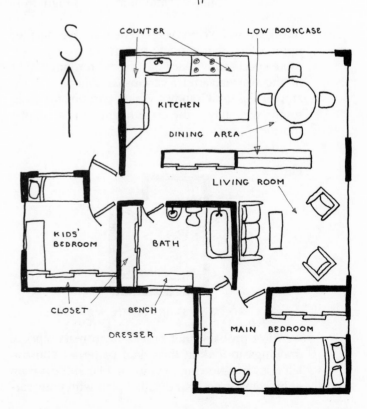

clarity. Detailed plans are questioned, adjusted, and revised much like other drawings. Begin to make your detailed plan by making scale cutouts of the furniture, cabinets, closets, and other items that must fit into your house. Move these around on a copy of your plan. Experiment with a variety of arrangements until you find one that seems spacious. If you compare Plan 5 with Plan 4, you will see that a house looks much smaller full of furniture than it does just as a line drawing.

Next, tentatively locate the windows. As Plan 5 illustrates, window location will be very much influenced by your layout of furniture, kitchen cabinets, doors, and storage. A window is wasted behind the refrigerator, but is perfectly placed between a comfortable chair and a beautiful view. Window heights will be effected by the layout too. Windows behind a counter, for example, begin three or four inches above counter height.

But the window location is mainly determined by the sun. In Plan 5, most of the big windows are on the south side, and to some extent the east and west sides, because that is where the sun is. Any house that depends on the sun for any fraction of its heating should follow this pattern. Windows will also judiciously face major and minor views. But if these views are to the north, the window area will be fairly small to avoid excessive heat loss.

REVISING THE DETAILED PLAN

You can analyze your tentative design from several angles.

Sunlight and Windows.   When you've decided upon a tentative window placement, you can see more specifically which parts of each room will be lit and warmed under various conditions. For example, Figure 32 shows which parts of the kids' room will have direct sunlight on a winter morning.

Fig. 32

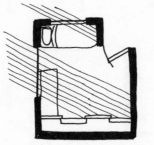

WINTER MORNING LIGHT, KIDS' ROOM

It is probably not necessary to make special drawings to look at these sun patterns. You can tell a lot by referring to your circular sun diagram or by comparing your detailed plan with your ear-lier sun analysis drawings. The point is: be sure the windows make good use of the sun and work well with what is inside the house.

Closet Location.   Closets make good acoustic and thermal insulation. When possible put them where they will divide rooms that should be sound-insulated. Closets should not be on walls that would be better used for windows. North walls and interior walls are good places for closets.

Doors.   It matters which way doors open. In Plan 5 the door to the kids' room should open in, because if it opened out, it would swing right into anybody coming into or leaving the house. Make sure a door won't cause a hazard or jam-up when opened.

Room to Move.   Often passages between rooms and around furniture are too small. Measure such passages with the architect's scale. A hallway that gets a lot of use should be 3 or 4 feet wide, though 30 inches will do if necessary. A passageway between pieces of furniture that will be used to get from one place to another must be at least two feet wide and ideally more like 30 inches.

Small Changes Make a Big Difference.   Often subtle changes make a huge difference. For example, consider the main bedroom. Figure 33 shows an initial layout next to the final arrangement. The main improvement is that the door to the bath has been reduced from 30 inches to 24 inches. This means that the dresser can be moved out of the northeast corner into the southeast corner, next to the smaller bathroom door. Then a tall window can go where the dresser was. These two changes — the smaller door and new window — may seem like nothing special, but they make the room better. The space where the chair is is now a real place — a special corner with nice light — instead of a piece of floor between the bed and the dresser that happened to accommodate a chair. Enough small changes like this can make a big difference in how big and comfortable a house feels.

TWO-STORY PLANS

If a house has two stories, make a separate drawing of the second floor. Levels that are only a few steps apart can be drawn on the same plan. Here are some considerations for second-floor layouts.

Plumbing.   If possible a second-story bathroom should be above a downstairs bathroom or the kitchen to economize on plumbing costs.

Noise.   Impact noise, such as footsteps, is easily transmitted through a ceiling. A noisy upstairs room should not be located over a quiet downstairs room.

Fig. 33

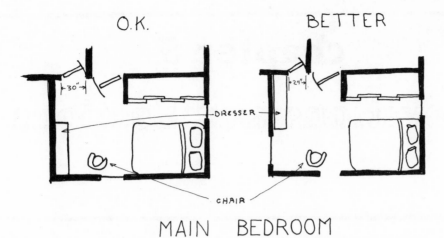

MAIN BEDROOM

Stairs.   If you plan to build a staircase, consult chapter twenty-one before completing your layout. Without careful planning it is easy to create a plan in which there will not be enough headroom.

KITCHEN LAYOUT

The kitchen layout deserves special attention. Your detailed floor plan should show kitchen cabinets, overhead cabinets, shelves, appliances, pantry, seating, and other details. These details should be subjected to the same process of questioning and revision you applied to the house as a whole.

How do you use a kitchen? If you like to eat in the kitchen, leave plenty of room for a table. You might not need a dining room at all. If you plan to do most of your entertaining in the kitchen, as I do, you might not need a big living room, but your kitchen should include a comfortable space for visiting. Make room in the kitchen for activities that will end up happening there whether you like it or not.

The kind of cooking you do will affect the kitchen layout also. If you bake a lot, you may want to include a baking area, with a counter for kneading bread and storage for grain and baking equipment. If children will be using the kitchen,

you may want a snacking spot. If you will be growing a lot of food, design your kitchen to handle and store raw unprocessed food. You may need space for a root cellar or freezer. You may need extra shelves to store large quantities of home-canned food. Sometimes a single pantry or pantry area is easier to build than a large number of cabinets for such purposes.

Kitchen Circulation.   The most efficient kitchens usually have the sink, refrigerator, and stove forming a more or less equilateral triangle, which saves a lot of walking. But there are other important considerations as well. Things should be stored near where they will be used. Plates should be near the sink so that they can easily be put away and near enough to the table to get out again. A slatted cabinet that drains into the sink is even better, because the dishes can be put away wet and will not have to be moved again when they are dry. Knives should be stored near the cutting board. Have a place near the refrigerator to put grocery bags when you bring them in. Have a place for dirty dishes separate from the food preparation area. In sum, match the layout to the specific activities that will happen.

Finally, the kitchen might border the main circulation area for entering or passing through the house, but it should not be the main traffic path.

chapter 5
Elevations and Sections

An elevation drawing shows a vertical or side view of the house from some point of view either inside or outside. A cross section or "section" shows a plane sliced through the house horizontally, vertically, or diagonally. Your next step is to make elevations and sections of your house. These help you design your roof, locate windows, and study how well different parts of the house will relate. These drawings will be developed and revised much like floor plans.

MAKING TRIAL ELEVATIONS

Make a set of four exterior elevations. If your house is oriented with the compass points, these will be labeled north, south, east, and west. Later you will make detailed elevations and sections to study particular design problems that come up,

such as staircases. The same hypothetical house is used here as an example.

Figure 34 shows elevations being projected from the floor plan, using the drawing method described in chapter three. These drawings could also be made by taking their horizontal dimensions from a floor plan with tracing paper. The initial elevations are open on top, since no roof is designed yet, but the windows and doors are shown, since they have been located in the floor plan. Usually the bottom edges of windows are determined by what is happening inside the house. The top edge is determined later, after the roof is designed.

Lay tracing paper over your elevations, and draw possible roof lines. Figure 35 shows some of the innumerable possibilities.

Fig. 34   PROJECTING ELEVATIONS FROM A PLAN

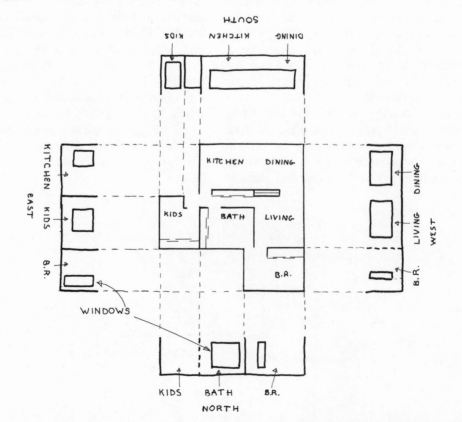

Fig. 35

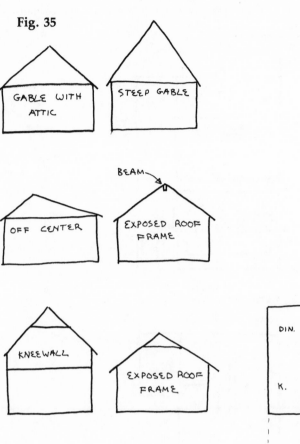

GABLE WITH ATTIC

STEEP GABLE

OFF CENTER

BEAM

EXPOSED ROOF FRAME

KNEEWALL

EXPOSED ROOF FRAME

CLEARSTORY

LOW PITCH SHED

HIGH PITCH SHED

FLAT

GAMBREL

The roof lines here differ in more than looks. They enclose different kinds of and amounts of space, they heat differently, and they afford different possibilities for windows. Some leave room for an attic. Some give a nice high ceiling. Some provide space for a loft. A high ceiling lets in more light but makes the space harder to heat. A steep roof sheds snow; a shallow one doesn't. A gable roof spans a longer distance than a flat or shed roof. A roof that is too low on the sunny side might block the sun. A roof that is high on the windy side may leave the house unprotected.

There is no set rule, but often a shed roof will rise to the south to catch the sun. In general any roof design should help you put sunlight where you want it. Figures 36 and 37 show two views each of four possible roof designs for our hypo-

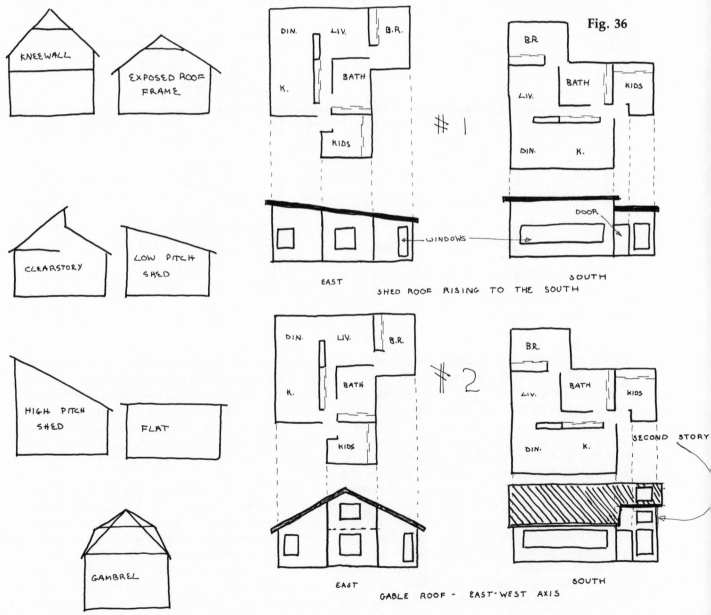

Fig. 36

#1

DIN. LIV. B.R. K. BATH KIDS

B.R. LIV. BATH KIDS DIN. K.

WINDOWS

DOOR

EAST

SOUTH

SHED ROOF RISING TO THE SOUTH

#2

DIN. LIV. B.R. K. BATH KIDS

B.R. LIV. BATH KIDS DIN. K.

SECOND STORY

EAST

SOUTH

GABLE ROOF - EAST-WEST AXIS

Fig. 37

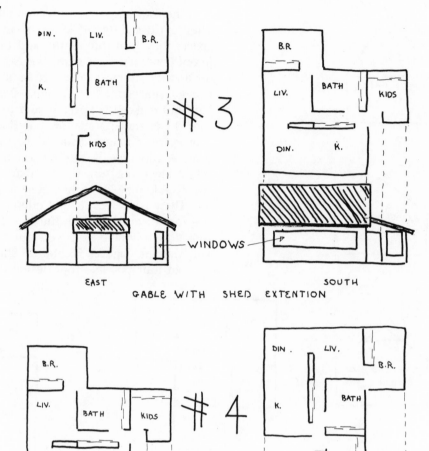

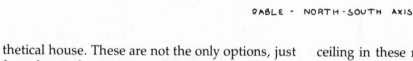

thetical house. These are not the only options, just four chosen for purposes of illustration.

All these designs are attempts to deal with the characteristic problem of this house: its relatively great width. Any sloping roof that covers it will enclose a large space; a second story of some kind will be created whether it is needed or not. In Design 1 I attack the problem by keeping the pitch of the shed roof at the lowest possible angle to minimize the cost and labor of covering the living area. But even this gentle slope results in a 12-foot kitchen ceiling. Design 2 goes the other way. Its steeply pitched roof ends up creating two or three new rooms under the highest part of the roof. Perhaps the roof of the kitchen and main bedroom will be left exposed, resulting in a high

ceiling in these rooms. Design 3 is a variation on this that attempts to reduce the expense of the extra space by eliminating the part of it above the kids' room, which gets a separate, lower shed roof. Design 4 has a more shallow pitch gable roof oriented 90 degrees the other way. This design also results either in very high ceilings or a useless attic.

Once you have chosen a roof design, you need to make a complete set of drawings for it. In this case I chose Design 3 — the gable roof with the shed extension — as most suitable for the floor plan. It provides height where needed but eliminates unnecessary space. It seems functional and economical, attractive and fairly simple. Figure 38 shows additional drawings necessary for visual-

Fig. 38

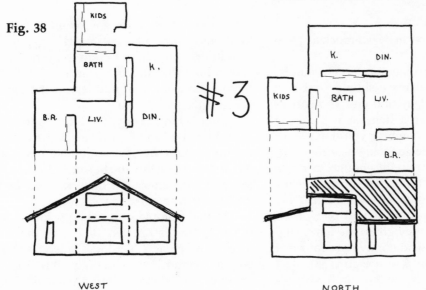

WEST

NORTH

#3

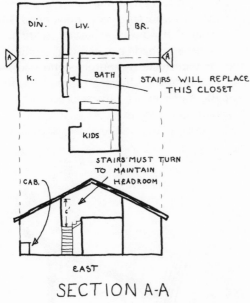

DIN.   LIV.   B.R.

A

A

K.   BATH

STAIRS WILL REPLACE
THIS CLOSET

KIDS

STAIRS MUST TURN
TO MAINTAIN
HEADROOM

CAB.

EAST

SECTION A-A

SECOND FLOOR PLAN

izing it as a whole. These include the two remaining elevations, north and west, a floor plan of the second story, and a section showing how the added staircase works in relation to the floor and roof. Figure 39 is a perspective drawing that shows what this design looks like.

Fig. 39   SOUTH   WEST

ANALYZING ELEVATIONS

Your elevations can be analyzed much as were earlier floor plans.

Circulation.   Vertical circulation is largely a question of staircases. The staircase should start at a convenient place downstairs and end at a convenient place upstairs. Often a staircase will start at a good place and end somewhere you don't want it to. Also there should be adequate headroom. In our design, the space was tight enough to make fitting a staircase in very tricky. The only place for it was where the hall closet had been. But if the stairs ran straight up, people would bang their heads on the roof when they got to the tenth step and the top of the stairs would only have four feet of headroom (see Section AA in Figure 38). So I made the stairs turn right at the ninth step — which is now a landing — because in that direction the headroom increases as the roof slopes up. If the stairs had turned earlier, the headroom of the first-floor hall would have been inadequate. Another problem was that the closet being replaced by the stairs was only 24 inches wide. To create a more spacious 30-inch staircase, I took 3 inches from the kitchen and 3 inches from the hall.

Light.   Appendix D shows how to gauge the elevation that the sun will reach in the sky during winter and summer. Use a sun diagram, as in Figure 40; to study how the sun will penetrate your house with different window heights and locations, with different overhangs or shading conditions, and in different seasons. Figure 40 shows how the sun comes into the kitchen of the hypothetical house at midday on the longest and shortest days of the year.

On the longest day, the roof shades the house at midday. But on the shortest day, the sun floods the house quite deeply. Both in summer and winter, the sun reaches further into the house in the morning and afternoon than at midday, because it is lower in the sky.

In the example, the ceiling is low (8 feet) and the overhang is angled down. If the overhang were as much as 2 feet long, it would start to cut out the winter sun at midday. But if the roof is rising or the ceiling higher, a relatively long overhang (about 4 feet) can be built that will shade the morning and afternoon summer sun, without interfering with the winter sun. If you have a lot of south windows and live in a place where summer shade is important, you may need such a wide overhang. If no roof exists to create an overhang, a special sunshade can be built, as shown in Figure 41. If you make the outer portion adjustable, you can change the shading to suit conditions. Some of the same effect can be achieved with curtains or bamboo screens.

Raising or lowering the top of the window

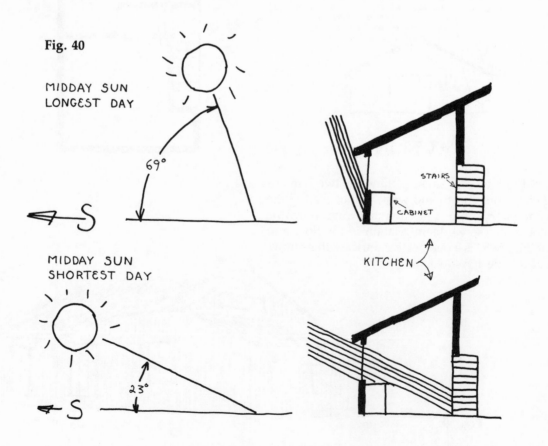

Fig. 40

MIDDAY SUN LONGEST DAY

69°

S

MIDDAY SUN SHORTEST DAY

23°

S

STAIRS

CABINET

KITCHEN

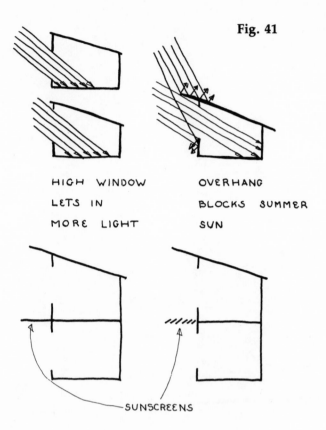

Fig. 41

HIGH WINDOW
LETS IN
MORE LIGHT

OVERHANG
BLOCKS SUMMER
SUN

SUNSCREENS

will also affect how much light and heat come in. In Figure 40 there is not really much room to maneuver because the ceiling is low. But in a roof with a higher ceiling, you can raise the window height to admit more light or lower it to limit light.

Appearance.   Your elevations also will show you what your house will look like. Make a set of elevations with the siding, trim, and any other details drawn in to scale. Usually the house will look good or it won't. Sometimes changing details will make a lot of difference. Horizontal siding will lower and spread a building visually, and vertical siding will make it look taller. Varying the size of casings, corner boards, overhangs, and other details can make the house look lighter, heavier, or otherwise improve its appearance. If you are not sure how the house looks from the drawings, make a scale model. Glue a set of the detailed scale elevations to cardboard, cut them out, make a roof piece in scale, and glue or tape the model together. Carry the drawings and the model to the site, and visualize how the house will look in place.

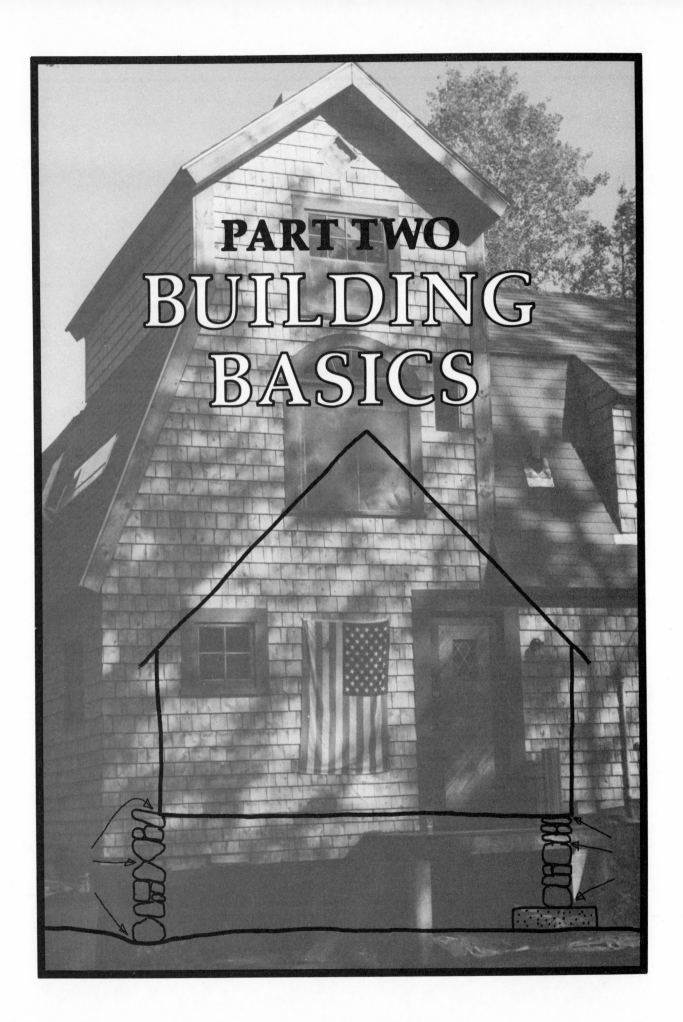

PART TWO
BUILDING BASICS

chapter 6
The Structure of a House

The first section of this book is called Design. This is a convenient title, but in fact a little misleading. Actually every part of building involves designing of some kind. The design covered in Part One involves choosing the kind and location of the spaces you want in your house. Next you have to design the structure that will make these spaces possible. What follows is an attempt to acquaint the reader with how a structure works, what makes it sound or unsound, and how to think about it usefully. You can build a house without understanding these concepts, but understanding them will help you build your house more economically and efficiently. More important, they can help you imagine and visualize possibilities that might not otherwise occur to you.

TENSION AND COMPRESSION

All questions of structure reduce to one basic problem: to design a house that will withstand the forces acting upon it. These forces include the weight of the house itself, the weight of snow, the weight of and the contents of the house, such as furniture and moving people, and wind.

The forces acting on a house may be differentiated according to how they act on a given part of a house. A compression force is one that tends to compress a piece, or shorten its dimensions. A weight resting on a column exerts a compression force on that column; the column is compressed between the weight and whatever the column is resting on. A tension force is a force that tends to pull apart or elongate something. A weight hanging from a wire exerts a tension force on the wire, stretching it between the weight at the bottom and its anchorage at the top (Figure 42).

Very few pieces of a house, however, are in pure tension or compression. Take a wooden beam with a heavy load at the center. It may seem to be purely in compression from the load, but a closer look reveals both kinds of forces acting at once. The top of the beam is in compression — it's being squeezed together. The bottom part is in tension — it's being stretched (Figure 43). The

Fig. 42

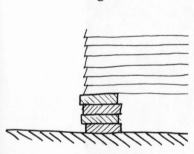

BRICKS IN COMPRESSION

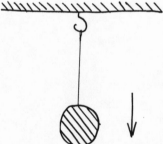

WIRE IN TENSION

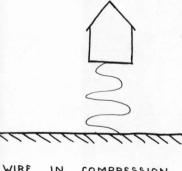

WIRE IN COMPRESSION

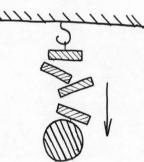

BRICKS IN TENSION

Fig. 43

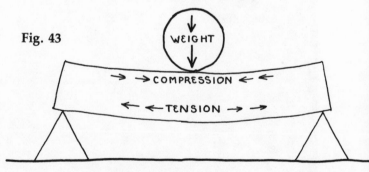

middle of the beam is not being strained much at all. The design of steel I-beams makes use of this fact, being wide at the top and bottom for strength,

Fig. 44

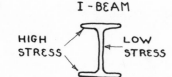

I-BEAM

HIGH STRESS   LOW STRESS

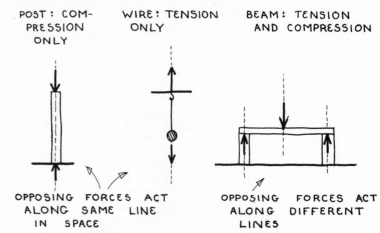

POST: COMPRESSION ONLY   WIRE: TENSION ONLY   BEAM: TENSION AND COMPRESSION

OPPOSING FORCES ACT ALONG SAME LINE IN SPACE   OPPOSING FORCES ACT ALONG DIFFERENT LINES

Fig. 45

yet narrow in the middle for lightness and economy (Figure 44).

Any structural member will be subjected to both tension and compression forces whenever the loads on the member are exerted along more than one line in space or tend to bend the piece. In the case of a weight on a column, there is an upward force from the base, and a downward force from the weight. These forces act in opposite directions along the same line in space. When a weight hangs from a wire, again the forces are in the opposite direction but along the same line. With a beam supported at the ends, the downward force is applied to the middle (or all along the beam) and the upward force is applied just at the ends, in the opposite direction but along different lines in space (Figure 45).

Different materials have different strengths under tension or compression. Masonry is very strong in compression, but not strong in tension. A pile of bricks will hold a huge weight in pure compression, but no weight at all in tension. Even when bricks are mortared together the tensile strength is not great. Concrete, which has low tensile strength, is often reinforced with steel, which has tremendous tensile strength. Bars or mesh can be cast into a concrete beam or wall where the tension loads will be greatest.

Perhaps an example will clarify this. A pile of bricks or a brick wall above ground might simply be subjected to a downward, compressive force. If that same wall is a basement wall, it will also be subjected to the sideward pressure of the earth. When forces are exerted on part of a building along

different lines in space, the part will be subjected to a combination of tension and compression forces. The wall is like a beam on its end, with the outside being in compression and the inside in tension. In masonry construction, this pressure on a basement wall can be small or large, depending on soil conditions. If the pressure is slight, as it might be in a well-drained soil, the pressure can be resisted simply by the weight of the wall, by mortaring the bricks together, or by making the wall thicker. If the pressure is greater, as it might be on a poorly drained site, the wall could eventually fail, as shown in Figure 46.

This sideward pressure can be resisted by making the wall thicker, by using mortar to strengthen the wall, or by using concrete, which is stronger because it is monolithic. Even greater strength can be gained by casting steel reinforcing bars into the concrete (Figure 47).

Wood, on the other hand, is strong in both tension and compression. A relatively slender wood column will support a huge weight in compression. A 4 × 4 post four feet long, for example, would probably be able to carry most of

Fig. 46   STRENGTH OF MASONRY MATERIALS

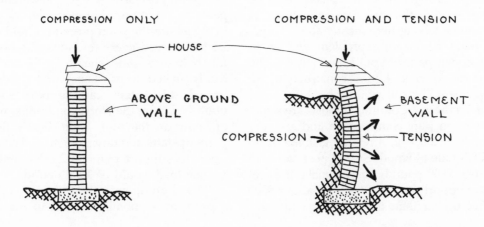

COMPRESSION ONLY   COMPRESSION AND TENSION

HOUSE

ABOVE GROUND WALL   BASEMENT WALL

COMPRESSION   TENSION

Fig. 47

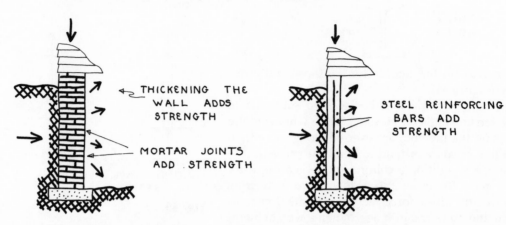

HOW MASONRY WALLS RESIST TENSION

THICKENING THE WALL ADDS STRENGTH

MORTAR JOINTS ADD STRENGTH

STEEL REINFORCING BARS ADD STRENGTH

the weight of a small house. You could hang a great weight from a ¼" dowel — hundreds of pounds — as long as the pulling force was straight and the joints at the end were strong. The joint would break before the wood. Wood is a good material for beams because it has both kinds of strength.

WHAT MAKES A STRUCTURE STRONG

We have said that a house must be designed to withstand the forces it will be subjected to. These forces are often called *loads*. Loads are of two kinds, live and dead. Dead loads are imposed by the building's own weight; for example, the weight of the roof is a dead load on its rafters. Live loads are other forces acting on the building, such as the weight of furniture, people on the floor, snow on the roof, and so on. When calculating the loads a structure will have to bear, it is important to take both kinds into account.

To withstand the loads on it, a house structure must meet three criteria. One, the individual members of the structure, such as beams, joists, and studs, must be strong enough. Two, the members must be attached to each other properly. The joints must be strong. Three, the pieces must be put together so that the structure as a whole is rigid. We will be talking here mostly about wood, since the main engineering problem will be to make the wooden parts of your house strong. The masonry parts in small-house construction are usually engineered by rule of thumb.

Strength of Timbers. Columns or posts are structural members in pure compression and are very strong. Consider a 4 × 4, 4 feet long, made from the cheapest grade of wood. Such a post can hold approximately 9800 pounds. If you make it 6 feet long it can support only a little less, about 9200 pounds. But higher than that, the capacity goes

down fast. At 8 feet high, the post can hold about 5000 pounds, at 10 feet, about 3000 pounds, and so on. As a column gets taller, it has an increasing tendency to bow out in the middle, as shown in Figure 48. That is the way columns fail. One way the strength of a column can be improved is to brace the middle in both directions to prevent its bending. If you have a 4 × 4, 8 feet long, well supported in the middle, it will hold as much as a 4 × 4, 4 feet long.

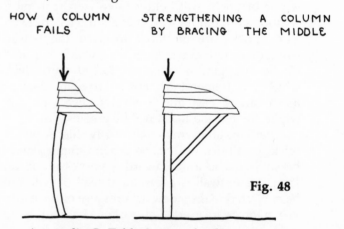

HOW A COLUMN FAILS

STRENGTHENING A COLUMN BY BRACING THE MIDDLE

Fig. 48

Appendix C, Table 8, gives loading capacities for timber posts. But in carpentry practice, it is rare that post size is even researched, because posts are so strong. For example, the 2 × 4 studs in a wall are the main posts that hold up a house. Each is braced every few inches, since the inside finish and outside sheathing of the house are firmly nailed to it. The worst grade of 2 × 4, braced this often, can support 3000 to 5000 pounds. Under the worst conditions, with five feet of snow on the roof, wide, heavy floors, and a party upstairs and down, each stud could be called upon to support perhaps 2400 pounds. A more normal load would be 1000 pounds.

Even an open, unbraced post is not much of a problem. Generally, a post in the middle of a room supporting one floor can be a 4 × 4, and a post supporting two floors can be a 4 × 6, 4 × 8, or 6 × 6. If you think the load on a post is extra large, you can compute the amount of load using Appendix A and find the column size by using Appendix C, Table 8. Usually a post size will be determined not so much by the load it must bear as by other considerations. For example, a post may be larger than the load demands for the sake of appearances or to make the joints at the top or bottom strong.

Members in pure tension are rare in most houses. Occasionally something will be hung from a wooden frame, but usually the only real tension members will be the collar ties that hold the rafters together (Figure 49). A tension member almost

Fig. 49

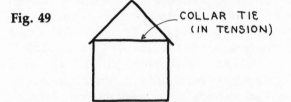

COLLAR TIE
(IN TENSION)

always fails at the joints at the ends. Therefore, the size of a tension member is usually determined by the size and shape of wood needed to make a strong-enough joint. The piece will be large not because the wood is weak, but to make the joint strong. For your purposes, follow rules of thumb given in this book unless your design has some unusual tension member. If so, get some experienced advice.

The timbers that require the most engineering from you are the horizontal beams, joists, and rafters that are subject to both tension and compression loads. These must be strong enough to carry their live and dead loads without breaking or deflecting (sagging or bouncing) too much. At the same time, they should be no bigger than necessary. Oversize timbers will cost more and be more work to put up.

The load a particular beam can carry depends on the size of the beam, the grade of wood in it, the span, and the location and size of the load on the beam. Appendix A shows how these elements are quantified and how you can use simple formulas to compute timber sizes. Here I will talk about some of the basic principles these formulas are based on.

1. The longer a beam is, the weaker it is. A 2 × 4 4 feet long will carry twice what a 2 × 4 8 feet long will carry, assuming both are supported at the ends.

2. The wider a beam is (B), the stronger it is. The strength is directly proportional to the width. A 4 × 4 will carry twice what a 2 × 4 will over the same span (Figure 50).

3. The deeper a beam is (D), the stronger it is by far. Mathematically, strength is proportional to the square of the depth. If you double the depth of a beam, the strength increases by 4 times (Figure 51). That is why most timbers are rectangular in cross section. The rectangular shape gives the most depth, hence the most strength, for the amount of lumber used (Figure 52).

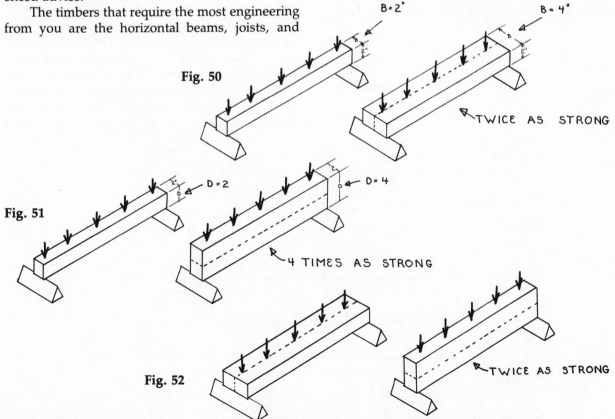

Fig. 50   B = 2"   B = 4"   TWICE AS STRONG

Fig. 51   D = 2   D = 4   4 TIMES AS STRONG

Fig. 52   TWICE AS STRONG

Fig. 53

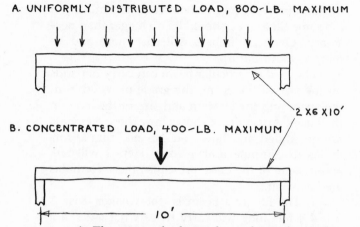

LOADING CONDITIONS

A. UNIFORMLY DISTRIBUTED LOAD, 800-LB. MAXIMUM

B. CONCENTRATED LOAD, 400-LB. MAXIMUM

2 x 6 X 10'

10'

4. The strength depends on how the timber is loaded. Figure 53 shows a 10-foot 2 × 6 under two different loading conditions. Figure 53–A shows the most common situation, a single span loaded more or less uniformly along its length. This kind of load is referred to as a *uniformly distributed load*. The people, furniture, snow, and most other loadings on floors and roofs are normally considered to be uniformly distributed loads, even though at times a part of such a load might be concentrated in one place or another. Under these conditions a typical 10-foot 2 × 6 can hold a safe working load of 800 pounds. Another way of saying this is that the maximum span of a typical 2 × 6, if it has a uniformly distributed load of 80 pounds per foot of beam, is 10 feet.

Fig. 54

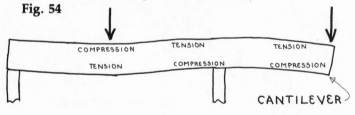

COMPRESSION   TENSION   TENSION

TENSION   COMPRESSION   COMPRESSION

CANTILEVER

A heavy weight, such as a wall, column, or a heavy machine, is called a *concentrated load* because its force is focused on a single area of a beam. If there is a load concentrated in midspan of the same 10-foot 2 × 6, it could carry only half as much, or 400 pounds, as shown in Figure 53-B. This does not mean that any 2 × 6 in the world will hold exactly these amounts. These figures, and the other examples mentioned below, are based on calculations for eastern spruce or a similarly strong timber. For other woods the figures might be proportionately higher or lower.

Cantilevered beams present a more complicated case. A cantilever is an overhanging end of a beam supporting a load, as in Figure 54. The cantilevered portion of a beam is much weaker than the same portion would be if it were supported at both ends. For example, a spruce 2 × 6 *spanning* 10 feet can normally carry a 600-pound distributed load. But a similar 2 × 6 *cantilevered* out 10 feet can only support a distributed load of 200 pounds, or one-fourth as much (Figure 55-A). If the load were concentrated at the end of the 10-foot cantilever, the maximum load would be only 100 pounds, or one eighth of the regular load (55-B).

Figure 56 shows this same mathematical relationship in a more usable form for carpentry purposes. In Figure 53 the maximum span was 10 feet for the 2 × 6 with a distributed load of 80 pounds per foot of beam. In Figure 56-A, the maximum cantilever is 5 feet, with the same loading of 80 pounds per foot of beam. In other words, a beam can cantilever half the distance it can span, if the distributed load per foot of beam is the same. Figure 56-B shows that if this load is concentrated at the end of the cantilever, the maximum cantilever will be 2½ feet, or one fourth of the normal span.

If you actually extended cantilevers to these maximums, they would be strong but quite

Fig. 55

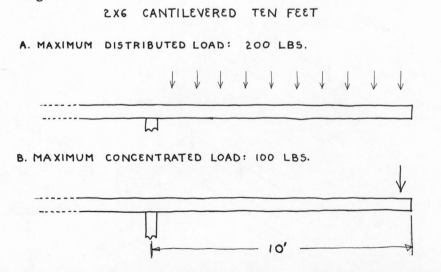

2 X 6 CANTILEVERED TEN FEET

A. MAXIMUM DISTRIBUTED LOAD: 200 LBS.

B. MAXIMUM CONCENTRATED LOAD: 100 LBS.

10'

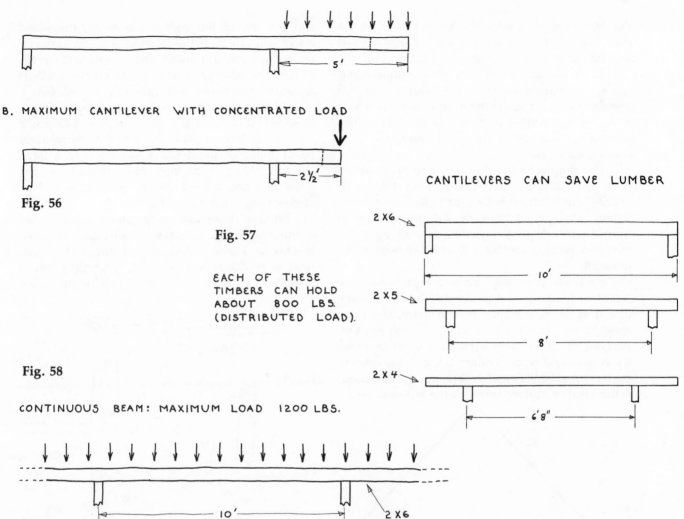

A. MAXIMUM CANTILEVER WITH 80 LBS./FT. LOAD

5'

B. MAXIMUM CANTILEVER WITH CONCENTRATED LOAD

2½'

Fig. 56

Fig. 57

EACH OF THESE TIMBERS CAN HOLD ABOUT 800 LBS. (DISTRIBUTED LOAD).

CANTILEVERS CAN SAVE LUMBER

2 X 6

10'

2 X 5

8'

2 X 4

6' 8"

Fig. 58

CONTINUOUS BEAM: MAXIMUM LOAD 1200 LBS.

10'

2 X 6

springy. In building terminology, they would *deflect*. So in practice it is unwise to push cantilevers to the limit. A common rule of thumb for distributed cantilever loads is that you can cantilever one third of the distance you could normally span between supports, assuming the same loading per foot of beam in both cases. In Figure 56-A, this means that in practice the maximum cantilever would be 3 feet, 4 inches (⅓ of 10 feet) instead of the theoretical 5 feet. The corresponding rule for concentrated loads is that you can cantilever one-sixth the distance you could normally span, assuming the same total load in both cases. In Figure 56-B, the maximum cantilever would be 1 foot, 8 inches, which is half of 3 feet, 4 inches and one sixth of 10 feet. These limits are shown in the drawing as dotted lines. Appendix A gives the formula for each kind of loading.

You might think that cantilevers are inefficient because they hold so much less than spans supported on both ends. But in certain situations cantilevers are actually more efficient.

Suppose you were building a deck 10 feet wide and the load was going to be, as before, 80 pounds per foot of beam. If you support the deck at the ends of the 10-foot span, you will have to use 2 × 6s. If you move the supports in one foot at each end, the span is now only 8 feet, so the joists can be 2 × 5s. If you push the cantilever as far as it will go, you can reduce the span to 6 feet, 8 inches and use 2 × 4s.

In addition to enabling you to reduce spans, the cantilever actually strengthens the beam inside the cantilever. You can see why in Figure 54. The force down on the end of the cantilever provides leverage to lift the load between supports, making the noncantilevered section stronger and stiffer. This means that the 2 × 4 in Figure 57 is actually somewhat stronger than the 2 × 6 above it.

This effect is put to use when a beam is continuous over a series of supports, such as in Figure 58. The downward force on each section of beam helps lift the adjacent sections. Thus the middle section of the 2 × 6 can now support 1200 pounds, which is 50 percent more than it could support with the same span without the cantilever effect.

Connections. Once you're sure the pieces in your house are strong enough, you must make sure they are strongly joined. The joints as well as the piece must carry the load. The kind of joint needed will be determined by the forces acting upon it.

To understand joints, you should understand *bearing*. A bearing surface is a surface where two members of a structure meet and through which a load is transmitted from one to the other. Any joint is, among other things, a combination of bearing surfaces.

The simplest kind of joint is one piece sitting on top of another, bearing down on it through gravity. An example is the stones in an old foundation. Each stone bears on the ones below to form a joint. A joint consisting of nothing but a common bearing surface will work if two conditions are met.

First, the joint must be in compression. The forces or loads on the joint must be in opposite directions along the same lines in space, and there must be no great forces tending to push the two parts of the joint away from each other or make them slide against each other. Second, the bearing surface must be big enough. In a stone foundation, if the bearing surface between the wooden house

and the top of the wall is too small, the wood fibers will crush. If the bearing surfaces between the stones are too small, the stones will break. And if the bearing of the stones on the earth is too small, the house will settle (Figures 59, 60).

Of course most joints are subjected to forces in several directions at once, so a mere piling will not suffice. Even a post supporting a second-floor beam could be accidentally subjected to a large sideways load. Therefore, most, if not all, the joints in a house need strong fastening as well as large-enough bearing surfaces.

Some of the common fastening devices used in building are nails, screws, bolts, glue, dowels, mortise and tenon, and pegs (Figure 61). Before nails were cheap and plentiful, carpenters had to fasten joints using wood alone. They did this using

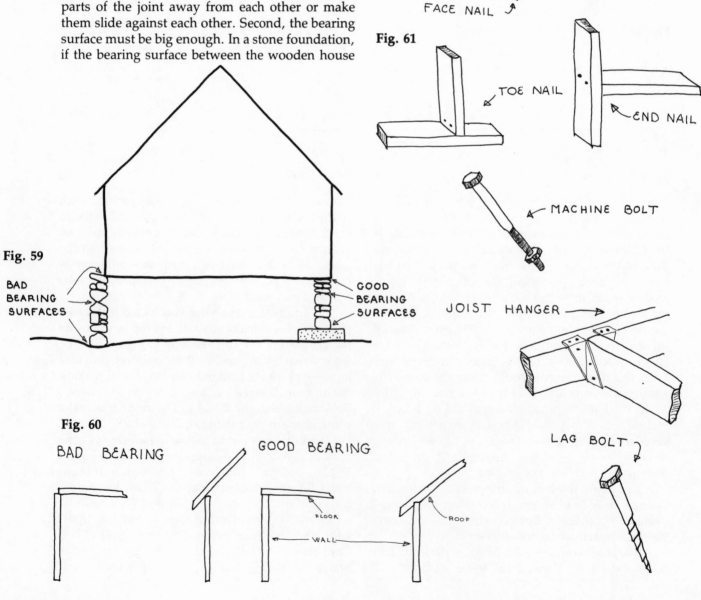

Fig. 59

BAD BEARING SURFACES

GOOD BEARING SURFACES

Fig. 60

BAD BEARING   GOOD BEARING

FLOOR

WALL

ROOF

Fig. 61

FACE NAIL

TOE NAIL   END NAIL

MACHINE BOLT

JOIST HANGER

LAG BOLT

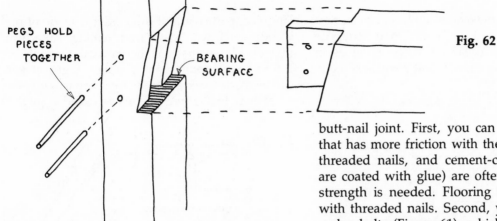

PEGS HOLD PIECES TOGETHER

BEARING SURFACE

Fig. 62

notches, dovetails, dowels, and similar techniques that depended on making complicated cuts in wood (Figure 62). But in a modern wood-frame house, most joints are held together with nails. The nails perform the same functions dowels or dovetails used to: they counteract forces that might pull the joint apart. Different nailing methods are used depending on the kind of joint and what the joint is doing. The most common joint is simply butt-nailing (Figure 63). The problem here is that

Fig. 63   BUTT-NAILING

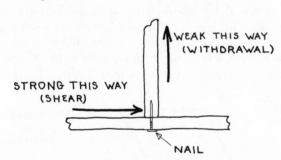

WEAK THIS WAY (WITHDRAWAL)

STRONG THIS WAY (SHEAR)

NAIL

such a joint is only really strong against some forces. If the top piece in the figure is forced upwards, parallel to the nail, the joint could come apart fairly easily because all that is holding it is the friction between the nail shank and the wood. The joint is much stronger against sideways forces, perpendicular to the nail. For the joint to break this way either the wood fibers must be destroyed or the nail must shear off at the mating surfaces between the two pieces. Technically speaking, butt-nail joints are much stronger in *shear* than in *withdrawal*.

Many of the joints in a house, however, are perfectly strong even though they are only butt-nailed, either because the nail joint is in shear or because the withdrawal load is fairly small. Siding and trim, for example, are only held to the wall by butt-nailing, but there is very little force pulling them off, so there is usually no problem.

There are many ways to improve on a simple

butt-nail joint. First, you can use a kind of nail that has more friction with the wood. Ring nails, threaded nails, and cement-coated nails (which are coated with glue) are often used when more strength is needed. Flooring is often laid down with threaded nails. Second, you can use screws or lag bolts (Figure 61), which hold even better. Third, you can toe-nail, as shown in Figure 64.

Fig. 64   TOE-NAILING

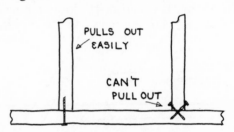

PULLS OUT EASILY

CAN'T PULL OUT

Toe-nailing is stronger because some of the nails will be in shear to some extent against a force in any direction. Any nail joint can be improved similarly simply by varying the nail angle. Fourth, you can strengthen a joint with a gusset. A gusset is a piece of wood nailed across two others ·to reinforce the joint between them. In Figure 65,

Fig. 65

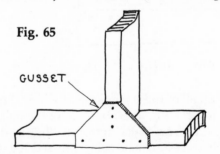

GUSSET

two 2 × 4s butt-nailed together are gusseted by a third piece. In this joint, a force in any direction will be resisted by some nails in shear, either the nails between the 2 × 4s or the nails between the gusset and the 2 × 4s.

Any piece well nailed across a joint between two others acts as a gusset. Most of the joints in the frame of a house are in effect gusseted by the sheathing and subflooring. Even if each individual nail joint is weak in some directions, the combination is strong.

Strength is especially important in the joints at the ends of a structural member in tension, such as the collar tie that holds a pair of rafters together and keeps the roof from spreading at the eaves.

Later I will discuss the overall subject of collar ties, but here I want to focus on the joint. Suppose you end-nailed the collar tie to the rafter as in Figure 66. The forces on the joint could easily pull

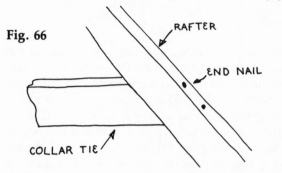

Fig. 66

RAFTER

END NAIL

COLLAR TIE

the nails out. The joint is weak in the one way it must be strong. It would help a lot to toe-nail the joint (Figure 67), but the nails could still pull out.

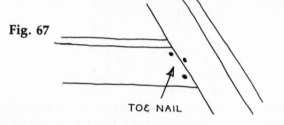

Fig. 67

TOE NAIL

A better solution would be to lap the collar tie onto the rafter, as in Figure 68, because the nails will then be in shear. Notice that the actual bearing

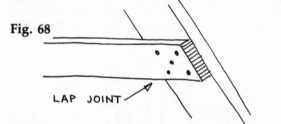

Fig. 68

LAP JOINT

surface in all of these joints is not where the wood pieces touch each other, but where the nails meet the wood. The nails transmit the load. The wooden pieces are not being pressed together at all, which means that the amount of bearing surface and the strength of the joint will depend on the number and size of the nails. In tension joints it is always important to use many nails and to use the biggest nails you can that won't split the wood.

Figure 69 shows how the same joint would be done with a gusset. This is just as good as the

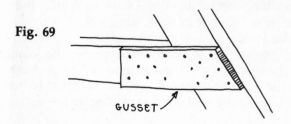

Fig. 69

GUSSET

lap joint, particularly if the gusset is made of plywood, which won't split from nailing. An advantage of using a gusset is that you can make it very big to accommodate lots of nails. A gusset joint can be made twice as strong by using two gussets, as shown in Figure 70. This is called a joint in

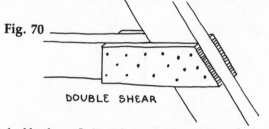

Fig. 70

DOUBLE SHEAR

double shear. It is twice as strong not only because there are more fasteners, but because the pull is symmetrical and there is less likelihood of the pieces turning a bit, which would allow the nails to withdraw slightly.

Rigidity.   Strong pieces strongly jointed do not necessarily make a strong structure. The forces acting on a house, if they do not break the pieces of the house, or the joints tying them together, can still distort the *shape* of the house. That is why you must design your house to be *rigid*.

A house is basically a box — or a combination of boxes. A box shape is not intrinsically rigid. It can fold up like a cardboard carton. The simple box that is your house can be distorted by a sideward force, like wind or movement in the house, or by the weight of its own roof (Figure 71). This

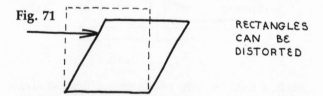

Fig. 71

RECTANGLES CAN BE DISTORTED

problem is solved with triangulation, often called diagonal bracing. Unlike a rectangle, a triangle will hold its shape against a force in any direction as long as the joints don't break apart (Figure 72).

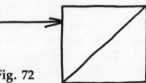

TRIANGLES ARE RIGID

Fig. 72

The way to make your house rigid is to introduce triangles into its basically rectangular shape. One way to do this is with diagonal bracing in the frame (Figure 73). Another way is to put your sheathing boards on diagonally (Figure 74). In fact, even horizontal boards provide some bracing, because every three nails not in a row form a small triangle (Figure 75). A house with horizontal

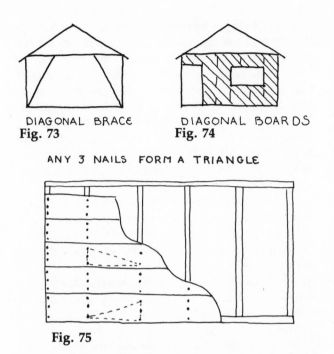

DIAGONAL BRACE
Fig. 73

DIAGONAL BOARDS
Fig. 74

ANY 3 NAILS FORM A TRIANGLE

Fig. 75

boards will in effect be braced with hundreds of little triangles. The bigger these are the more effective the bracing is. That is why the most effective bracing is plywood or other materials that come in large sheets. They form hundreds of large triangles, which give the best possible bracing.

You also need rigidity in the roof structure. An ordinary gable roof is shaped like a triangle with one side missing (Figure 76). If you put such

Fig. 76

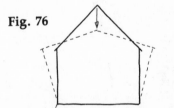

a roof on top of the walls of a house, you will soon find (as many have found) that the roof tends to spread at the eaves as its weight pushes down. The roof will cave in, and the walls will be pushed out. Figure 77 shows three possible ways to solve this problem.

The first solution is through some kind of exterior bracing or *buttress*. This is usually impractical, unless you're building a cathedral. The second solution is to support the ridge with a *bearing wall* or *beam*. This holds up the ridge of the roof and prevents it from moving downward. This is perfectly satisfactory, although it does require that the ridge beam (or wall) be properly supported at the ends. The most common solution is to install *collar ties* between the two rafters to hold them together. In many houses the attic floor joists will serve the purpose. This keeps the bottoms of the rafters from spreading outward, and thus the roof itself cannot change its shape. The roof becomes a stable structure exerting a downward force on the walls.

EVALUATING STRUCTURAL SOUNDNESS

Keeping these three principles in mind — strong pieces, strong joints, and rigidity — you can now evaluate your house design structurally. You can't make the precise calculations a structural engineer would, but you can get an intuitive sense of whether the house is designed to stand up to the loads placed on it. Since most of the loads in a house occur in a downward direction, start at the top, following the loads from the roof down to the earth. Every link in the structural chain must be strong. Every downward load must be transmitted all the way down to the earth. As you follow the loads down, ask yourself: (1) whether the pieces can support the loads passing through them, (2) whether the joints connecting the pieces are strong enough, and (3) whether the structure will retain its shape.

For example, Figure 78 shows a typical small two-room structure. To evaluate this design structurally, you would first figure out the live and dead loads on the roof. The dead load is the roof's weight. The live load includes snow and people occasionally walking about on the roof. These loads are supported by the roof sheathing (boards or plywood, probably), which in turn is supported

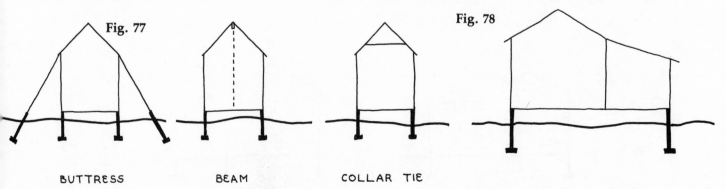

Fig. 77

Fig. 78

BUTTRESS

BEAM

COLLAR TIE

by rafters. Your first task is to make sure the sheathing is thick enough so that it won't sag or break. How thick it needs to be depends on how wide the rafters are spaced. For example, 1/2-inch plywood will span 2 feet, but will sag over a 3-foot span (a typical carpenter's rule of thumb).

Next, consider the rafters. They must be big enough to carry the load of the roofing, the sheathing, and their own weight over the distance they span. Appendix A shows how to calculate rafter sizes for specific situations. You also have to make sure your roof structure is rigid. The structure in Figure 78 is not. The weight of the gable tends to spread it at the eaves. Using collar ties to fix this will solve the rigidity problem — but only if the collar ties are strongly attached to the rafters. The outward spreading force of the rafters will put the collar tie in *tension*, so you must give special attention to the joints attaching it. The collar tie has to be nailed or bolted to the rafters.

The strong, stable structure created by the collar ties gives us a stable, straight-down load resting on the exterior wall to the left and the interior wall to the right. Our next concern is the bearing surface where the rafter meets the wall. Usually a special notch called a bird's mouth is cut in the rafter to enable it to sit flat on the wall and transmit the load downward (Figure 79).

Next, study the walls themselves. Walls are columns being compressed between the roof at the top and the floor at the bottom. Columns have tremendous strength in pure compression, so there should be no problem there. But whenever you have a column, you must make sure the structure it sits on is as strong as the column itself. The left-hand sketch in Figure 80 shows a strong column over a strong foundation, with a structure between them that is not strong enough to transmit the load. In the right-hand sketch blocking is added to solve the problem.

Next, look at the right-hand side of the gable roof. This rests on a bearing wall, which in turn rests on the middle of the first-floor beam. In theory the beam could be large enough to carry the concentrated load, but such a beam would have to be absurdly huge. Any reasonably sized beam would sag as shown in Figure 81-A. The practical solution is a foundation post directly under the bearing wall (Figure 81-B).

To complete the chain, make sure the bearing surface between the foundation and the earth is big enough. On a rock base, a foundation column by itself would probably have enough bearing. But on a base of soil, the weight of the house might drive such a column right into the earth like a stake or cause uneven settling. A footing is needed to distribute the load. The softer the soil the bigger the footing has to be.

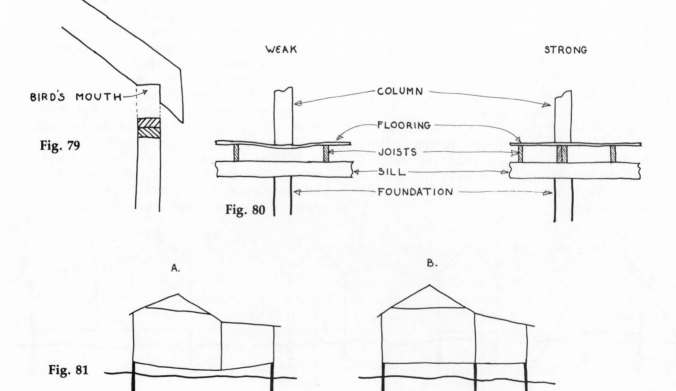

BIRD'S MOUTH

Fig. 79

WEAK   STRONG

COLUMN

FLOORING

JOISTS

SILL

FOUNDATION

Fig. 80

A.   B.

Fig. 81

chapter 7
Wood

THE NATURE OF WOOD

Most people will be building houses that consist largely of wooden parts. Even a stone house will be partly wood. Wood is an easy and forgiving material. It is light, yet strong. It is soft enough to cut easily, but hard enough to last a long time.

There are two problems with wood. First, there are many different kinds, and not every wood does every job well. Some kinds are strong, some are weak; some are hard, and some soft; some are durable and some are not; some rot quickly and some resist rot. Second, though wood is dead when you use it, it seems to have a life of its own: it shrinks and expands continually, it splits and cracks, it warps, and, if not kept dry, it rots. Designing a house consists partly of contending with the varieties of wood and the changes all wood goes through when you use it. If you are fully aware of these factors, you can build your house more easily, and it will look and function better. Furthermore, you can lower your building costs significantly by using less expensive grades of wood in most parts of your house.

Shrinkage. A tree is full of water, like any living thing. When it is sawn into lumber, the moisture slowly starts to evaporate into the surrounding air. This process is accelerated if the surrounding air is warm, if the air is relatively dry, or if the air is moving. The process is slower if the air is cold, humid, or stagnant. The drying-out process continues until the moisture content of the wood comes into equilibrium with the air. If the humidity drops, the wood starts to lose moisture. If the humidity rises, the wood starts to absorb moisture. Since the humidity of the air frequently changes, wood is often absorbing or losing moisture. The process is important to anyone building a house because when a piece of wood gives off moisture it shrinks and when it picks up moisture it swells. Since the humidity constantly varies, the wood in your house is always slowly changing size.

Wood dries out in two phases. The first phase is the initial seasoning, in which most of the water is removed from the wood permanently. This usually takes a year at most. The second phase is the more minute variations that continue indefinitely as the humidity varies. Indoors, in a heated house, these second-phase variations are essentially seasonal. In the winter months, the heating system dries out the house and the wood shrinks to its minimum size. When the heat goes off in the spring, the wood gradually starts to expand, particularly if the weather is wet. Even your varnished furniture will go through these seasonal changes, only more slowly than raw wood does. Outside or in unheated buildings the variations may be more frequent since the outside atmosphere varies in temperature and humidity much more often. When it rains your siding will swell. When the sun comes out it will shrink again.

Lumber shrinks mainly across the grain — that is, in width and thickness. The lengthwise shrinkage is negligible. An 8-foot 1 × 10 board can shrink 1/8 inch in thickness and 1/2 inch in width, but the length will not change measurably. The

Fig. 82   SHRINKAGE PATTERNS

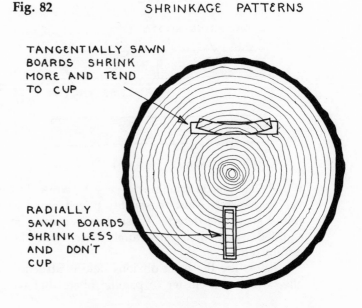

TANGENTIALLY SAWN BOARDS SHRINK MORE AND TEND TO CUP

RADIALLY SAWN BOARDS SHRINK LESS AND DON'T CUP

amount of shrinkage is affected by how the board is positioned in the log. As Figure 82 shows, a board sawn out tangentially to the growth rings will shrink more than one sawn out radially. A tangentially sawn board will also cup away from the center of the tree as it dries. Since most boards will inevitably be tangential to some extent, most boards can be expected to cup slightly when dry.

Carpentry practice takes these facts into account continually. Wood is usually carefully seasoned until it is in equilibrium with the air in the place where it will be used. Since houses are drier inside than out, boards to be used inside are dried more thoroughly than boards to be used outside. Since humidity varies seasonally, it is the usual practice to dry wood to match the driest conditions that will occur. Many construction methods are specifically designed to permit wood to shrink and expand without causing cracks or other problems. For example, wood clapboards can slide by each other when they change size. Shingles are usually nailed up with spaces between them so that when they are soaked by the rain they can swell without buckling.

Structural Defects in Wood.   Big, tall, straight trees tend to produce straight-grained, knot-free lumber with little tendency to warp. Lumber from big redwood or Douglas fir trees is sometimes so uniform that the lines of the grain are almost perfectly straight and evenly spaced (Figure 83).

Fig. 83   STRAIGHT GRAIN

DEFECTS

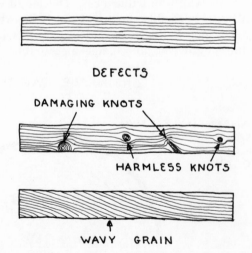

DAMAGING KNOTS

HARMLESS KNOTS

WAVY GRAIN

Wood like this is strong and easy to work, but very expensive. Most reasonably priced wood is full of structural defects. These defects cannot be avoided, but their structural effect can be minimized.

Knots are the most obvious defect. Structurally, wood is a cluster of parallel fibers that we see as the *grain* of wood. A knot interrupts and weakens this structure. How much of a problem a knot will cause depends on its size and on where it is located. A knot on the upper, or compression, side of a beam is less harmful than a knot on the tension side, at least if the knot is tight in its hole. A knot in the center of a piece usually presents no problem because the center of a beam is not really under stress. A knot near the end of a piece weakens the piece less than a knot in midspan. When you build, put knots where they will do the least damage. Select and cut the wood so that the best pieces are used for heaviest loads and longest spans and the worst pieces are cut up for shorter spans or nonstructural uses. Place the bigger knots on the compression side. Only the worst pieces need to be eliminated outright.

A second defect is wavy or angular grain. A piece is strong as long as the grain is more or less parallel to the piece, even if it is quite wavy. But when the grain actually bisects the piece (Figure 83), it will be weak. When no grain lines can be followed from one end of the piece to the other, don't use the piece as a beam.

Warps do not weaken wood, but they do make it harder to use. Warping can mean cupping — which is to some extent unavoidable — bowing, or twisting (Figure 84). Bowing and twisting are

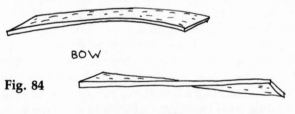

BOW

Fig. 84

TWIST

particularly likely to occur in boards sawn from crooked trees. Such a tree is full of tremendous strains in every direction, like crooked sticks tied together in a bundle. When the tree is sawn into lumber, these tensions are released and the lumber warps. Usually this warping happens as the lumber dries. If wood is carefully dried in straight stacks (see pages 48–49), the amount of distortion will be reduced. Warped lumber is still usable up to a point. Often 1-inch boards can be simply forced into position and nailed down flat. Framing lumber is much harder to use warped or twisted, and you can usually count on some of your framing lumber being useless for this reason. When native lumber from small, relatively crooked trees is being used, the framing members are often nailed up green, before the warping occurs, and allowed to season in place. The pressure of the adjacent framing keeps them from warping. The effect of a warp can be reduced by cutting and using the piece in shorter lengths.

Kinds of Wood.   Wood falls into two categories: hardwood and softwood. Hardwoods come from broad-leaved trees, which shed their leaves in winter. Softwoods are evergreens. Maple, oak, beech, and ash are hardwoods. Spruce, fir, pine, and hemlock are softwoods. While most hardwood is in fact harder than most softwood, there are some very hard softwoods and some very soft hardwoods. Butternut, a hardwood, is softer than yellow pine, a softwood. Softwoods are used for house frames, siding, flooring, paneling, trim, and in fact for every part of a house. Hardwoods are commonly used in building only for certain specialized purposes: flooring, door sills, and occasionally for paneling and trim. Hardwood is difficult or impossible to nail through without drilling a hole first and takes much longer to saw. It warps more as it dries. For all these reasons, softwood is the basic housebuilding material.

HOW LUMBER IS PROCESSED

Sawmills saw logs into boards, planks, and timbers of various sizes. A log might be sawn entirely into 2 × 4s or perhaps into a variety of sizes according to what the sawyer thinks is the best use of the particular log. The lumber is now in the rough, which means it has the rough surface left by the sawmill blade. It is approximately full size; a 2 × 4 is about 2 inches by 4 inches. The lumber is not perfectly uniform, however, since a sawmill saw is not a precision machine. A 2 × 4 may vary as much as ½ inch from the nominal size.

At this point, the lumber is full of moisture or green. Lumber is sometimes used in this form, particularly for framing and for boards that will later be covered, such as subflooring. Rough, green lumber is usually bought directly from local sawmills. But much lumber has to undergo two further steps before use: drying, to minimize further shrinkage, and planing, to increase uniformity.

Drying.   There are several ways of drying lumber. The simplest is called air-drying. Sometimes it is done by local sawmills and it is the way you would dry native lumber yourself. The lumber is stacked outdoors under cover in specially spaced piles to allow air to circulate freely all around each board. Air-drying will take from a few weeks to several years, depending on the type of wood, the drying conditions, and how the wood will be used. Lumber can also be kiln-dried in a huge storage room where heat and moisture are controlled to dry out the wood as fast as possible without damaging it. Much of the wood available at lumberyards has been kiln-dried.

Planing.   Wood is planed or milled to uniform dimensions by feeding the pieces through huge planers. A rough 2 × 4 will be milled down to 1½″ × 3½″. A 1 × 8 board will end up ¾″ × 7¼″. The actual thickness will generally be at least ¼ inch less than the nominal thickness and the actual width ½ inch to ¾ of an inch less than the nominal. In addition, some lumber will be milled to special shapes for flooring, molding, door frames, and other items.

PRICING

Lumber is sold by the board foot. The easiest way to think of a board foot is as a piece of wood 12″ × 12″ × 1″ or any equal volume (144 cu. in.). A 1-foot length (one running foot) of 1 × 12 contains 1 board foot. So does a running foot of 2 × 6 (half as wide but twice as thick) or of 3 × 4. A running foot of 2 × 4 is two-thirds of a board foot, because its cross section is only two-thirds that of a 2 × 6 (8 square inches instead of 12). One method of figuring board feet in a piece is to find the board feet per running feet and then multiply by the number of running feet. Say you have an 8-foot 1 × 6. A 1 × 6 contains ½ of a board foot for each running foot; one half times 8 is 4, or 4 board feet.

Another method is to multiply the width of a piece in inches, times the thickness in inches, times the length *in feet*, and divide the result by

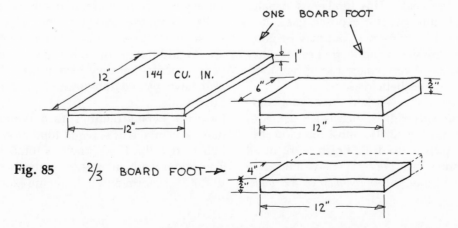

ONE BOARD FOOT

12″   144 CU. IN.   1″

12″

6″   ¾″

12″

Fig. 85   ⅔ BOARD FOOT →   4″   ½″

12″

12. If you have a 2 × 8 that's 10 feet long, you multiply 2 × 8 × 10 to get 160, and divide by 12, which comes out to 13⅓ board feet.

Board measure is figured for pricing *before planing*. Thus a planed 1 × 12 is still one board foot per running foot, even though the piece is only 3/4″ × 11½″ after planing. Any wood under 1 inch thick is considered 1 inch thick for pricing purposes.

Large quantities of lumber are sold by the thousand board feet. A price of "180 a thousand" means $180 per 1000 board feet. That price would be written on a price list as $180/M and would be the equivalent of .18 per board foot.

SOURCES

In most areas there are two main sources of supply. Local sawmills sell mostly green or air-dried rough lumber from local trees. Lumber yards sell mostly planed, kiln-dried lumber imported from the large forests of the Pacific Coast. The source you choose will have a big influence on the appearance and cost of your house.

Lumber Yard Wood.   Yards stock different items in different parts of the country, but the following description is typical.

The 2 × 4s, 2 × 8s, and other framing lumber are usually spruce, hemlock, white fir, hem-fir, (hemlock and white fir mixed), or S–P–F, (spruce, pine, and fir mixed). This lumber is planed, dry, straight, fairly economical, and strong. These qualities vary considerably with the grade of lumber. Though yards usually refer to their framing lumber as *construction grade*, there are actually several construction grades of wood, of which the most common are (in descending order of quality) *Select Structural, #1, #2,* and *#3*. Select Structural, #1, and #2 are the premium grades. Number 3 is the cheap grade, which is generally inferior.

The construction grades are usually covered up by the finish materials of the house, except when used for decks or other somewhat rough work. Lumber yards also sell Douglas fir, redwood, yellow pine, or other species in a special *clear* or *appearance grade*. This lumber is usually knot-free and is intended for exposed uses. It is much too expensive for framing but may be good for railings, windowsills, window frames, or other jobs where you need very straight knot-free lumber for practical or aesthetic reasons.

Lumber yards also sell kiln-dried, planed 1-inch boards in various widths, such as 1 × 4, 1 × 6, 1 × 8, 1 × 10, and 1 × 12. The most common species is pine, which is used for finish work of all kinds. This comes in a very expensive knot-free *clear grade* and a more knotty *common* or *#2 grade*,

which costs about half as much but is more trouble to work with. Redwood, Douglas fir, cedar, and yellow pine boards are also often available, particularly in a *clear grade*.

Lumber yards also sell specially milled pieces for specific purposes. Stock for door frames, window frames, and moldings is usually made of clear, white pine. Stair treads and door sills come in oak or clear Douglas fir. Siding materials (shingles, clapboards, shiplap siding, etc.) are available in pine and in rot-resistant cedar or redwood. And of course lumber yards sell a lot of plywood for sheathing, subfloors, cabinets, etc. Plywood usually comes in 4 × 8 sheets and in thicknesses from ¼ inch to an inch. It is expensive, but goes up fast if the house is framed for it. In addition, lumber yards often supply other building supplies, such as sheetrock, insulation, concrete blocks, nails, etc., and sometimes hardware and tools as well.

Sawmill Wood.   Sawmills are local institutions. They sell whatever wood grows nearby. In the northeast this usually means pine, spruce, hemlock, and smaller amounts of hardwoods like oak, maple, birch, and cherry. In parts of the south, certain hardwoods, such as oak, are so plentiful that they are sold by sawmills as framing material. The quality of the wood depends on the quality of the local forests and the way the logs are treated by the mills.

The framing lumber is usually green and rough. Some mills stock a variety of sizes and lengths, but often mills custom-saw logs into the particular sizes you need, including large timbers, such as 6 × 8s. Usually timbers are sold at a standard board-foot price, irrespective of the size of the pieces. (At lumber yards, the larger timbers are usually much more expensive). Some sawmills also have planing equipment and sell framing lumber planed to uniform dimensions.

The boards sawmills sell are often unplaned and green like the framing lumber. Often these boards are sold *random-width, random-length*. If you buy 1000 board feet of boards, some will be long, some short, some wide, and some narrow. Other mills sort out the sizes you need, which is essential for some purposes and convenient for others.

In addition, some mills have a supply of last year's boards that they have air-dried. Some may also have planed tongue and groove or shiplap boards.

Sawmill Versus Lumber Yard Wood.   The primary advantage of sawmill lumber is that it costs half to two-thirds as much as lumberyard wood. The primary advantages of lumber yard wood are that it is uniform and light (being planed and dry) and convenient to obtain. All you do is call the lumber yard, tell the clerk what you need, and the next morning the lumber will be delivered to your site. Whether this convenience is worth the extra price depends on what the lumber is being used for.

For framing purposes, sawmill wood has several advantages. First, you can save a lot of money, especially with large-size timbers like 4 × 6s or 6 × 10s, since lumber yards charge a premium for these big pieces. Second, unplaned sawmill lumber is bigger, and therefore stronger, all other factors being equal. Third, rough framing lumber looks better exposed. Ordinary construction-grade wood from a lumber yard is not usually very presentable. Fourth, a sawmill will saw lumber to the exact sizes and lengths you want.

If you use rough lumber for framing, you'll have to put up with some disadvantages. It is heavier than lumber yard stock because it is green. It usually has to be ordered in advance, especially when custom-sawn to your order. Finally, rough-sawn lumber is not as uniform in dimension, which makes it harder to work with. You may, for example, have to trim each joist with a saw or hatchet to make the floor come out flat.

My experience is that for heavy timbers like floor joists, sills, and rafters, rough lumber is worth using, even if you do have to spend extra time. Its appearance and economy outweigh the disadvantages. But walls should be framed with planed timber, because they are finished on both sides and will be uneven if the studs are irregular. Also, windows and doors take much longer to install in an uneven wall. If a sawmill has planing equipment, this is not a problem.

With boards there are even stronger reasons for using native lumber. One-inch boards bought from a sawmill are considerably cheaper, about half the price of #2 pine or plywood. For the most part sawmill boards are perfectly adequate especially if they are dried and planed. If a sawmill sells planed, dry boards, there's probably no reason to buy any boards at all from a lumberyard, except for special projects that require clear stock, like window frames.

If your local sawmill offers only rough, green boards, you can still use them as is on many parts of the house. Subfloors and sheathing can be made of green boards because they will be covered later. So can board-and-batten siding, since the cracks that appear between the boards are covered by the battens. But visible boards, like paneling, finish flooring, door and window frames, and trim should be dried and planed. If the sawmill can't plane the boards you should find one that can. If they come green, you'll have to air-dry them yourself — and if they are to be used inside, you will need to dry them further by stacking them in a heated place for a few weeks. All this moving and stacking and drying and restacking takes time and planning. But what you get may be worth it in beauty and economy.

BUYING NATIVE LUMBER

Visiting Sawmills.   Before you buy native lumber, visit several sawmills to see what's available. They are usually small, informal operations, and you can find out much of what you need to know by talking to the owners. Here are the main questions to ask:

1. What species are available? Different woods have different appearances, and some are stronger than others (see Appendices A and B).
2. What can the mill supply? Will it custom-saw to your specifications? Does it sell batches or boards the same lengths and width or random sizes? Does it have extra-wide boards? Does it sell large timbers? Can you get air-dried boards?
3. *When* can it supply what you need? Can it promise you a specific date? How far in advance do you have to order?
4. What special milling operations can it perform? Some mills offer only rough-cut lumber. Others have planers that can plane the pieces smooth and uniform. Some do special work such as tongue and grooving or shiplapping, valuable for floors or horizontal siding. Some can mill boards down to 1/2 inch thick. Some make clapboards.

You can check out a number of questions yourself if you bring a ruler and square with you to the mill.

1. *Squareness*. Lay a square on some of the larger timbers — 4 inches or 6 inches thick. Sometimes they will be sawn so that they look like parallelograms in cross section.
2. *Straightness*. Take a board or a 2 × 4 and sight down an edge with one eye. Do this with pieces from different piles. Twisted pieces are hard to use. Bowed pieces are generally usable but only with trouble, and they are harder to fit tight. Cupping is not so serious and to some extent is unavoidable.
3. *Strength*. Look at the structural pieces. How straight and parallel to the piece is the grain? How knotty are the timbers? All framing lumber has knots, but too many, especially along the edges, can seriously weaken a beam.
4. *Uniformity*. Take a board or timber and measure the width at both ends to see if they're the same. Compare different boards with one another. A difference of plus or minus an eighth is common on rough-sawn board width. Plus or minus a quarter is about the maximum tolerable width. For board thickness, plus or minus a sixteenth is about the

limit. If you are using native 2 × 4s unplaned, check the consistency of the dimensions, especially the 4-inch dimension. On tongue and groove or shiplap boards, check the fit of the edges with each other. Bad milling makes wood hard to use.

5. *Waste.* Check the ends of boards and timbers to see how much will have to be cut off. Parts may be marginally usable due to knots, splitting, or sloppy sawing. Sometimes the sawyer uses a log that's a little too thin and part of the piece won't be square.

6. *Appearance.* If you're planning to expose any of the wood, look over its surface. Some wood may be blemished by rot or fungus, although interesting grain patterns or colorations can be a positive asset. Check if the surface of planed lumber is smooth or chipped.

Planning and Ordering.   A lot of preparation is necessary to use native lumber. Start visiting sawmills as soon as you think you might be using native wood. It's worth it to buy some 1-inch boards even before you know exactly what your design will call for. Mills may have a supply of last year's boards already air-dried, or you can arrange in advance to have the mill dry boards for you.

It helps to have a schedule, so you can work the various steps of the lumber-getting process into your overall building scheme. An ideal schedule might be to visit sawmills in summer or fall, make your plans over the winter months, order in the early spring, and do your drying in the spring and early summer while working on the foundation. Don't count on your lumber being ready at a given time unless you know the mill is a reliable one. Ask around to get some idea. Some mills are slow but dependable. Others will promise work soon but rarely deliver on time. It's not a bad idea to fix a delivery date a few weeks in advance of the time you'll actually need the wood.

When you order, give the sawmill operator a detailed list. For framing, specify the exact sizes of the pieces you need and order a few extras of each size. For boards, the order should show the total board feet needed, along with any other dimensions you can specify. Show which items you need dried, which should be planed and how they should be planed. Finally, the list should show when you need each item. Keep an exact copy for yourself to keep track of what has been delivered and how much money you owe the mill.

DRYING NATIVE LUMBER

Framing Lumber.   It is usually best *not* to dry framing lumber. As it dries it tends to warp and twist and become unusable. Thicker timbers — 4 inches or 6 inches — will almost certainly warp terribly if they are air-dried. Two by fours are less likely to warp, but there is still a risk. Therefore framing lumber should be prevented from drying if possible, and used green. Stack the lumber tightly in a pile off the ground, and cover it with plastic so it will not dry out much. However, make sure the pile does not get so damp that rot can start. Inspect the pile periodically by moving a few

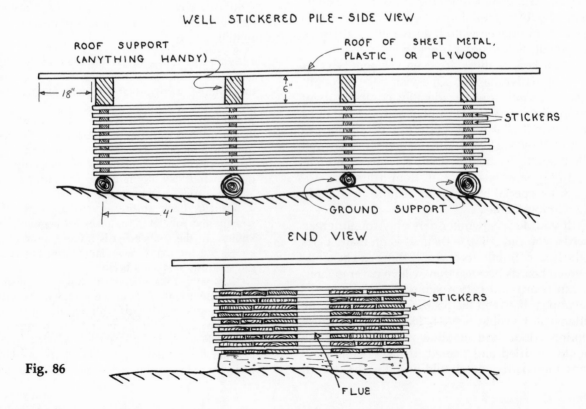

Fig. 86

pieces around and looking for stains or other signs of decay and dampness. If you find any, air out the pile enough to dry the surfaces and cover it up again. If you have a stack of 2 × 4s sitting around for a long time you might try to air-dry them, using the stickered-pile method described below for boards.

Air-Drying Boards. Wood is air-dried by being stickered in a pile. Stickers are long strips of wood about 1 inch thick, used to separate lumber in a pile so that each board is surrounded by currents of air that carry moisture away. Figure 86 shows a properly stickered pile, which is made as follows: Find a breezy spot, since the wind will definitely accelerate drying. A drafty barn with the doors open will do, or simply a spot outside. The ground should be flat, but it need not be level. In fact, if the pile slopes, the boards will shed water better. Next, put down logs or other ground supports, 4 feet to 6 feet long, every 4 feet, to keep the pile off the ground. If you're drying hardwood the supports should come every 2½ feet. If you take the trouble to elevate the entire pile 18 inches off the ground, the lumber will dry faster. If the logs vary in thickness, the variance can be used to compensate for any unevenness in the ground. Have the tops of the supports form a flat bed for the pile. Sight along the tops to make sure.

Now put a layer of boards on the logs, spacing them at least 1 inch apart. If you have a pile containing over 500 board feet, create vertical flues in the middle of the pile as shown in Figure 86, by leaving a wider 4-inch to 6-inch space every 15 inches or 2 feet. Next put a row of stickers on top of the boards, directly above the ground supports. Put down another row of boards, again leaving spaces between the boards. Put the next row of stickers directly above the first row, add another row of boards, and so on. The pile can be very high, but 4 feet is a good height.

Protect the pile from rain with a roof of plywood, plastic, or old tin roofing. Leave 6 inches between the roof and the top row of boards so that the flues will work. The roof should overhang 18 inches.

Figure 87 shows a badly stickered pile. Notice

BADLY STICKERED PILE   **Fig. 87**

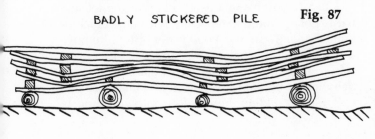

that the stickers aren't lined up, some are thicker than others, some of the boards are unsupported at the ends (not always avoidable), and the log foundation is not flat. All this makes for bending and sagging in the pile. Any kind of sags will become permanent features of the boards as they dry.

Well-stickered softwood boards will usually air-dry about as much as they ever will in six to ten weeks of hot, dry summer weather. Colder, wetter weather will slow the process tremendously. You can test the dryness of the pile by including in it some short sample pieces that can be measured for shrinkage. As you build the pile, include about eight pieces 2 or 3 feet long. Draw a line across each one, and measure the width to the nearest 1/64th of an inch. Write the width next to the line. These samples should be chosen from boards cut tangentially since boards of this kind shrink more than those cut radially. Place the sample pieces where they can be fairly easily removed, perhaps with a crowbar. After the pile has been exposed to a month of good drying weather, remove a few of the test boards and remeasure their width. If your test board is 8 inches wide and has not shrunk at least 1/4 inch, the pile is probably not dry yet. If the test board is 6 inches wide, look for a shrinkage of at least 3/16 of an inch. You can also measure test pieces several weeks in a row. When the pieces stop shrinking, they are as dry as they'll get outdoors.

You can also make an estimate of the further shrinkage you can expect. Take two or three of your test boards and cut 1-inch strips across the center of each one, as shown in Figure 88. Measure

Fig. 88

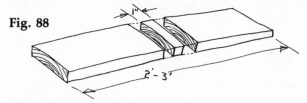

the width of the 1-inch strips precisely. Put the strips in a spot that has similar humidity to the part of the house where the wood will be used. For siding or exterior uses, place the strips in direct sunlight for three hot days, or until they stop shrinking. Rotate the pieces periodically, and keep them from getting covered with dew or rain, which will slow down the test. To test lumber to be used indoors, place the sample in a heated place, directly above and near a heat source. If the heat is not on yet, put the sample in the oven with the pilot on. Rotate the pieces for 2 days, or until shrinking stops, and take a second accurate measurement of the width. The difference in width before and after will approximately equal the further shrinkage you can expect and therefore the size of cracks you can expect to see between boards.

The following chart gives a rough idea of how much shrinkage is acceptable under various conditions. Many buildings are built with wider spaces, and time schedules will not always permit perfect drying procedures. Dry wood as thoroughly as you can without making the chore a nuisance.

	Max. Shrinkage:
Board and batten siding	1/4″
Shiplap or tongue in groove siding	1/8″
Vertical square edged board siding	1/16″
Shiplap or tongue and groove paneling	1/16″
Window casings and trim	1/32″ or 0″
Door and window jambs	1/32″
Flooring	1/32″ or 0″
Ceilings	1/8″

Shrinkage is proportional to board width. If your boards are wider than the test pieces, the cracks between boards will be greater. If the boards are narrower, the cracks will be proportionately smaller.

I have talked so far only about outdoor air-drying. But no matter how long you air-dry boards outside, they will shrink further when used in a heated house. This shrinkage may be within acceptable limits for ceilings or paneling, especially if the boards are relatively narrow. But for flooring, trim, and paneling, I think an additional drying period indoors in a heated part of your new house is worth it. This extra drying is equivalent to the kiln drying done by lumber companies and is just as effective. Sticker up the boards again inside, preferably in a loft or upstairs area that will be quite warm. The boards should probably be left this way for about six weeks. However, as before, the best method is to test 1-inch sample pieces exactly as you would with air-dried lumber. An alternate method is to use a few of the boards just as you will later use the whole pile. Pick a location near the heat, and observe the cracks after two weeks.

Boards dried this way should be used in the winter or spring, before humid summer weather causes them to swell again. If your boards must sit around in hot, humid weather, wrap the pile with plastic to minimize swelling.

The point at which you move boards indoors may also be the time to have shiplapping, tongue and grooving, or thickness planing done. Do this *after* the boards have been air-dried so that once planed they won't shrink much more, but *before* bringing them indoors, to minimize moving piles around.

OTHER SOURCES OF LUMBER

Having Your Own Lumber Sawn.   If your land has tall, straight softwood trees at least 12 inches in diameter, you can have them sawed up into lumber by a sawmill. This service will cost about .04 per board foot, as opposed to about .20 for bought lumber. However, you must include in your figuring other expenses you will incur. First you must buy or borrow a chainsaw to cut down the trees. Next you need a jeep, horse, bulldozer, or farm tractor to drag the logs out of the woods. Then you must find or hire a truck or wagon to haul the logs to the mill and haul the lumber back. All this costs money and takes times. Usually it will cost enough money to make getting your own logs sawn a marginal economy at best. If your plans already include a chainsaw for wood heat, a tractor for farming, or a truck for general purposes, doing your own logging may be practical if you have the time.

If you decide to do logging, you should definitely get an experienced logger to teach you. Logging is a dangerous trade, perhaps the most dangerous.

Used Lumber.   You can get used lumber in two ways. You can buy it from a salvage company for about half the cost of new wood. This wood varies greatly for appearance and usability. It may be already dry. But it often takes more work to use than new wood. You can demolish decrepit buildings yourself to recycle the wood. Sometimes people will sell cheap or give you the wood from an old barn if you promise to demolish the building cleanly and completely. Lumber from such a source is cheap and sometimes beautiful, but it takes a long time to demolish a barn. If you build entirely with used lumber, you can probably expect your labor time to be about 50 percent more than with new wood.

Before you make a deal to buy or demolish a barn, poke around extensively with an icepick or knife to make sure the wood is not rotten. Remove a few boards to make sure they do not conceal rotten timbers. After all, the building is being demolished because it is defective. Make sure you will not be building these defects into your house.

chapter 8
Heat

HEAT SOURCES

Central Heating Systems. In a central heating system the heat from a main furnace is transported to each part of the house. In a forced hot water system, water is heated in a boiler and carried by pipes to radiators in each room. These can be the old-fashioned upright radiators, but today most systems use baseboard radiators. Some houses are built with the hot water pipes embedded in a concrete floor so the entire floor becomes the radiator. In a forced air system, air instead of water is heated by the furnace and transported to grates in each room through sheet-metal ducts installed in the framing.

A central heating system has two particular advantages. First, the heat can be uniform because it is so widely distributed. Second, the temperature is controlled automatically by thermostats. The main disadvantage is the high installation cost. A hot water system for a small house will cost about $2300 installed. A hot air system for a small house will cost about $1700 installed. If you do the work yourself, the cost will be about half in both cases. Both hot air and hot water have their advocates. A hot air system is less expensive and can be combined easily with central air conditioning. A hot water system is simpler and more compact.

Either system can be used with a variety of fuels. Furnaces can run on wood, oil, gas and even electricity. Wood furnaces are uncommon, but are coming back into popularity, especially in areas where the cost of wood is low enough to justify the effort of gathering wood and stoking the furnace every day. Of the other heat sources, oil and gas are similar in cost and electricity is much more expensive.

Space Heat. In a space heating system, a few smaller heaters are distributed throughout the house. The fuel, rather than the heat, is transported throughout the house. These heaters can be wood stoves, electric heaters, or gas or kerosene space heaters. In a small house a single heater may serve the whole house. A larger house may have two, three, or more. Usually a heater will not be needed in every room.

These systems are cheaper because they are simpler. There is little or no ductwork or plumbing, perhaps only a gas line bringing gas to the heater and a chimney of some type. For the same reason, space heaters are easier to install. These systems have important disadvantages. Since the heat sources are widely separated, the heat is less uniform; there will be hot and cold places. Only certain house layouts heat efficiently with space heat, since the heat is concentrated near a few heat sources. A reasonably compact two-story house works well because the heat rises automatically to the second floor. A small cabin or house will heat fairly well because no part of it is far from the stove. But heat from a space heater will not travel far horizontally and will be blocked by closed doors. A large, horizontally spread out one-story house may need many heaters to maintain reasonably even temperatures. In such cases a central system may be more economical.

This does not mean that a large, one-story house cannot use space heat, particularly if it is tight and well insulated. The heat can be distributed effectively with fans. Some space heaters come with fans built in. Gas floor furnaces, which are gas space heaters mounted under the floor, sometimes have an air-return duct that brings cooled air from the far side of the room back to the heater. You can accomplish much of the same purpose with ordinary fans. A 20 × 20 window fan located above the stove and operating on low speed will distribute the heat throughout a large area without much noise or breeze.

At one time many space heaters burned kerosene. Kerosene heaters are dangerous and illegal in some places. Today the most practical space heaters are gas heaters and wood stoves. Both come in many sizes and varieties. Wood stoves can be cook stoves as well as room heaters.

My favorite heating system combines wood stoves with one or two gas space heaters. The wood stoves provide the bulk of the heat, but a gas heater or two keeps the house somewhat warm when no one is home or when the wood-stove dies down in the early morning.

Electric Heat.   Electrical heating systems include regular furnaces, baseboard radiators, wall-mounted space heaters with fans, and radiant panels that cover the entire ceiling. Electric systems combine the uniformity and controllability of central systems with the simplicity of installation and operation of space heat systems. There are no pipes, no chimney, no dirt, and almost no maintenance. Installation is usually simpler and more economical than with other central systems. The problem is that electricity is more expensive by far than any other fuel. In cold climates electric heat is not practical except for small spaces such as bathrooms or as supplementary heating.

Solar Heat.   There may be some confusion about the term solar heat. Solar heat can mean using ordinary building materials and techniques to maximize the extent to which a house is heated by the sun so that the load on the regular heating

system will be reduced. This is *passive solar heat*, which will be the most practical approach for most people. The second kind of solar heat uses a complex system of rooftop solar collectors as the main heat supply (Figure 89). In a passive system, the sun supplements the furnace. In a collector system, a small furnace supplements the solar system.

To heat a house with the sun's diffuse energy you must collect heat from a large area and concentrate it. In a typical rooftop collector system an entire roof is oriented to face the sun and covered with a series of collectors. A collector is typically a box with a glass surface on the outside, an air cavity in the middle, and a black metal heat-absorbing surface on the inside. Like a greenhouse, the inside of the box heats up when the sun is up, even if the sky is overcast. The black inner surface maximizes this effect. Bonded to the metal surface is a network of pipes filled with water. The water heats up from contact with the hot black surface and is pumped to a heavily insulated storage tank. The large insulated mass of water is the heat storage mechanism. It stays warm up to a few days even when no fresh heat is coming in. (Sometimes the water mass will be combined with a masonry mass, which may be simply a tankful of rocks or a fireplace through which the water pipes flow.) The water from the colder portions of the tank is pumped up to the roof to continue the cycle. Another set of pipes reverses the collection process to heat the house. These pipes pick up the hottest water from the storage tank and circulate it to radiators distributed throughout the house.

In many systems the heat is circulated throughout the house by air instead of water via a system of air ducts much like the ductwork in a conventional forced air system, only larger in size. As in a conventional system, the air is forcibly circulated by a fan. A heat exchanger transfers the heat from the hot water to the air. This is essentially a coil or a network of small pipes something like a radiator, located inside the air ductwork, through which the hottest water circulates. The cool air blows across the coil or network of hot pipes, cooling the water and heating the air.

A solar collector system is at first glance tremendously attractive because it offers virtually free heat. In reality the first costs are huge, because your roof is covered with plumbing and plumbing is the most expensive part of any building. The cost of commercially available collectors alone could be as much as $10,000 for a medium-sized house (800 to 1000 square feet, two stories tall). This is in addition to the cost of the storage system, the distribution system, the pumps, and installa-

SOLAR COLLECTOR SYSTEM

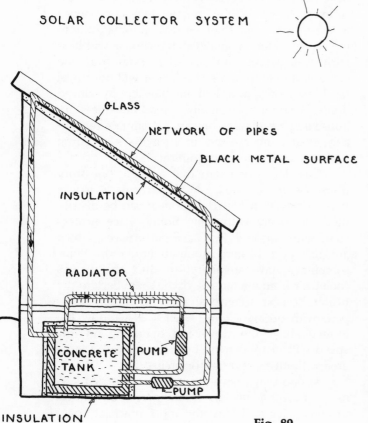

GLASS

NETWORK OF PIPES

BLACK METAL SURFACE

INSULATION

RADIATOR

CONCRETE TANK

PUMP

PUMP

INSULATION

Fig. 89

tion. If you make your own collectors, just the materials for the collectors could cost $1000 or more. The expense means that a solar collecting system you buy will only represent a reasonable proportion of your building cost if you are building an expensive house, say, over $40,000. You can design and build your own system from scratch, but it is a major undertaking.

HEATING EFFICIENCY

Though few can afford a rooftop collector system, anyone building a house can have an energy-efficient house by applying a few basic heating principles thoroughly. Taking pains with a hundred small details, each unimportant in itself, can result in saving about half the fuel costs. These conscientious efforts are not just for economy's sake. An efficient house is more comfortable. Being sunny, bright, relatively uniform in temperature, and relatively free of drafts, your house will have a feeling of warmth even when the room temperature is low.

Weather Orientation.   Your building site should be well open to the sky on the south, east, and west, because that's where the sun shines. The southern quadrant is particularly important, since the sun is there in the winter.

The house should also be protected from winter winds (though not necessarily from summer breezes) by hills, plantings, and outbuildings, because the wind-chill factor cools a house just as much as it does a person outdoors.

The house must have sufficient window area, especially to the south, to let the heat in when the sun is up.

Surface Area.   As important as how you heat your house is how you minimize *heat loss*. The heat loss of anything is proportional to its surface area. That is why radiators, which are designed to lose their heat, have fins or other irregularities to maximize their surface. In a house, you want to do the opposite, minimize the surface presented to the outside weather. The simpler the structure the more heat-efficient it will be. I am not recommending that you build a spherical or cubical house, because heat efficiency is only one of your design goals. Many factors should influence the shape of your house. But a relatively compact shape will be easier to heat than a complex one.

Insulation.   Most materials used to insulate buildings are efficient for the same reason down garments are warm. Both are full of small pores or cavities — dead air spaces — that trap air and impede the transfer of heat. Chapter nineteen discusses different kinds of insulation. Appendix E treats insulation ratings in a more technical way.

The main idea is simply that heat loss is reduced by using more insulation. The effectiveness of any insulation is proportional to its thickness.

The most common and economical insulation is fiberglass. Until recently, the rule of thumb has been to use 3 inches in the walls and 6 inches in the roof and floor. Now many people are exceeding these amounts, because fuel has become so expensive. For about $100 or so you can add an extra 3 inches of fiberglass insulation to your roof, as long as the rafters are deep enough to hold it. Increasing the depth of the rafters by 2 or 3 inches might cost an extra $30 or $50. You can frame the walls with 2 × 6s instead of 2 × 4s to double the insulation space. This might cost about $150 for the extra insulation and $100 for the extra framing. If at the same time you expanded the interval between wall studs from 16 inches to 24 inches, it would not cost you anything for extra framing. For a cost of something like $400 for a medium-sized house you can permanently reduce your heating bills by approximately 15 percent.

Window Placement and Insulation.   Windows lose heat about ten times as fast per square foot as do walls or roofs. Even a moderate window area can account for 40 percent of your total heat bill. One of the keys to heating efficiency is to minimize this avenue of heat loss. You should first eliminate superfluous or inefficient window area. You need south, east, and west windows for solar heat and light. You need north windows to see outside. But you do not need entire walls of glass. Your south, east, and west walls should have enough window for solar heat but not too much more. You should be even more circumspect about north windows, because these give no heat back even with the sun out. North windows should therefore usually be relatively few and relatively small.

Next, use storm windows, insulated glass (Thermopane) or some other system of double glazing. This one step will cut the heat loss through the windows in half, which means an overall savings of around 15 percent. Even with double glazing, however, windows will still pour out heat at night or on overcast days when there is no compensating solar heat gain. Heavy curtains will go a long way toward solving this problem, especially if they are quilted and fit tightly against the wall. Insulated shutters are even better. Removable or hinged shutters with 1 or 2 inches of rigid foam insulation can insulate almost as well as a wall. If you use a shuttering system scrupulously you can save another 15 percent on your heat bill.

Infiltration.   Infiltration means the actual flow of warm air out and cold air in. This leakage can be through small cracks in the siding, or around windows and doors, especially through cracks between the jambs and the studs. It can also be simply from opening and closing doors. Infiltration can account for anywhere from 10 to about 40 percent of the total heat loss. There are several ways to keep infiltration down. Under the siding there should be some sort of continuous seal, such as plywood or 15-pound felt paper, to keep the wall tight. Cracks around windows and doors should be caulked. Before you do finish work you should stuff cracks with insulation. Weatherstripping helps seal openings around doors and windows. A vestibule or double door at an entry helps prevent large masses of cold air from coming in when people enter or leave. These precautions can save perhaps 15 percent of your total heat loss.

All of these percentages are of course approximate. What they amount to is that if you locate, design, and build your house with these features in mind, you can save tremendously on heating costs.

Passive Solar Heat.   All these factors can be quantified, and there are engineering methods to compute them. When a house is engineered to maximize heating efficiency, the result is called *passive*

solar heat or *solar-tempering*. A solar-tempered house may also include a simple system to store solar energy between sunny periods. Such a system will usually consist of a large masonry mass inside the house that is warmed up slowly by direct exposure to the sunlight. When the sun goes down, the masonry mass gradually emits heat into the surrounding room. Such a mass can be a stone or concrete floor insulated underneath or a vertical mass such as an interior masonry wall or fireplace. One effective way to solar-temper is to build a large stone or brick wall perhaps 4 or 5 feet inside a south wall with a large glass area, as shown in Figure 90.

Readers interested in solar engineering can pursue the subject with Appendices D and E and with books listed in the bibliography. Remember that solar efficiency, though valuable, is not your only design goal. Some people get so involved with making their house energy-efficient that they forget other equally important or more important needs. Most of the benefits of passive solar heat can be achieved by following the sensible design practices described here. Space needs, good views, or your own tastes should not be sacrificed for further, marginal reductions in heat loss.

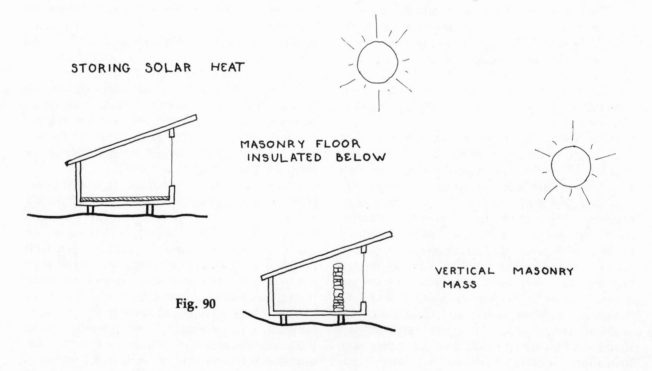

STORING SOLAR HEAT

MASONRY FLOOR INSULATED BELOW

VERTICAL MASONRY MASS

Fig. 90

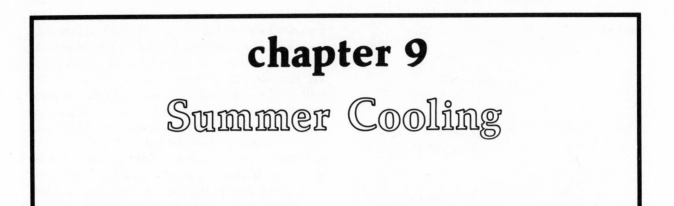

chapter 9
Summer Cooling

In northern climates you can keep your house cool by opening a few windows, but in most of the United States you will need to do more. The key is to do the opposite of what you did to keep the house warm.

SITE CONDITIONS

Since most houses face the sun, you will need shade trees. Shade trees are broad-leaved trees — hardwoods — that shed their leaves in winter when you need maximum sun.

Summer breezes are equally important. Often the prevailing wind direction varies seasonally. By consulting radio stations and neighbors, and by making your own observations, you can find the pattern at your site. Build your house where hills, plants, and outbuildings will obstruct the winter but not the summer wind. Of course you may have to remove or add plants and trees to do this.

You might want to live in your house for a season before removing too many large irreplaceable trees. The temperature of the wind will be affected somewhat by what it passes over immediately before it reaches the house. If it passes over a street or driveway, it will be warmed. A pond or vegetation will cool it and therefore help cool your house.

Insulation. The insulation that keeps the winter heat in also keeps out the summer heat. Effective insulation — especially in the roof — is as important for summer cooling as for winter heating.

South Window Area. You need enough south windows to collect the sun's heat, but too much south-facing glass will make the inside intolerable in summer and increase your winter heat loss too. Use common sense to determine what the right amount of glass is. Observe other houses in the area. You can add or remove windows later to make adjustments based on your experience.

Ventilation. Winter leaks you don't want are called infiltration. The leaks you do want in summer are called ventilation. Ventilation can consist of open doors and windows, but you can also add supplementary screened vents. Vents are almost a necessity in houses with fixed windows. Whatever type of opening you use, the principles are the same (Figure 91). The air should enter on the windward side where possible and exit on the opposite leeward side for cross ventilation. The wind is the fan driving the air through. If the inlet is low on the windward side, and the outlet higher on the leeward side, the house acts like a chimney. A natural draft is set up, so air will move even without the wind. Finally, the airflow will be more effective if the outlet size is larger than the inlet size. Chapter fifteen discusses the construction of windows and vents.

Architectural Shading. In some climates a stra-

VENTILATION

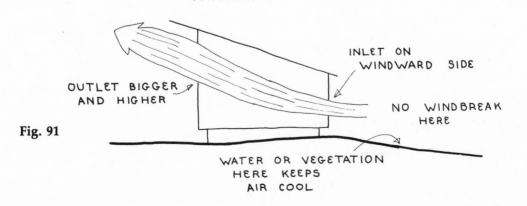

OUTLET BIGGER AND HIGHER

INLET ON WINDWARD SIDE

NO WINDBREAK HERE

WATER OR VEGETATION HERE KEEPS AIR COOL

Fig. 91

Fig. 92

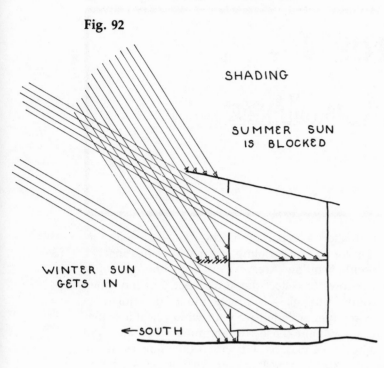

SHADING

SUMMER SUN
IS BLOCKED

WINTER SUN
GETS IN

← SOUTH

tegically located shade tree will be all the shading you need. In hotter climates you may need to build the shade into your house. Figure 92 shows shading provided by extending the overhang of the roof on the south side. The sun is higher in summer than in winter. The goal is to find an amount of projection that lets in the winter midday sun but blocks out the high midsummer sun. You can determine the amount of overhang you want by studying the sun angles in your latitude (Appendix D), but usually the correct overhang for a relatively horizontal roof will be about 4 feet.

When a roof does not provide convenient shading you can devise a projecting sunshade such as is shown in Figure 92. If such a shade is spaced or louvered the summer breeze will be more free to flow. Make the outer portion adjustable so you can vary the overhang with conditions.

Readers interested in a more scientific approach can consult *Low Cost Energy Efficient Shelter*, edited by Eugene Eccli (see bibliography).

chapter 10
Plumbing and Water Systems

Water supplies and the laws that govern them vary tremendously from place to place. When you construct your water system, follow local practice. In looking at local systems, don't just investigate those popular with contractors. Check out how farmers get their water. Farmers of necessity are experts on cheap but reliable water systems. If you don't find a certain type of system in local use, the chances are it has been tried and found impractical.

A water system has four parts: the source, the pipe that goes from the source to the house, the plumbing in the house, and the sewer system.

SOURCES OF WATER

When there is no town water, most people have a well drilled by a huge truck-mounted drill that looks something like a crane. This rig cannot maneuver on soft ground or in confined areas such as dense woods, so make sure the machine can get close enough to your house before planning on a well. The machine drills a 6-inch hole and keeps drilling until it hits an adequate supply of water. Drilling costs around $10 per foot. The depth at which water is found is notoriously unpredictable, although you can get some idea by finding out how deep other wells in the neighborhood are.

In most parts of the country, well water is pumped by a submersible pump located at the bottom of the well and hung from a rope or pipe. Usually this pump and the other hardware that goes with the well cost at least $700.

A drilled well is not only expensive, but indeterminately expensive. Less expensive sources should be investigated first. Still used in some areas is the *dug well*, which is the old-fashioned hole in the ground lined with stone, wood, concrete, or steel. Usually such a well will be at least 3 feet in diameter. This kind of well works when the water-bearing soil or rock is within about 30 feet of the surface. Another inexpensive type of well is the *driven well*, which consists of a perforated pipe with a special tip called a well point that you drive into the ground. This type of well can be 50 or 60 feet deep, but will only work where the water is above bedrock.

Usually a source at or near the surface is more economical than any type of well. The simplest of all is an unpolluted stream, river, or lake. If you have such a source nearby, have the water tested. Usually some branch of the state government will test the water free.

Springs are a more common source. A spring is a place where water from underground surfaces. Sometimes it will be obvious because it creates a swamp or stream. Other times the ground will just seem damp. Often ferns, cedar trees, or other wet-ground vegetation will signal its location.

When you are looking at a spring, bring along someone familiar with local water systems to help you evaluate what you find. Begin by digging out the spring with a shovel to see how much water there is, unless there is obviously enough. Have the water tested. Find out if it runs year-round.

Springs can be developed as a water system in a variety of ways. A temporary method is to dig out a hole and put in a garbage can full of holes as a liner. Surround the can with rocks and cover the can with its regular lid, making sure the top of the can is several inches above ground level. A more permanent arrangement is to dig a large hole 4 to 10 feet deep at the spring and install spring tiles, round sections of concrete pipe 2 feet long and typically 4 feet in diameter. The top tile sticks a foot or so above the ground and is covered with a concrete lid.

A surprisingly effective secondary source in some places is a rain barrel that catches the water from the roof gutter. This can amount to a lot of water as an emergency or supplementary supply, or a main source for cabin or outbuilding. The water is surprisingly clean and often fit for washing or for animals, though not always for drinking.

MOVING THE WATER TO THE HOUSE

Whatever the source, the water usually will be brought to the house in flexible black plastic water pipes, which cost about 7 cents per foot in the ½-inch size. For a summer house, the pipes can simply run across the surface of the ground or be buried in a shallow trench. In a freezing climate the pipes must be buried in a trench below the frost line so they won't freeze up. The frost line is the maximum depth to which the ground freezes. Usually there will be a local rule of thumb that you should follow (Appendix I). If the spring is far from the house, the trench will usually be dug by a backhoe, which is a tractor with a digging shovel on the back. The trench may be a major expense, so find out from a backhoe operator what yours will cost. A trench across open fields may not be

too expensive. In the woods you will have to clear a road wide enough for the machine to work in. If a trench is too long or too hard to dig, the spring may not be worth using.

Water will flow by gravity as long as the source is above the house, even if the pipe rises above the source in some places. When it does it is called a siphon (Figure 93). If the source is below the house, it must be pumped.

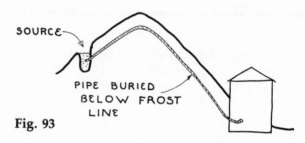

GRAVITY FLOW WITH SIPHON

Fig. 93

 Fig. 94   UNDERGROUND PUMP HOUSE

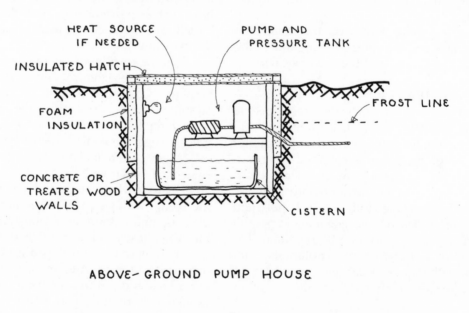

ABOVE-GROUND PUMP HOUSE

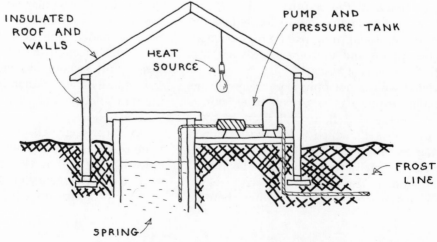

Pump Location and Protection. Pump location will often determine the type of pump used. A pump can be submerged in the water at the source or placed above but within a few feet of the source. It can also be located in or near the house, as long as the house is not too far above the source. Here we come to the characteristic problem with pumps: though they can push water hundreds of feet above themselves, they can only suck water from about 20 feet below themselves. That means the pump can only be about 20 feet in elevation above the water source, though the horizontal distance can be much greater.

In cold climates the pump must be protected from freezing, so your water supply is not cut off or the pump does not crack. There are four ways to protect a pump. First, you can locate it deep underground, submerged in the water source. Second, you can put it in the house, in a heated basement or utility room. Third, you can build a pump house. This can be an insulated box on top of the ground built much like a wooden house, or an underground box with an insulated lid. The underground type will tend to be warmer, since the earth is warm. An above-ground pump house will be more accessible, which may be important if the pump is a type that doesn't operate automatically. In either case, you will probably need some sort of heat source hooked up to a thermostat to keep the pump house warm in extreme weather. This heat source may be an electric heat tape, an electric bulb, or a small electric heater, depending on the severity of the weather. With a buried pump house covered with snow, a light bulb will provide plenty of heat even in a very cold climate. The fourth method of protecting the pump is to drain it of all water after each use. This may not be too much of a problem if you only use the pump every few days to fill a tank in the house, but I think most people will find the process too aggravating to put up with indefinitely.

Types of Pumps. Pumps can be operated by hand, by wind, by the hydraulic power of a stream, by a gasoline engine, or by electricity. The type you choose will depend on the power sources you have, the type of water source, and the lay of the land.

The old-fashioned hand pump is probably the simplest and can be quite practical if the water source is fairly near the house. One common type has the pump mechanism located right at the handle. Below this is a pipe leading to the source. Since a pump can only pull water by suction from about 20 feet below itself, this type of hand pump must be no more than 20 feet above the water. At the handle there will either be the familiar spout, or a second pipeline leading upward from the pump to a cistern (holding tank) from which it can flow into the plumbing (Figure 95).

A type of hand pump called a deep-well pump can be used to retrieve water from a source more than 20 feet down, as long as the source is directly below the handle. The handle at the top is connected by a long shaft within a pipe to the pumping valve so that the valve itself is within 20 feet of the water. Because of the shaft, this type of pump is only for use in wells (Figure 96).

If your source is a flowing stream or river, water can be pumped by the stream's own power. You do this with a special pump called a hydraulic ram. Write the Rife Hydraulic Engine Manufacturing Company, P.O. Box 367, Millburn, N.J. 07041. A ram uses the flow of the stream or river to pump a small fraction of the water up to the house.

DEEP WELL PUMP

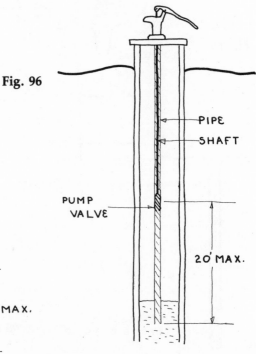

Fig. 96

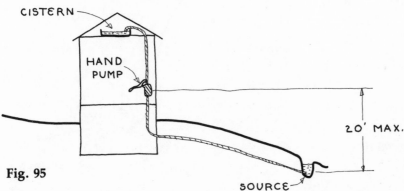

Fig. 95

Wind used to be a pump power source. A windmill seems like a simple practical way to pump water, and before electricity came along windmill pumps were common, particularly in the Midwest, where many abandoned windmills can still be seen. Windmills today are simply much too expensive to be taken seriously as a power source.

Pumps can also be powered with gasoline motors. If you had a gas-powered pump, you would periodically — perhaps every few days — start up the pump and fill a large 200 to 500 gallon tank in the attic. You might also fill an even larger water tower with thousands of gallons. In either case, the water would flow from the tank to your plumbing by gravity. You will have no freezing problem if the pump is in the house. Outside, you would have to protect the pump as described under Pump Location and Protection on page 59 and illustrated in Figure 97.

The most convenient and perhaps most economical solution is usually an electric pump. A common pump for deep wells is a *submersible pump* located right down at the bottom of the well (Figure 98). For other water sources, the *jet pump* is the popular type. A pump salesclerk can help you pick the right kind for your situation. Usually an electric pump is combined with a small tank called a pressure tank, which stores a small supply of water under pressure so the pump doesn't have to go on every time someone gets a glass of water.

If the water source is nearby, the pump and pressure tank can be right in the house (Figure 99). Otherwise you may need a pump house. This is usually located right at the source (Figure 100), but it occasionally happens that you can't get an electric power line to the source economically. If so, one solution is to have the water flow from the source in a pipeline by gravity to a lower elevation to which you can more easily run an electric line. The water collects in a cistern consisting of a galvanized metal stock-feeding tank or (more permanently) a concrete tank. To prevent overflowing, the cistern has a float valve which, like the valve in a toilet tank, cuts off the water flow when the tank is full. The cistern is located in a pump house with an electric pump and pressure tank. These send the water on to the house when

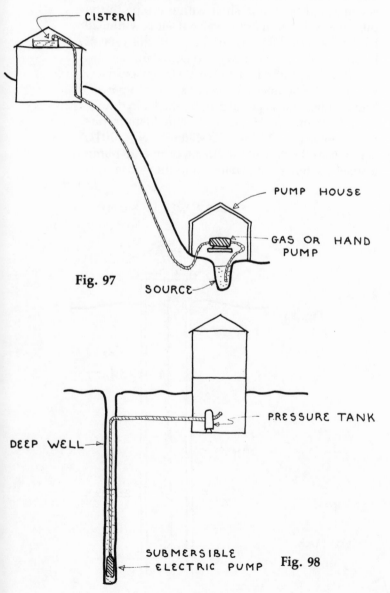

Fig. 97

CISTERN

PUMP HOUSE

GAS OR HAND PUMP

SOURCE

DEEP WELL

PRESSURE TANK

SUBMERSIBLE ELECTRIC PUMP   Fig. 98

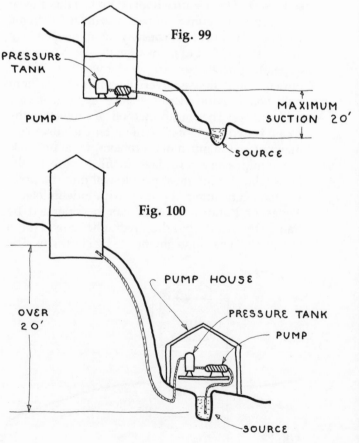

Fig. 99

PRESSURE TANK

PUMP

MAXIMUM SUCTION 20'

SOURCE

Fig. 100

OVER 20'

PUMP HOUSE

PRESSURE TANK

PUMP

SOURCE

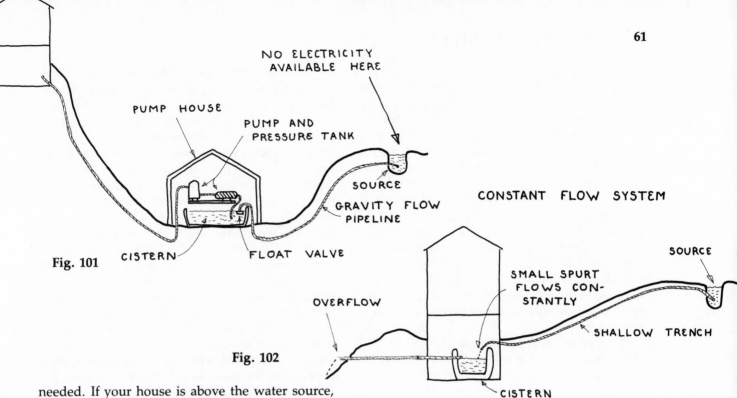

Fig. 101

NO ELECTRICITY AVAILABLE HERE

PUMP HOUSE

PUMP AND PRESSURE TANK

SOURCE

GRAVITY FLOW PIPELINE

CISTERN

FLOAT VALVE

CONSTANT FLOW SYSTEM

OVERFLOW

SMALL SPURT FLOWS CONSTANTLY

SOURCE

SHALLOW TRENCH

Fig. 102

CISTERN

needed. If your house is above the water source, but the cellar is slightly below it, all this hardware can be in the basement (Figure 101).

Constant Flow and Runback Systems. Sometimes none of these arrangements will work because distance, expense, or bedrock make it impossible to dig a trench deep enough to avoid freezing. There are two ways to solve this problem, both based on the principle that water moving continuously in a pipe will not freeze. When water flows to the house by gravity, you can use a constant flow system, as shown in Figure 102. The water flows to the cellar, and spurts constantly into a cistern through a small hole, perhaps as big as a pencil lead, in the end of the pipe. Though the flow is small, it is enough to prevent freezing, so the pipeline can be buried in a shallow trench. Even a small flow will amount to thousands of gallons if it never stops, so you will need an overflow pipe to carry the excess water over the edge of a nearby hillside.

When the water is being pumped uphill in a pipe, you can use a runback system, as shown in Figure 103. Here there is a hole in the bottom end of the pipeline, either in the pump house or (with a deep well) down in the well just above the pump. Each time the pump stops running, the water in the pipeline flows back into the well or cistern, so there is nothing left to freeze. There must be no dips in the pipeline, because water will be left behind there to freeze. The runback system is commonly used with wells where bedrock is near the surface. The problem with both of these methods is that if the flow stops for even one minute in winter, the line will freeze and you will have no water till the ground thaws.

Fig. 103 RUNBACK SYSTEM

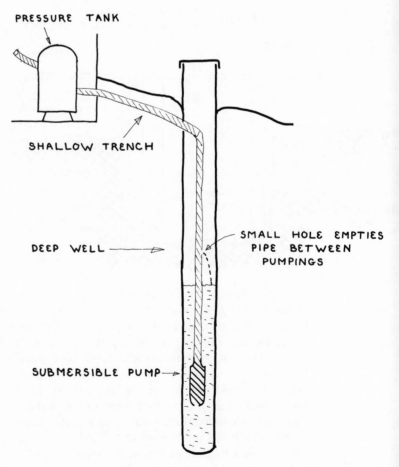

PRESSURE TANK

SHALLOW TRENCH

DEEP WELL

SUBMERSIBLE PUMP

SMALL HOLE EMPTIES PIPE BETWEEN PUMPINGS

HOUSE PLUMBING

Plumbing in the house includes the supply system, which consists of the hot and cold water lines, and the waste system (technically called the drain-waste-vent system), which usually leads to the town sewer or a septic tank. The supply begins with the pipe that enters the house from the water source. You must get this pipe into the house without exposing it to freezing temperatures. If you live in a warm climate or have a furnace in the basement, this is no problem. If you live in a moderately cold climate and do not have a heated basement, it may be sufficient to wrap the supply pipe in thick insulation and firmly attach an electric heat tape to the vulnerable portion of pipe. A heat tape is a heating element with a built-in thermostat.

Sooner or later this system will fail in very cold climates and you will find yourself with no water and perhaps a burst pipe. In such a climate the supply pipe should emerge from the earth and enter the heated part of the house through a fully insulated and heated chamber called a *hotbox* (Figure 104).

Fig. 104   HOTBOX

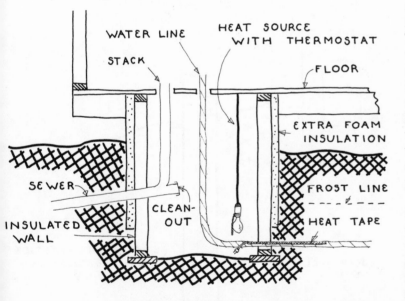

For a house on a post foundation, this may mean building a small, insulated basement of treated wood or concrete block just for the pipes' entrance. The hotbox goes below the frost line. It is protected on the outside with rigid foam insulation and on the inside with rigid foam or fiberglass. The heat source can be one or two light bulbs, located at or near the bottom of the hotbox. Leave a peek-hole into the house so you can make sure the bulb has not burned out. The heat source can also be a furnace or hot water heater.

Even with these precautions, water pipes may freeze, during a power failure, for example. Therefore the box should be at least big enough to permit you to work inside it, perhaps 30 inches square. This dimension also allows the sewer line to exit through the hotbox, protecting the sewer from the cold and giving you access to the sewer cleanout. It is a good idea to install a section of heat tape on the first few feet of pipe that enter the earth, as shown in Figure 104. If a freeze-up happens, the inaccessible section is likely to freeze along with the section in the hotbox itself, and the tape gives you an emergency method of thawing it. (Normally, this heat tape would be left unplugged.) In a house with an unheated basement, wall off one corner of the basement as a hotbox.

Once the water is in the house and past the pump, it will divide into two lines, one heading directly to the cold water taps, the other leading through the hot water heater to the hot water taps. These supply lines will be either copper, which is excellent but expensive, or PVC plastic, which is good, and cheaper and easier to put in. Plastic is not legal everywhere, so consult the local plumbing code.

Supply lines are usually run through the walls and floors. You install them after the walls are framed and before they are covered on the inside. The actual fixtures are installed after the finished wall and the floor surfaces go in. In cold climates, supply lines should be in interior walls, because they can freeze in the exterior walls. In wood- or space-heated houses in extreme climates, supply lines should not be concealed even in interior walls, because the house will not be uniformly warm and the risk of freezing is great. Exposed supply lines will be warmer and can be easily repaired if they do freeze.

Though plastic is not always legal for supply lines, it is becoming standard for waste lines. The waste system of a house is centered around one or more stacks. A stack is a 3½- or 4-inch pipe going from the sewer underground up through the framing in the walls and on up through the roof. Where it goes through the roof, it is the vent that lets out sewer gas.

Each fixture (sink, toilet, etc.) has a drainpipe that pitches downhill all the way to a stack so that waste can flow away by gravity. A toilet drain will be 3½- or 4-inch pipe, and a sink drain will be a 1¼- to 2-inch pipe. An S- or P-shaped trap will be between the fixture and the drain, and it stays full of water all the time. (In a toilet, the trap is built into the toilet itself.) Traps provide a seal to prevent sewer gas from entering the room through the fixture.

Every fixture needs a vent, which is a pipe that starts from the drain below the trap and goes upward and out the roof. Vents do two important jobs: they allow sewer gas to exit into the outside air instead of into the house, and they prevent the traps from being emptied by suction. Fluids flowing down the drains act like a pump to create suction in the system. In a vented system, the suction pulls outside air in through the vents instead of through the traps at each fixture, which would cause the traps to empty. If a fixture is very close to the main stack, the stack itself will be the vent. But any fixture even a few feet away from the stack should have its own vent pipe.

The maximum distance between a fixture trap and the nearest vent depends on the type of fixture, the drainpipe diameter, and the floor the fixture is on. Local plumbing codes will give standards to follow. Usually a sink, tub, and perhaps other fixtures will have a common vent pipe, as in Figure 105, which will reenter the main stack above the topmost drain or go through the roof separately. In an economical house the toilet will be located right adjacent to the main stack, because large-size pipes are expensive and you want to avoid having to provide a special vent.

Lay out plumbing location to minimize materials and plumbing labor. Ideally this means locating all the pipes in one wall with the kitchen and bath back to back or one on top of the other. Then all fixtures can feed into the same stack. Another good arrangement is to have a centrally located room containing most of the house machinery such as pipes, electrical panels, furnace,

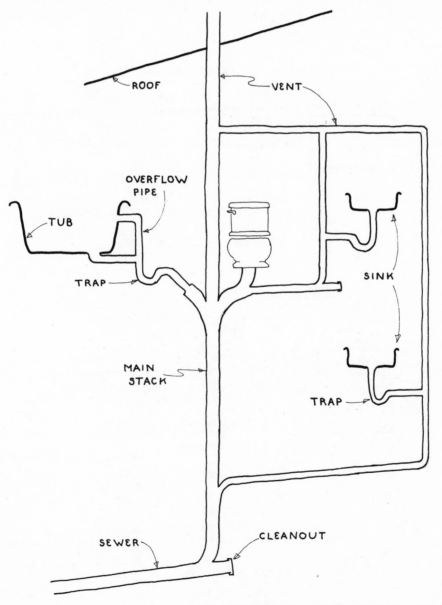

ROOF

VENT

OVERFLOW PIPE

TUB

TRAP

SINK

MAIN STACK

TRAP

SEWER

CLEANOUT

DRAIN-WASTE-VENT SYSTEM   **Fig. 105**

hot water heater, laundry equipment, and so on. The bathroom and kitchen would be adjacent to the machine room. This machine room has no interior wall covering, so the plumbing pipes will always be accessible for repair or remodeling.

SEWER SYSTEM

If there is no town sewer, the sewer system will consist of a pipe leading from your stack to the septic tank nearby, the tank itself, the pipe leading to the drainage field, and the drainage field. The pipes are all pitched to flow by gravity, and do not need to be below the frost line.

The sewer pipe will be a 4-inch pipe with

sealed joints. Different types are used in different places. The septic tank is a large sealed tank with an inlet opening near the top for the sewer line, an outlet on the opposite end leading to the drainage field, and a removable hatch for inspection and pumping out. You can buy these ready-made of concrete or tar-covered steel, or build one out of concrete block. Probably the most common and practical is a ready-made 1000-gallon concrete tank, which will be delivered and placed in its hole by a special truck.

The tank should be on the same level as the house or below it, since the pipes must flow by gravity. It can be within 20 or 30 feet of the house to economize on the cost of the sewer line, but if

Fig. 106   SEPTIC   SYSTEMS

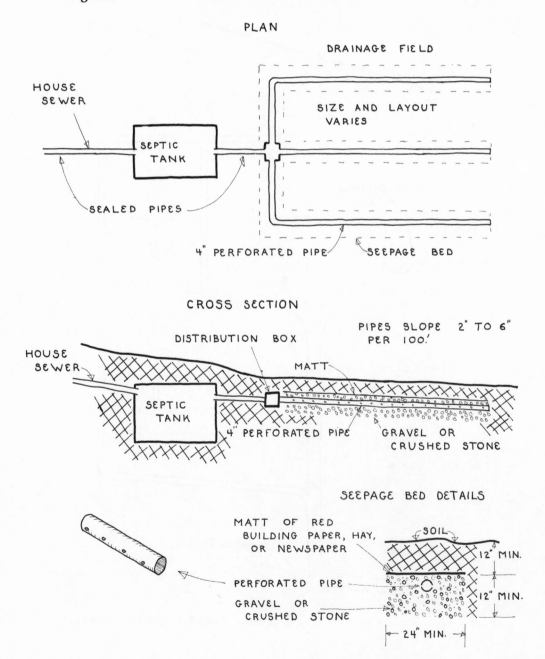

PLAN

DRAINAGE FIELD

HOUSE SEWER

SIZE AND LAYOUT VARIES

SEPTIC TANK

SEALED PIPES

4" PERFORATED PIPE — SEEPAGE BED

CROSS SECTION

DISTRIBUTION BOX

PIPES SLOPE 2" TO 6" PER 100.'

HOUSE SEWER

MATT

SEPTIC TANK

4" PERFORATED PIPE   GRAVEL OR CRUSHED STONE

SEEPAGE BED DETAILS

MATT OF RED BUILDING PAPER, HAY, OR NEWSPAPER

SOIL

12" MIN.

PERFORATED PIPE

12" MIN.

GRAVEL OR CRUSHED STONE

24" MIN.

possible put it where heavy vehicles will not drive over it. The concrete tank can take the weight, but you want to avoid disturbing the alignment of the pipes.

The sewage flows into the tank, where, if the system is working right, bacteria will attack the sewage and transform it into a less noxious liquid, which flows out of the tank through another pipe into the drainage field. This is a network of nearly level pipes with rows of holes in the sides to let the treated sewage percolate back into the soil. The drainage pipes rest in a seepage bed of coarse gravel covered with a matt of red building paper, newspapers, or hay. Over this is topsoil. The matt keeps the topsoil from clogging up the system, without preventing ground water from sinking into the earth.

Some systems have two sewers coming from two stacks. The toilets feed one pipe, which goes to the septic tank. Everything else feeds into the other sewer line, which by-passes the septic tank and goes directly to the drainage field. This prevents nondegradable detergents from ruining the bacterial action in the septic tank, but it is not legal everywhere.

The location of the drainage field is important. It must be level with or downhill from the house and septic tank, because everything flows by gravity. Like the septic tank, it should be located where it won't be driven over, if possible. The field should be below the water source and at least 100 feet away from it. Equally important, the soil must be porous enough so that the wastes can percolate back into it.

You have to make sure the soil is suitable for a septic system when you plan your house site (see chapter 1). Septic systems must be built right to work well. The right materials must be used. The tank must be big enough to handle the amount of flow. The drainage field must be big enough to handle the outflow in the given soil conditions. In many places septic systems must be designed or approved by the town. Sometimes a building permit will not be issued at all until a sanitary specialist has made test borings in the soil or conducted a perc test to measure empirically how well the soil absorbs liquid. Legal requirements vary, so check local regulations before you buy a piece of land.

Many legal requirements for rural building are pointlessly restrictive. But I think septic systems should be carefully controlled because they must be engineered right to work well, or even to work at all. Many individuals and some contractors have put in expensive systems that don't work and have to be pumped out periodically.

ALTERNATIVE WASTE DISPOSAL SYSTEMS

There is a lot of interest today in alternative systems for waste disposal that pollute less, use less water, and are otherwise considered ecologically better. One such system is the composting toilet, such as the Clivus Multrum, which was developed in Sweden. This is a tank that fits under the house. Excrement and garbage go directly into the tank, but waste water from sinks, tubs, and washing machines does not. The Clivus is designed so that the excrement and garbage are turned into a rich humus through the action of various microorganisms over a period of months. Water use is cut in half, since there is no toilet flushing and the septic tank is eliminated. Unfortunately a Clivus costs $1500 to $1700 installed, often more than the cost of a septic system. In addition, you need a way to dispose of water waste from sinks and showers. If the amount of water isn't huge, a small drainage field or a dry well (a perforated underground seepage tank) will suffice. However, many places require a septic tank even for these wastes, which makes the Clivus quite uneconomical. Some people like the Clivus because it is nonpolluting. Actually, a properly built septic system is nonpolluting too.

If you have a small budget and want to avoid a septic system, the best solution is the old-fashioned outhouse, which is still legal in some rural areas. A properly built outhouse is hygienic, uses no water, does not pollute the soil, and can be built with scrap materials and a minimum of labor. You can use a covered potty chair or chamber pot — emptied daily — for nighttime or cold weather use.

WHO SHOULD DO THE WORK?

A big question is whether to do the water system, plumbing, and septic system yourself. Some local laws may actually prohibit you from doing this work, but in most places you can do it as long as you have it inspected. It doesn't make sense to do the digging yourself, because a backhoe is so much faster. But it may make sense to do most or some of the rest. The manual tasks of plumbing are easy, especially with plastic pipe. The biggest part is learning to do the job right. As far as I know, there is no complete, clear, plumbing book. You will have to study how to do the plumbing in a way that will work properly and last a long time: collect what books you can, review the local plumbing codes, and talk to people. I know from experience that plumbing is one area where a novice cannot just barge in and learn as he or she works. There are principles, techniques, rules of thumb, and building codes that must be followed or the system will not work well and will not be approved by the inspector.

Though you can save money doing your own plumbing, you should also think about saving energy. You have to learn many new skills when you build your house, including the skill of managing and supervising the whole project. Some people have the energy to take on plumbing too, but others may find it worth paying others to do the work. A good compromise is to have someone on the job who knows about plumbing and whom you can work with. This might be a builder or carpenter you hire to work on the entire project or a hired plumber who is willing to teach you plumbing skills.

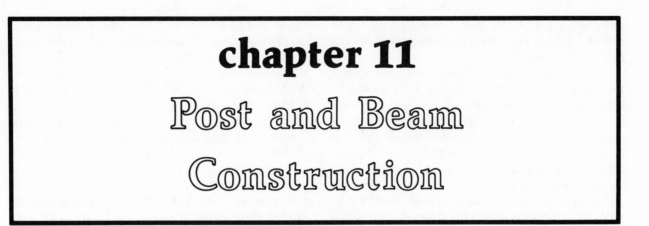

chapter 11
Post and Beam Construction

Most houses today are built using studwall or stickbuilt construction. In a stickbuilt house, the load-carrying frame consists of a profusion of small, closely spaced framing members such as 2 × 4s or 2 × 6s spaced at 16- or 24-inch intervals and concealed inside the floor, walls, and roof. Framing is done in stages from the ground up: first a floor, then walls on top of it, then another floor, then more walls, and finally a roof. Most of Part Three, Construction Methods, describes stickbuilt framing.

At one time, most houses were built using the post and beam system, in which the loads are carried by a few large, widely spaced, and usually exposed heavy timbers such as 8 × 8s. Colonial houses are probably the most well known example of post and beam construction. Today many owner-builders are turning to modern versions.

Figure 107 shows one example. In the photos in the introduction, houses 6, 9, and 10 have post and beam frames.

When I started building I believed, as many new builders do, that post and beam construction was the key to economical building. I liked the feeling of a big visible frame, and I believed that with intelligent design a post and beam system could save enormous amounts of money and time. After building several post and beam houses, observing many more, and discussing the subject with many other builders, I have come to the reluctant conclusion that though post and beam methods are economical in particular cases, and though specific post and beam techniques are widely usable, a post and beam structure will often take more work and cost extra money. As most builders have known for years, I discovered that

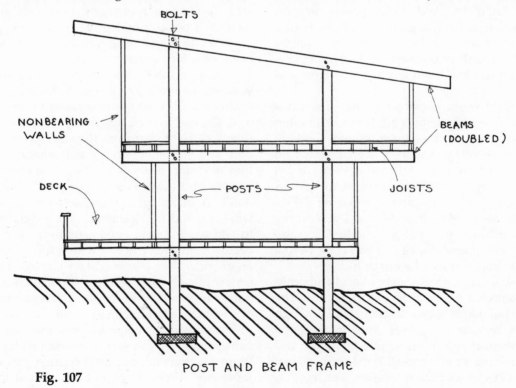

POST AND BEAM FRAME

Fig. 107

nothing goes up faster than 2 × 4s and plywood; nothing is stronger either, even though those big timbers may look it.

So this book does not contain an exhaustive manual on post and beam construction, though in early drafts it did. Instead you will find extensive instructions on conventional framing methods and on particular post and beam techniques that can easily be combined with conventional wall framing. Since post and beam framing is very practical for certain specific designs, and since some people will simply prefer to build post and beam, I provide here a general introduction to the subject and some suggestions about how to go about designing a post and beam style house.

Post and beam framing has many advantages. The frame, having few parts, goes up fast. You can put the roof on early, to provide a covered place to work. The walls that fill in between the heavy timbers are not load-bearing. Window openings can be put anywhere and can be any size, and the walls can be easily altered or removed when your needs change. With an exposed frame you eliminate a lot of time-consuming finish work.

However, I think the major appeal of post and beam is aesthetic. The frame is big, obvious, and exposed. To me, and I think to many people, this exposed frame looks good and gives a house a reassuring feeling of strength and permanence. The simple frame is easier for many people to understand and visualize. You can easily imagine extending the posts upward or the beams outward to create interesting and useful nooks, alcoves, lofts, cupolas, or overhangs that might be harder to conceive of with regular framing. These can be and are built with conventional framing, but it is often easier to think them through with post and beam.

Post and beam construction has disadvantages too. Those big timbers are heavy. You often need a real crew to move them around. Framing details can be tricky. Members are cut down on the floor and have to fit right when they are put up. Joints may be more complex, with various notches often replacing simple butt-nailing. Framing errors are costlier. If you cut a 2 × 8 wrong you can go to the pile and get another, and use the short one somewhere else. If you cut a 14-foot 6 × 8 too short you may be out of luck.

The simplicity and economy of post and beam is often canceled out by *structural duplication*. The walls you build in between the framework, though they carry no important loads, must be designed for insulation. If you are using fiberglass, you will end up building a conventional 2 × 4 studwall just to create bays to hold the insulation. But this 2 × 4 wall could carry the weight of the house by itself, so the heavy posts become somewhat superfluous. You have built a strong structure to hold up the house and then an equally strong structure just to hold insulation. One way around this duplication is to build a wall of light, thin, home-fabricated, foam-insulated panels, but, either way, you will lose some of the economies achieved with the simple frame.

Post and beam construction demands more overall planning. Studwall construction is additive; you build one part at a time and what you do in one place doesn't necessarily affect what you do 10 feet away. But post and beam framing is systematic. There is a single framework and everything is interrelated. You must detail everything in advance. You have to plan where your wiring and plumbing will go, because they can't necessarily run through the walls just anywhere. You can't cut joists as freely to accommodate staircases. In general, your layout and structure must be unified and orderly if post and beam methods are to be a help rather than a hindrance. There is room for improvisation, but it must be done within a system.

Post and beam will also demand more from you as a designer. Since post and beam is the exception rather than the rule in American building, there are few standard ways of doing things and few special products to help you. There are as many ways to build post and beam as there are ways to attach two pieces of wood together (Figure 108). You have to find your own system, and your own solutions to problems. For some people, the inventiveness and resourcefulness that post and beam calls for is part of its fascination.

Some people settle on post and beam construction before they even start designing. If you find post and beam systems easier to understand, or if, like me, you are simply a post and beam fan, this is all right. But from the standpoint of economy and efficiency, do not automatically assume that post and beam is the right approach. Some houses lend themselves to post and beam; others don't. A house on a hilly site with lots of large windows and no basement, and which you plan to add to, will be a good candidate for post and beam. A one-story house with a full basement or an irregular floor plan might well be easier to build conventionally. I have often found that a combination of post and beam and conventional methods works well. Sometimes just a few heavy posts or beams will solve special problems, such as an extra-long span. Familiarize yourself with post and beam methods so that they become part of your repertoire. Then use them to the extent they suit

Fig. 108   ATTACHING 2 BIG PIECES OF WOOD

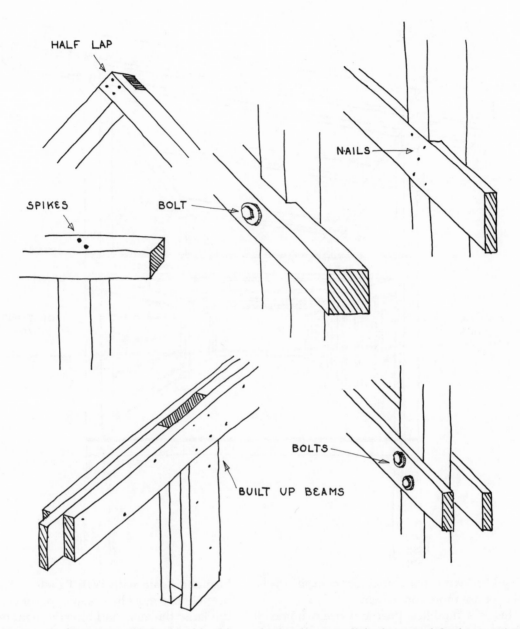

HALF LAP

SPIKES   BOLT

NAILS

BOLTS

BUILT UP BEAMS

your layout, site, preferences, and the local building code.

POST AND BEAM FRAMING METHODS

As I have explained, post and beam framing must be systematic and unified, and everyone has to work out his or her own system. I could have presented one or more systems I have seen or used, but they would be *my* solutions to *my* design priorities and might not fit your layout, site, lumber supply, or taste. Complete how-to information would require an entire book, so I have chosen to summarize briefly a few of the most common and practical post and beam approaches. Elsewhere in

the book you will find most of the basic principles and technical information you need to work out your own system. A few books in the bibliography may be helpful. You can also get someone experienced at post and beam to go over your design with you.

Frame Built One Story at a Time.   Figure 109 shows a heavy timber frame built in stages. The first level consists of concrete foundation posts with sills joining them on top. Over the sills goes a floor frame as in a conventional house. Then a heavy timber wall frame, one story high, is built on the floor. The second floor rests on this frame and then a second wall frame is built on that. The roof can be framed in any fashion. The walls can

Fig. 109

POST AND BEAM FRAME BUILT ONE STORY AT A TIME

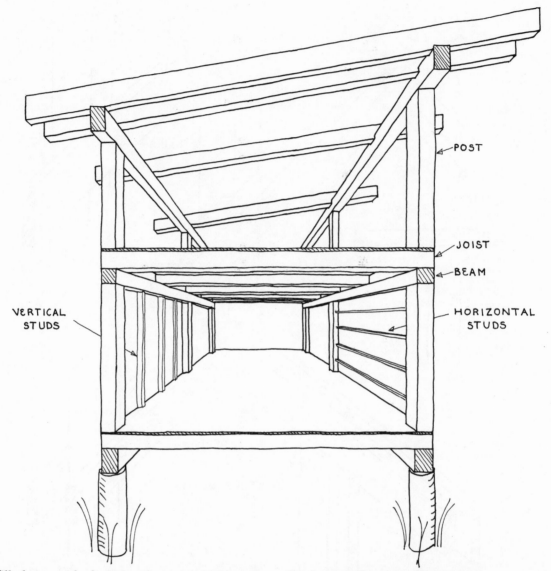

POST

JOIST

BEAM

VERTICAL
STUDS

HORIZONTAL
STUDS

be filled in with horizontal or vertical studs, whichever are more convenient.

This is a modified post and beam frame. It combines the overall strategy of post and beam with some features of studwall construction. The joints are simple. The timbers are smaller and easier to handle than ground-to-roof posts would be. Each floor provides a platform for doing the next story.

Colonial Frame.   Figure 110 shows a Colonial house frame built entirely with wooden joints. There are no nails, only mortises and tenons, notches, and dowels. Some of these joints are detailed in Figure 111. This is the most ambitious kind of post and beam frame and takes great skill. It is, to me, about the most satisfying way to build a house, but I would not suggest it to anyone in a hurry.

Post and Beam with Wall Panels.   Any post and beam house must have some sort of walls between the large timbers. As I already mentioned, building regular studwalls to do this is wasteful. An alternative is to use thin, lightweight home-prefabricated wall panels, as shown in Figure 112. These consist of a core of 1 or 2 inches of rigid foam insulation sandwiched between an inner layer of sheetrock, plywood, or Homasote and an outer layer of plywood or insulation board. The inner layer becomes the inside wall finish, and the outer layer becomes the sheathing or siding. The panel has a framework around its edge the same thickness as the insulation. With 2-inch foam, the frame would be made of 2 × 2s.

This framework provides a way to nail the panel to the house and siding to the panel. The panels can be made up quickly on the floor in

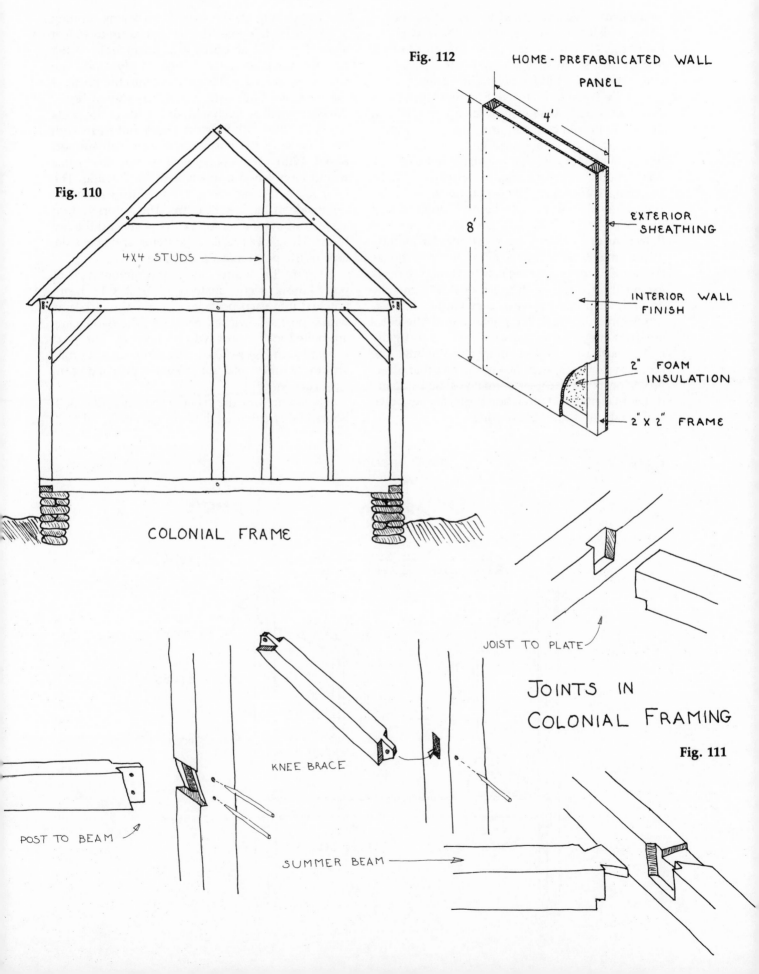

Fig. 112

HOME - PREFABRICATED WALL
PANEL

4'

8'

EXTERIOR
SHEATHING

INTERIOR WALL
FINISH

2" FOAM
INSULATION

2" X 2" FRAME

Fig. 110

4X4 STUDS

COLONIAL FRAME

JOIST TO PLATE

JOINTS IN
COLONIAL FRAMING

Fig. 111

KNEE BRACE

POST TO BEAM

SUMMER BEAM

convenient sizes and nailed to the outside of the posts, which are spaced to receive them. One virtue of this system is that it eliminates much of the tedious inside finish work, since the joints between panels are hidden behind posts and do not have to be taped or battened. The problems, however, are several. One inch of foam is insufficient insulation in cold climates, and 2 inches is expensive. Foam is flammable and gives off poisonous fumes when it burns. You may have to build special window units to match your thin walls. Plumbing and wiring that would normally be inside the walls will have to be exposed or run in the floor.

Pole House.   Perhaps the most popular method of post and beam construction is the pole house (Figure 113). In pole house construction, the posts extend from the roof all the way down into the ground, where they serve as the foundation. They can be pressure-treated to prevent rot. If the holes are deep enough, the posts will be held so rigidly by the earth that they will brace the building. The economy of this system lies in the fact that a few heavy posts do the jobs normally done by many different elements: foundation posts, anchor bolts, wall studs, and diagonal bracing.

Depending on the size of the beams running across them, the poles can be spaced up to 16 feet apart. Eight feet on center is a convenient spacing for any modular material such as plywood. The beams are often 2 × 12s notched into the posts. If the walls are built with 2 × 4s (as shown here), the beams will be flush with the inside of the posts wherever they will support floors and flush with the outside of the posts where they will support a roof. With a foam panel wall system, the beams would be notched in flush with the outside. The floor joists rest on a 2 × 4 ledger strip nailed to the inside of the 2 × 12 beam. The rafters rest on a 2 × 6 sitting flat on top of the posts and the top beam. This piece is called a stiffener and keeps the tops of the posts in a straight line.

Figure 107 shows another common type of pole house. Here, instead of a 2 × 12 beam notched into each post, you have pairs of beams with a post sandwiched between. The two beams are bolted to the post with no notches. The joint is detailed in Figure 108, lower right. This is probably the simplest and fastest kind of post and beam construction.

References in the bibliography describe pole house construction methods in greater detail.

Fig. 113

POLE   HOUSE

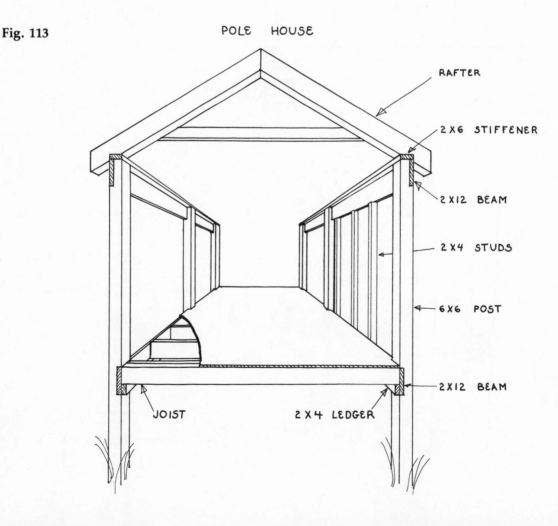

RAFTER

2 X 6 STIFFENER

2 X 12 BEAM

2 X 4 STUDS

6 X 6 POST

2 X 12 BEAM

JOIST

2 X 4 LEDGER

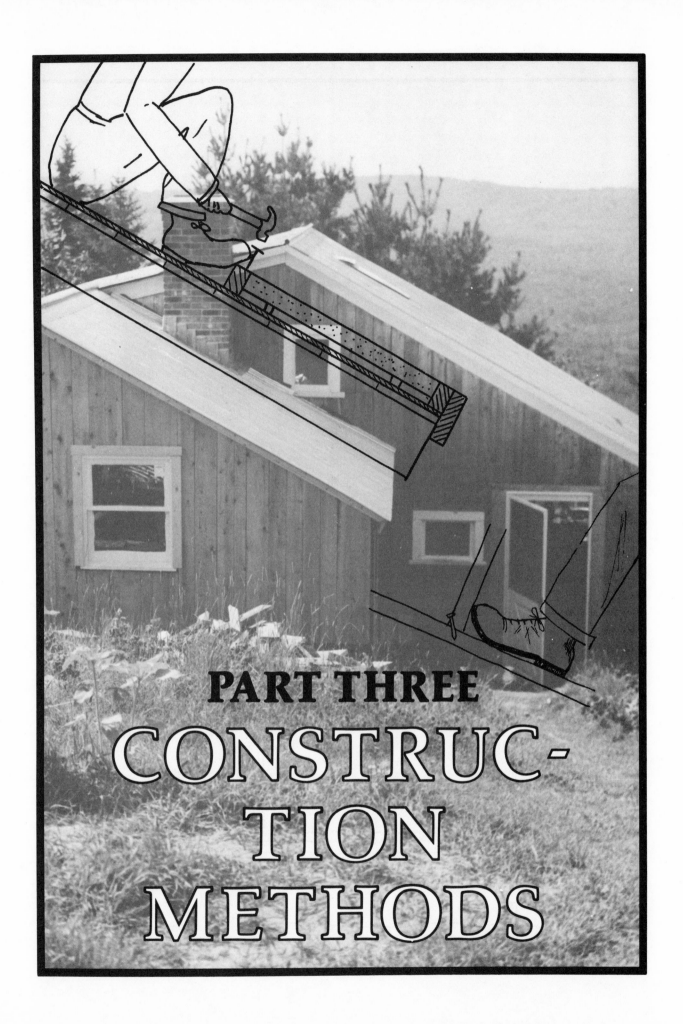

PART THREE
CONSTRUC-
TION
METHODS

Introduction

Figure 114 shows the typical order in which a house is built. This section describes how each step is accomplished, usually with several variations. I do not try to give every possible method but just a variety of straightforward and economical choices.

Each chapter in this Construction section takes a part of a house and looks at it three ways. First there is a general discussion of the design objective. Second, I describe a variety of construction methods and compare their advantages and disadvantages. Third, I give examples of the kind

Fig. 114 TYPICAL STEPS IN BUILDING

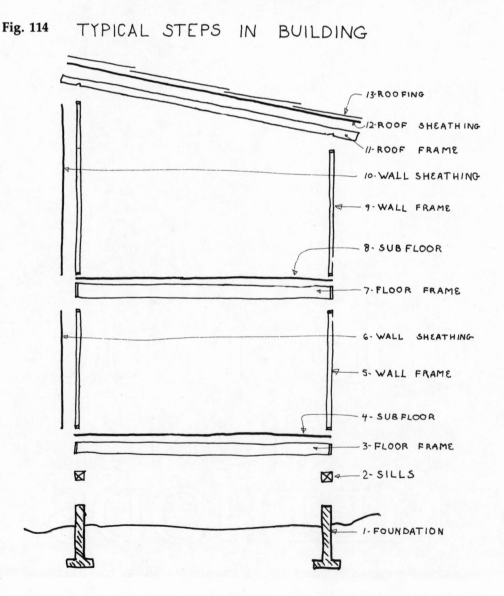

13·ROOFING
12·ROOF SHEATHING
11·ROOF FRAME
10·WALL SHEATHING
9·WALL FRAME
8·SUBFLOOR
7·FLOOR FRAME
6·WALL SHEATHING
5·WALL FRAME
4·SUBFLOOR
3·FLOOR FRAME
2·SILLS
1·FOUNDATION

of working drawings and materials lists you will need to do the work.

Figures 115 and 116 illustrate typical working drawings. Figure 115 is a floor framing plan. Figure 116 is a detail drawing, which clarifies how some elements of a house fit together. The working drawings do three jobs. First, they help you figure out how the house will be constructed. Second, they are the easiest tool for making the materials lists complete and accurate. In Figure 115

you can quickly count the number of 2 × 6s of each size needed to frame the floor shown, including blocking, headers, doubled joists, and other elements you might easily forget if you were trying to make the list with no drawing. Third, the drawings help you keep track of your design while building is underway.

Since Part Three refers to many different kinds and sizes of nails, you may wish to look at Appendix L, which outlines nail types.

Fig. 115

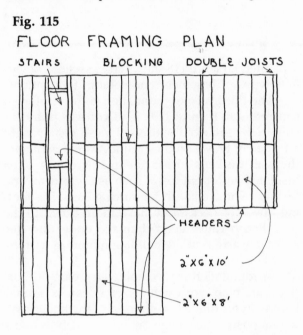

FLOOR FRAMING PLAN

Fig. 116

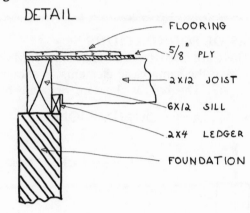

DETAIL

chapter 12
Foundations

TYPES OF FOUNDATIONS

There are many types of foundations, Most of them have the same basic elements as shown in Figure 117. The bolt at the top, or some other

PARTS OF A FOUNDATION

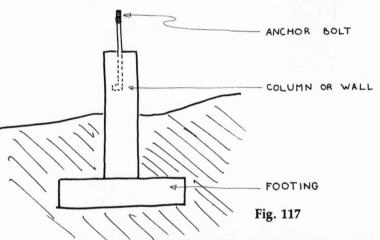

ANCHOR BOLT

COLUMN OR WALL

FOOTING

Fig. 117

strong connector, holds the building tightly to the foundation. The weight of the building is carried to the earth by rows of columns, or by foundation walls. The concrete footing at the bottom distributes the weight of the house to prevent settling. This footing has to be below the frost line, that is, the depth to which the ground freezes.

There are three basic types of foundations. One is a column foundation, which consists of several rows of columns (posts) sunk into the ground and connected at the top with heavy wooden beams called *sills*. These columns can be of either treated wood or concrete. The second type is the basement foundation. This consists of a continuous wall of block, concrete, stone, or treated wood resting on footings below the frost line. A variation on this is the crawlspace foundation, which has the same walls but no basement, just a crawlspace about 1 to 3 feet high. (Since the crawlspace type is built essentially the same way as a basement foundation, I have not discussed it

separately). Figure 118 shows cross sections of various types of basement and column foundations.

The third type of foundation is the reinforced concrete slab (Figure 119). This consists of a concrete slab reinforced with steel mesh resting right on a bed of gravel on the ground. At the perimeter the slab thickens into a footing, which is often insulated with rigid foam, such as Styrofoam, and further reinforced with reinforcing bars. The footing does not necessarily have to go down to the frost line because good drainage under the slab and the warmth of the building minimize harmful frost heaves.

A foundation can combine elements of more than one type. For example, there can be a small basement for utilities, with most of the house resting on posts. The garage can be on a slab. A house need not rest on a single foundation as long as each part of the house is properly built.

CHOOSING A TYPE OF FOUNDATION
Column Foundation Versus Basement Walls. A column foundation is both quicker and more economical to build than a basement foundation. The materials for a column foundation for a small house can cost as little as $100, compared to perhaps ten times that for a concrete cellar. A column foundation can be put in by two or three people in a few days. No bulldozer will tear up the landscape because the digging can usually be done quickly by hand. As a rule, a house with a low budget should have a column foundation.

If a full foundation is an expensive way to hold up a house, it is inexpensive as *space*. A poured concrete foundation — the most expensive type — can be built by a basement contractor for $6 to $10 per square foot. A wooden room above ground will cost at least $8 per square foot for materials alone. If a basement can satisfy some of your space requirements, you should definitely consider building one. Anyone planning central heat, a laundry, a shop, and a darkroom, for

Fig. 118 COLUMN FOUNDATIONS

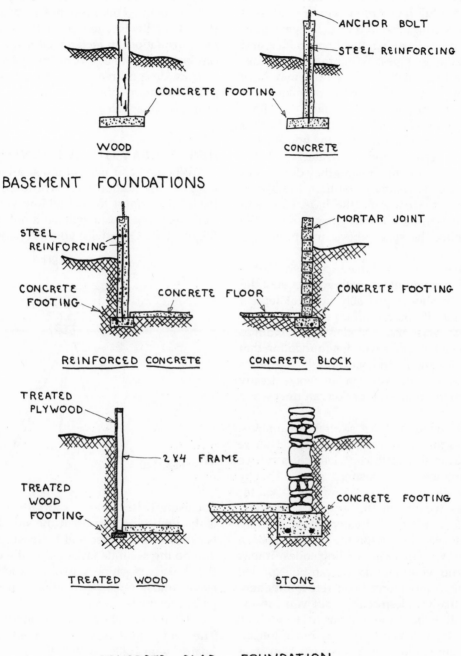

ANCHOR BOLT

STEEL REINFORCING

CONCRETE FOOTING

WOOD

CONCRETE

BASEMENT FOUNDATIONS

STEEL REINFORCING

CONCRETE FOOTING

CONCRETE FLOOR

REINFORCED CONCRETE

MORTAR JOINT

CONCRETE FOOTING

CONCRETE BLOCK

TREATED PLYWOOD

2×4 FRAME

TREATED WOOD FOOTING

CONCRETE FOOTING

TREATED WOOD

STONE

Fig. 119 CONCRETE SLAB FOUNDATION

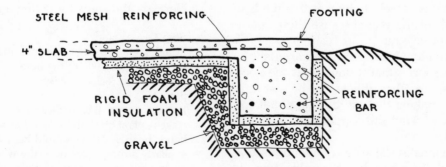

STEEL MESH REINFORCING

FOOTING

4" SLAB

RIGID FOAM INSULATION

REINFORCING BAR

GRAVEL

example, should find a basement economical.

If you live in a very cold climate, you may want to build a full foundation even if you don't need the space. The wind and cold can get under a house on posts, making the floor colder and perhaps freezing the pipes. To minimize this problem you have to insulate the floor. You may have to build a skirt around the crawlspace to keep out the wind. And you probably will have to build a small wooden or concrete basement or hotbox through which the pipes can enter the house without freezing. These methods of dealing with the cold work, but in extreme climates they don't work as well as the most common solution, the heated basement. A furnace warms the basement, and the basement becomes a warm zone under the house, warming the space above and protecting the pipes.

If you live in a cold climate, plan on central heat, and a basement fits in with your overall design, then you should probably build at least a partial basement if you can afford it.

Wood Versus Masonry.   Modern preservatives make it possible to build a wooden foundation that is virtually permanent. Today even full basements are being built of wood. You can buy wood already pressure-treated against rot, or you can treat wood yourself.

Wood foundations have several advantages. They cost less than masonry foundations. They're faster and easier to install, especially for a novice with no experience in masonry work. They're light, which means less back-breaking labor for you and less weight on the ground. However, many people don't think treated-wood foundations will last. For this reason they have not been accepted yet by many local building codes. It may be true that no wood foundation can be expected to last as long as a reinforced concrete foundation, which is virtually indestructible. But you can expect well-built wooden foundations to last without trouble for sixty years and probably much longer.

Wood foundations may be impractical in areas where treated posts are expensive or hard to obtain. I do not think a wood foundation should be used in soil that isn't well drained or that tends to stay wet much of the year, because these conditions may encourage rot.

Slab Foundations.   The special characteristic of the slab foundation is that it doubles as the floor. Heating pipes and other utilities can be cast right into the slab, making the entire floor a radiator. Then it can be covered with carpet, tile, or similar flooring.

In warm climates slabs are commonly used as an economical floor-foundation combination. In cold climates they are not usually used under living areas because the floor tends to be cold near the perimeter. This need not be a problem if the slab is totally isolated from the cold with rigid foam insulation. In fact, a well-insulated floor slab can become a storage bank for solar heat. This is a tricky design area, so if you are considering a slab foundation in a cold climate I suggest you get professional advice.

HOW TO LAY OUT A FOUNDATION

Whether you use columns, a basement, or a slab, the foundation will have to be laid out precisely. If a contractor is building you a basement foundation, he or she will lay it out using a transit (Figure 120). Otherwise you will do your own lay-

TRANSIT

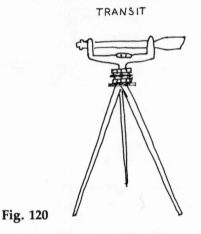

Fig. 120

out using batter boards and strings. Usually this is the first thing you do at the site. However, if a backhoe or bulldozer will be used for excavation, you do the accurate layout after the digging, since the heavy machinery would knock down the stakes and strings. Excavation can be done with an approximate layout.

Figure 121 shows batter boards and strings. The string locations are marked on the batter boards with nails so that the strings can be removed when they are in the way and put back in exactly the same positions.

Here are the steps for laying a foundation:

Step 1.
Rough layout: Using a compass and a 50-foot tape, lay out roughly where the house will be. Mark the corners with rocks or stakes.
Step 2.
Put up stakes: About three feet outside of these stakes, plant the tall stakes that will support the batter boards. These should be 2 × 3s, 2 × 4s, or similarly strong poles from the woods. They must be as high or higher than the foundation because

Comparative Foundation Costs.
These approximations are based on average 1977 costs. Actual costs will vary from place to place.

Type	Cost	Cost of Typical 20' × 30'
Wood column	$1.50/ft. of column	$110
Wood column, columns treated by owner	$.50–$1/ft. of column	80
Concrete column, made with Sonotubes	$2/ft. of column	160
Block foundation, including footing, no floor slab	$4.50/running ft. of wall	450
Reinforced concrete by contractor, no floor slab	$30/running ft. of wall	3000
Reinforced concrete by owner, no concrete floor	$8/running ft. of wall	800
Reinforced concrete crawlspace foundation (frost-wall) by contractor	$7.50/running ft. of wall	750
Concrete basement floor, by contractor	$.60/sq.ft.	360
Concrete basement floor, by owner	$.40/sq.ft.	240
Concrete slab foundation, by contractor	$1/sq.ft.	600
Concrete slab foundation, by owner	$.70/sq.ft.	420
Stone (very approximate figure)	$3/running ft. of wall	300

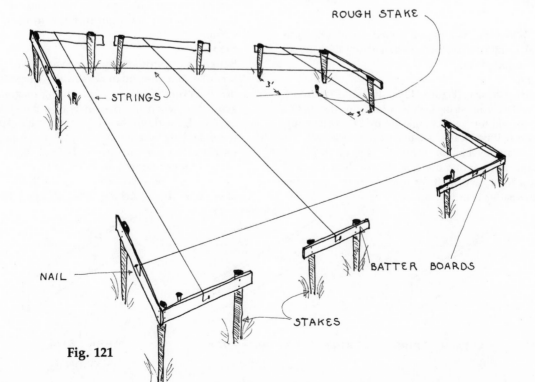

Fig. 121

the batter boards are set at the level of the foundation top. The foundation height will often be about 6 inches above the ground at the highest corner. You can point the stakes with a hatchet and drive them into the ground with a sledgehammer. If you are building a column foundation with a row of columns down the middle of the house, provide stakes to support batter boards to mark this row of columns.

Step 3.

Attach batter boards: When the stakes are in, nail 1 x̄ 6 rough boards onto them as shown in Figure 121. The top edge of these boards should be at the level of the top of the foundation. Level the batter boards with a water level, which you make yourself with a gallon jug and clear plastic tubing from the hardware store (Figure 122). Chapter twenty-four explains exactly how to use a water level.

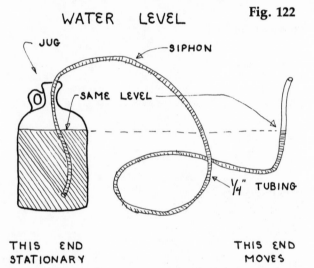

WATER LEVEL   **Fig. 122**

JUG

SIPHON

SAME LEVEL

¼" TUBING

THIS END STATIONARY

THIS END MOVES

When the boards are nailed on at the right height, sight across them to make sure they are all in a single plane.

Step 4.

Attach Strings (Figure 123): If your house is 16' × 24', the strings you attach to the batter boards will form a rectangle 16' by 24'. Your foundation will be located relative to this rectangle.

Using eyeball or compass, set up the first string, representing the first side of the rectangle. Pull it tight, and tie it off to nails in the top edge of the batter boards.

Next, attach the opposite, parallel string in the approximately correct spot. You will need a 50-foot tape and someone to help you. Make the second string equidistant from the first at both ends. The string should be drawn tight over the board and tied to a nail on the bottom outside edge of the board. This allows you to adjust the string back and forth until it is exactly parallel to the first string and exactly the right distance away. When the second string is just right, mark the batter board by putting a nail into the *top* edge where the string comes across. You can now remove the string when necessary and replace it accurately.

Next, put up the third string approximately square to the first two, using a framing square to make a right angle. Do not set the final location of this string yet. Figure 125 shows the relationship of all four strings.

The fourth string will be parallel to and opposite the third, just as the second was parallel to and opposite the first. Measure and mark where the fourth string should go by tying marker strings onto the first and second strings (Figure 124). You

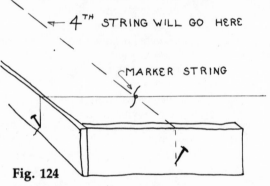

4ᵀᴴ STRING WILL GO HERE

MARKER STRING

Fig. 124

can slide these little markers back and forth until they are exactly the right distance from the third string.

Step 5.

Squaring the strings: The dimensions will now be accurate, but the squareness of the shape may be off. Squaring is done by measuring diagonals. In geometry, when the diagonals of a parallelogram are equal, the figure has to be a rectangle. Equalize the diagonals by moving strings 3 and 4 back and forth *together from the same ends* until the diagonal measurements are within ⅛ of an inch.

You can now lay out strings for interior rows of columns by stretching other strings parallel to

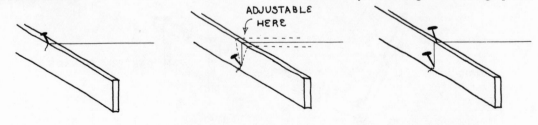

ADJUSTABLE HERE

Fig. 123   ATTACH FIRST STRING   ATTACH OTHER STRINGS   MARK EXACT LOCATION

Fig. 125

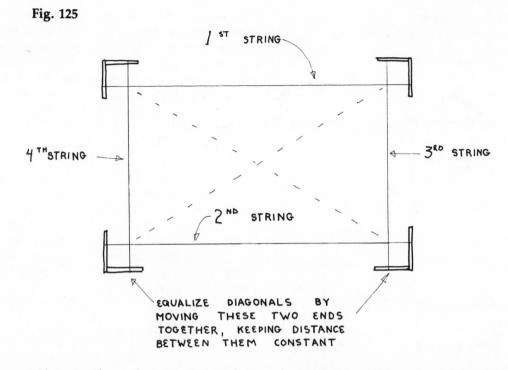

1ˢᵗ STRING

4ᵀᴴ STRING

3ᴿᴰ STRING

2ᴺᴰ STRING

EQUALIZE DIAGONALS BY
MOVING THESE TWO ENDS
TOGETHER, KEEPING DISTANCE
BETWEEN THEM CONSTANT

the outside ones. If your layout is L-shaped, U-shaped, or some other odd shape, divide the shape into rectangles and lay out one rectangle at a time. When all the strings are right, mark the positions permanently with nails at the top of the batter boards.

BUILDING A COLUMN FOUNDATION

Wooden columns will consist of 6-inch — or bigger — square or round posts treated against rot. These can be bought already pressure-treated — which is the most effective method of treatment — or you can treat the posts yourself (see Appendix G).

Concrete columns are poured in place in special cylindrical cardboard forms, often known by the trade name Sonotubes. One-story houses, with each column supporting an area of 150 square feet or less, can be built on 8-inch columns. Use 10-inch columns if the columns are less frequent, if the house has two stories, or if the columns stick more than 3 feet above the ground.

Layout and Design. Foundation posts are always arranged in rows. On top of each row is a sill, a heavy timber such as a 6 × 8 that bridges the posts and is a main carrying timber of the house. The floor beams or joists rest on the sills and span between them (Figure 126). For purposes of illustration the column height is exaggerated in the drawing. Usually the columns will be as low as possible.

Figure out how many rows of posts you will need and how many columns should be in each row. If there are too many columns, the work and cost of putting them in is too high. If there are too few — and the distance between them too large — the timbers that connect the posts will have to be impractically large. For most designs, rows should fall about every 8 to 12 feet, which is an efficient length for floor joists to span. Sixteen feet should be the maximum distance between rows. Within a given row, columns should be spaced 8 to 10 feet apart, and not more than 12 feet apart. Work out a grid of posts that approximates these ideal spans and otherwise fits your design.

A foundation plan must accommodate any special loads that come down inside the building. If part of the roof or second-story floor is resting

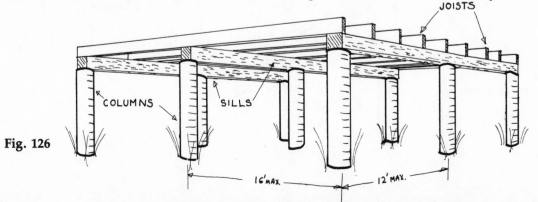

JOISTS

COLUMNS SILLS

16' MAX. 12' MAX.

Fig. 126

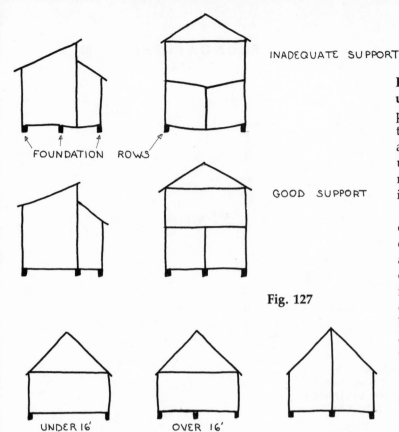

INADEQUATE SUPPORT

FOUNDATION ROWS

GOOD SUPPORT

UNDER 16'   OVER 16'

Fig. 127

on walls or posts inside the house, these walls or posts should be directly supported by strategically located sills or posts (Figure 127).

Finding the Sill Size. Once the foundation is arranged, you can figure out what size sill will be necessary. The longer a sill is and the more weight it supports, the larger the timber. A two-story house will need bigger sills than a one-story house. Appendix A explains how to compute what size timber is needed for any situation. I recommend that you spend a few hours mastering that material, because it will give you a better understanding of how a house structure works and enable you to make your own design more efficient. The sill size table in Appendix C also gives sill sizes for different cases.

Figuring Out How the Sill Will Sit on the Column. The sill should be centered as much as possible on the column without sticking out where the rain can collect and rot it. With a narrow sill and a wide column, centering the sill on the column will sometimes cause a water trap. If so, move the column over until the siding just covers it (Figure 128).

Figure 129 shows how to calculate where the center of the column should be with a 4-inch sill on a 10-inch column. The siding and sheathing add up to 2 inches. The strings mark the outer edge of the sill. If the column is positioned with its outside edge flush with the siding, the center of the column will be 3 inches inside the string. Use a plumb bob (Figure 130) to locate the center of the column on the ground, and mark the spot with a small stake.

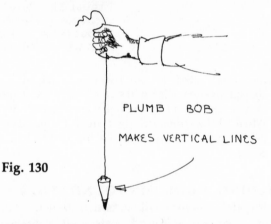

PLUMB BOB

MAKES VERTICAL LINES

Fig. 130

Digging. You can dig the holes yourself, or hire a backhoe at fifteen or twenty dollars per hour to do the digging. I suggest you dig a test hole. If it takes more than an hour or two, the backhoe will save a lot of time and aggravation if you can afford it. If a backhoe is to do the digging, put up the batter boards after the backhoe finishes as noted earlier. The backhoe digs a big hole, so it can work

Fig. 128

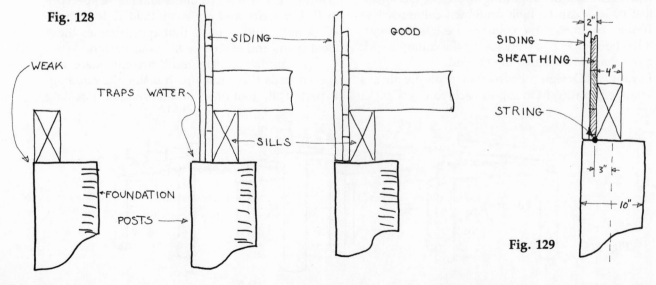

WEAK

SIDING

GOOD

SIDING

SHEATHING

TRAPS WATER

SILLS

STRING

FOUNDATION

POSTS

Fig. 129

from an approximate, quick layout done with stakes and a 50-foot tape. The accurate layout can be done later.

If you dig yourself, you will need:

a shovel
a posthole digger (rentable)
a mattock for roots
a pick for rocks
a 5-foot crowbar for prying out boulders

Make your holes 1½ to 2 feet in diameter at the top; the sides should go straight down or, if possible, splay out at the bottom. Dig the holes below the frost line. You can find out where this is by asking local builders or by referring to Appendix I. If you hit bedrock, you can pour the footing on that. The diameter of the hole at the bottom is determined by the size of the footing.

Footings. The footings consist of reinforced concrete puddles poured in the bottom of the holes. Their diameter depends on the amount of weight each column must hold and the bearing capacity of the soil. In general, a one-story house can have footings 20 inches or 24 inches in diameter, and a two-story house can have footings 30 or 36 inches in diameter. The footing thickness depends on the diameter, as follows:

Diameter	Thickness
20″	6″
24″	8″
30″	10″
36″	12″

The steel reinforcing can be four ½-inch reinforcing bars placed in a tic-tac-toe shape about 2 inches up from the bottom of the footing. For a 36-inch footing, use 6 bars.

You can have ready-mixed concrete delivered by huge cement mixing trucks. Use it if possible to save a lot of backbreaking labor and because the economy made by mixing your own is not great. You may need to mix your own concrete if footing volume is smaller than the minimum you can get delivered or if you are building in an inaccessible place.

Mixing Concrete. Prepared concrete mix comes in bags, but it is much cheaper to make your own. Here is a good recipe.

one part portland air-entraining cement
two parts fine aggregate (clean sand)
three parts coarse aggregate (gravel)

A lumber yard can sell you the cement in 94-pound bags, which is one cubic feet of cement. The aggregates can be bought from a sand and gravel company. The fine aggregate must be clean sand. The coarse aggregate ideally should be a mixture of particles ¼ inch to 1 inch or 1½ inches in diameter. But often peastone is used — this is uniformly about ¼ inch or ³/₈ of an inch in diameter. What you want is a mixture that contains an even gradation of particle sizes if possible. Tell the person at the gravel pit what you are doing, so he or she can give you the right materials. Sometimes concrete is made with a single, ungraded bank-run gravel dug right out of the hillside and used as is. If you use bank-run gravel, make sure it contains an even gradation of particle sizes and not mostly small or large pieces. Eliminate pieces over about 2 inches in diameter, because they will make the mix harder to work with.

You can mix concrete in a rented electric mixer or make your own mixing pan out of a 4 × 8 sheet of plywood and some 1 × 4 or 1 × 6 boards, as shown in Figure 131. If you use an electric mixer,

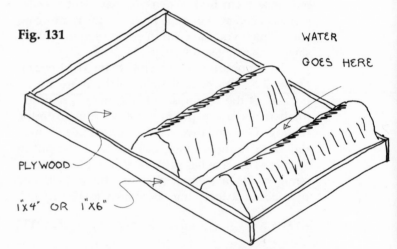

Fig. 131

WATER GOES HERE

PLYWOOD

1″×4″ OR 1″×6″

first mix the ingredients dry, then add water until the mix reaches the right consistency. It's hard to describe what the right amount of water is, but the mix should be stiff without being dry. Every particle should be wet, and the mix should get shiny when you whack it with the back of a shovel. It should not be runny because a wet mix makes weak concrete.

If you mix in a wooden pan, the trick is to mix the ingredients as you fill the pan. Sprinkle a shovelful of cement lightly around the pan. Then sprinkle two shovelfuls of sand and then three shovelfuls of coarse aggregate. Do this ten times. After a few passes with a shovel or hoe, the dry ingredients will be mixed. Then use a hoe or shovel to form two mountain ranges with a deep valley between them.

Pour some water in the valley. Take the hoe and gently pull part of the mountainside into the water, spreading it out with a pulling stroke. Keep this up until your mountains have been eaten away and the water is used up. Add water if needed. Then keep mixing until the batch is well mixed. Keep track of the amount of water you use to reach the right consistency. On the next batch, put in all the water at once, which will make the work easier.

Pouring Concrete.   Concrete trucks run on a tight schedule and have to dump their loads quickly. If you are using ready-mixed concrete, you will have to be completely prepared with a crew of three or four people all set to work. Line the bottom of each footing hole with old newspapers, felt, paper, or plastic to prevent the water in the mix from leaching into the soil and weakening the concrete. Put the concrete into a wheelbarrow or buckets and transport it to the hole. As you pour the footing, try to keep dirt from the sides of the hole from falling into the concrete. You can stretch the concrete by throwing in rocks you have dug up, but rinse them first. When you have put about 2 inches of concrete into the hole, put the reinforcing bars, which you have cut in advance with a hacksaw, in the tic-tac-toe shape.

Finish pouring the concrete to the right depth. Use a 2 × 4 to pack it tight so there are no air pockets. If the columns will be concrete, reinforcing bars should be put in to tie the column to the footing. On a relatively flat site, a single ¹⁄₂-inch rod 12 to 18 inches long will do. It can be put in after the concrete has set enough for it to stand up straight. On a sloping site, use three L-shaped rods about 2 feet long, as shown in Figure 132.

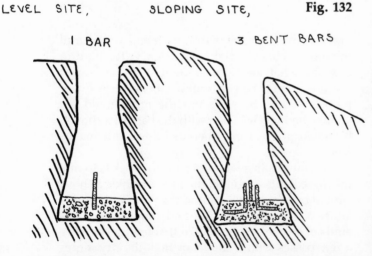

LEVEL SITE,   SLOPING SITE,   **Fig. 132**

I BAR   3 BENT BARS

These must be placed immediately after you finish pouring the concrete. Wire them together or use sticks to hold them up while the concrete sets. Whether you use one bar or three, set up the layout strings to make sure they emerge from the footing within the circle where the column will be.

Cutting the Columns.   You must cut your wooden columns (or cardboard forms if your col-

umns are concrete) so that each of them will come to exactly the same level. Since the bottoms of the holes will not be at the same level, each column will have a different length.

Number the holes so that the columns don't get mixed up. Next, measure and record the length required for each column. In theory, the layout strings represent the top level of the columns, but I suggest making the columns ¹⁄₂ inch shorter (or lower) than the layout strings so that the columns don't push the strings out of line. One way to find column height is to measure down from the strings. If you use this method, make sure the strings are tight. Even so you should add about ¹⁄₄ inch to the measurement of the middle columns to compensate for the slight sag that will inevitably exist.

A better method is to use the water level. (Consult chapter twenty-four to see how the water level is used.) Set the reservoir of the level at the column height, ¹⁄₂ inch below the strings and batter boards. Get a stick, such as a 1 × 2, at least as tall as the tallest column, to use as a ruler. (You will not need a tape measure at all.) Take the stick to hole 1, set its bottom on the footing, and hold it as straight up as you can by eye. Put the free end of the level's tube next to the stick and make a mark opposite the water level in the tube. Write 1 next to the mark. Take the stick over to hole 2, put it on the footing, straighten it, mark it in the same way, and put a 2 next to the mark. Continue the procedure until your stick has a mark for each column.

You are now ready to mark the columns or cardboard forms. The stick is the ruler. Make sure the columns or forms are cut square. If they're cardboard tubes for concrete, make several measurements around the perimeter and connect them freehand; then cut along that line with a hand saw or saber saw (Figure 133).

Sonotubes come in 10-foot pieces, which cost about .75 a running foot. You can avoid waste by taping the scraps together with duct tape. Put the taped joint within 1 foot of the top or underground so that the weak place at the joint won't cause trouble.

Setting the Columns.   Cardboard forms or wooden columns are set in the ground similarly. One person holds the column or cardboard form at the right place relative to the layout strings at the top. Another person uses a 2-foot, or longer, level, held vertically, to adjust the bottom of the column or form until it is plumb (exactly vertical). Read the level on two different sides of the column.

When the column or form is vertical and lines up with the strings, place a few inches of dirt in

 MEASURING STICK

Fig. 133

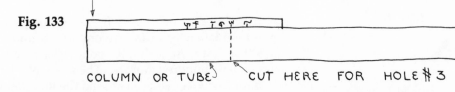

COLUMN OR TUBE⌐ CUT HERE FOR HOLE ⧣3

the hole, and pack it down carefully with a 2 × 4 without moving the bottom of the column in the process. When the bottom is positioned, one person continues to hold the top in place while the other fills in more dirt. About every 6 inches, pack the dirt down with a 2 × 4. Rocks or other rubble may be added to fill the hole since the dirt will run short.

Pouring Concrete Columns. If your foundation is wooden, it is now done. If you are using concrete columns, these can now be poured the same way that the footings were. Any tubes that stick above ground more than 30 inches will have a tendency to wave back and forth when they are full of heavy concrete, so the tall ones should be braced to the ground or to the batter boards to keep their tops positioned.

Any column that sticks more than 3 feet above the ground should be reinforced with 3 pieces of 1/4-inch #2 reinforcing rod. The rods can be cut to fall just short of the top of the tube, so they won't be in your way later. Put them in after you have poured the concrete about 2 feet deep.

Agitate the concrete as it is going in to prevent air pockets which will weaken the column. This may be done several ways. A 2 × 4 can be used to pack down the concrete as it goes in, shovelful by shovelful. You can drum on the sides of the tube with your fists, which will free a lot of air. If the tube is reinforced, you can wiggle the reinforcing rod vigorously to set up a vibration like a tuning fork to settle the concrete.

When a tube is full, install a special L-shaped bolt called an *anchor bolt*. This will later hold the sill firmly to the column. The trick is to hold the anchor bolt in the right position long enough for the concrete to set (Figure 134). Put the L-shaped

4X4 BEING USED TO POSITION ANCHOR BOLT WHILE CONCRETE SETS

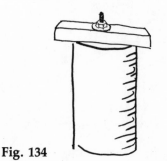

Fig. 134

end down. The bend in the bolt prevents it from being ripped out of the hardened concrete by a violent event. The anchor bolt should sink at least 5 inches into the concrete and should be centered.

Setting the Sills on the Column. Before the sills go on they should be treated with wood preservatives (see Appendix G). The more thoroughly you do this the better, since sills are particularly subject to rot.

Locate the resting place of the sills. Even if there is some inaccuracy in the location of the columns, set the sills exactly. The outside edges of the sills should fall right on the layout strings. Set up the strings, and mark on the column exactly where the sills should go. If the columns are wood, the sills can be placed on the marks and toe-nailed in with 20d nails. In places where severe windstorms are possible, reinforce this connection with some perforated metal strapping from a hardware store. Buy the type that is about 1/32 of an inch thick and nail it to both sill and column with 1 1/2-inch roofing nails (Figure 135).

PERFORATED METAL STRAPPING

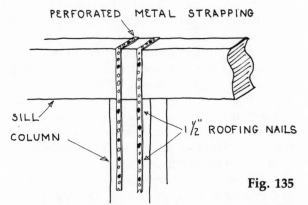

SILL

COLUMN

1 1/2" ROOFING NAILS

Fig. 135

If your columns are concrete, wait until the next day to set the sills, since the concrete must set. Even then be gentle with the concrete, which only gradually cures to its full strength. Once it sets, locate the sills by marking the columns exactly where the strings pass over them. Then drill holes in the sills for the anchor bolts. To locate the holes you will have to measure from the end of the row to the center of the bolt and from the layout string to the bolt, since the anchor bolt may not be perfectly centered. Since it is hard to measure precisely where these holes should be and the anchor bolts may not be perfectly straight, drill oversize holes to allow a little play. Use a 1-inch hole with a 1/2-inch anchor bolt, and then put a large-size washer under the nut. The holes can be

BIT BRACE   SPADE BIT

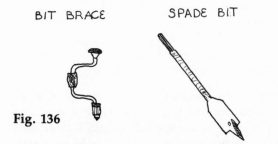

Fig. 136

drilled with a brace and bit or a spade bit in an electric drill (Figure 136). Since the spade bits are only 5 or 6 inches long they will not drill all the way through the sill. You can drill from both top and bottom of the sill and hope the holes will meet in the middle, or get a drill bit extension from the same place you bought the spade bits. In either case, have a friend hold a square on the sill next to the drill to make sure that you are drilling straight.

The sill should not be installed in direct contact with a concrete column, since masonry attracts dampness. Before you put the sills on, cut a piece of sheet aluminum bigger in radius than the column, make a hole in it for the anchor bolt, and place it on top of the column as a shield against moisture. Put the sills on loosely and check them for level. Check too that they are exactly the right distance apart and that the diagonals are equal within ⅛ of an inch if possible. Make adjustments, and bolt the sill in.

What to Do if the Foundation Is Inaccurate.   Your foundation can be out of whack in two ways. First, the column heights can be a little off. If a column is too high, notch the sill above it by the same amount. If the column is too low, add to the column with mortar mix or wood scraps of the right thickness. Separate the wood from the masonry with a layer of aluminum flashing.

Second, the columns can be out of line. If the discrepancy is an inch or two, line the sills up where they should theoretically go and let them sit a little incorrectly over the columns. If a column is more than 2 inches out, you need advice from an experienced person.

BUILDING A BASEMENT FOUNDATION

A basement foundation is a more ambitious undertaking than a column foundation. I describe four types of basement foundations: poured concrete, block, stone, and wood. Readers planning to build any of them will need to consult the references in the bibliography. Evacuation, layout, and building footings will be identical for all types except wood.

Excavation and Layout.   A cellar hole can be dug

by a backhoe or bulldozer. If you're doing your own foundation you can hire one for around $15 or $20 an hour. At such rates your cellar hole will cost a few hundred dollars. There should be a corridor 2 or 3 feet wide all around the foundation, so that you will have room to build the foundation walls. A 16 × 20-foot house needs a hole about 22 × 26 feet.

Put up batter boards and strings after the hole is dug. Because the hole is oversized, these must be set further back than they would be for a column foundation. Otherwise, the layout strings are set up exactly as for column foundations (pages 78–81). If you're having a contractor do the foundation, he or she will do the layout and no batter boards will be needed.

Building Footings.   Any masonry foundation wall will need the type of footing shown in Figure 137. The footing should be as deep as the wall is wide and its width twice that.

FOOTING SIZE

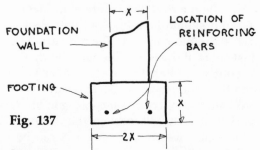

FOUNDATION WALL

LOCATION OF REINFORCING BARS

FOOTING

Fig. 137

Step 1.
Building forms: The simple forms for a footing are shown in Figure 138. These forms must be level. An easy way to locate them is to place an extra string on the batter boards right above where the outside edge of the footing will be. Measure down with a plumb bob to locate the outside of the footing. The first plank of the form will go there. Measure down from the string to find the correct height of the footings. The top edge of the form's plank goes here. Measure at the corners, where the strings won't sag appreciably. When the first plank is set and leveled, it can be held in place with

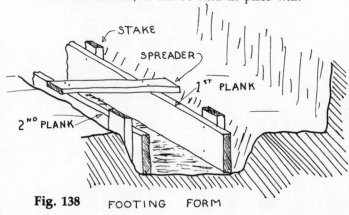

STAKE

SPREADER

1ST PLANK

2ND PLANK

Fig. 138   FOOTING FORM

stakes. The second, inside plank can be located the proper distance in from the first and leveled with a carpenter's level. After the two planks are staked down, nail scraps of lumber called *spreaders* on top to hold them the right distance apart.

Step 2.

Tamping: Before pouring the footing, pack the loose earth inside down hard with a tamper (Figure 139).

Fig. 139 TAMPER

Step 3.

Moistening the Soil: If the soil is dry, it will absorb water from the concrete too fast and weaken the mix. Sprinkle water in the bottom of the footing to dampen the soil.

Step 4.

Pouring Concrete: Pages 83–84 explain how to mix your own concrete. Ready-mixed concrete, delivered to you all ready to go, costs under $100, at $30 per cubic yard, for the footings for a small house. This expense is small compared to the labor of mixing it by hand. (See page 91 to figure out how much concrete to order.)

When a concrete truck comes, be ready. These trucks are on schedule and charge extra for any time they spend idle. Have a crew of at least four people prepared with shovels and a good strong wheelbarrow. The truck will need a good, fairly flat road right up to the hole. Plan exactly how the mix will be brought to the forms from the truck. Fill the part of the form farthest from the truck first, and work back toward the truck.

Step 5.

Reinforcing: Though many footings are put in unreinforced, 1/2-inch reinforcing bars laid in the concrete will strengthen the footing against shifting. When the concrete is 2 inches deep, lay in two bars parallel with the footing (Figure 137) and then continue pouring.

Step 6.

Screeding: When the forms are full, use a board to level the concrete with the top of the forms. This is *screeding*. The concrete should be level, but it need not be smooth. In fact, if you pour concrete walls above, the roughness will help the wall adhere.

Step 7.

Tying the wall to the footing: If you pour concrete walls on your footings, use short pieces of rein-

forcing bar to tie the two parts together. Cut pieces of 1/2-inch reinforcing bar about 16 inches long with a hacksaw. Place the bars sticking up out of the center of the footing every 2 feet. They can be stuck into the concrete as soon as it has stiffened enough to hold them up.

Step 8.

Protecting concrete from the sun: In hot weather, the sun and heat can cause the concrete to dry too fast, which weakens it. Keep the concrete damp until it has fully set — at least 24 hours. Cover it with plastic between soakings.

Poured Concrete Foundation Walls. Concrete foundations are cast in one piece in special forms. Since there are no joints to break or leak, they are both stronger and tighter than any other type of foundation. Reinforced with steel they are indestructible.

If you have chosen a poured concrete foundation, I recommend having all of the work done by a foundation contractor. If you do it yourself, you can save half the cost, assuming you can reuse your form material, but I don't think it is an efficient use of your time. The plywood forms you build must be super-strong, and you must build them piece by piece — a job you have never done before and probably will never do again. The plywood you make the forms from will be coated with a thin film of concrete and will dull any tool you use to cut it with. The contractor, who has done it all before, has special forms that can be put up in a morning and reused again and again. A labor that will take you weeks will take the contractor two days. Concrete foundation work is one place where a contractor's services are worth the premium they cost. If you want to build your own foundation, I suggest you build a block or treated-wood foundation.

Block Foundation. A block foundation costs about 60 percent as much as a poured concrete foundation you build yourself and about 25 percent as much as a concrete foundation a contractor builds for you. Block is definitely the most inexpensive way to build a masonry foundation in a reasonably short time. These foundations are not as strong or watertight as reinforced concrete because they are not monolithic. They are more likely to develop leaks and are more susceptible to damage caused by settling or frost. But they work well in a well-drained soil.

If you wish to build a block foundation, get someone experienced with block construction to help you design your foundation and to show you how to lay block. The Audel's guide on the subject has an excellent, detailed description of block construction (see bibliography).

Block construction is modular. Every dimension in every direction is, or should be, a multiple of 4 inches. The standard block, called a *stretcher*, is $7\frac{5}{8}'' \times 7\frac{5}{8}'' \times 15\frac{5}{8}''$. With a standard $\frac{3}{8}$-inch mortar joint, each block occupies a space $8'' \times 8'' \times 16''$ (Figure 140).

Eight inches is a standard thickness of a block wall. Other common thicknesses are 4 inches — used for nonbearing partitions — 10 inches, and 12 inches. These extra-thick walls are used where extra strength is needed or desired. For each thickness of wall, there is a large variety of blocks for special situations, such as corners, window location, $\frac{1}{2}$ length, and $\frac{3}{4}$ length (Figure 141).

A block foundation should be designed to avoid cutting any blocks. A wall 16 feet long will be 12 blocks long and easy to build. A wall 16 feet, 2 inches long will require a lot of block cutting and make the work longer. Usually the corners are laid first in a bed of mortar on the footing and are staggered back as shown in Figure 142. Strings are then stretched from one end of the wall to the other to line up the block courses (rows) in between. All the blocks are carefully plumbed and leveled to keep the wall straight and accurate. Anchor bolts are embedded in the top course to hold down a 2-inch-thick sill.

A modern variation on block construction that is becoming popular is *surface bonding*. In a surface-bonded wall, the first course of blocks is set in mortar. After that the courses are stacked with no mortar at all. Then both sides of the wall are plastered with a special cement such as Block-bond, which is reinforced with glass fiber. Though this construction might not seem strong, tests have been conducted which show that a surface-bonded wall is stronger than a conventional block wall. The mortar joints in a regular wall do not actually hold the block together very strongly. But the glass fibers in the surface bonding make the plastered surface into a continuous film with considerable tensile strength. The surface is also more waterproof.

Surface bonding should be faster than a conventional block construction, particularly for the amateur, and is probably one of the best methods for building your own basement.

Stone Foundations. A stone foundation, like a block foundation, is susceptible to frost damage and uneven settling. On a good footing and in well-drained soil, this will not be a serious drawback. The major disadvantage of stone construction is that it is the slowest possible way to build. I do not want to discourage anyone from learning

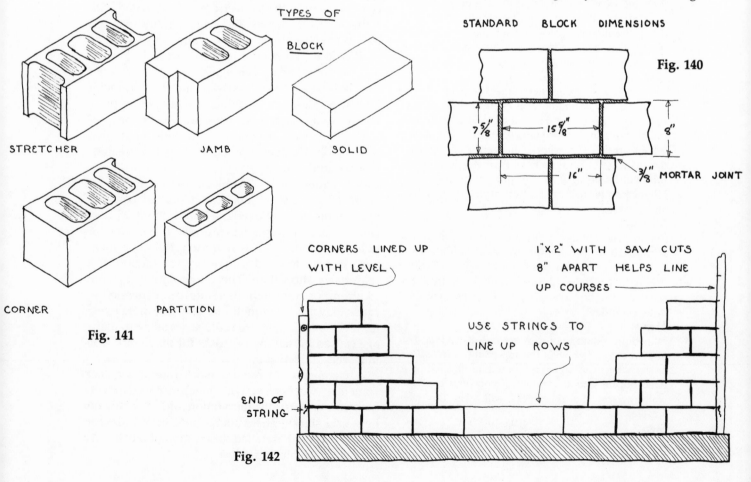

TYPES OF BLOCK

STRETCHER   JAMB   SOLID

CORNER   PARTITION

Fig. 141

STANDARD BLOCK DIMENSIONS

Fig. 140

$7\frac{5}{8}''$ $15\frac{5}{8}''$ $8''$

$16''$ $\frac{3}{8}''$ MORTAR JOINT

CORNERS LINED UP WITH LEVEL

1"X 2" WITH SAW CUTS 8" APART HELPS LINE UP COURSES

USE STRINGS TO LINE UP ROWS

END OF STRING

Fig. 142

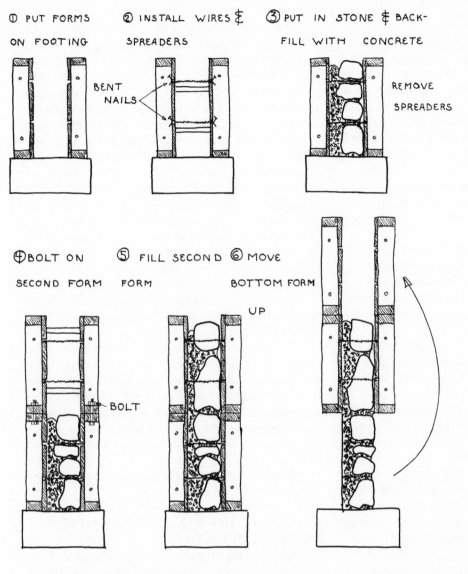

① PUT FORMS ON FOOTING

② INSTALL WIRES & SPREADERS

BENT NAILS

③ PUT IN STONE & BACKFILL WITH CONCRETE

REMOVE SPREADERS

④ BOLT ON SECOND FORM

BOLT

⑤ FILL SECOND FORM

⑥ MOVE BOTTOM FORM UP

Fig. 143

stonework. To me it is one of the most satisfying kinds of building, perhaps the most satisfying. And it is a skill you can learn without being a professional. But do it for the pleasure in the work and in the result, not because you think it will save you money. Stone construction will only produce significant dollar savings in very mild climates, where wall insulation is not important. In cold climates, stone walls must be insulated, and this means building, in effect, a wooden wall inside the stone wall. The stone primarily saves the cost of siding, which is not very much anyway. The tremendous extra labor of stone construction will usually offset any dollar savings, unless you have very little money and a great deal of time. Should you take up stonework, hire a local mason to teach you the art.

One type of stonework suitable for an amateur is the slip form or the Nearing method, pictured in Figure 143. Stones are laid against the wall of a movable form (Figure 144) on the side of the wall

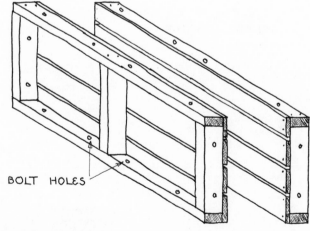

BOLT HOLES

Fig. 144

BASIC SLIPFORM

that will be exposed. Concrete is poured behind the stone. When the concrete sets, the forms are removed and repositioned further up the wall. The bibliography gives references that describe the Nearing method in detail.

Treated Wood Foundations. The American Plywood Association has developed a full basement foundation built of pressure-treated wood. It consists of an ordinary studwall built with treated studs, covered with treated plywood on the outside, and resting on a treated 2 × 8 used as a footing. The outside of the wall is sealed with plastic film and asphalt. A bed of crushed rock, covered with plastic film, fills the cellar hole. On that rests a concrete slab floor, which holds the foundation in position at the bottom. A sump or drain within the slab area provides drainage for the cellar itself and for the perimeter of the foundation walls (Figure 145).

The wood foundation costs almost exactly the same amount for materials as a block foundation, and I suspect it is as durable. Its two advantages are that (1) it is the fastest full foundation to build and (2) that for many people wood is a more familiar material than stone.

The American Plywood Association will supply a free manual on request explaining exactly how the wood foundation is built (see bibliography).

Drainage. When you build any basement, you must keep the water out of it. Figure 145 shows common ways to do this. The first objective is to keep as much water as possible away from the foundation in the first place. If there is a hill behind the house, you may need a drainage ditch of some kind to divert water coming down the hill toward the house. The earth near the house should slope away from the foundation. Finally, gutters and downspouts can be installed. Your house may need all or none of these provisions, depending on the contour of the land and the porosity of the soil.

The second objective is to remove water that does find its way to the cellar walls. Special 4-inch perforated pipe is placed in the bottom of a trench just beside the footing. This pipe surrounds the house and is carefully laid almost level, at a pitch of about 1 inch in 12 feet. The pipe is covered with crushed rock to catch the water. The crush rock is covered with a double layer of red building paper, which keeps the crushed rock and piping from getting clogged with earth. The pipe continues at a downward pitch, till it emerges from the ground to daylight or flows into a dry well or a drainage field similar to the leach field of a septic tank. Exactly how you provide drainage will depend on the conditions at the site. Seek reliable advice. Often a bulldozer or backhoe operator will know a lot about drainage systems.

To keep the remaining water out of the basement, coat the outside of the foundation with a special tarlike foundation coating.

If water still finds its way into the cellar, you can provide a *sump*, which is a concrete tank below the basement floor, where the water can collect (Figure 146). From the sump water can flow to a dry well, drainage field, or daylight, or if absolutely necessary, be removed with a sump pump. However, if the drainage in your site is so bad as to require a sump pump you should consider a different site, or perhaps a column-type foundation.

WORKING DRAWING AND SAMPLE MATERIALS LISTS

Foundation Drawings. For both design and estimating purposes you will need a plan and a cross section of your foundation. Show the dimensions

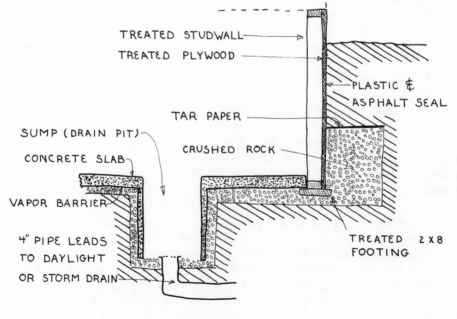

Fig. 145

WOOD FOUNDATION WALL

Fig. 146

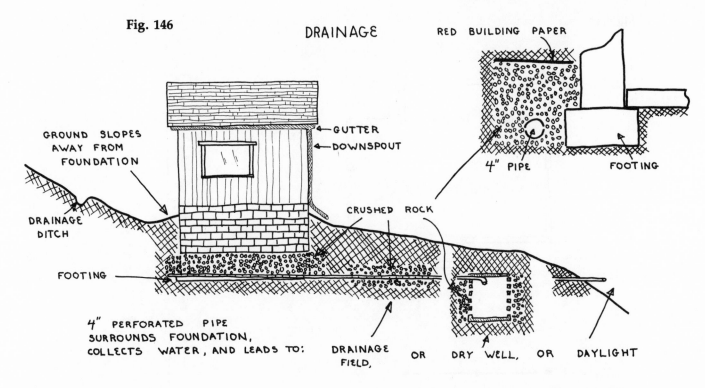

DRAINAGE

RED BUILDING PAPER

GROUND SLOPES
AWAY FROM
FOUNDATION

GUTTER
DOWNSPOUT

4" PIPE

FOOTING

DRAINAGE
DITCH

CRUSHED ROCK

FOOTING

4" PERFORATED PIPE
SURROUNDS FOUNDATION,
COLLECTS WATER, AND LEADS TO: DRAINAGE   OR   DRY WELL,   OR   DAYLIGHT
FIELD,

of the foundation, plus any special details such as anchor bolts and reinforcement. For a post foundation, list the estimated heights of the various columns. Figure 147 shows typical plans and sections for 2 common types of foundations.

Figuring Concrete Materials.

Step. 1

Figure volumes in cubic feet: To figure out the volume of foundation walls, multiply the area times the thickness, measuring both in feet. An 8-inch concrete wall 10 feet wide and 8 feet high will have a volume of $10 \times 8 \times \frac{2}{3}$ cubic feet because 8 inches is $\frac{2}{3}$ of a foot.

Volume of round column footings:

Diameter	Depth	Volume in cu. ft.
20"	6"	1.1
24"	8"	2.1
30"	10"	4.1
36"	12"	7.1

Volume of round columns:

Diameter	Volume in cu. ft. per foot of height
8"	.35
10"	.55

Step 2.

Volumes for ready mix: Divide cubic feet by 27 to convert to cubic yards for ordering ready-mix concrete.

$$\frac{\text{cubic ft.}}{27} = \text{cubic yards}$$

Volumes for mixing your own concrete: Computing the volume of materials is complicated by the fact that 1 cubic foot of cement, plus 2 cubic feet of sand, and 3 cubic feet of peastone will not add up to 6 cubic feet of concrete. To some extent the smaller particles will occupy the spaces between the larger particles. For estimating purposes you can roughly figure that the sand in your concrete formula will disappear into these spaces. One cubic foot of cement, 2 cubic feet of sand, and 3 cubic feet of stone, for example, will make approximately 4 cubic feet of concrete. Cement is sold by the cubic-foot bag, which weighs 94 pounds. Stone and sand are sold by the cubic yard.

For a mix of 1 part cement, 2 parts sand, and 3 parts peastone (1:2:3), order:

Cement: .25 bag/cu.ft. of concrete
Sand: .5 cu.ft. sand/cu.ft. of concrete
Peastone: .75 cu.ft. peastone/cu.ft. of concrete

For a mix of 1 part cement, 2 parts sand, and 4 parts peastone (1:2:4), order:

Cement: .2 bags/cu.ft. concrete
Sand: .4 cu. ft./cu.ft. concrete
Peastone: .8 cu. ft./cu.ft. concrete

Convert sand and peastone figures to cubic yards by dividing by 27, and add 15 percent for waste.

Fig. 147

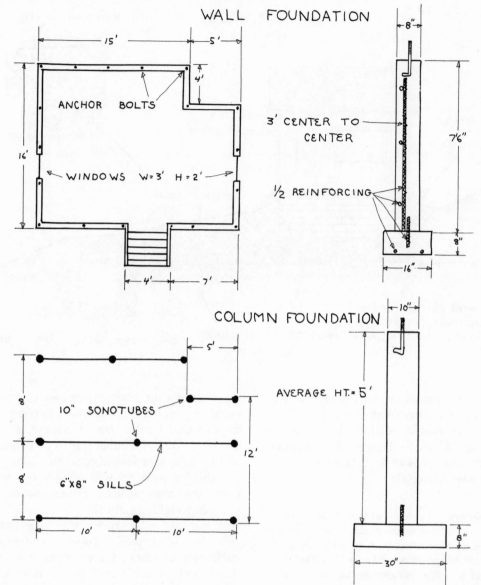

WALL   FOUNDATION

15'   5'

ANCHOR   BOLTS

4'

16'

WINDOWS   W = 3'   H = 2'

4'   7'

8'

3' CENTER TO
CENTER

7'6"

½ REINFORCING

8"

16"

COLUMN FOUNDATION

5'

10" SONOTUBES

8'

6"X8" SILLS

8'

10'   10'

12'

10"

AVERAGE HT. = 5'

8"

30"

Sample List: Layout Materials

Item	Quantity	Price/Unit	Total Cost
Large ball of string	_____	$ _____ /ball	$ _____
Rough 1" boards for batter boards and miscellaneous purposes	300 bd.ft.	$ _____ /bd.ft.	$ _____
Stakes, either 2"- or 3"-diam. poles or cheap 2 × 3s	_____	$ _____ /stake	$ _____

Sample List: Wooden Post Foundation

Item	Quantity	Price/Unit	Total Cost
Portland cement	_____ bags	$ _____ /bag	$ _____
Clean sand (fine aggregate)	_____ cu. yds.	$ _____ /cu. yd.	$ _____
Peastone (or coarse aggregate)	_____ cu. yds.	$ _____ /cu. yd.	$ _____
Wooden posts, 6" min. size, square or round	_____ ft.	$ _____ /ft.	$ _____
Preservative, if posts not pressure treated, approx. $\frac{1}{2}$ gallon/post	_____ gal.	$ _____ gal.	$ _____
Galvanized strapping to secure sill to column			

Sample List: Concrete Post Foundation

Item	Quantity	Price/Unit	Total Cost
Portland cement	_____ bags	$ _____ /bag	$ _____
Clean sand (fine aggregate)	_____ cu. yds.	$ _____ /cu. yd.	$ _____
Peastone (or coarse aggregate)	_____ cu. yds.	$ _____ /cu. yd.	$ _____
Sonotube concrete forms	_____ 10' pieces	$ _____ /10' piece	$ _____
Duct tape	_____ roll	$ _____ /roll	$ _____
Anchor bolt	_____ bolts	$ _____ /bolt	$ _____
$\frac{1}{2}$" reinforcing to tie posts to footings, and to reinforce footings	_____ 20' pieces	$ _____ /20' piece	$ _____
$\frac{1}{4}$" reinforcing, to reinforce tall columns, 3/tall column	_____ 20' pieces	$ _____ /20' piece	$ _____
12" aluminum flashing for tops of columns	_____ ft.	$ _____ /ft.	$ _____

chapter 13
Floors

PARTS OF A FLOOR

Figure 148 shows the most common type of floor framing, used with both column and basement foundations. Figure 149 shows floor details that go together to complete the floor.

Joists. Floor joists are the main beams that support the flooring. They span between the sills either by resting on top of them or by being hung between them on a ledger strip or joist hangers. Joists are usually spaced 16 inches or 24 inches center to center (o.c.) to match insulation, plywood, and other materials. Joists are doubled where they carry extra weight around stair openings, or under walls, partitions, and bathtubs.

Headers. Headers are what joists butt into. They run perpendicular to the joists. They hold the joists in position and provide support for flooring and walls around the perimeter of the house. Spe-

cial headers are provided wherever joists will be cut for a staircase or other opening. They pick up the ends of the cut joists.

Blocking. These are short pieces of wood that run between joists. They are used with joists over 10 feet to stiffen the floor in midspan and space the joists.

Reinforcing Blocks. Reinforcing blocks are scraps of the joist material nailed to a joist under the area in which a major load-bearing column will be located. These transmit the column load firmly down to the foundation or sill.

Insulation. In any but the most moderate cli-

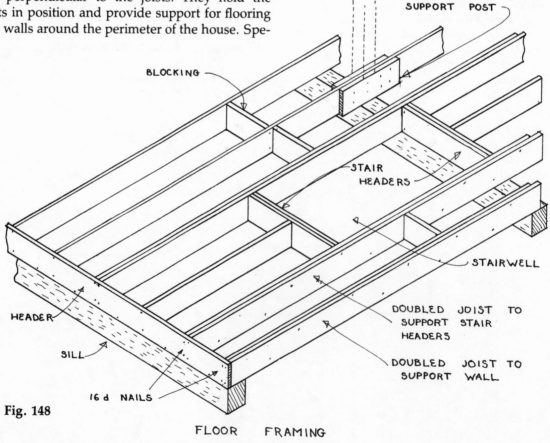

Fig. 148

FLOOR FRAMING

Fig. 149

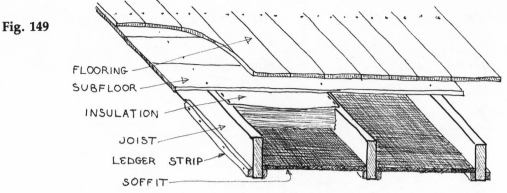

FLOORING
SUBFLOOR
INSULATION
JOIST
LEDGER STRIP
SOFFIT

FLOOR DETAILS

mates, a floor over an unheated area needs to be insulated. Conventionally, 6 inches of foil-backed fiberglass would be used in a cold climate, and 3½ inches in a warm climate. These standards will give you a well-insulated and efficient floor. With the price of fuel rising, you may want to use even more insulation, if there is room for it in the floor frame and if you can afford it. Some people are using 8 or even 10 inches of insulation, figuring that the extra cost will be offset by fuel savings in a few years.

Subfloor. The first layer to go down on the joists, the subfloor, is made of ¾-inch particle board, cheap 1-inch boards, or ½-inch or ⅝-inch plywood. It stiffens the floor and provides a surface to work on while building the rest of the house.

Vapor Barrier. The foil on the insulation is an effective vapor barrier, but often a layer of .004-inch plastic film will be used in addition, either right under or right over the subfloor.

Soffit. The insulation needs support or it will soon fall out. When the floor is built above a cellar or enclosed crawlspace, the insulation can be supported by wire or wire mesh. But if the area below is exposed to the weather, the insulation should be protected from the wind with a soffit made of insulation board or any cheap material that comes in 4′ × 8′ sheets.

Finish Flooring. This is the final flooring layer. Installing the finish floor is usually delayed as long as possible to minimize the amount it gets scarred up by the building process. The finish floor will usually be good-quality dry softwood or hardwood boards laid over a layer of 15-pound felt (tarpaper) to prevent squeaking and reduce drafts. You can also use tile, carpet, linoleum, and other materials as a finish flooring if the subfloor is ¾-inch plywood or particle board and all the joints are supported by joists or blocking. A subfloor can be painted and used as a temporary finish floor. Particle board is very hard, takes paint well, and can be used as the permanent finish floor if you like a painted floor.

HOW TO BUILD A FLOOR

Designing the Frame. Your first job is to determine what size joists to use. The common sizes are 2 × 6, 2 × 8, 2 × 10, and 2 × 12. The size will be influenced by the joist span and spacing. A wider spacing may require a deeper joist. If you are using a subfloor plus wooden flooring, 24-inch spacing will be most economical if building codes permit it. A 16-inch spacing should be used when there is no finish flooring layer or when the finish flooring is tile, carpet, or another nonstructural material. The tables in Appendix C show what size joists to use for different situations, and Appendix A shows how to make these computations for yourself. When you are planning the floor, remember all the extra joists, headers, and blocking shown in Figure 148.

If the house is wide, a single joist may not span the house, in which case two sets of joists will butt together over a sill in the middle of the house. When such a beam is located in a cellar, it is called a *girder*. Joists meeting over a sill or girder should be positioned with a row of blocking and tied together either with joist scraps or ¹/₃₂-inch perforated metal strapping, as shown in Figure 150. This can be omitted if a plywood or particle board subfloor will tie the two sides together.

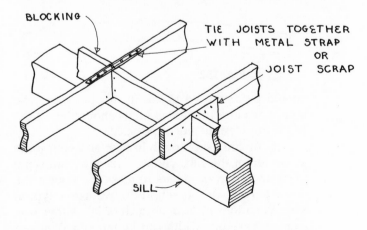

BLOCKING

TIE JOISTS TOGETHER WITH METAL STRAP OR JOIST SCRAP

SILL

JOINING JOISTS OVER A SILL **Fig. 150**

Fig. 151   FRAMING A FLOOR TO MINIMIZE BUILDING HEIGHT

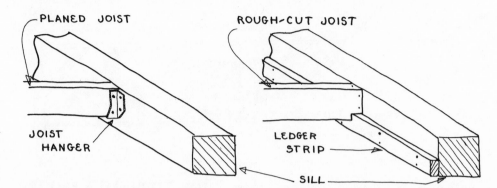

Joists can be installed two ways. First, they can rest on top of the sill and butt into a header flush with the outside edge of the sill (Figure 148). Second, when you want to minimize the height of the house, you can hang the joists between sills, with the sills and joists flush on top. Joists made of planed lumber can be hung on special metal brackets called *joist hangers*. Rough-cut joists can be supported by a 2 × 4 ledger strip nailed firmly to the sill. Often the latter method will require notching the joists (Figure 151).

Cutting Joists and Headers.   As long as the sills are parallel and square to each other, you can cut all the joists to the same length all at one time (see page 97 if your sills are out of line). Chapter twenty-four describes cutting methods. If the joists rest on the sills, their length will equal the distance across the house minus the thickness of the 2 headers. If the joists hang between the sills, the joist length will equal the distance between the sills; the sills themselves will serve as headers.

Before you cut each joist, sight down it to check for straightness. If there is a slight crown (convex bow), plan to place that up, as in Figure 152. A joist that bows as much as the one shown

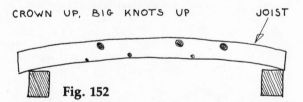

Fig. 152

should be discarded or cut up for blocking. The bigger or more numerous knots should be on the top (compression) side if possible.

If you are using rough lumber and your joists sit on top of the sills, you may have to trim some joists and shim up others to make the floor come out flat. To do this, first find the average or typical size. Variations of 1/8 of an inch or less either way from the average width can be ignored. You can trim oversize joists on the bottom where they will

rest on the sills by using a hatchet or saw. Narrow joists can be shimmed up with a shingle or scrap of the right thickness. The headers have to be flush too, so make them from pieces of average width. The headers should also be pieces of uniform thickness, so that the joist lengths can be constant.

If the joists run between the sills, your problem is to make them come out flush with the top surface of the sill. This is easy if you are using joist hangers. But with ledger strips, the trick is to match the notch location with the ledger strip location accurately. Figure out the proper notch size by making a scale cross section through the sill. As Figure 153 shows, the notch should remove no

Fig. 153

more than one third of the joist depth or the joist will be weakened. If your joists are 2 × 8s, for example, you might have a 2-inch notch with 6 inches of wood remaining. When you mark the joists for notching, do not measure 2 inches up from the bottom. Measure down 6 inches from the top. This will automatically compensate for any variation in the size of the joists. I find it easiest to cut a template to use as a ruler. In this case it would be a 6-inch-long 1 × 1 or 1 × 2. The template makes measuring mistakes almost impossible. Use the same template to position the 2 × 4 ledger strip on the sill. That will guarantee that the joists come out flush with the sill.

Installing Joists and Headers.   Your first step is to lay out the joist locations (Figure 154). If the

Fig. 154

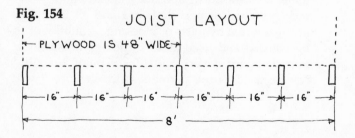

joists are resting on top of the sills, mark the headers. If the joists are hung between sills, the marks will be on the sills themselves. In either case, hook the end of a long tape measure on one end of the header (or sill) and make a mark every 2 feet. Do *not* measure 2 feet, make a mark, measure 2 feet more from that mark, and so on. You will get a cumulative error. Hook the tape on one end and make a mark at 2 feet, at 4 feet, 6 feet and so forth. If your interval is 16 inches instead of 24 inches, you will probably find that the 16-inch intervals on the tape are numbered in red or boxed for convenience. Your marks indicate the *centers* of the joists, except for the first and last in the row. For these two, the edge of the joist will be flush with the end of the header or sill as in Figure 154.

If you're using a 2 × 4 ledger strip you can now attach it to the sills. Use a ruler or template piece to position the ledger strip just the right distance down from the top of the sill. Nail the strip in with two 20d (20 "penny") common nails, one right over the other, every 10 or 12 inches.

If the floor will be insulated, and the space below the floor is cramped, now is the time to nail the small 1 × 1 or 1 × 2 ledger strips that will hold up the soffit to the joists. These strips can be attached with almost any 5d, 6d, or 8d nail (Figure 149).

The joists are now ready to go in. If your joists rest on top of the sills, toe-nail both joist and headers to the sill with 8d common nails or 10d box nails. End-nail rough-cut headers with 20d common nails, and planed headers with 16d or 20d common nails (Figure 155). If your joists rest on 2 × 4 ledgers, toe-nail everything together with 8d common nails, or preferably 10d box nails. If you find toe-nailing hard because the joist tends to move around, secure the joist temporarily by nailing a block behind it as shown in Figure 155. If your joists are supported with joist hangers, use a joist scrap to position the hangers, and then nail them to the sills on one side only with 8d common nails. Slide a joist in, and nail the other side of the hanger to the sill with 8d common nails, being sure the hanger fits the joist snugly. Then tack the hanger to the joist with 1-inch roofing nails.

As Figure 148 shows, stairwells and other large holes through the flooring will require doubling the adjacent joists and putting in doubled headers to support the cut joists. If one joist will be cut, and the header will therefore be 4 feet long or less, install the header before you double the joists. End-nail the headers in position through the joists with numerous 16d or 20d common nails, and then add the second joist. If the header is over 4 feet long the joist should be reinforced using one of the two methods shown in Figure 151. Large joist hangers that are made to fit a 4-inch beam are simplest to use. If the header is rough-cut and will not fit in the hanger, you can notch it slightly. Alternatively, the header can be notched on the bottom and supported on a 2 × 4 ledger strip 2 or 3 feet long nailed to the joists. If you do this, reinforce the joint further by toe-nailing the header directly to the joists once they are in place.

Framing to Correct Errors in Sill Location.   If your sills are not parallel or are the wrong distance apart, find out if they can be adjusted by loosening the bolts and moving them around. Recut the bolt holes if necessary. Try to make the sills level, square, parallel, and the right distance apart. Even if you spend a whole day making corrections, you will save more time later. Inaccurate sills can cause trouble all the way up to the roof. If you can't completely correct the problem by adjusting the sills, you can still make adjustments.

If the joists are the type that rest on the top of the sills, the trick is to build a square floor on top of crooked sills. Make the joists all the same size, exactly as specified in your design. In some places around the perimeter, the sills will stick out past the floor frame; in others the floor will overhang the sills. Where the sills are in, scraps can be nailed to them to pad them out flush with the framing. Where the sills stick out, you can omit sheathing where the bulge would be.

If the joists hang between the sills, you will have to cut the joists individually to different

Fig. 155   NAILING   JOISTS

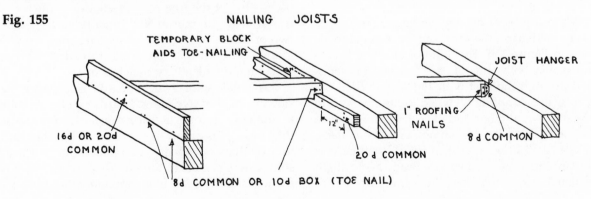

TEMPORARY BLOCK
AIDS TOE-NAILING

JOIST HANGER

1" ROOFING NAILS

8d COMMON

16d OR 20d COMMON

20d COMMON

8d COMMON OR 10d BOX (TOE NAIL)

lengths. Later, when you build the first-floor walls, build them the lengths they should be according to your plans, and set them on the uneven platform square and parallel.

All this assumes that the greatest discrepancy is no more than an inch or so. If the error is larger, you will probably have to build a slightly crooked house. This is not a serious problem except that some jobs may take a little longer. With care the error will not be visible by eye. The main difficulty is that the rafters may have to be of varying lengths. This will greatly add to your roof-framing work, which is tricky enough with accurate framing. Sometimes the walls can be brought back parallel at the roof line by allowing one of the walls to tilt in or out a little.

Putting in the Soffit. If the floor is to be insulated and exposed below to the weather, now is the time to put in the soffit. Use ½-inch bracewall insulation board, or any cheap material that comes in 4 × 8 sheets. If there is room to work below the floor, the soffit can be nailed from below with 6d common nails. If the space below is too cramped to work in, the soffit material can be cut into strips and dropped onto the 1 × 1 ledger strips that you have installed earlier for this purpose as shown in Figure 149. The soffit can simply rest on the ledgers. Leave a 2-inch space at the end of each bay for venting purposes, and staple screening over it to keep out mice.

Blocking. Blocking may be needed in four possible places: (1) you need blocking where two rows of joists meet over a sill in the middle of the house, (2) it is a good idea to put a row of blocking in midspan if the joists are over 10 feet long, (3) provide blocking under the joints in a plywood subfloor, if there is not going to be a structural finish floor, or the floor will sag at the joints, (4) you need reinforcing blocks wherever load-carrying posts will be located in order to transmit the column load to the sills and foundation. This reinforcing should be at least as wide as the post. It can consist of blocking between joists or of pieces of scrap nailed flat to the joist, as shown in Figure 148.

When the blocking only serves to stiffen the floor in midspan, the row can be staggered as shown in Figure 156. This kind of blocking is easiest, because both ends of each block can be end-nailed through the joist with 16d nails. When the blocking also supports plywood joints, they go in a straight row, and one end of each block will have to be toe-nailed with 8d common or 10d box nails. It might seem to be easiest to cut all the blocking in advance to a specified length. But to avoid slight cumulative errors that can throw the joists out of

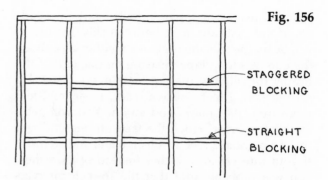

Fig. 156

STAGGERED BLOCKING

STRAIGHT BLOCKING

line, cut the blocking individually and periodically sight down the joists to make sure they are straight.

Wiring. Any wiring that will be run in the floor should be put in before the floor is insulated and before the subfloor is put in.

Insulation and Vapor Barrier. Six-inch insulation usually comes in 4-foot-long pieces called *batts*, and 3½-inch insulation comes in rolls. Buy the kind that has a foil backing. If you have decided to use more than 6 inches of insulation in the floor, the extra that you add to the 6-inch batts should be the kind without aluminum-foil backing. It can have a paper backing or no backing at all. Pieces with no backing are called *friction batts*. Cut the insulation to length by laying it on its back, foil side down, on a flat wooden surface you don't mind scarring up. Cut it with a utility knife. Install the insulation snugly so no drafts will come through. If you have an un-backed layer, put it in first, and then put in the foil-backed layer with the foil up. Neatly staple the paper tabs to the tops of the joists.

Next comes a layer of 4-mil (.004) plastic to keep moisture from getting through. This plastic comes folded up in long rolls and should go on in as few pieces as possible. Unroll the roll to the right length, cut it, unfold the cut section, and staple it onto the joists. This layer can also be put down later over the subfloor.

Subfloor. Any subfloor will go down quickly, but a plywood or particle board subfloor will go down particularly fast because the pieces are big. The trick is to get the first few sheets down flush and square with the frame. Nail them tentatively with two or three nails until you are sure they are well located. Then use 7d plywood (threaded) nails or 8d common nails every 8 inches or so.

A subfloor of 1-inch boards is cheaper but slower. Inexpensive green boards can be used for a subfloor, as long as they are fairly uniform in thickness (plus or minus 1/16 of an inch). The really thin or thick boards in your pile should be used somewhere else. Nail the boards perpendicular to the joists. Only a fair fit is required, since they will

Fig. 157 NAILING BOARDS TO JOISTS

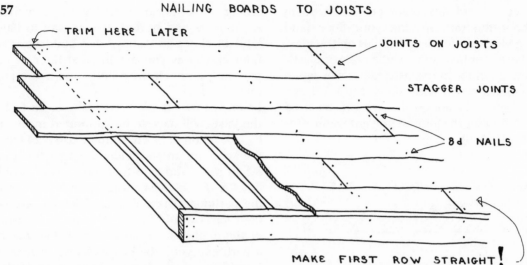

TRIM HERE LATER

JOINTS ON JOISTS

STAGGER JOINTS

8d NAILS

MAKE FIRST ROW STRAIGHT!

be covered up later. Usually the ends of sawmill boards are ragged, so they must be squared. Often subflooring boards are allowed to hang out over the edge of the floor frame as much as is necessary and trimmed off all at once later with a skillsaw. Use two or three 8d nails at each joint (Figure 157).

Some of the boards will be warped and will have to be forced into position. Place the warped board as shown in Figure 158 and nail one end down. Have a friend force the other end in tight, while you nail the board down working from the tight end to the loose end.

Figure 159 shows two other handy ways to draw boards tight. In the first method, you place a chisel next to the board at the joist with the bevel of the chisel touching the board. Tilt the chisel to one side and pound one point of it into the joist about ¼ of an inch. Then lever the chisel over to force in the board.

If the board is only ⅛ or 3/16 of an inch out of line, you can usually bring it over just by toe-nailing the board to the joist as shown in the picture.

Fig. 159 FORCING WARPED BOARDS

DRIVE POINT OF CHISEL INTO JOIST, THEN LEVER BOARD OVER

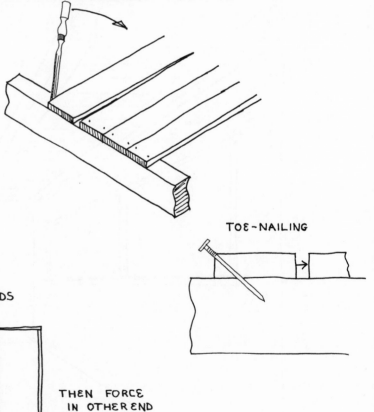

TOE-NAILING

Fig. 158 NAILING WARPED BOARDS

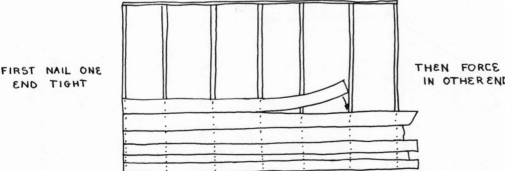

FIRST NAIL ONE END TIGHT

THEN FORCE IN OTHER END

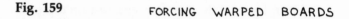

Rain Cover.   From this point on you have to worry about the rain soaking your floor (and everything else) and forming puddles on the plastic vapor barrier or insulation. Cut a piece of plastic larger than the floor to use as a rain cover when needed. Hold it down with a few 2 × 4s. If one piece of plastic will not cover, two can be used with a 2 × 4 under the joint to prevent water running in (Figure 160).

Fig. 160

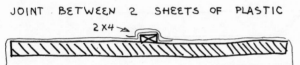

JOINT BETWEEN 2 SHEETS OF PLASTIC

BUILDING A SECOND FLOOR

In a conventional house, the second floor is usually framed just like the first floor. Joists span from one wall to the other and rest on top of the walls. A floor is nailed down on the joists from above: first a subfloor, then a finish floor. A ceiling is installed from below — most often a sheetrock ceiling. There is no insulation, since both spaces are indoors and heated. If you plan to have this kind of closed-in ceiling, just build your second floor exactly as you did the first floor. If you are planning a sheetrock ceiling, space the joists 16 inches o.c.

Long Spans.   If the house is over 16 feet wide, the joists will have to be supported in the middle by a partition or beam. If the house is 24 feet wide, the space might be divided by a partition into an 8-foot room and a 16-foot room. You would then have a 16-foot joist meeting an 8-foot joist over the partition. These would be joined just as first-floor joists would be joined over a sill, using one of the methods shown in Figure 150. Since such a partition would be load-carrying, it must be located over a sill. If the second-floor joists meet over a horizontal beam, the posts that support the beam should be located over a foundation wall or column and the space under the post between the subfloor and sill should be filled with reinforcing blocks.

Exposed Frame Ceiling.   Figure 161 shows an ex-

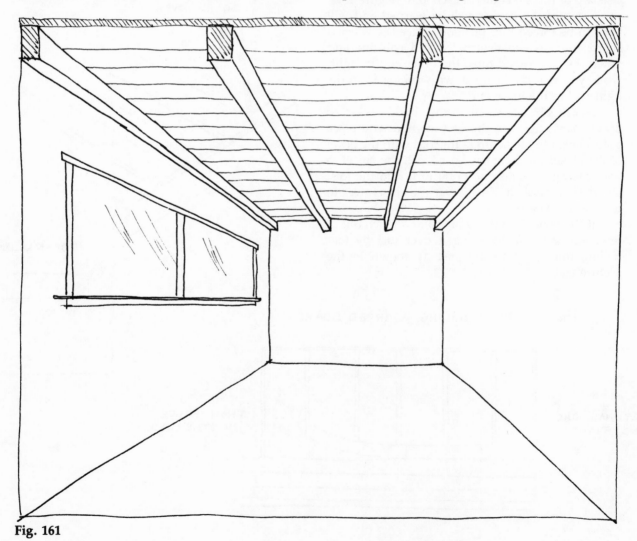

Fig. 161

posed frame second-floor structure that in my opinion is cheaper, easier to build, and better looking than the regular system. The joists consist of rough sawmill timbers 3 or 4 inches thick and 3 or 4 feet on center. No ceiling is nailed to the bottom of these joists. The ceiling consists of the underside of the subfloor, which is made with dry, good-looking boards. Over the subfloor goes a layer of Homasote or ½-inch insulation board for sound insulation. The finish floor is laid on top of the insulation board parallel to the first layer of boards.

This system is inexpensive because no extra-finish ceiling needs to be built. It is quick because everything is nailed down from the top, which is faster than nailing up from the bottom.

To build this ceiling/floor, first find the correct joist size by using the formula in Appendix A. Or use the same depth of joist you would use in a conventional floor and increase the width as you increase the spacing. If a regular floor would have called for 2 × 8s every 2 feet, you could use 3 × 8s every 3 feet or 4 × 8s every 4 feet. This system should not be used with a spacing over 4 feet. Joist tables can be found in Appendix C.

The floor is put together much like a conventional floor. The joists will butt into a 2-inch thick header flush to the outside of the wall framing. Nail the header to the joists with 20d nails, and toe-nail both joists and header to the top of the wall. Put 1 inch of rigid foam insulation board against the inside of the header. Cover this with an extra row of blocking (Figure 162), which can be nailed through the foam into the header and

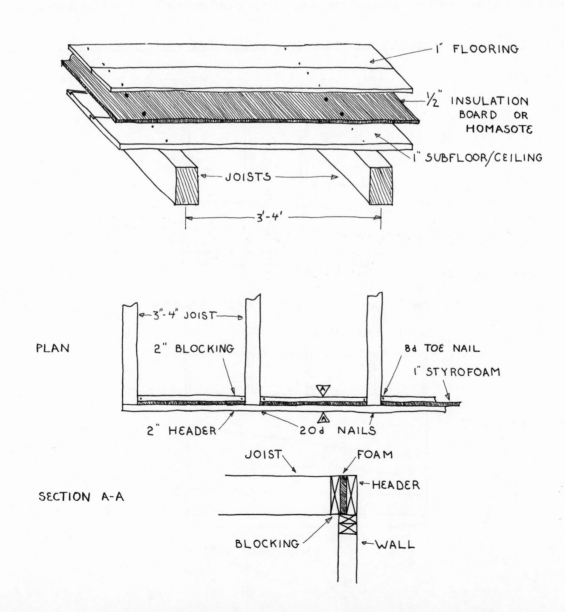

Fig. 162   EXPOSED-FRAME CEILING DETAILS

carefully toe-nailed to the joists. Do this nailing neatly, since these nails will show. The blocking conceals the foam, stiffens the joists, and trims the top of the inside wall surface.

Next comes the subfloor. Since it will be visible from below it should be made of good-looking wood. Ideally, the boards should be dry to minimize cracks from shrinkage. Like the joist timbers, these boards should probably come from a sawmill for reasons of both beauty and economy. Shiplap boards or extrawide pine boards are excellent. These second-story floorboards are nailed down like first-floor subflooring except that you want to take more care with them, as they will be visible.

Put the best side of the board down. Make sure the first row is straight by aligning it with a chalk line or by sighting down the row before it is finally nailed. Use two 8d common nails into each joist, or three if the board is over 6 inches wide. If it takes more than one board to make up a row, choose boards close to the same width. Extra-thin or extra-thick boards should be set aside to use for some less visible job. Fit each board as tightly as possible to the previous row.

Boards vary somewhat in width from one end to the other, and often the flooring will be out of parallel with the house frame by the time you get halfway across. Every few rows, measure the remaining distance across at both ends to see if you're still parallel. If not, make corrections by putting the wider ends of the next few rows at the end that needs to be expanded (Figure 163).

On top of the subfloor goes a layer of black insulation board or Homasote. Black or gray will reduce the visibility of any shrinkage cracks that appear from below. Wherever you can, nail the Homasote through the subfloor to the joists with 8d nails and elsewhere into just the subfloor boards with 1-inch roofing nails, which have large heads. The finish floor will go on later, parallel to the subfloor.

The same exposed framing system can also be used in combination with a single-layer floor of tongue and groove 2 × 6 decking from the lumber

Fig. 163

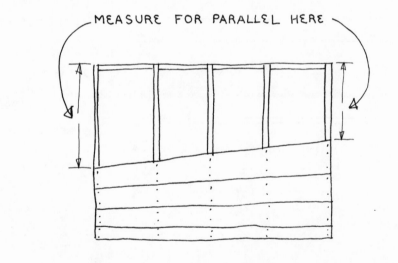

MEASURE FOR PARALLEL HERE

THEN ADJUST WITH NEXT BOARDS

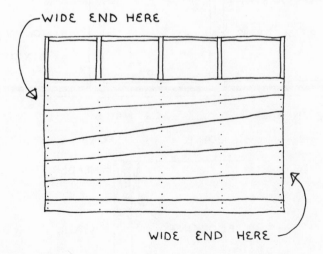

WIDE END HERE

WIDE END HERE

Fig. 164

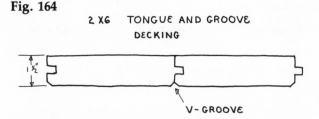

2 X 6   TONGUE AND GROOVE
DECKING

V-GROOVE

yard (Figure 164). This system is as fast or faster than the one just described. Decking is flat on top and has a V-groove pattern on the bottom.

The decking can span up to 6 feet, although anything over 5 feet may be too springy for a floor. If you buy decking, look over the stock carefully, because quality varies. Decking must be dry to

work well. Make sure it has not been sitting around outdoors in a lumber yard picking up moisture for several months.

SAMPLE FLOOR WORKING DRAWINGS AND MATERIALS LIST

You will need two simple scale drawings of your floor. One is a plan view that shows the layout of the joists. The second is a cross section showing how the soffit and insulation fit in and what will be used for subfloor and flooring. If your joists are going to be hung between the sills, a third drawing should show what size ledger will be used and what size notch will be taken out of the ends of the joists (Figure 165).

Fig. 165

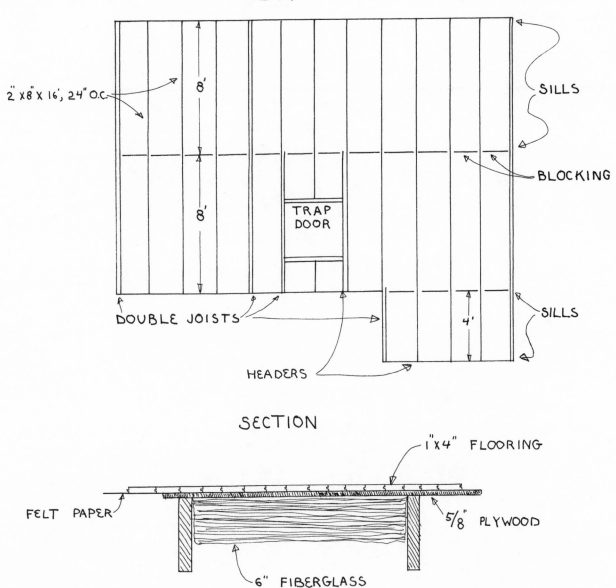

FLOOR

PLAN

2" X 8" X 16', 24" O.C.

8'

8'

TRAP DOOR

4'

SILLS

BLOCKING

SILLS

DOUBLE JOISTS

HEADERS

SECTION

1" X 4" FLOORING

FELT PAPER

5/8" PLYWOOD

6" FIBERGLASS

Sample List of Materials

Item	Quantity	Price/Unit	Total Cost
Joist material (itemize, taking lengths from drawing with architect's scale) Joists Blocking Headers	_____ bd.ft.	$ _____ /bd.ft.	$ _____
Soffit material, if any	_____ sheets	$ _____ /sheet	$ _____
1/32" perforated strapping	_____ rolls	$ _____ /roll	$ _____
1 × 2s to hold up soffit (approx. twice length of joist needed)			
Insulation: 6" foil-back batts, either 16" or 24" (same quantity as area of floor in sq.ft.)	_____ sq.ft.	$ _____ /sq.ft.	$ _____
Vapor barrier: 4 mil. plastic (same area as floor, plus waste, in a convenient-size roll)			
Subfloor (if plywood, figure # of sheets from plan)	_____ sheets	$ _____ /sheet	$ _____
Subfloor (if boards, figure area of floor plus 15% waste)	_____ bd.ft.	$ _____ /bd.ft.	$ _____
Finish floor of good-quality dry boards (figure area of floor plus 15% waste	_____ bd.ft.	$ _____ /bd.ft.	$ _____
(Note: Nails will be figured later)			

chapter 14
Walls

The simplest and most common type of wall building is 2 × 4 studwall construction. You build a wall frame on the floor, as in Figure 166, then tilt it into position in one piece. This is called platform framing. Some people are substituting 2 × 6s for 2 × 4s in their walls to make room for 6 inches of insulation. The theory behind this is that the additional first cost is less than the long-run savings in heating costs. Readers wishing to consider this new system should consult Appendix E. A 2 × 6 wall can be built using exactly the same methods described here for 2 × 4s.

PARTS OF A STUDWALL

Figure 166 shows the parts of a typical studwall.

Studs. The studs are the vertical 2 × 4s which support the house and provide nailing surfaces for the exterior and interior wall coverings. Studs are usually 16 inches o.c. or 24 inches o.c. There is no structural reason for the closer spacing, although it is still required by some building codes.

Plates. The plates are the horizontal 2 × 4s to which the studs are nailed. The top one is doubled for extra strength and to make it possible to interlock the corners of adjacent walls (Figure 167).

Rough Openings. The openings left for windows and doors are called rough openings because they are usually about 1 inch larger than the window or door frames that will be used. This allows the window or door to be adjusted exactly plumb and level when it is installed.

Headers. The headers support the top plate where windows and door openings have caused studs to be removed. They usually consist of a pair of 2 × 6s or 2 × 8s on edge with a shim of some kind between them to make their combined thickness equal the width of the studs (Figure 168).

Fig. 166   STUDWALL

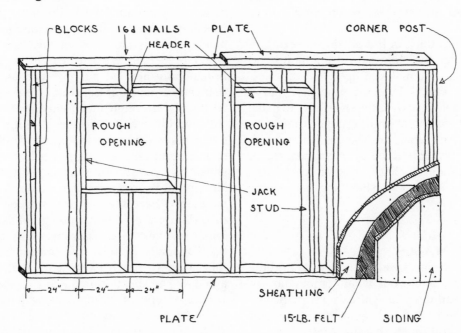

Fig. 167

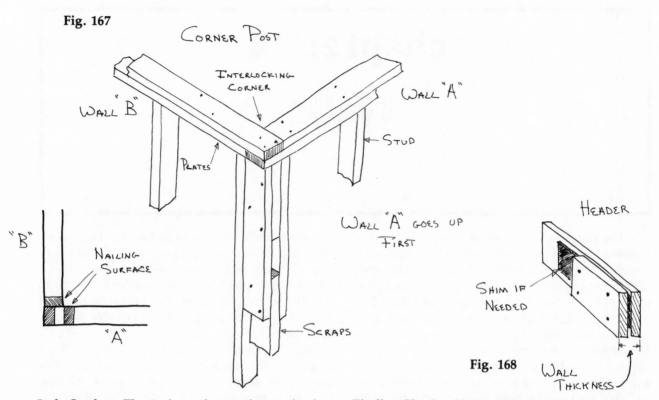

Fig. 168

Jack Studs.   The jack studs are the studs that support the headers over doors and windows.

Corner Post.   The corner posts consist of two studs separated by a row of 2 × 4 scraps. The scraps position the inner stud where it can serve as a nailing surface for the interior wall surface (Figure 167).

When two walls meet at a corner of a building, only the one erected first (marked A in Figure 167) needs a completely built-up corner post. The wall erected second (marked B) can end in a single stud. Figure 167 also shows the combined corner post.

Sheathing.   Sheathing is the outside covering of the house under the siding. It strengthens and braces the house and makes it tight.

Fifteen-pound Felt.   Fifteen-pound felt paper (tarpaper) is often used over the sheathing to make the wall more watertight and to reduce drafts.

Siding.   Many materials are used as siding, such as horizontal or vertical boards, clapboards, or shingles. Sometimes a single layer of special textured plywood is used as sheathing and siding combined.

DESIGNING WALLS

When you design a wall you must (1) find the header sizes, (2) figure out what combination of siding and sheathing you will use, (3) plan how the wall will be braced, (4) figure out the rough opening sizes, and (5) make a drawing.

Finding Header Sizes.   Headers above windows and doors must be designed to hold the loads they will carry, which may include a second story or roof. Consult the chart in Appendix C or make the computation yourself using the method in Appendix A.

Choosing a Sheathing-Siding Combination.   You can sheath your house with plywood, black insulation board, or horizontal boards. Plywood is very fast, provides excellent diagonal bracing, and makes the house very weathertight and warm. The main problem with plywood is that it is expensive. Half-inch insulation board provides good diagonal bracing and is an excellent weather seal. But it won't hold nails, so it can only be used with a horizontally applied siding, such as clapboards, that can be nailed at the studs. One-inch horizontal boards are often much cheaper than plywood and provide a better nailing base for siding than either plywood or insulation board. When a layer of 15-pound felt paper is put between siding and sheathing, boards also make a good weather seal. Horizontal boards take many times longer to put up than either plywood or insulation board, and they do not provide nearly as good diagonal bracing as plywood. Sometimes board sheathing is put up diagonally to solve the bracing problem, but this takes so much extra work that you should avoid it. The sheathing you choose should fit well with the type of siding you will use. (Chapter eighteen discusses siding in detail.) Here are some workable sheathing-siding combinations:

One layer of ³/₈-inch or ¹/₂-inch plywood only. A single layer of plywood can serve as sheathing and siding both. Special kinds of textured plywood, such as T–111 and Weldtex, are made for this purpose. This is probably the most economical approach all around.

Plywood plus any kind of siding. Half-inch plywood makes a sufficient base for shingles, clapboards, tongue and groove boards, or any type of horizontally applied siding. Board and batten siding can be nailed to ¹/₂-inch plywood if many nails are used, and every opportunity is taken to nail to horizontal framing members. Vertical boards without battens should be used over ⁵/₈-inch plywood.

Horizontal 1-inch rough or planed board sheathing with any siding. Boards, covered with 15-pound felt, make an excellent base for any siding material.

Half-inch insulation-board sheathing with horizontal siding. Black insulation board can be covered with any continuous horizontal siding that can be nailed to the studs, such as clapboards, horizontal shiplap boards, or novelty siding.

Plan Bracing. Any two-story house, and a one-story house subjected to extreme weather, such as hurricanes or earthquakes, will require diagonal bracing. It is a good idea to check local building codes, if any, to find out what kind of diagonal bracing is accepted. Plywood sheathing provides excellent bracing. Half-inch insulation board also provides adequate bracing, particularly if sheets of ¹/₂-inch plywood are substituted at the building corners to supplement it. With horizontal-board sheathing, bracing is provided by notching diagonal 1 × 4 or 2 × 4 pieces right into the wall frames, as shown in Figure 169. There should be 2 braces in each wall, and if possible they should

Fig. 170

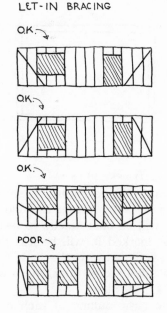

LET-IN BRACING

go from the bottom to the top of the wall. Create bracing triangles as large as the window and door locations will permit. Figure 170 shows some possible arrangements.

Determine Rough Opening Sizes. If you are buying new windows and doors in their frames, each unit should have a specified rough opening (R.O.) that you can get from the lumber yard. Usually rough openings can be about 1 inch bigger than the window or door frame. If you are building your own windows or doors, see chapter seventeen.

Making a Layout Drawing. To clarify your wall design and make ordering materials easier, make a quick scale layout drawing showing the parts of the wall frame. First clarify for yourself how long

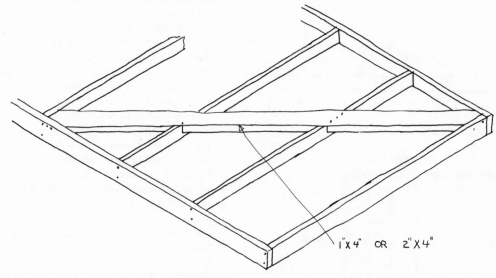

1" X 4" OR 2" X 4"

Fig. 169 LET-IN DIAGONAL BRACING

Fig. 171

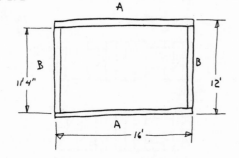

WALL A GOES UP FIRST

each wall frame will be. Figure 171 shows the wall lengths of a 12' × 16' house. The two long walls, marked A, will be built exactly 16 feet long. The short walls, marked B, will be less than 12 feet because they fit between the long walls. If the studs are a full 4 inches thick, the B walls would be 11 feet, 4 inches long.

Get the basic outline of each of your wall framing plans by making a tracing from your exterior elevation drawings. Then draw the regular intervals where the studs will be centered. This should be 24 inches, unless local codes require 16-inch centers. The intervals should always start at the corner of the building. On A walls, this will also be the end of the wall frame, but for B walls, which are erected after A walls, the intervals should be offset by the stud width, as shown in Figure 172. Finally, mark all the doubled studs, corner posts, diagonal braces, jack studs, and headers on your drawing (Figure 173).

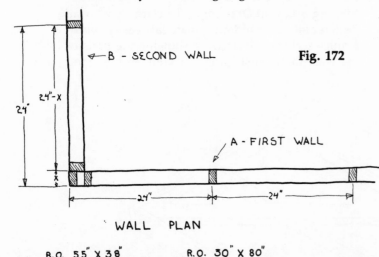

B - SECOND WALL   **Fig. 172**

A - FIRST WALL

WALL PLAN

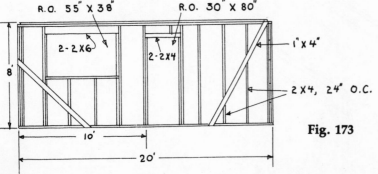

R.O. 55" X 38"   R.O. 30" X 80"

2-2X6   2-2X4   1" X 4"

2 X 4, 24" O.C.

8'

10'

20'

Fig. 173

BUILDING A STUDWALL

Step 1.
Cut studs: Figure out how many vertical full-length studs there are, and cut them all at once with a power or hand saw.

Step 2.
Cut plates: Cut 3 plates to length. Remember that the top plate will be a different length than the other two because of the corner interlock detail shown in Figure 167. Set the top plate aside.

Step 3.
Lay out plates: Lay the two remaining plates next to each other on the horses with the ends flush. Lay out the 16-inch or 24-inch intervals on the plates, remembering to set the zero hook of the tape at a point representing the corner of the building, which may or may not be the end of the plate itself. If a wall sits 4 inches in from the corner of the building, have someone hold the tape 4 inches out from the end of the plate as you do the layout (Figure 174).

With a square, mark both plates at once at the appropriate interval (16 inches or 24 inches). These marks represent the centers of the studs (Figure 175).

Mark the plates where the rough openings will be. Often for convenience a rough opening will start at a 16-inch or 24-inch interval. Mark an X to indicate on which side of these marks the jack studs go. You now have two kinds of marks on the plates. Simple lines that indicate the center of a stud, and lines with X's to indicate one edge of a stud.

Mark another X outside of each X to show the stud that doubles up with the jack stud.

Mark the plates for corner posts, and any other special details.

Step 4.
Frame the walls: Lay the plates and studs on the floor, with the studs on the layout marks. This should be done in a position that will allow you to lift the wall directly into position, just like opening a door (Figure 176).

When the studs are in position, nail through the plates into the studs with 2 16d nails at each joint. If your studs are over 1¾ inches thick, it might be better to use 20d nails. Make the joints square and flush by eye. The trick to nailing studwalls together is somehow to prevent the studs from jumping around every time you hit the nail. The simplest system is to hold the stud down with one foot while you nail through the plate. If the stud and plate are not flush, shim the lowest one up on a shingle while you nail. Another nice trick is to nail a scrap temporarily to the floor next to the plate you aren't nailing through to keep the entire unassembled wall frame from sliding away as you hammer.

Step 5.
Complete the frame: Working from your drawings, cut and fit in any extra studs or headers to complete the frame.

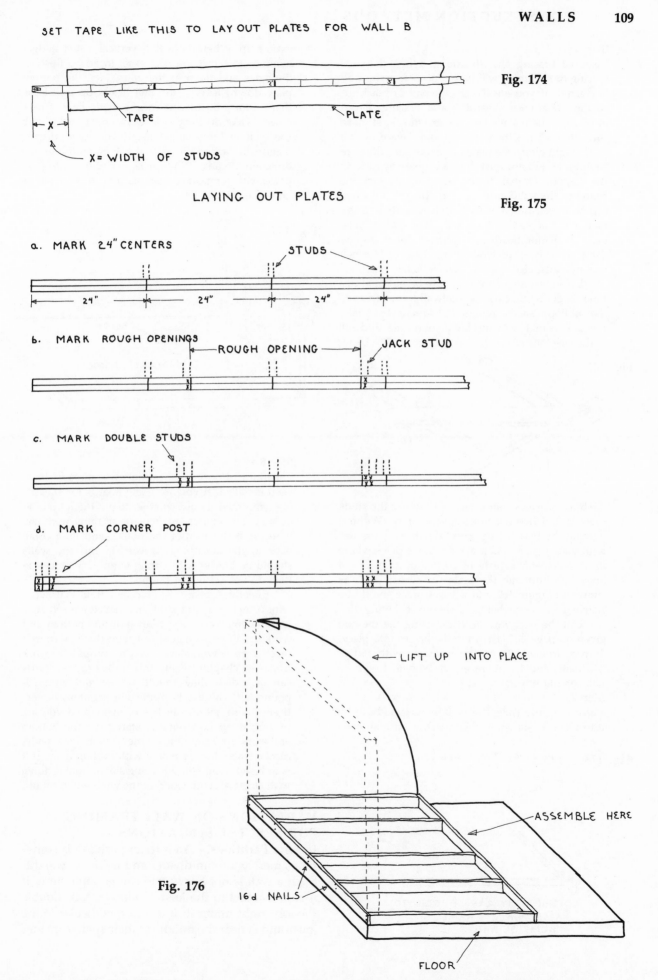

Fig. 174

TAPE

PLATE

X= WIDTH OF STUDS

LAYING OUT PLATES

Fig. 175

a. MARK 24" CENTERS

STUDS

24"   24"   24"

b. MARK ROUGH OPENINGS

ROUGH OPENING   JACK STUD

c. MARK DOUBLE STUDS

d. MARK CORNER POST

LIFT UP INTO PLACE

ASSEMBLE HERE

Fig. 176

16d NAILS

FLOOR

Step 6.

Diagonal bracing and sheathing: Often diagonal bracing or sheathing will be put on before the wall is erected. If you are using plywood or black insulation board for sheathing and bracing, it can most easily be installed on the ground. First make sure the wall is sitting straight and square on the floor. Sight along the plates to make sure they are straight, and then adjust the wall square by making the diagonals equal. If necessary, lightly tack the frame to the subfloor to hold it straight. Plywood can be nailed down every 8 inches, with 8d common nails or special threaded 7d plywood nails. Black insulation board can be nailed down with 6d common nails, or preferably large-headed 1½-inch roofing nails, also spaced about 8 inches apart.

Let-in bracing (if any) can also be put in at this time. Begin by bracing the studwall frame down to the subfloor exactly straight and square. Then take two 2 × 4s or 1 × 4s and lay them on the studwall in the best location you can find (Figure 177). Using

Fig. 177

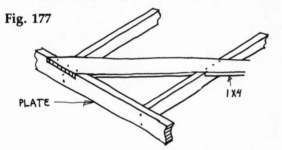

PLATE

1 X 4

the brace piece as your ruler, mark where the studs must be notched out to accept the brace. Without moving the brace piece, kneel down, reach under with your pencil, and mark the brace piece where its ends meet the plate or corner post. A 2 × 4 brace can butt into the plates or corner post, as shown in Figure 169, but a 1 × 4 brace should be notched in everywhere, as shown in Figure 177.

Cut the necessary notches, using the method given on page 205. Then tap the braces into place. Two-by-four braces can be nailed in with 16d or 20d nails, and 1 × 4 braces can be nailed with 8d nails or 10d box nails.

Step 7.

Putting up the wall: The wall is now ready to lift into place as shown in Figure 178. You may need

Fig. 178   LIFTING THE WALL

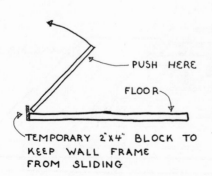

PUSH HERE

FLOOR

TEMPORARY 2"x4" BLOCK TO
KEEP WALL FRAME
FROM SLIDING

extra help. When the wall is vertical, use a sledgehammer to tap it into the exact location, flush at the sides and flush at the ends. Nail the bottom plate down, leaving the nail heads up a little so that minor adjustments can be made later if necessary. Take the longest level you have and plumb the wall in both directions. If you have already diagonally braced the wall, it will be plumb in one direction already. When it is just right, hold it in place with temporary diagonal braces attached as shown in Figure 179.

Fig. 179

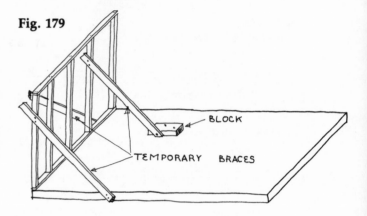

BLOCK

TEMPORARY   BRACES

Step 8.

Sheathing: Plywood sheathing will already have been installed. If you are using boards for sheathing, you must choose whether to put them up now or later. Sometimes, particularly in rainy weather, it seems better to roof the house, and then come back to the sheathing. If you do this the walls should be braced with strong temporary braces so they do not get out of plumb.

Sheathing boards should be cut so that every joint comes at a stud, and then nailed at each stud with 8d common nails. Start from the bottom and work up. When you get to a height that you cannot reach from sawhorses, build a scaffold to work from (see chapter twenty-three). Before the boards can be sided, they should be covered with 15-pound felt. This can be applied horizontally or vertically, with about 6 inches of overlap. If you are putting it up horizontally, start from the bottom and work up. Felt, which comes in rolls 3 feet wide, can be stapled on or nailed with roofing nails. If it is to be left long without being sided, hold it down with strips of scrap wood or the wind will rip it off.

VARIATIONS ON WALL FRAMING FOR SPECIAL SITUATIONS

Interior Partitions. An interior partition is sometimes merely a room divider and holds no weight. Such a wall is not heavy and can go anywhere. If it runs parallel to the joists underneath it, double the joist right under it. If it is perpendicular to the joists and is near the middle of their span, consider its weight when you compute the size of the joists. A partition that carries roof, rafters, or second-floor joists should be located over a sill. If such a partition is perpendicular to the sills, the joist beneath it can be doubled or tripled to make in effect an extra sill. These interior partitions are made exactly like exterior walls.

Studwalls Constructed in Place.   Sometimes it is inconvenient to build a studwall on the ground and erect it in one piece. This is particularly true of irregular walls, such as those that meet a sloping rafter at the top (Figure 180). They can be built

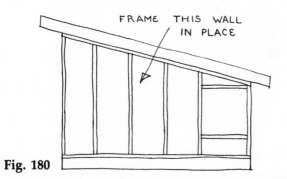

FRAME THIS WALL IN PLACE

Fig. 180

after the rafter is up. First put the bottom and top plates in place with 16d or 20d nails. Then lay out the stud locations on the bottom plate. Place a stud a little longer than necessary on a layout mark and plumb it with a level. The stud should be offset as shown in Figure 181. With the stud

MARKING STUDS IN PLACE

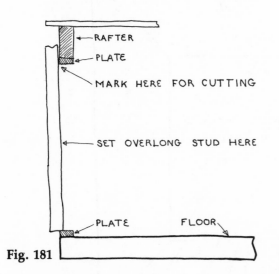

RAFTER
PLATE
MARK HERE FOR CUTTING
SET OVERLONG STUD HERE
PLATE   FLOOR

Fig. 181

plumb, mark it for cutting at the correct angle, and mark the top plate to show where the stud will fit when cut. Cut the stud to size, and toe-nail it in (Figure 182).

Studwalls for Houses with Kneewall Design. Some houses have a gable roof sitting on a short 3- or 4-foot-high second-story wall called a *knee-*

TOE-NAILING
Fig. 182
SUPPORT STUD WITH FOOT WHILE NAILING
SECTION

wall. This kneewall cannot be built as a separate short studwall. Part of its job is to help hold in the roof, which has a tendency to spread. To do this the kneewall and the wall below it are built in one continuous piece. The studs go from the first floor right up to the roof (Figure 183).

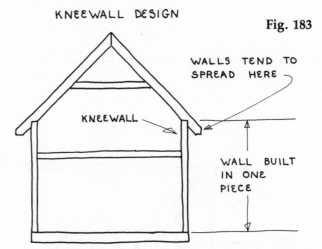

KNEEWALL DESIGN   **Fig. 183**
WALLS TEND TO SPREAD HERE
KNEEWALL
WALL BUILT IN ONE PIECE

These continuous side walls are held together by the second floor, which can be built using one of two methods, as shown in Figure 184. In either method, the strength of the structure depends on a strong joint between the wall stud and the floor joist.

SUPPORTING INSIDE LOADS ON POSTS AND BEAMS

Sometimes the second floor or roof needs support inside the house but a partition would be in the way. Such a load can be carried on a horizontal beam, the ends of which are carried on posts. Compute the side of such beams using Appendix A. The posts can be exposed 4 × 4s, 4 × 6s, double 2 × 4s concealed in a wall, or for a very large load, triple 2 × 4s concealed in an existing studwall. Locate these posts right over the foundation. There should be solid wood at least 6 inches wide between the post and the foundation (Figure 185).

Fig. 184

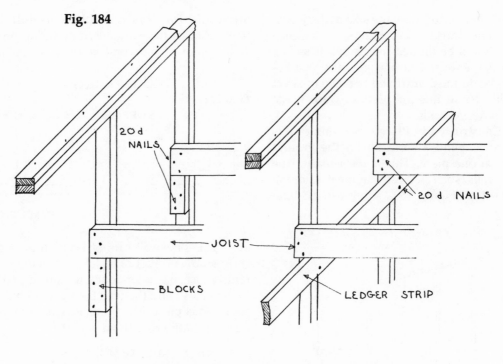

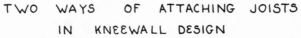

TWO WAYS OF ATTACHING JOISTS
IN KNEEWALL DESIGN

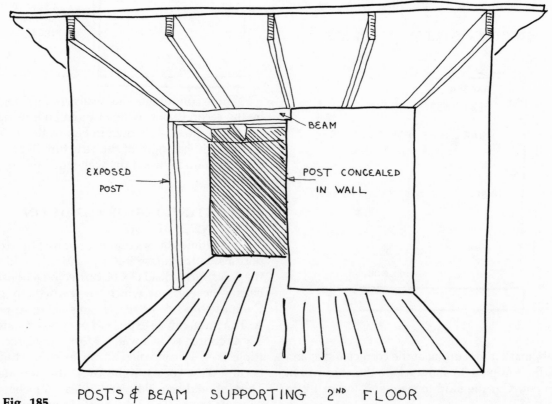

Fig. 185   POSTS & BEAM SUPPORTING 2ND FLOOR

WORKING DRAWING AND SAMPLE MATERIALS LIST

A simple elevation of each wall frame — traced from your elevations of the house — is all that you need for working drawings and estimating wall materials. A typical framing plan is shown in Figure 173.

Sample List Materials

Item	Quantity	Price/Unit	Total Cost
2 × 4s			
Studs (itemize)			
Plates (itemize)			
Jacks (itemize)			
Total running feet			
of 2 × 4 × $^2/_3$ gives			
total board feet	_____ bd.ft.	$ _____ /bd.ft.	$ _____
Diagonal braces (1 × 4 or			
2 × 4)	_____ bd.ft.	$ _____ /bd.ft.	$ _____
Headers	_____ bd.ft.	$ _____ /bd.ft.	$ _____
Sheathing (if boards,			
order 15% extra for waste	_____ bd.ft.	$ _____ /bd.ft.	$ _____
15-lb. felt (order 1 roll			
per 250 sq.ft.)	_____ rolls	$ _____ /roll	$ _____

chapter 15
Roofs

The roof is the most complicated and tricky part of a house to frame. Yours should be as simple as possible.

TYPES OF ROOF STRUCTURE

Almost all roofs are structurally either shed roofs or gable roofs. Figure 186 shows the basic structure of each. A shed roof is a flat, sloping roof. A gable roof is the common A-shaped roof, which can be built in almost any size and pitch. More complex-looking roofs are usually variations or combinations of these basic types (Figure 187).

The structure of a shed roof consists of rafters laid across from one wall to another. A gable roof,

Fig. 186   ROOF STRUCTURE

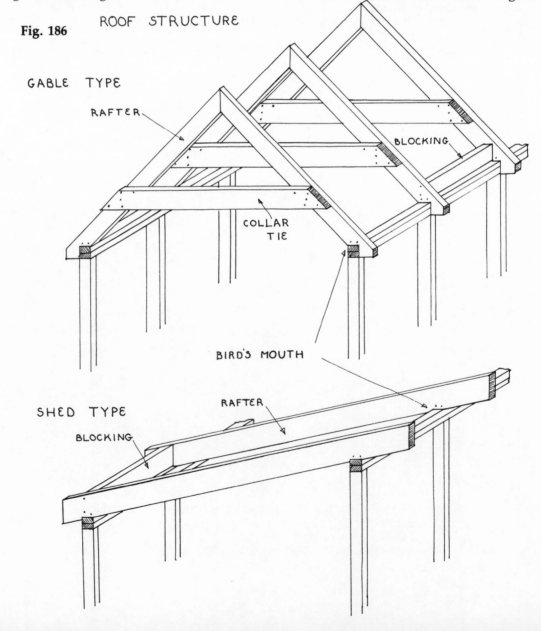

GABLE TYPE

RAFTER

BLOCKING

COLLAR TIE

BIRD'S MOUTH

RAFTER

SHED TYPE

BLOCKING

Fig. 187

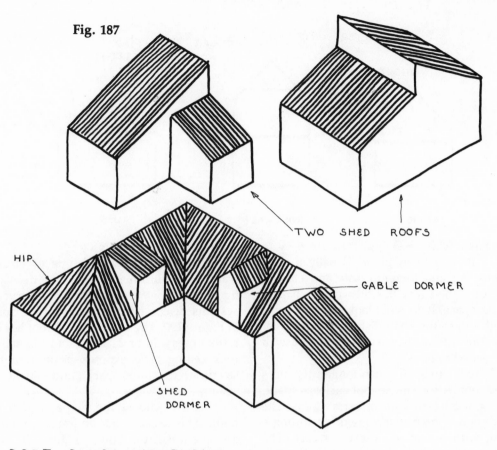

TWO SHED ROOFS

HIP

GABLE DORMER

SHED
DORMER

ROOF SHAPE VARIATIONS

however, consists of more than rafters, as it must be triangulated to be stable. Without a crosspiece to hold the bottom ends of the rafters together, they will spread apart from the weight of the roof (Figure 188). These crosspieces are called *collar ties*.

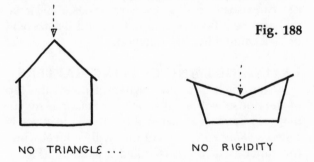

Fig. 188

NO TRIANGLE ...

NO RIGIDITY

There are several main types of gable roof, each of which solves the problem of triangulation in a slightly different way. These are shown in Figure 189. In the *attic* design, the collar ties are located where the rafters meet the walls and double as attic floor joists. In an attic design, the rafters are put up individually against a ridge board at the top. The collar ties/attic floor joists are put down first, and then the floor is laid on them as

a work surface for putting up the rafters. In a small house the attic may be useful only for storage because the headroom is poor. But in larger houses the attic can be living space if the roof pitch is steep enough.

In a small house the area under the roof can be made usable by using the story-and-a-half or kneewall design. Here the collar ties are located farther up the rafter to create headroom; they cannot be above the midpoint, however, or they will be ineffective. The little walls extending up past the second floor are the kneewalls. The added height they yield makes the space usable as a second floor. In this type of design, the rafters and collar ties are often assembled into units called *rafter units*, which are hefted into place in one piece. The second floor provides a convenient work platform.

A third type of gable-roof frame, which I don't discuss in detail but which is worth mentioning, is the *truss* (Figure 189). A truss roof consists of a series of triangles assembled into a frame. These frames are generally bought ready made from lumber yards.

A shed roof is simpler and faster to build than

Fig. 189   GABLE ROOFS

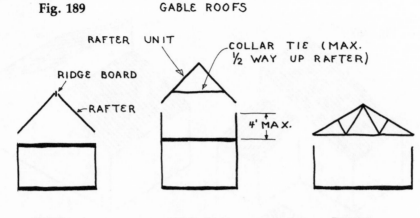

ATTIC   KNEEWALL   TRUSS

a gable. It has fewer pieces and they are easy to figure out, cut, and fit in place. Usually a shed roof is pretty flat and therefore safe and easy to work on. But a shed roof has drawbacks. It provides no attic space. It does not look good on every house. And it does not span distances much over 16 feet without intermediate support from a wall or beams inside the house.

A gable roof can span much longer distances than a shed roof. Also, a gable roof encloses space, which can be used as an attic or extra rooms. The kneewall design is particularly good for adding a story along with a roof at little extra cost. The primary disadvantage of a gable roof is that it is more work to build. There are more pieces, they are trickier to lay out and cut, and they take more time to install. If the pitch is steep, working on the roof can be dangerous (although this can also apply to a steep shed roof).

The truss roof has great strength, and is particularly useful where you need long spans — say over 20 feet — with no intermediate support. Trusses are usually used with relatively low pitches, since the attic space is obstructed anyway.

One way to achieve a gable-roof shape without collar ties is to put a heavy beam at the ridge, supported at its ends, to hold the top ends of the rafters. This makes the roof structure in effect two shed roofs. The ridge cannot move down, there is no outward thrust, and the collar ties can be omitted.

Each of these basic roof types can be built in many sizes and at many angles or *pitches*. How do you decide which to make for your house? The best method, I think, is to let the roof type be determined by your space needs in the house, the general character of the site, the sun orientation of the house, and similar nonstructural considerations. Find the roof shape that fits your overall plan. Chapter five describes how to choose a roof shape this way.

DESIGN DECISIONS

Once you know the type of structure you want, you still must make some decisions. First, figure out how to cover the roof structure. Two systems discussed later in detail are summarized in Figure 190. The conventional roof has concealed rafters every 16 or 24 inches and usually a sheet-rock ceiling. The exposed-beam roof has large-sized rafters widely spaced and usually a wooden ceiling.

Second, choose the shape of your roof overhang. This decision has an important effect on the appearance of the house. Figure 191 shows four typical shapes. Consider, too, the *amount* of overhang. This can protect the walls from the weather and perform an important shading function. (For more on shading, see chapters five and eight).

Third, find the rafter size that suits the design by using the formula in Appendix A, or by referring to Tables 1, 2, or 3 in Appendix C. The collar ties can usually be 2 × 6s. Sometimes a collar tie will also be a floor or ceiling joist and its size will be determined by that function.

LAYING OUT AND CUTTING RAFTERS

The notch in a rafter where it meets the top of the house wall is called a *bird's mouth*. Any cut that will be vertical when the rafter is in place is called a *plumb cut*. Any cut that will be level when the rafter is in place is called a *level cut* (Figure 192).

In carpentry, roof angles are measured not in degrees but in "rise and run." In Figure 193, for example, the roof pitch is a rise of 8 feet in a run of 12 feet, or 8:12. You rarely need to know the roof pitch in degrees.

There are many ways to lay out rafters for cutting. Two are given here. Pick the one that will be simplest for you, or adapt one to suit your own requirements. If your roof is too complex for these

Fig. 190   CONVENTIONAL ROOF

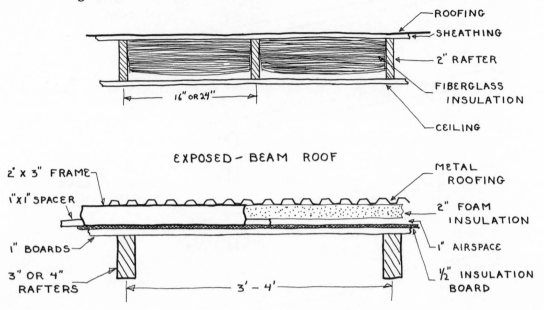

- ROOFING
- SHEATHING
- 2" RAFTER
- FIBERGLASS INSULATION
- CEILING

16" OR 24"

EXPOSED - BEAM ROOF

- 2" x 3" FRAME
- 1"x 1" SPACER
- 1" BOARDS
- 3" OR 4" RAFTERS
- METAL ROOFING
- 2" FOAM INSULATION
- 1" AIRSPACE
- ½" INSULATION BOARD

3' – 4'

Fig. 191   ROOF OVERHANG

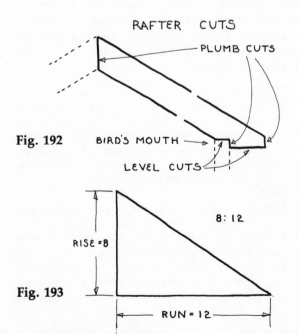

RAFTER CUTS

- PLUMB CUTS
- BIRD'S MOUTH
- LEVEL CUTS

Fig. 192

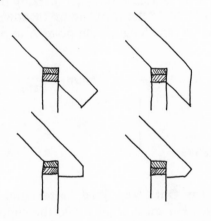

8 : 12

RISE = 8

RUN = 12

Fig. 193

methods, learn to use a rafter square, the traditional carpenter's computer for roof framing and other complex framing problems. Stanley rafter squares come with a good book on the subject, *How to Use the Stanley Steel Square*, by L. Perth.

How to Lay Out Moderate Pitch Shed Rafters. When a shed roof has a pitch of about 4:12 or less, the rafters can be marked for cutting with no measuring at all (Figure 194).

Step 1.
Lay out the rafter positions on the top of the wall plates. They will normally be 16-inch or 24-inch centers for a roof with an inside ceiling and 3-foot or 4-foot centers for an exposed frame. Then take an uncut rafter and hoist it up onto the two wall plates. Put it on two corresponding marks where it will actually sit.

Step 2.
Take the level to the lower end and mark a plumb (vertical) line on the rafter even with the outside of the frame. Make another vertical line at the top even with the inside of the wall.

Step 3.
Rest a piece of 1-inch board on the wall plate, right against the rafter. Use it to mark a level or horizontal line on the rafter 1 inch above the plate. Do this at the bottom also. These two lines show where to cut the bird's mouth. While the rafter is there you can decide how far out at the top and bottom you want to let it overhang. Mark the rafter at those spots. If you want that overhang cut plumb, mark a vertical line with a level.

Step 4.
Take the rafter down and cut on the marks you

118

Fig. 194

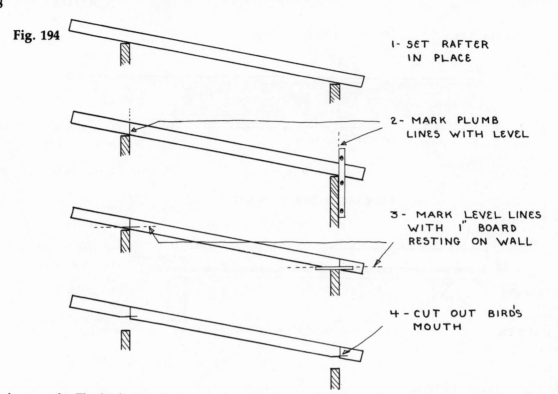

1- SET RAFTER
IN PLACE

2- MARK PLUMB
LINES WITH LEVEL

3 - MARK LEVEL LINES
WITH 1" BOARD
RESTING ON WALL

4 - CUT OUT BIRD'S
MOUTH

have made. The bird's mouth cuts can be started with a circular saw but must be finished with a hand saw.

Step 5.

If your wall framing is uniform, this rafter can be used as a template to mark all the others once you are sure it fits. Simply lay it on the next rafter you must cut and trace. Use the original rafter as the template each time, to avoid a cumulative error. If rough, nonuniform lumber is used, line up the template piece with the rafter flush on the *top* side. This way variations in the width of rafters won't affect where their top edges sit, so the roof will be flat.

Sometimes your template rafter will not fit everywhere, because the wall framing is not uniform. If this is the case, first try to make the framing uniform so that all the rafters can be cut identically. Sometimes a slight warp in a wall can be forced back into line as you install the rafters. Sometimes a wall will be out of plumb, and you can readjust temporary braces to cure the problem. Try to find a way to straighten out the walls and make them parallel on top.

If a correction can't be made, measure each rafter as you did the first by hefting it up, marking it, and bringing it down again to cut it. Or, to avoid this extra hefting, measure each rafter length with a tape measure. Measure from point A to point B, as shown in Figure 195, which represents the distance between the plumb cuts of the bird's mouths. Similarly, measure between the corresponding points of your first rafter, which has already been cut. Then use the first rafter as a

marking template, but after marking the top bird's mouth, slide the template up or down as needed to adjust the length from point A to point B.

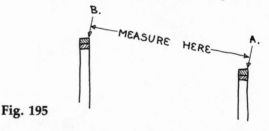

B.

MEASURE HERE

A.

Fig. 195

To Lay Out Steep Shed Rafters and Gable Rafters. For most other roofs, the simplest way to mark rafters is by making a full-scale drawing of the roof frame right on the new floor (Figure 196). A gable roof built with rafter units is used in the example, but the identical method can be used with almost any roof.

Step 1.

Using a chalk line, make a base line representing the level of the top of the walls. On this line, lay out the width of the house, from the outside of the framing on one side to the outside of the framing on the other side. Below the line, at the appropriate place, draw the studwalls themselves.

Step 2.

Find the midpoint of the base line you have made, and draw a vertical (perpendicular) line up from there. From this midpoint to the outside of either studwall represents the run of the roof. The vertical line will represent the rise of the roof. Measure up the rise line an amount equal to the rise you want and make a mark. The distance from this mark to

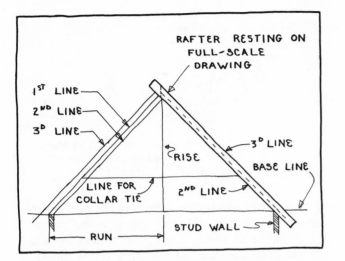

FULL-SCALE DRAWING OF RAFTER UNIT (DRAWN ON SUBFLOOR)   Fig. 196

the left end of the base line (at the top of the wall) should equal the distance from the mark to the right end of the base line. If not, the rise line is not square to the base line and should be adjusted.

Step 3.

Make a chalk line going from the left-hand end of the base line up to the mark at the roof peak. This chalk line should begin at the outer top corner of the left-hand studwall, since that is where the run is measured from. In Figure 196, this line is marked *1st line*. Make another similar line on the right-hand side.

Step 4.

Inside each of the two lines you just made, make a second and parallel line intersecting the *inner* top edge of the wall. The bottom edge of the first rafter you mark will rest on these lines, marked *2nd line* in Figure 196.

Step 5.

Make a horizontal line to represent the bottom edge of your collar tie. In some designs the collar-tie line will be the base line itself; in others it will be another line higher up.

Step 6.

Place an uncut rafter with its bottom edge on the line marked *2nd line* in Figure 196. You will mark this rafter for a plumb cut at the top, a bird's mouth, and the overhang shape by transferring lines up from the chalk lines on the floor. The line for the plumb cut at the top will be the rise line on the floor. Place a straightedge on the rafter above the rise line. You can use a rafter square on the floor to make sure the straightedge is directly above the chalk line. When the straightedge is aligned, draw the plumb cut on the rafter. Take your straightedge and use the same method to mark the bird's mouth and the overhang shape.

Step 7.

Cut the rafter on the lines you have made. Flip it

over, and place it on the corresponding position on the other side of the roof. It should fit perfectly. The whole procedure may seem a little confusing to read about, but when you have a full-scale drawing made and the wood and tools in hand, it will be fairly easy. If you are building the type of roof frame that has a ridge board, use the same method, but draw the ridge board on your full-scale drawing and adjust the rafter size accordingly.

Step 8.

Use the first rafter as a template to mark all the rafters to avoid a cumulative error. With rough lumber, line up the *top* edge of the template with the top edge of the piece being marked to keep the roof flat.

Step 9.

When you have two identical rafters, place them on the drawing. When they look just right, and fit right at the bird's mouth, make a third parallel line on the floor along the outer edge of each rafter. This line is labeled *3d line* in Figure 196 and represents the outside edge of the roof frame. Later, when you assemble the rafter units, they will be assembled in this position on these two lines to guarantee that all units are identical.

Step 10.

While the first two rafters are in position on the floor, take the piece of stock you are using for a collar tie — usually a 2 × 6 — and place it on top of the rafters, right above the line on the floor that represents the collar tie. Mark where to cut the collar tie to length, and mark on the rafters where the tie will go. This piece can be cut, tested, and then used as a template for marking the other collar ties.

When you make all the rafter units identical, you presuppose that the wall framing is accurate. It sometimes happens that by the time you get up to the roof, the house will vary an inch or two in width. The goal then is to frame the roof in a way that disguises these inaccuracies without spending too much extra time. If the variation is under 2 inches, the rafters can be made to fit the widest dimension. This will mean that although the walls vary, the roof is uniform and straight. Since each bird's mouth will sit slightly differently on the wall, you may find that the interior and exterior trim near the eaves will be tricky to fit but the framing will proceed quickly. Usually this is the simplest solution. If the discrepancy is much over 2 inches, I suggest you get a skilled carpenter to help you find the simplest solution. Usually it will involve cutting each rafter unit to slightly different dimensions to match the fluctuation in the run of the roof.

Improvising a Roof Framing Method. Sometimes neither of the systems mentioned here will be convenient. The roof may be too steep to heft the rafters into place, yet there may not be enough room on the floor for a full-scale drawing, for example. In that case you can improvise some way of finding the angles of the cuts and the distances between the cuts. The essential trick is to find or make a line along which to measure and from which to read the angles. This might mean stretching a string from one point to the other so that you can find the angles of the cuts with your angle bevel. Alternatively, you can put lightweight piece such as a 1 × 6 in place, mark it as you would a real rafter and then use it as a template. The advantage of the latter approach is that if you make an error you have not ruined a valuable rafter piece. Sometimes the trick is to find the right *place* to measure from so that you can measure along a line parallel to the rafter. In Figure 197 you cannot

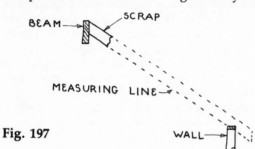

Fig. 197

measure from the top wall to the bottom because the line would not be parallel with the rafter. However, you can find the angle of the top plumb cut by making a scale drawing, or simply by reading the angle from an existing scale drawing with your angle bevel. Take a scrap of the rafter material — or any scrap of the same width — and cut it to that angle. Place it in the position shown, and mark the wall at the bottom of the scrap. This point establishes the top end of a line that will be parallel to the rafter and that you can measure along.

INSTALLING RAFTERS

How you put up your rafters depends on what type of roof structure you have. The process ranges from very simple to tricky and awkward. **How to Put Up Shed Rafters.** Shed rafters can be hefted into place, lined up on the right spacing, and toe-nailed in with 8d or 10d common nails. If the roof overhang is more than 2½ feet, the wind could conceivably get underneath in a hurricane and rip the roof off. To prevent this, reinforce the joint with metal straps called rafter tie-downs, which you can buy through lumber yards or make yourself with mending plates from the hardware store (Figure 198).
How to Put Up Rafter Units. If you are using assembled rafter units instead of individual rafters, you will assemble the units first. Lay the pieces on the full-scale drawing used for the layout. Nail

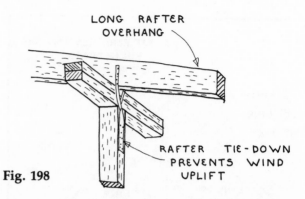

Fig. 198

some 2 × 4 blocks to the outside of the 3rd line in Figure 196. These will help position the rafters while you nail them. Place two rafters on the drawing right on the 3rd line against the blocks. Nail a gusset of plywood or 1-inch board (Figure 199) across the rafters at the ridge, then lay the collar tie on top, over the right line. If the rafters are 2 inches thick, nail the collar tie in place with the 10d nails arranged in a neat pattern, as shown in Figure 199. The joint will be strengthened if you

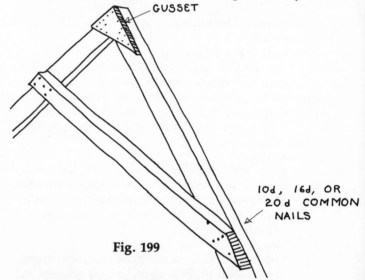

Fig. 199

drive the nails at slightly varying angles. The 20d nails may tend to split the collar tie. Eliminate the problem by predrilling the collar tie (not the rafter) with a drill bit about two-thirds or three-quarters the size of the nail.

If your roof is an exposed-frame type with 3- or 4-inch thick rafters every 3 or 4 feet, the collar ties can still be 2 × 6s, but the joints must be stronger, since a smaller number of ties will have to contain the outward thrust at the eaves. First nail the collar tie on just as with 2-inch thick rafters, but using only 4 nails. Then prop the rafter unit up on blocks and drill a ½-inch hole through the center of the joint and install a ½-inch machine bolt or carriage bolt (and washers) to reinforce the nail joint.

Fig. 200   INSTALLING RAFTER UNITS

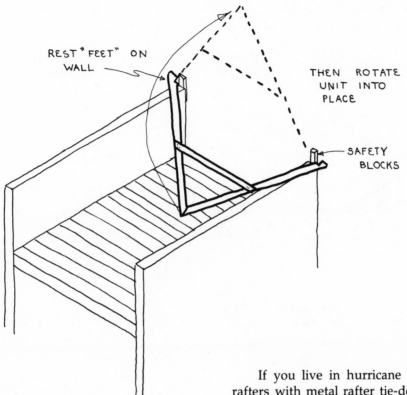

REST "FEET" ON WALL

THEN ROTATE UNIT INTO PLACE

SAFETY BLOCKS

Once assembled, rafter units can be rotated in position much as a studwall is. Lay the unit on the floor, and lift up one of the lower corners onto the top of the kneewall. Then lift the other corner up. The unit is now upside-down, with its feet in the right place, as in Figure 200. Nail a block at the end of the wall to keep the unit from sliding off. With some friends, rotate the unit up and into place using props, ropes, and any other devices you need. How hard this is and how many people it takes depends on how heavy the rafter units are. If they are heavy, you should probably get some experienced help.

When the first unit is up, it can be plumbed with a plumb bob and braced in position. As you did the first, tip each unit up into vertical position. However, when you get down toward the end of the row you will run out of floor to stand on. When this is about to happen, the rafter units already on the walls can be stacked together at one end and moved back into position later. Once a unit is vertical, it can be moved back and forth along the wall plates fairly easily if one or two people hold the top in position with some kind of brace and someone else walks the bottom ends along with gentle taps of a sledgehammer. When the units are all in position, plumb and brace them strongly.

If you live in hurricane country, secure the rafters with metal rafter tie-downs (Figure 198) if the overhang exceeds 2 feet.

How to Install Gable Rafters Using a Ridge Board.

Step 1.
Install the ceiling joists (attic floor joists), which are also the collar ties (Figure 201). When you lay out joist locations on top of the wall, remember that they will rest *beside* the rafters. Toe-nail them to the walls with 3 10d nails in each joint.

Step 2.
Lay a subfloor on top of the joists. This will be your work surface for framing the roof. Leave out the first and last foot or so of the subfloor to avoid obstructing the rafters.

Step 3.
Position the ridge board in place temporarily at just the right height, which you can get from your full-scale drawing, using whatever lumber is at hand.

Step 4.
Put up three pairs of rafters, one pair at each end and one in the middle. These will stabilize the ridge board. Nail them to the floor joists at the bottom with 5 10d nails for planed lumber (1½ inches thick) and 5 16d or 20d nails for rough-cut lumber. At the top, use a few 8d nails in whatever way seems easiest. Since this joint is in compression, the nails serve mainly to hold the pieces in position.

Step 5.
Install the rest of the rafters following Step 4. Install metal rafter tie-downs if the overhang exceeds 2 feet (Figure 198).

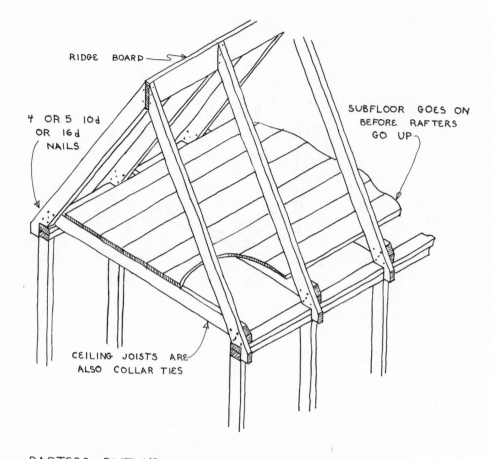

RIDGE BOARD

4 OR 5 10d
OR 16d
NAILS

SUBFLOOR GOES ON
BEFORE RAFTERS
GO UP

CEILING JOISTS ARE
ALSO COLLAR TIES

Fig. 201 RAFTERS PUT UP SINGLY AGAINST RIDGE BOARD

COVERING THE ROOF FRAME

Figure 190 shows two basic approaches to covering the roof frame: (1) the conventional roof, which has 16-inch or 24-inch o.c. rafters, fiberglass insulation between the rafters, and a ceiling covering everything from below and (2) the exposed-beam roof with a wooden ceiling and large, heavy-timber exposed rafters.

In the conventional system, you install the rafters as you earlier installed joists or studs. Then you sheathe it on the outside with plywood or boards. Any kind of roofing can be used over that. Inside, you stuff 6 inches or more of fiberglass insulation between the rafters and then attach a ceiling — usually sheetrock — to the underside of the rafters.

This type of roof is most economical in materials and provides the best insulation for a reasonable cost. Its main disadvantage is that it is very awkward to put up a sheetrock ceiling, particularly for the amateur, and particularly if the ceiling is high. The difficulty of working overhead also makes it hard to do a good job on the sheetrock joints.

In the exposed rafter system, you put up the rafters first as you would conventionally, though they are larger. You then install a layer of wooden boards on top of the rafters. These function as sheathing and finish ceiling combined. A layer of ½-inch black insulation board goes over the boards. Next comes a 1-inch airspace — created with 1 × 1 spacers — and then 2 inches or more of foam insulation in horizontal rows, separated by 2 × 3 strips. Galvanized roofing goes on top, right on the foam.

The primary advantage of the exposed-beam system is its appearance from the inside. But it is also a very fast and easy way to build a roof — quite a bit faster than the conventional method. This is because everything is done in layers from the bottom up, working from above. You do not have to work over your head in an awkward position. Perhaps even more important, all the joints in the ceiling boards are concealed behind the rafters. You get a ceiling that looks very trim and well fitted from the bottom, but you don't have to do much of the careful, precise work you would normally do to make it look that way. You save the time you would otherwise spend on finish work.

With 2 inches of foam an exposed-beam roof costs just about what a conventional roof does.

But though exposed-beam insulates well, its 2 inches of foam do not insulate as well as the other's 6 inches of fiberglass. With the best foam — urethane — the foam design is about 85 percent as efficient. Less expensive foams will make the system only 65 percent as efficient. You can solve the insulation problem by using 3 or even 4 inches of foam, but then the cost will be significantly more than the cost of the conventional roof.

How to Cover a Conventional Roof. As usual, you must plan some of the important design details. You will have already decided on a shape for the roof overhang at the eaves. These rafters can be left open, as in Figure 202, or boxed in with a fascia and soffit, as in Figure 203. This is largely

a matter of looks. In either case, a crack must be left for a vent so air can enter the insulation space between the rafters and carry off excess moisture. In a shed roof, the same venting detail can be used at the high end of the roof to create the air circulation above the insulation (Figure 204). In a gable roof, this will not work, and some other venting method should be provided at the roof peak, at least ideally. Figure 205 shows two methods. In one a tunnel is created just under the peak by installing an extra row of small collar ties. Louvered vents are provided at the gable ends of this tunnel to let out the moisture-laden air.

Another method is called *ventridge*. An opening is created all along the peak of the roof, so that

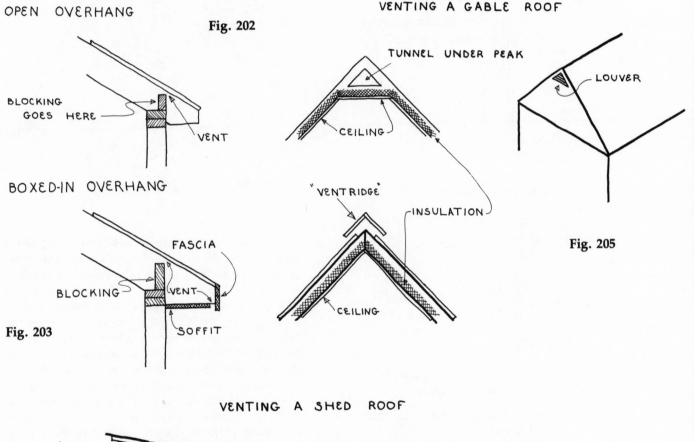

OPEN OVERHANG
Fig. 202
BLOCKING GOES HERE
VENT

BOXED-IN OVERHANG
FASCIA
BLOCKING
VENT
Fig. 203
SOFFIT

VENTING A GABLE ROOF
TUNNEL UNDER PEAK
CEILING
"VENTRIDGE"
INSULATION
CEILING
LOUVER
Fig. 205

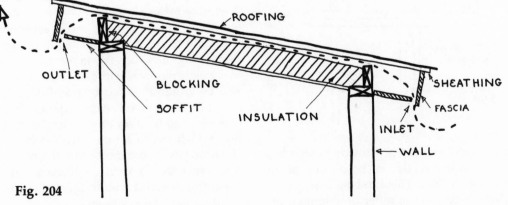

VENTING A SHED ROOF
ROOFING
OUTLET
BLOCKING
SOFFIT
INSULATION
SHEATHING
FASCIA
INLET
WALL
Fig. 204

the moisture-laden air can escape more directly. This crack is protected from the rain with a tiny roof of its own. You can build a ventridge out of wood protected on top with roll roofing or buy a specially made and unobtrusive metal ventridge from a lumber yard.

After planning for ventilation, you must decide on the overhang at the side of the roof parallel with the end rafters. It is not always necessary to have a large overhang at the end walls of the house. In fact, providing one is extra trouble since the rafters do not stick out there. It is possible simply to run the sheathing and siding up over the end rafter as in Figure 206. However, a small

MINIMAL OVERHANG

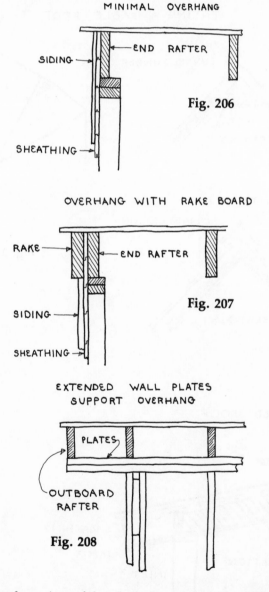

Fig. 206

SIDING
END RAFTER
SHEATHING

OVERHANG WITH RAKE BOARD

Fig. 207

RAKE
END RAFTER
SIDING
SHEATHING

EXTENDED WALL PLATES
SUPPORT OVERHANG

PLATES
OUTBOARD RAFTER

Fig. 208

overhang *is* useful and can be provided by nailing an extra rafter called a *rake* on the outside of the end rafters (Figure 207). This can be a 2-inch thick piece nailed directly to the rafter or shimmed out

1, 2, or 3 inches. Or it can be a 2-inch board or extra rafter nailed to the outside of the sheathing. It would then serve to trim out or "stop" the siding at the top as shown in the figure.

Greater overhang can be provided by running the top plates of the wall out in midair a foot or so to support a real outboard rafter (Figure 208). Sometimes short 2 × 4s perpendicular to the rafters are notched into the first rafter to create a large overhang as in Figure 209.

FRAMING A LARGE OVERHANG

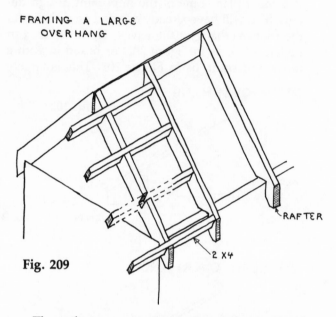

RAFTER
2 X 4
Fig. 209

These features may be easier to figure out if you make scale cross sections showing the overhang at the eaves and the rake details. If the roof is steep, high up, or otherwise hard to get at, you will need a scaffolding (see chapter twenty-three).

Begin by installing the blocking between the rafters at the eaves, leaving a venting crack at the top (Figure 202). Usually if the blocking is cut from the same size stock as the rafters, a ½-inch crack will automatically be left at the top. Toe-nail the blocking in with 8d nails. Do the rake next, installing whatever pieces you need to create an overhang at the end wall, parallel to the rafters. This may mean simply a rake board nailed to the sheathing or something more complicated. The soffit and fascia, if any, can be put on now or later, depending on which is convenient.

You can now sheathe the roof. Your sheathing will be either air-dried boards (rough or planed) or ½-inch plywood with exterior glue. Boards make a good base for any roofing except roll roofing, which needs a more even surface. Plywood sheathing will cost more, but the savings in time will probably be worth the extra expense. The sheathing method will be the same used for your subfloor (see pages 98–99).

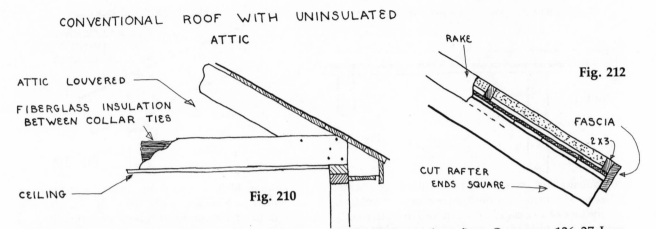

CONVENTIONAL ROOF WITH UNINSULATED ATTIC

ATTIC LOUVERED

FIBERGLASS INSULATION BETWEEN COLLAR TIES

CEILING

Fig. 210

RAKE

Fig. 212

FASCIA

2 X 3

CUT RAFTER ENDS SQUARE

When the sheathing is done, you should put the roofing on as soon as possible to protect the house from the weather. Roofing procedures are discussed in chapter sixteen. Later, when the building is all closed in, you will insulate the roof by laying rolls or batts of 6-inch fiberglass insulation between the rafters from underneath (see chapter nineteen). The last step will be the inside ceiling and trim (see chapter twenty).

If the house is to have an uninsulated attic, you do not need to insulate between the rafters. Instead, you can lay the insulation between the attic floor joists, which is easier. If you do this you must vent the gable end walls with louvered vents you can buy from lumber yards. One square foot at each end will do (Figure 210).

How to Cover an Exposed Beam Roof.

The following instructions are for use with

galvanized metal roofing. On pages 126–27 I explain how to adapt them to asphalt roofing materials. Figure 211 shows the basic components of the system. The rafters are exposed at the eave. The rake and fascia pieces are attached to the 2 × 3 frame that holds the foam sheets. The ends of the rafters are cut square rather than plumb to fit tight with the fascia (Figure 212). The overhang at the rake is created by extending the 2 × 3s out past the end-most rafter (Figure 213). If you plan the amount of this overhang carefully, the galvanized roofing will go up in full sheets, which will save a lot of work (see Chapter 16, p. 129).

Step 1.
Blocking: Install double blocking between the rafters with a layer of 1-inch Styrofoam between, as shown in Figure 214. These pieces should be fit carefully and caulked tight with an expensive

Fig. 211

EXPOSED-BEAM ROOF COMPONENTS

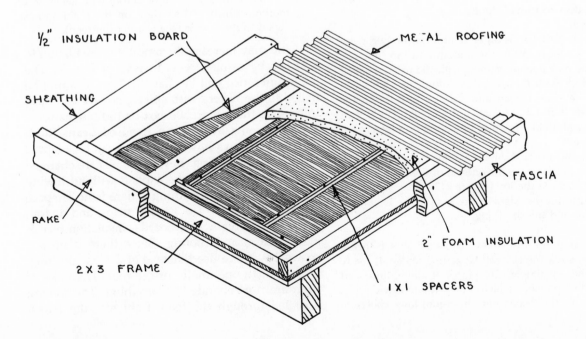

½" INSULATION BOARD

METAL ROOFING

SHEATHING

FASCIA

RAKE

2" FOAM INSULATION

2 X 3 FRAME

1 X 1 SPACERS

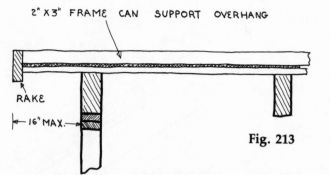

Fig. 213

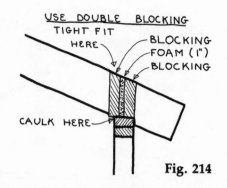

Fig. 214

caulking such as silicone, butyl rubber, or Pheno-seal. The foam and caulking are needed because the lack of a fascia and rake around the rafter-ends leaves the blocking covered outside by only a single layer of siding.

Step 2.

Sheathing: Sheathing boards should be dry and good looking because their underside will be your finish ceiling. These boards should be installed neatly and tightly with the good side down. Chapter thirteen, page 102, gives more detailed instructions on how to do this in an analogous situation. Overhang the boards at the end wall and trim them all at once with a skill saw.

Step 3.

Insulation board: Cover the boards with a layer of ½-inch black insulation board. Nail it at the rafters with 8d nails and elsewhere with 1-inch or 1¼-inch roofing nails every 8 or 10 inches. Then make a chalk line directly over the center of each rafter. You will need this line later to find where to nail down the 2 × 3s.

Step 4.

Plastic vapor barrier: Install a layer of clear 4 mil plastic over the insulation board as a vapor barrier. Put it on in as few pieces as possible for a complete seal. On a steep roof the plastic will be slippery to walk on, but you can nail temporary cleats to the roof deck to provide footholds.

Step 5.

2 × 3s: Nail 2 × 3s on edge around the perimeter of the roof deck. At the bottom and top they can be toe-nailed to the framing with 10d nails or nailed through with 6-inch spikes. Along the sides you will have to nail up into the 2 × 3s through the boards with 6d or 8d galvanized nails. The 2 × 3s that will divide the rows of foam go up later.

Step 6.

Rake and fascia: Nail 2 × 6 rake and fascia pieces at the perimeter to the outside of the 2 × 3s, flush with them at the top (Figure 212). They will cover and protect the edges of the 2 × 3s, the insulation board, and the sheathing.

Step 7.

Preparing for insulation: While all this is being done, someone else can be getting materials ready for roof insulating. Cut pieces of aluminum-faced building paper — which comes in 3-foot-wide rolls — to fit the 2-foot-wide by 8-foot-long sheets of foam insulation. Attach the aluminum to the foam with 1-inch roofing nails. Since the foam is soft, you can push the nails in with your thumb. Also rip scrap boards into strips approximately 1" × 1" or ¾" × 1" on a table saw. These will be used as spacers to hold the foam slabs up off the black insulation board, as shown in Figure 211.

Step 8.

Insulation (Figure 215): Start with the bottom row, at the eaves. Place or lightly tack 2 horizontal rows of 1 × 1 spacers on the insulation board to support the first row of foam, which will go against the 2 × 3 at the eaves. Place two strips perpendicular to these, i.e., above each of the outermost rafters. Cut these pieces to 24 inches or slightly less. Their purpose is to block off the ends of the airspaces so cold air can't leak in from the uninsulated eaves. Caulk these strips top and bottom (Figure 211).

Lay one row of foam slabs on the spacers with the foil side *down*. The foam need not extend into the overhang areas. Cut to size a second row of 2 × 3s to fit above the foam and put them in place.

Sitting above them on the roof, press them against the layer of foam to get a tight fit — a tight fit is important with foam — and nail them down to the rafters with 6-inch spikes. Repeat this procedure until the whole roof is insulated.

The roof is now ready to roof with galvanized roofing, which will sit right on the foam and be nailed to the 2 × 3s (see chapter fourteen).

You may increase the amount of insulation to 3 inches by using 2 × 4s instead of 2 × 3s. The main difference will be that the 2 × 3s cannot be nailed to the rafters with spikes, so you will have to toe-nail them with 10d box or 16d box nails.

Variation on Covering an Exposed-Beam Roof. Figure 216 shows how the system can be adapted to asphalt roll roofing. Several details are changed to provide nailing for the asphalt without having to add an exterior sheathing. There is no airspace below the foam, no 1 × 1 wood strips, and no foil, just a tight sandwich of boards, insulation board, plastic foam, and roofing. Since there is no airspace, 2 × 2s are used instead of 2 × 3s, and they only go at the perimeter of the roof. The rows of foam are not separated by anything. The roofing is nailed through the foam right into the 1-inch

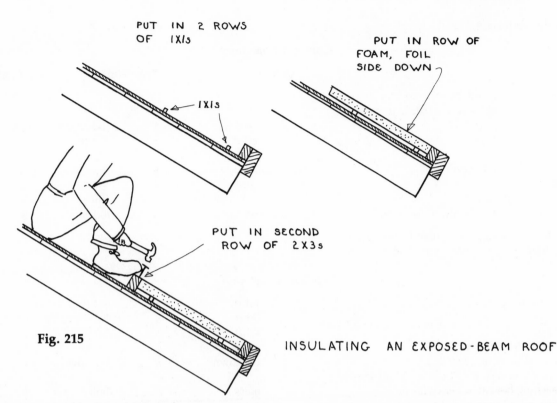

PUT IN 2 ROWS OF 1X1s

1X1s

PUT IN SECOND ROW OF 2X3s

Fig. 215

PUT IN ROW OF FOAM, FOIL SIDE DOWN

INSULATING AN EXPOSED-BEAM ROOF

boards. The nails must be long enough to penetrate the boards without coming out on the bottom. The nail to use is 3½-inch roofing nail, or failing that, a 16d galvanized common nail. If you use the common nail, use more nails than normal to hold the roofing down because the nail heads are smaller and have less holding power. Since there are no 2 × 3s, and the sheathing will carry the roof load directly, space the rafters no more than 3 feet o.c., unless the roof pitch is 4:12 or more, and will therefore shed snow.

DRAWINGS

Making scale drawings will save time in the end by helping keep the details clear. The draw-

ings you may need include:

1. An elevation, showing the basic rafter or rafter unit shape, the length of the rafters, and the shape of the overhang (example, Figure 210)
2. A plan view, showing the number and arrangements of the rafters seen from above
3. A cross section showing the size of the rafters, their spacing, the type of insulation, the kind of sheathing, the kind of ceiling, and the kind of roofing (example, Figure 190)
4. A cross section through the eaves, showing soffit, bird's mouth, blocking, fascia, and roofing details (examples, Figures 201, 202)
5. A cross section through the end rafter, showing the rake board, overhang, sheathing, and siding details (examples, Figures 207, 208)

VARIATION ON EXPOSED-BEAM SYSTEM

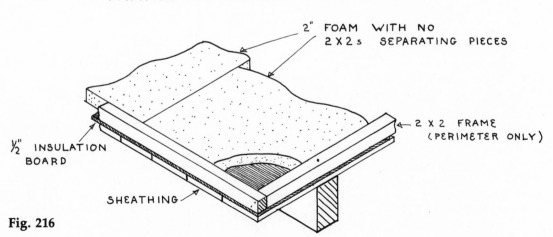

2" FOAM WITH NO 2 X 2s SEPARATING PIECES

½" INSULATION BOARD

SHEATHING

2 X 2 FRAME (PERIMETER ONLY)

Fig. 216

Sample Materials List

Conventional Roof

Item	Quantity	Price/Unit	Total Cost
Rafters (Itemize, and be sure to buy enough lumber for at least one extra, in case one gets cut wrong)	_____ bd.ft.	$ _____ /bd.ft.	$ _____
Collar ties (2 × 6)	_____ bd.ft.	$ _____ /bd.ft.	$ _____
Blocking			
Rafter tie-downs, if needed	_____ tie downs	$ _____ /tie down	$ _____
Ceiling material	_____ sq.ft.	$ _____ /sq.ft.	$ _____
Sheathing, if plywood	_____ 4 × 8 sheets	$ _____ /sheet	$ _____
Sheathing, if boards, order 15% extra	_____ bd.ft.	$ _____ /bd.ft.	$ _____

Insulation, roofing, and vapor barrier are included on other lists, pages 136 and 165.

Exposed-beam roof

Item	Quantity	Price/Unit	Total Cost
Rafters (order 1 extra)	_____ bd.ft.	$ _____ /bd.ft.	$ _____
Collar ties	_____ bd.ft.	$ _____ /bd.ft.	$ _____
2 × 3's	_____ bd.ft.	$ _____ /bd.ft.	$ _____
Black insulation board	_____ 4 × 8 sheet	$ _____ /sheet	$ _____
Rafter tie-downs, if needed	_____ tie down	$ _____ /tie down	$ _____
Bolts for collar ties, 6½" or 7" × ½" carriage or machine bolt, two per collar tie	_____ bolts	$ _____ /bolt	$ _____
Aluminum building paper, same area as roof	_____ rolls	$ _____ /roll	$ _____
Caulking	_____ cartridges	$ _____ /cartridge	$ _____
Inexpensive stock for 1 × 1s	_____ bd.ft.	$ _____ /bd.ft.	$ _____
1" foam to insulate between two layers of blocking	_____ 2' × 8' sheets	$ _____ /sheet	$ _____
Plastic vapor barrier, same area as roof	_____ rolls	$ _____ /roll	$ _____
Blocking	_____ bd.ft.	$ _____ /bd.ft.	$ _____
6" nails	_____ lbs.	$ _____ /lb.	$ _____
1" roofing nails to hold foil to foam	_____ lbs.	$ _____ /lb.	$ _____

Roofing and insulation are included on other lists, pages 136 and 165.

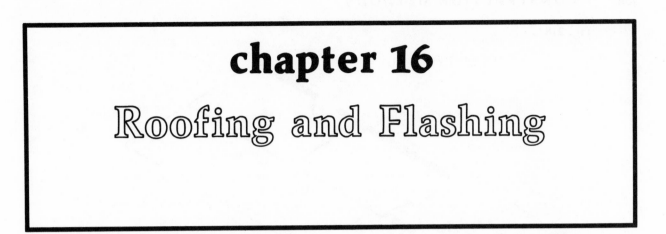

chapter 16
Roofing and Flashing

The more levels and planes a roof has, the more complicated and laborious will be the roofing process. A simple shed or gable roof can be roofed in a day, but a roof full of hips, valleys, skylights, chimneys, and other interruptions will be a major production. This is another reason to keep your roof as simple as possible.

TYPES OF ROOFING

The least expensive roofing is ordinary roll roofing, which consists of 3-foot-wide rolls of asphalt-impregnated felt coated with shiny sandsized mineral particles (Figure 218). The mineral surface protects the roofing by reflecting sunlight away, particularly if the mineral is a light color. Roll roofing comes in 45-pound, 60-pound, and 90-pound weights. Heavier roofing lasts longer.

Since it comes in such big sheets, roll roofing is quick to install. It can be laid horizontally on shallow roofs with a pitch of 2:12 or greater (Figure 217). However, above about 6:12, the material

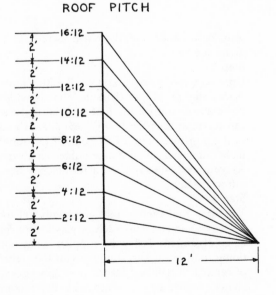

ROOF PITCH

Fig. 217

slides around so much that it is probably not worth using. It can be used vertically on steep roofs with a pitch of about 10:12 or steeper. Roll roofing costs about $10 for 100 square feet coverage (one square).

Double coverage roll roofing is the same as regular roll roofing except that each piece laps the next one halfway (see Figure 219). The upper half of each sheet is not mineralized, because it will be covered with the lower half of the next sheet up. This kind of roofing is more durable than ordinary roll roofing because of the wide lap and because there are few if any exposed nail heads where leaks can start. The wide lap also makes it possible to use double coverage on roofs as shallow as 1:12. Like ordinary roll roofing, it will be awkward to install on roofs over 6:12. At about $20 per square, double-coverage roll roofing is the least expensive top-quality roof you can install.

The most common roofing material is asphalt shingles, made of the same material as roll roofing (Figure 220). The self-tabbing types have a dab of tar under each shingle. After the shingles are up, the sun melts the dab and glues each shingle to the one below. Asphalt shingles are more expensive to buy and more time-consuming to install than roll roofing, but they are easier to handle on steep roofs. They can be used when the pitch is 4:12 or greater, and they cost about $25 per square.

Metal roofing is made of many metals, but galvanized steel is the most satisfactory all around (Figure 224). It is more expensive than asphalt roofings (about $32 per square), but with good planning it can be installed very fast. Since it is quite stiff, it does not need continuous support, so savings on sheathing are sometimes possible. It can be used when the slope is 3:12 or steeper.

Number 1 wood shingles (Figure 226) make one of the most beautiful and durable roofs. Unfortunately they cost more than other common roofings (about $85 per square) and take much longer to put up.

Fig. 218

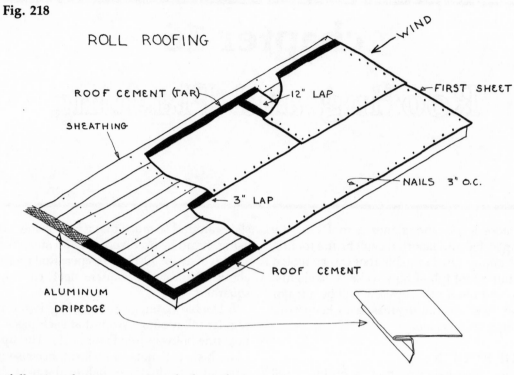

The following chart summarizes the basic facts about the different types of roofing:

	Roofing Types		
	Cost per 100 sq.ft.	Minimum pitch	Amt. of work to install
90-lb asphalt roll	$10	2:12 (6:12 max)	fast
Double coverage roll	17	1:12 (6:12 max)	fast
235-lb. asphalt shingles (self-tabbing)	22	4:12	medium
Galvanized metal	32	3:12	fast
No. 1 Wood shingles	85	4:12	slow

HOW TO PUT UP ROOFING

Follow the directions that come with the brand of roofing you buy.

Regular Roll Roofing.

If roll roofing is to have a long life, it should be laid over a sheathing of plywood or dry tongue and groove boards. Square-edged boards will not present a smooth enough surface, and green boards will move around and perhaps cause premature leaks. Wear your oldest clothes, because you will be working with tar. Have some paint thinner or turpentine on hand for cleanup. Figure 218 shows the procedures for roll roofing.

Step 1.

Begin by nailing a special aluminum flashing, called a *dripedge*, to the edges of the roof sheathing with aluminum roofing nails. Nail the dripedge at the bottom first, and lap the side pieces over the bottom. With a shed roof, there will also be a dripedge along the top.

Step 2.

Unroll a roll of roofing, and cut it with a knife into pieces slightly longer than the roof is wide. Lay these sheets out on the roof deck so that the sun can warm and flatten them. Each sheet should sit in the sun for about a half-hour. If the roofing is nailed down too soon it may bubble as it expands. As you roof, always keep a few pieces stretched out in the sun.

Step 3.

The tarry roof cement that goes with roll roofing goes by various names such as plastic roof cement or cold cement. Tell your supplier what you are doing, and he or she will give you the right kind of cement. It will be a black, incredibly sticky substance. Sometimes it comes with the roofing. In cold weather, warm the cans in the sun or in a warm room to make the cement easier to use.

Spread a bed of the roof cement 3 or 4 inches wide, along the bottom edge of the roof, on top of the dripedge. Do the same along each side, starting at the bottom and going up 3 feet. Spread the tar with a piece of shingle or a scrap board.

Step 4.

Place the first sheet of roofing along the bottom edge of the roof, as shown in Figure 218. Overhang the dripedge around ⅛ of an inch at the bottom. Smooth it carefully, and nail it down along the bottom edge with 1¼- or 1½-inch galvanized roofing nails every 3 inches. These nails have large heads to hold the roofing firmly. The row of nails should be close to the bottom edge of the roofing without missing the sheathing. Nail down the ends of the sheet in the same way. Every exposed nail in roll roofing should go through a bed of roof cement after it goes through the roofing, because the roof cement seals the hole.

Step 5.

With a chalk line, make a line 3 inches down from the top edge of the first sheet and parallel to it. This line represents where the bottom edge of the second sheet will be and shows where to put the roof cement that holds down the bottom of the second sheet. Spread a ribbon of roof cement 3 inches wide above this chalk line. Also put a ribbon of roof cement under where the ends of the next sheet will be, along the rake. Place the second sheet with its bottom edge on the chalk line, smooth it, and nail it as before with 1 nail every 3 inches. Locate the nails ¾ of an inch to 1 inch in from the edge of the sheet.

Step 6.

Continue placing, cementing and nailing sheets until you get to the top of the roof. The ridge of a gable can be covered with a half sheet folded over the top. Vertical joints should be lapped 12 inches

and placed so that the prevailing wind will not lift the upper sheet.

Double Coverage Roll Roofing. Like regular roll roofing, double coverage is laid in sheets working from the bottom up to the ridge, but many of the procedures are different. Figure 219 illustrates the basic steps.

Step 1.

Install a dripedge as described in Step 1 for roll roofing (see page 130).

Step 2.

Also as before, unroll a roll or two, cut pieces to length, and stretch the sheets out in the sun to warm and flatten them.

Step 3.

Spread a bed of roof cement on the dripedge at the eave and along the edge of the roof with a shingle or a scrap board.

Cut 1 sheet in half lengthwise, separating the mineralized from the unmineralized part. Set aside the mineralized part for later use. The unmineralized part will be a starter strip. Nail it down along the eave using the procedures given in Step 4 for roll roofing.

Step 4.

Here is the main difference in method between double coverage and regular roll-roofing: nail all the sheets in place — through the top half only — before you apply the roof cement to the joints. The only places that gets roof cement at this point are the metal dripedges. After all the sheets are nailed down, you fold them back one at a time to apply the roof cement.

Take a full width sheet and place it along the eave overlapping the dripedge ⅛ of an inch and covering the starter sheet. Nail the sheet through the upper half only with 1½-inch galvanized roof-

DOUBLE COVERAGE ROLL ROOFING

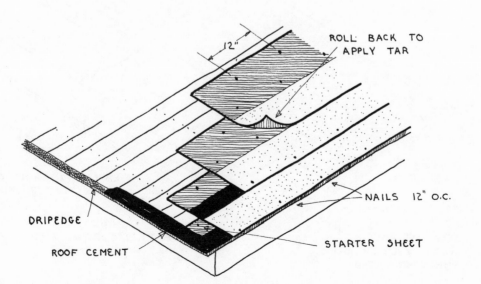

Fig. 219

ing nails every 6 inches in a staggered pattern as shown in Figure 219.

Step 5.

Continue on up the roof, nailing down the sheets through their upper half only and lapping each sheet half way. Lap vertical joints 6 inches, with the upper sheet to windward.

Step 6.

When all the sheets are laid, take a chalk line and mark the bottom edge of each sheet.

Step 7.

Starting from the top, fold each sheet back, and spread an 8-inch band of roof cement just above the chalk line. The more neatly you do this, the better looking the roof will be. Make sure you use roof cement at all vertical joints and along the dripedge. The best tool for this is a notched trowel, which can be bought at hardware or flooring stores.

Step 8.

After you cement each joint, fold the top sheet down, smooth it out, and nail it with one roofing nail every foot.

On very shallow roofs, pitched between 1:12 and 2:12, it is probably a good idea to change the procedure slightly to eliminate all exposed nails.

Use the same method, but rather than spread an 8-inch bed of tar, coat the entire unmineralized half, or as much of it as you can coat without risking a crease in the folded sheet. Then fold the sheet down and flatten it. Nail the vertical joints and the ends of the sheets only. The horizontal joints will be held just by the tar.

Asphalt Shingles.   Figure 220 shows a standard asphalt shingle and Figure 221 shows typical installation details.

Step 1.

Install a metal dripedge along the bottom edge of the roof.

Step 2.

Cover the roof with a layer of 15-pound felt, lapping the pieces as shown in the illustration. Nail the felt down with the minimum number of roofing nails that will hold it. On a steep roof you may find it more convenient to apply only the first row or two of felt now and the rest as you work your way up the roof.

Step 3.

Install a dripedge at the sides of the roof, along the rake. If the roof is steep, this also can be done one section at a time as you move up the roof.

Step 4.

In cold climates install a single strip of 60-pound roll roofing along the eaves under the shingles as protection against ice dams. The eave is often colder than the rest of the roof, since it is removed from the heat of the house. Melted snow can flow down the relatively warm roof, hit the cold eave, and refreeze. This creates the ice dam, which can cause water to back up under the shingles and leak in. The 60-pound roll roofing provides an extra barrier against this. It can be installed using Steps 3, 4, and 5, pages 130–31.

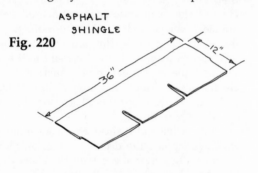

ASPHALT SHINGLE

Fig. 220

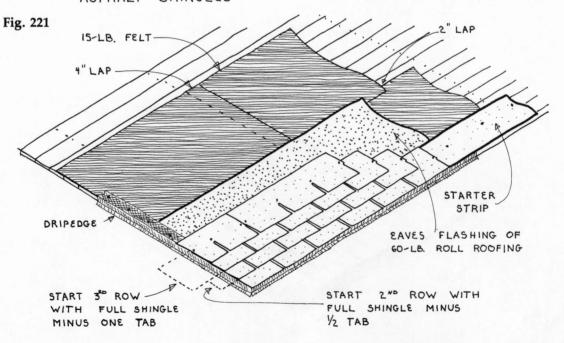

ASPHALT SHINGLES

Fig. 221

15-LB. FELT

4" LAP

2" LAP

DRIPEDGE

STARTER STRIP

EAVES FLASHING OF 60-LB. ROLL ROOFING

START 3ᴿᴰ ROW WITH FULL SHINGLE MINUS ONE TAB

START 2ᴺᴰ ROW WITH FULL SHINGLE MINUS ½ TAB

Step 5.
The first row of shingles must be doubled. This is often done by nailing a special starter strip along the eave, over the 15-pound felt and 60-pound roll roofing, if any. The strip is the same as the shingle material, only without slots.

Step 6.
Nail the first row of shingles over the starter strip with 4 1½-inch galvanized roofing nails per shingle, as shown in Figure 221. Locate the nails about 1 inch above the top of the slots. The shingles should overlap the dripedge side and bottom by about ⅜ of an inch.

Step 7.
Establish a few chalk lines, starting from the shingle slots and running up to the top of the roof parallel to the sides of the roof. These will help you keep the slots aligned as you move up the roof.

Step 8.
Asphalt shingles are laid with 5-inch exposure to the weather. Five inches comes just below the top of the slots, so the rows can be aligned using the slots as a guide. Periodically use a chalk line to make sure the rows are straight and parallel to the roof deck.

Start the second row with a shingle from which you have removed one half of a tab. Cut the shingle with a knife from the back side. Start the third row with a shingle from which you have removed a full tab. This procedure keeps the slots staggered.

If the roof is too steep to walk on, you can support planks to work on with pairs of special shingle brackets (Figure 222). These brackets are

Fig. 222   SHINGLE   BRACKET

nailed to the roof sheathing with 3 8d nails each. Locate the metal plate of the bracket where a tab from the next course of shingles you install will cover the nails to prevent leaks. Remove the brackets when all the roofing is done. The teardrop-

shaped holes in the metal plate allow you to remove the bracket without disturbing the shingles too much. Wiggle or tap the bracket toward the ridge ¼ of an inch or so to release it. Lift the tab above the nail and drive the nails flush.

Fig. 223   BOSTON RIDGE

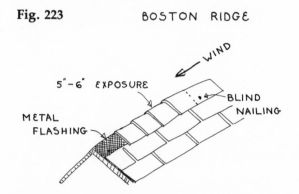

Step 9.
Cover the peak of the roof with a Boston ridge as shown in Figure 223. First cap the ridge with a strip of aluminum flashing 8 inches wide, folded over the ridge. Then cut shingles into thirds, and blind-nail them as shown over the metal flashing. Blind-nailing means the nails you use to hold down one piece are covered by the subsequent piece. To protect the ridge from the wind, start laying the shingles on the leeward end and work toward the prevailing wind. Lay the pieces with 5- to 6-inch exposure to the weather, i.e., all but 5 or 6 inches of each piece should be covered by the subsequent piece.

Galvanized Metal.   On roofs pitched below 4:12, the sheathing under galvanized roofing should be plywood or continuous dry boards. Above 4:12, the sheathing can be dry 1 × 4s spaced 4 inches apart, or dry 1 × 6s spaced 6 inches apart. Here are the procedures (Figure 224).

Step 1.
First figure out what lengths of roofing to buy. The goal is to avoid any cutting, which is noisy, unpleasant, and time-consuming. Sometimes a slight adjustment in overhang size or fascia thickness will enable you to do this. The sheets should overhang a fascia board by 2 to 3 inches. On roofs where a single sheet will not reach from top to bottom, the upper sheet should overlap the lower by at least 4 inches. On a gable roof the roofing usually must fall short of the peak by around 4 to 6 inches to accommodate the special ridge roll that will cover the peak. Similarly, where the roof meets a wall at the top, the roofing must fall short of the wall by 4 to 6 inches to accommodate the end-wall flashing that will seal that joint.

The roofing comes in a variety of lengths, such as 7, 8, 9, 10, 12, 14, 16, and 20 feet. Find out what lengths your brand comes in and how much clearance is necessary for ridge rolls or end-wall flash-

Fig. 224

METAL ROOFING

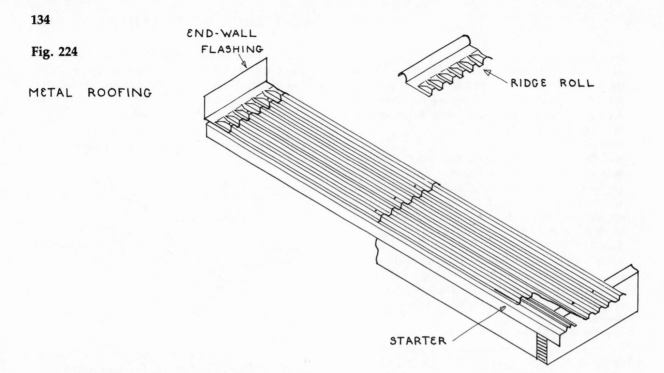

ings, if you need them. Then look at the elevation of your roof. If the distance from the peak to the eave, including the fascia, is approximately the same as one of the standard roofing lengths, often you can adjust the overhang slightly to make things come out right. For example, one brand of roofing might call for the roofing to fall short of the ridge by 4 inches. If your rafters are 12 feet long, you could add a 2-inch fascia and then a 12-foot sheet would leave the necessary 2-inch overhang at the bottom.

There is less of a problem if your roof will take a double row of sheets, because you can vary the overlap between sheets.

Step 2.
Figure out the width of roofing. Again the goal is to avoid cutting. For example, in one brand called Paneldrain, the sheets are 32 inches wide and overlap 2 inches. To avoid cutting, the roof should be some multiple of 30 inches plus 2 inches. The extra 2 inches is for the unused overlap (Figure 225). Find the specifications of your roofing and adjust the design of your roof overhang to match. Of course, don't make a major change in your overhang if it would compromise other important aspects of your design. In that case it is better to cut the roofing.

Step 3.
When everything is carefully planned, nail up the first sheet on the lower left-hand corner of the roof. Just nail it tentatively with one or two nails. Always nail through the hump, never in the valley. These first nails should be in the right-hand half of the sheet, because soon you will lift the left-hand half to slide a starter piece under it. The nails should not be nailed through the hump on the far right, because the next sheet must fit tight over this hump. The nails you use are galvanized roofing nails with neoprene or lead-headed washers attached to seal around the nail head where it punctures the roofing.

Step 4.
Make sure the first sheet is in the right place and parallel to the edges of the roof.

Step 5.
Take a starter strip and slide it under the left-hand edge of the roofing.

Step 6.
Nail the first sheet down with the starter piece. There should be a horizontal row of nails at least every 2 feet on center, with one nail going through every other hump, except the hump that will be lapped by the next sheet. Use a chalk line to locate where to nail, because a neatly nailed roof will look much better.

The big hazard is that you will miss the nail and hit your thumb. This is particularly likely when the nail must puncture two or more layers of roofing, which requires a heavy hammer blow. This is one of the most painful injuries you can have (I speak from experience), particularly if you hit the same thumb twice. These bruises take months to heal. To avoid them, hold the nail with a stout pair of pliers, especially if you are going through more than one layer. Make sure the neoprene or lead

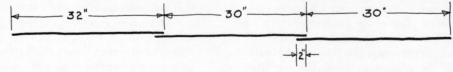

Fig. 225

washer is crushed against the roofing, but don't dent the roofing.

Step 7.

Nail the remaining sheets and finish with another starter strip. Watch that the overhang at the bottom stays more or less constant. If there is a double row of sheets, do the whole bottom row and then the top row. Ridge rolls and end-wall flashings can be nailed on later using the same method. If the first pieces are well aligned, you should have no trouble. If cutting the roofing is necessary, you will find that regular tin snips do not work well. Instead, use an abrasive blade on a portable circular saw or a type of tin snip called a *pipe and duct snip*.

WOOD SHINGLES   **Fig. 226**

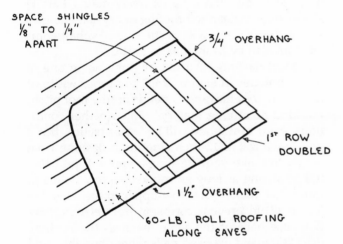

SPACE SHINGLES ⅛" TO ¼" APART

¾" OVERHANG

1ˢᵀ ROW DOUBLED

1½" OVERHANG

60-LB. ROLL ROOFING ALONG EAVES

Wood Shingles (Figure 226). Wood shingles can be nailed to a sheathing of ½-inch exterior plywood or air-dried boards. Use #1 red cedar or redwood shingles. Sixteen-inch shingles can be laid with a 4-inch exposure on roofs of 4:12 to 5:12. On steeper roofs, the exposure can be increased to 5 inches. No metal dripedge or felt underlayment is necessary, but in cold climates there should be a 3-foot-wide strip of 60-pound roofing along the eaves to prevent ice damming.

Step 1.

The first row of shingles should be doubled. Begin by nailing a row of shingles along the eaves with 2 5d galvanized box nails per shingle. Locate the nails about ¾ of an inch in from each side and about 6 inches up from the bottom edge of the shingle. Overhang ¾ of an inch at the ends and 1½ inches at the bottom. Space the shingles ⅛ to ¼ of an inch apart for expansion, with the wider spacing next to the wider shingles.

Step 2.

Put another row of shingles over the first, carefully staggering the joints. Nail the shingles as in Step 1, locating the row of nails about 1½ inches above where the butt line of the next row of shingles will be. With a 4-inch exposure, the nails will be about 5½ inches up from the bottom.

Step 3.

Use a chalk line to locate the bottom of the next course of shingles and nail them up as before. The joints should be at least 1½ inches away from the joints in the first row.

Step 4.

Proceed on up the roof following Steps 2 and 3. The trick is to quickly find a shingle the right width so that the joints will be 1½ inches away from the joints in the next row down and 1 inch away from the joints in the second row down. These staggerings are minimal and should be exceeded in general. When you have to cut a shingle, use an electric saber saw or a hatchet in combination with a small block plane for trimming. If the roof is too steep to work on, use shingle brackets as described on page 133.

Step 5.

Finish the ridge using a Boston ridge made of 6-inch-wide shingles, blind-nailed, over an 8- or 10-inch-wide bent metal flashing (Figure 227).

BOSTON RIDGE   **Fig. 227**

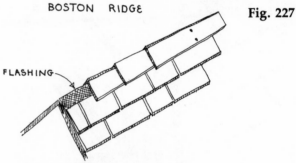

FLASHING

FLASHING

Whenever a roof meets a wall or another roof, or is penetrated by a chimney or a vent, there must be some sort of flashing. A flashing is a piece — usually made of sheet metal — that prevents leaks at the joint. Flashings are also sometimes needed on walls where the type of material changes, such as where the siding meets a window or door casing. Figure 228 shows several typical flashings. Each follows the basic principle of roofing: the upper piece laps the lower. Figure 228–A shows the kind of flashing used above the casings of windows and doors. This flashing, which you can buy ready-made, goes under the siding and over the casing. Part B shows the flashing that seals where a roof meets a wall at the top. It goes under the siding and over the shingles. This is a flashing you would make yourself by bending 12-inch sheet aluminum to the right angle (Figure 229). You can buy this in rolls from the lumber yard. When wood shingles meet a wall at the side, use step flashing (C), shown with the siding removed for clarity in the illustration. You can make

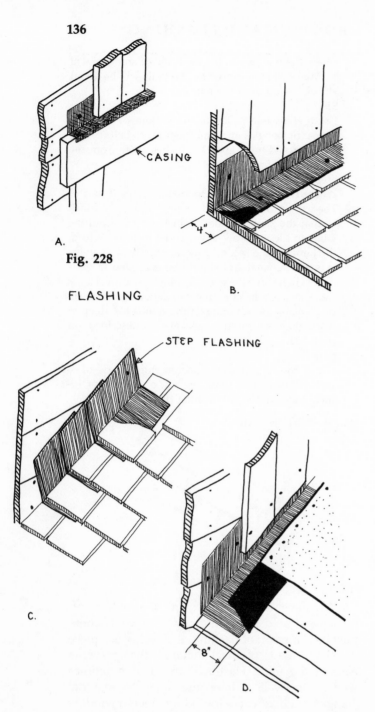

CASING

A.

Fig. 228

FLASHING

B.

STEP FLASHING

C.

D.

Fig. 229

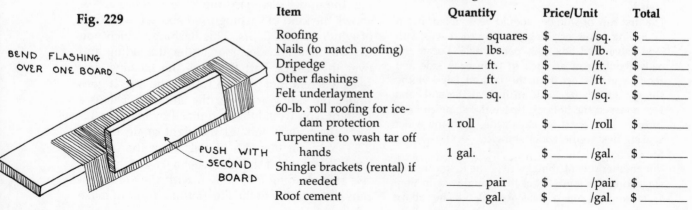

BEND FLASHING OVER ONE BOARD

PUSH WITH SECOND BOARD

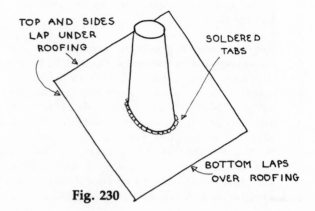

TOP AND SIDES LAP UNDER ROOFING

SOLDERED TABS

BOTTOM LAPS OVER ROOFING

Fig. 230

step flashing squares by cutting up rolls of 8-inch aluminum flashing with tin snips, but it is also possible to buy the squares ready-made. Part D shows how to flash roll roofing or asphalt shingles where they meet a wall at the side. Asphalt shingles can also be flashed as in Part C.

Most flashing jobs can be done using one of the techniques in Figure 228. The proper width of lap in any roof flashing depends on the roof pitch, the kind of roofing material, and weather conditions. Your best guide will be local practice. But if you buy a roll of 12-inch aluminum flashing from which to make your flashings, you will probably not go wrong as long as you keep a few points in mind: (1) make sure the upper piece laps the lower, (2) to prevent corrosion from electrical action, use nails of the same metal as the flashing used, (3) avoid exposed nails where possible, and seal all exposed nail heads with roof cement.

Some flashings are too complicated to make yourself. Good examples are the stovepipe flashing shown in Figure 230 and the flashings used around skylights. Sometimes such flashings are available ready-made, but a tinsmith can also make them to fit your specifications.

SAMPLE MATERIALS LIST

See page 161 to figure the number of bundles of wood shingles.

Item	Quantity	Price/Unit	Total
Roofing	_____ squares	$ _____ /sq.	$ _____
Nails (to match roofing)	_____ lbs.	$ _____ /lb.	$ _____
Dripedge	_____ ft.	$ _____ /ft.	$ _____
Other flashings	_____ ft.	$ _____ /ft.	$ _____
Felt underlayment	_____ sq.	$ _____ /sq.	$ _____
60-lb. roll roofing for ice-dam protection	1 roll	$ _____ /roll	$ _____
Turpentine to wash tar off hands	1 gal.	$ _____ /gal.	$ _____
Shingle brackets (rental) if needed	_____ pair	$ _____ /pair	$ _____
Roof cement	_____ gal.	$ _____ /gal.	$ _____

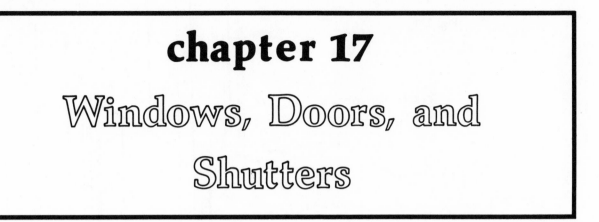

chapter 17
Windows, Doors, and Shutters

Install windows and doors after the roof but before the siding. Later the siding seals the cracks around the window and door frames. This order of work gets your house closed in as soon as possible.

WINDOWS

Windows are the most complicated and precisely built part of a house. This is because windows do many contradictory jobs. They let in the summer breeze yet keep out the winter wind. They let in the sun's heat but keep out the winter cold. They let in air but keep out bugs. Many types of windows exist to do these jobs in varying degrees. There are fixed windows, which don't open at all. Then there are various kinds of opening windows. Sliding windows include double-hung windows, which slide up and down, and horizontal sliders. Hinged windows include casements, which are hinged at the sides, awning windows, which are hinged at the top, and hoppers, which are hinged at the bottom.

Windows are a main avenue of heat loss in a house, because glass is a very poor insulator. Various methods are used to make windows keep the heat in better. The most common is double glazing, in which two layers of glass are separated by an airspace. This can be done with a removable storm sash, a permanently installed second pane of glass, or thermal (insulated) glass, which consists of two panes with a factory-sealed airspace. Even with two layers of glass, windows can account for half of the heat loss in a house. The heating efficiency of windows can be further improved by adding heavy curtains or insulated shutters to insulate the window at night or when not in use.

You can get windows three ways. You can buy new ready-made window units, complete with jamb, stops, sash, glass, storm windows, and screens, ready to install in the wall. You can buy used ready-made units, which have been removed from buildings being demolished or remodeled. You can make your own windows.

The fastest thing to do is buy ready-made units from lumber yards or millwork companies. Double-hung windows cost $50 or so. More complex types of units such as casements cost about $100 to $300. New ready-made units can be installed in an hour or two each.

Used window units can be bought through classified ads or from salvage companies for about half the cost of new units. Sometimes you can scrounge them for almost nothing where people are demolishing or remodeling a building. They will take longer to put in than new windows, because repairs will usually be needed.

Making your own windows means one of two things. First, you can install fixed panes between the regularly spaced wall studs. This is a simple and economical project that inexperienced builders should not have much trouble with. Second, you can build window units much like those you would buy, complete with frame, sill, sash, hardware, and trim. For this you will need a table saw, and you will have to know how to use it to make various angle cuts. Expect to put a lot of work into each unit. Building all the windows for a medium-sized house could easily require several weeks, but the extra work might save perhaps 60 percent to 70 percent of opening window costs. You should probably not plan to build a large number of opening windows until you have built one or two to find out whether the savings are worth it.

For most people, the best plan is to combine the above approaches. Use fixed windows as much as possible. These you can make yourself quickly and cheaply, in any size, shape, or combination. As you design and build your house, locate as many good used windows as you can. Buy or make the remaining opening windows you need.

Fig. 231

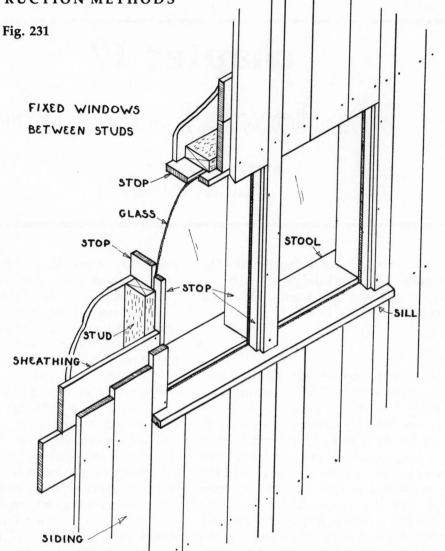

FIXED WINDOWS
BETWEEN STUDS

STOP

GLASS

STOP

STOOL

STOP

STUD

SHEATHING

SILL

SIDING

How to Make Fixed Windows Between the Studs. Figure 231 shows a row of fixed windows mounted directly between the regularly spaced wall studs. You can make an individual window or a whole row. This is the simplest window to make. It is especially practical in a cold climate, where doors and a few strategically located opening windows can provide enough ventilation. In warmer climates fixed windows can be combined with separate opening ventilators, which can be closed in winter with tight insulated doors. Figure 232 gives the basic idea (see chapter seven, Summer Cooling).

Though fixed windows can be built with a separate frame such as you would build for an opening window, mounting the pane directly on the studs has advantages. It simplifies your framing because no rough openings and no headers are needed; the glass fits between the regularly spaced studs. Because the framing is simpler, you can create a large bank of windows quickly and economically.

Figure 233 shows the parts of this system. The sill at the bottom supports the glass and slopes to the outside to shed water. The stops hold the glass in place. The bottom, inner stop is called the stool. It supports the casings, which together with the apron seal the cracks between the wall studs and the stops.

Step 1.
Blocking: Put a row of horizontal 2 × 4s between the vertical studs just below and just above where your window will be (Figure 234). The sill will sit on the bottom blocking, and the top stops will be nailed to the top blocking. Install the blocking level, straight and square.

Step 2.
Sills: Sills should be made of planed, dry, knot-free, 2-inch lumber. Two by eights or 2 × 10s from the lumber yard are fine if you pick ones with a minimum of knots. Design the sill to stick out about 1 inch past the siding and to reach to the inside edge of the framing at least. The sill is notched around the studs and sheathing at the ends. This

Fig. 232   FIXED WINDOWS WITH VENTS

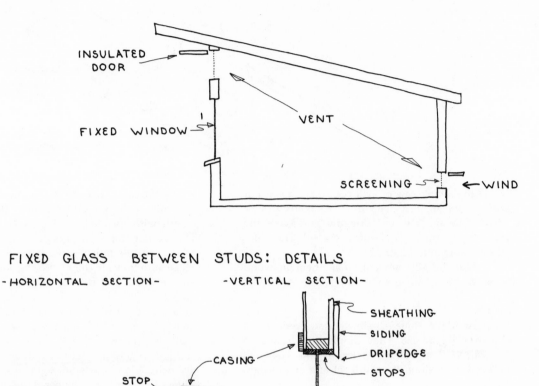

INSULATED DOOR

VENT

FIXED WINDOW

SCREENING

WIND

Fig. 233   FIXED GLASS BETWEEN STUDS: DETAILS

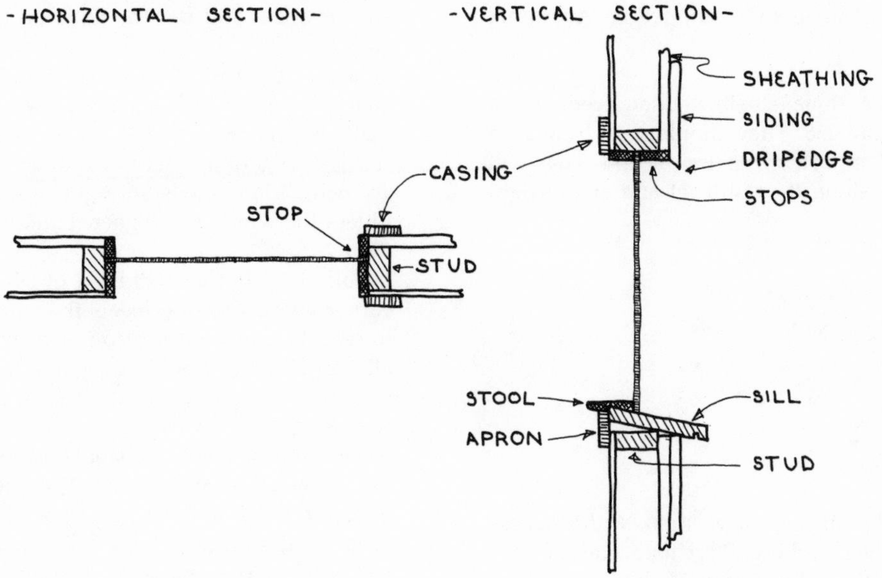

-HORIZONTAL SECTION-   -VERTICAL SECTION-

SHEATHING

SIDING

DRIPEDGE

CASING

STOPS

STOP

STUD

STOOL

SILL

APRON

STUD

BLOCKING

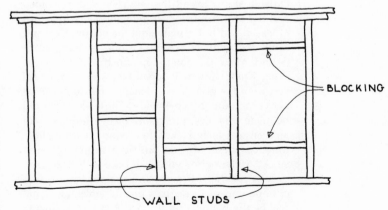

BLOCKING

will leave "ears" sticking out on the ends of the sills. These will later support the outside trim boards, called *casings*. If there are several windows in a row, they can share a common sill. In that case there will be additional notches in the middle for each intermediary stud. Since the sill will rest at a 15-degree angle, all notches will have to be cut at a 15-degree angle to match. The notches at the ends can most easily be cut with a sharp hand saw. To cut intermediary notches, if any, saw into the sill with a sharp hand saw, and chop out the notch with a hammer and chisel.

WALL STUDS

Fig. 234

Fig. 235   SILL   SILL FOR DOUBLE WINDOW

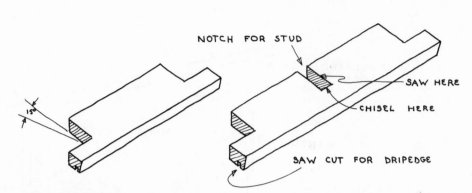

Using a table saw or skill saw, make a saw cut about ⅛ of an inch deep near the bottom outer edge of the sill. This is a dripedge and keeps the water from running back under the sill. These details are shown in Figure 235.

When the sills are cut, soak them in wood preservative for an hour or more (see Appendix G).

Step 3.

Wedges: Make some small wooden wedges, as shown in Figure 236. They should vary from zero to about ⅜ of an inch at the narrow end. They will be used to position the sill level and at the right angle.

Fig. 236

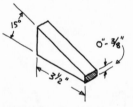

WEDGES SUPPORT SILL

Step 4.

Install sills: Place the sill in position, with the ears tight against the sheathing. Place the wedges under the sill, and slide them around until the sill is straight and level. Drive 16d finish nails down through the sill and wedges. Nail through the part of the sill that will later be covered by stops.

Step 5.

Outside stops: Install the outer stops at the sides and top of the opening. If the window is 20 inches or less in width, I usually omit the bottom stop and caulk the joint later with silicone caulking compound. Make the outer stops flush with the sheathing. Their width will depend on where on the sill you want the glass to sit. Usually, the stops will be between 1 and 2 inches wide. These stops should be made from dry, preferably planed lumber ¾ of an inch to 1 inch thick. Often leftovers from sheathing can be used. You can rip a supply of "stop stock" to the right width all at once on a table saw.

To cut the side stops to the right length, first cut one end to 15 degrees on the table saw. That will be the bottom end. In fact, it is a good idea to cut several at once to 15 degrees to minimize re-

setting the saw. Measure the length the stop should be, and cut the top end square at the appropriate length with the table saw or a small hand saw. These outer stops can be nailed into the studs with 6d galvanized finish nails every 8 or 10 inches. Make sure they are flush with the sheathing on the outsides. Cut and nail the top stop the same way.

Step 6.

Measure for glass: The glass should be approximately ¼ of an inch smaller in width and height than the opening. Glass can be bought in single strength (¹⁄₁₆ of an inch) or double strength (⅛ of an inch). I buy single strength, which is cheaper, unless the window is bigger than about 2' × 4'.

Step 7.

Install glass: Put a small bead of latex caulk in the corner where the stop meets the stud, just enough to seal the crack but not so much that it oozes out all over when you put in the glass. Put in the glass, pressing it carefully into the bed of caulking.

Step 8.

Stool: In most cases, the stool and the inside stops are not installed at this time. The inner stops go in after the stool, and the stool goes in after the interior wall surface, which is often done when all the outdoor projects such as siding are done. So take some short scraps of stop material and nail them temporarily to the studs to hold the glass in position until you get back to the job, a month or two later. A few short scraps will hold the glass well enough. However, for the sake of continuity, I will describe how to install the stool and inside stops here.

STOOL

Fig. 237

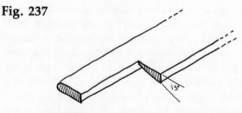

Figure 237 shows the shape of the stool. An angled notch fits over the top corner of the sill, and ears like those on the sill go around the sheetrock or paneling. These ears should be wide enough to support the interior casing that will later surround the window, plus ½ inch or 1 inch. The inside edge is often rounded off for looks. The notching is done on a table saw, and the rounding off can be done with a hand plane, router, or even with sandpaper.

When the time comes to install the stool, use a caulking gun to put a bead of silicone caulk along the bottom edge of the glass. Set the stool down on the sill against the glass. Then nail the stool to the sill with 4d finish nails.

Step 9.

Stops: Put in the interior side and top stops, made of the same material you used for exterior stops. Make them wide enough to come flush with the inside finish wall surface. Nail them with 4d finish nails. The small nail size will reduce the likelihood of breaking the glass with your hammer. Three nails per stop will be enough. No caulking is needed.

Step 10.

Casing: Inside casing is discussed in chapter twenty, since casing is part of the finish work you do later. Outside casings are done along with siding and are discussed in chapter eighteen.

How to Make Window Units.   Figure 238 shows the basic parts of any window assembled into a unit and installed in one piece. The frame consists of a sill at the bottom and the jambs at the side and top. The width of the jambs is critical. Jambs

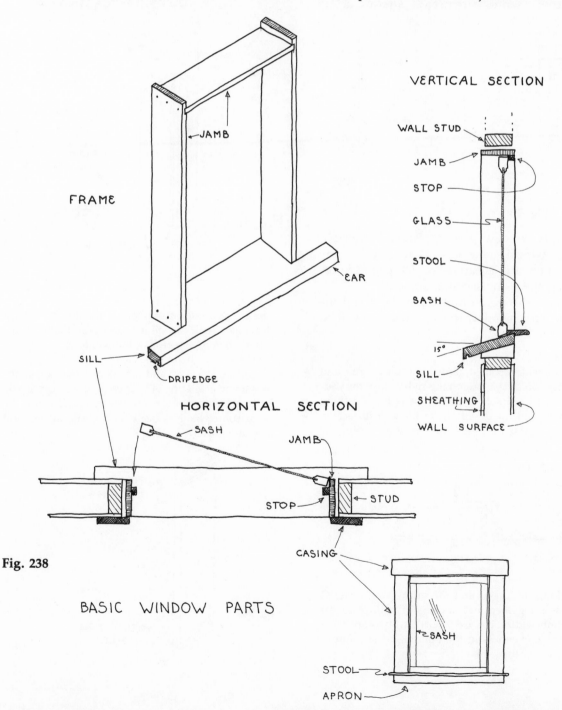

Fig. 238

BASIC WINDOW PARTS

must come flush with the sheathing on the outside and with the interior wall surface on the inside. Next comes the sash, the wooden frame that holds the glass. If the sash is on hinges, it will close against wooden stops. If the sash is a slider, it will slide in a track consisting of stoplike strips. A fixed sash can simply be sandwiched between two rows of stops. The window unit as a whole is installed in a rough opening framed into the wall. If the siding is vertical boards, there will be no exterior casing because the siding will serve that purpose. But with horizontal sidings there usually will be a casing, and this can be installed on the jambs before the unit goes in the wall (Figure 239).

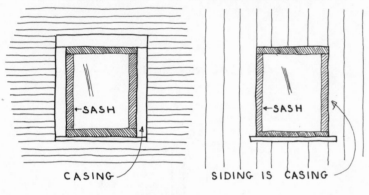

NO CASING NEEDED WITH VERTICAL SIDING

Fig. 239

The one window part you should probably not make yourself is the sash. Glazed sash is inexpensive new and cheap used. See page 150 on scrounging and using secondhand sash.

Here are the procedures for making and installing the basic window frame. Variations will be discussed later.

Step 1.
Take some dry, planed, fairly knot-free boards, and rip them on a table saw to the right width for your jambs. Jambs should come flush with the sheathing on the outside, and with the inside wall surface on the inside (Figure 240). Add the stud width, the

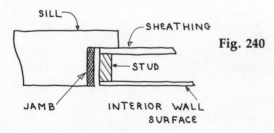

Fig. 240

sheathing thickness, and the inside wall material thickness together, and add 1/16 of an inch to get the jamb width. The extra 1/16th will compensate for any unevenness in the building or any future shrinkage of the jamb.

Step 2.
For each window, take a piece of the jamb material and draw a picture of the window parts in cross section right on the wood. This picture should look like the cross section in Figure 238. This is the easiest way to figure out all the dimensions.

Step 3.
Make the sill as described in Step 2 on page 138. Use dry, knot-free wood at least a full inch thick. It should have ears on the ends for the casing to sit on. Plan the length of the ears so that the outside casing will come flush with the end of the ears (Figure 241). The sill should overhang the siding 1 inch and come flush with the jamb on the inside.

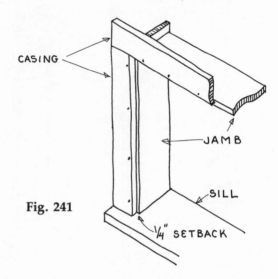

OUTSIDE CASING

Fig. 241

Make a saw cut on the bottom outside edge for a dripedge. Soak the sill in wood preservative thoroughly before assembling the window.

Step 4.
Notch the top jamb and the sill into the side jambs as shown in Figure 242. These notches can easily be made with a table saw or router. They can be made somewhat less easily with a skill saw or hand saw and chisel.

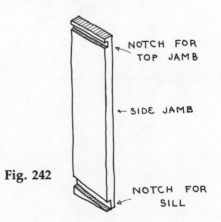

Fig. 242

Step 5.

Put some high-quality caulking such as Phenoseal, Silicon, or PL 200 in the notches and nail the frame together with 6d nails.

Step 6.

If you are using vertical boards for siding there will be no outside casing because the boards themselves will case the window. But with most kinds of horizontal siding there will be a casing attached to the frame before it is installed. Figure 241 shows what outside casings look like.

Casing will be easier if you lay the window unit down flat on a table or a pair of sawhorses. Cut the casings from dry, straight, planed boards ³/₄ of an inch or preferably 1 inch thick. Often casings will be 1 × 4 or 1 × 5 boards, but the width is really a question of appearance. Notice that the casings are set back ¹/₄ inch on the jamb. Cut the side casings first. Make a 15-degree cut on the bottom end, then cut the top square to overlap the top jamb ¹/₄ inch. Nail each side casing to the jamb with 4 or 5 8d galvanized finish nails. Then cut the top casing flush at the ends with the outside edges of the side casings, and nail it to the jambs in the same way. The top casing is made flush to avoid having to notch the siding later. As you nail, make sure the frame is square. Turn the completed unit over and caulk the joints on the inside with silicone, butyl, or some other high-quality caulking.

Step 7.

The next step is usually to attach the sash. We'll discuss how to attach sash for different types of windows in a moment. For now, let's assume the sash is attached and proceed to the installation of the assembled unit, since installation is the same with any type of sash.

Step 8.

(*For cased windows.*) Place the unit in its rough opening from the outside. The casing will automatically align the jambs flush with the sheathing. Use a level to make sure the sill is level. If not, slide a shingle under the low end. If the window has been built square, the sides will be vertical when the bottom is level. Tack the casing tentatively to the sheathing with 2 or 3 8d galvanized finish nails. Leave the nail heads up in case adjustments are necessary. Check sides and bottom again with a level, and make sure the sash opens and closes right (if an opener). Then nail the casing to the studs permanently with 4 to 8 of the 8d galvanized finish nails. Caulk where the casing meets the sheathing.

Step 8.

(*For uncased windows.*) Uncased windows can be put in their openings from the inside. They must be adjusted plumb and level by using pairs of shingles as shims between the jamb and the studs on either side. Begin by making sure the bottom sill is level. If not, slide a shingle under the low end. Also slide shingles or scraps under the sill as needed for support. Then slide 2 or 3 pairs of shin-

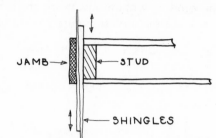

Fig. 243   ADJUST JAMB PLUMB BY SLIDING SHINGLES

gles between one jamb and the adjacent stud, as shown in Figure 243. Slide the shingles back and forth until the jamb is straight and plumb. At the same time, use a long straightedge to make sure the jamb is flush on the outside with the sheathing. Nail the jamb through the shingles with 2 or 3 16d galvanized finish nails, leaving the heads up a little so that corrections can be made later if necessary. Shim, straighten, and nail the opposite jamb. When the entire window is positioned correctly, nail each jamb with about 6 16d galvanized finish nails.

This procedure can be used with any window or door frame. If you are installing a hinged door or window, shim and attach the hinged side first.

How to Mount Sash.

WINDOW UNIT WITH A FIXED SASH. You usually put a fixed sash into a window unit when you want a large-size fixed window or have some specially beautiful odd-sized sash you want to mount fixed, such as a salvaged stained-glass window: If so, the sash can be mounted simply between a pair of stops as shown in Figure 244. These stops

Fig. 244

can be 1 inch × ³/₄ inches or any convenient size. It will be somewhat easier if you put the side stops in before the top. If the sash fits the sill tightly, omit the bottom outer stop and caulk the joint thoroughly.

OUTWARD OPENING CASEMENT. Casement windows are hinged at the side. For several reasons, an outward opening casement is one of the most widely used types of windows. First, like all casements, it opens 100 percent. With a sliding window, one sash slides behind another to leave at best a 50 percent opening. Second, since it opens outward, the sash is not in the way when open. Third, the window sash can act as a scoop to catch the breeze.

The problem with an outward opener is that the screen, which must be on the inside, is always in the way of opening and closing the window. To get around this the screen must be hinged or removable, or you must use special crank hardware to open the window without disturbing the screen. These choices are pictured in Figure 245. In either

TWO WAYS TO OPEN CASEMENT

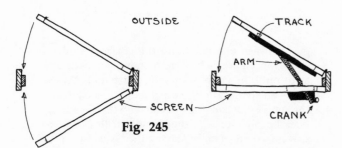

- SCREEN OPENS IN -   - CRANK OPERATOR-

OUTSIDE

TRACK

ARM

SCREEN

CRANK

Fig. 245

case, all the dimensions — such as the width of the stops — must be figured out in advance for the window to work right. Figure 246 shows typical casement dimensions.

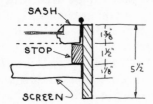

- TYPICAL CASEMENT DIMENSIONS -

SASH

STOP

SCREEN

1⅜"
1½"
⅛"
5½"

Fig. 246

Figure 247 shows two ways to mount the hinges. If the sash is flush with the outer edge of the jamb, the hinges can be mounted between the sash and jamb as in Part A. Part B shows an easier method, which can be used when the sash is set back. In either case, use 2″ × 2″ loose-pin, galvanized butt hinges if possible.

If you use a casement crank operator, you will find it cannot pull the sash tight enough for win-

Fig. 247 TWO WAYS TO MOUNT HINGES

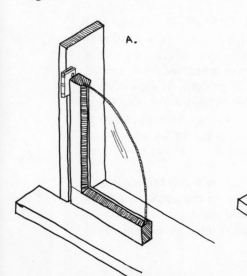

A.   B.

ter. In winter the screen is removed (perhaps replaced with a storm sash) and the sash is pulled tight with some type of latch (Figure 248).

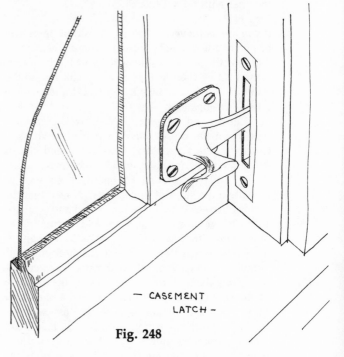

- CASEMENT LATCH -

Fig. 248

All this may seem like a lot of trouble to go through to open a window, but a window that does everything is always complicated. The trick is to find a fairly simple type of window that will do most of what you need well enough.

INWARD OPENING CASEMENT. An inward opening casement is simpler than an outward opener because the screen can be mounted fixed on the outside and the sash can open inward with no complex hardware. There are two ways to set up. First, the screen can be installed permanently between stops, as shown in Figure 249. Second,

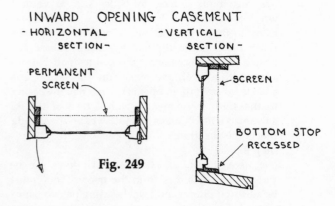

INWARD OPENING CASEMENT

- HORIZONTAL SECTION -   - VERTICAL SECTION -

PERMANENT SCREEN

SCREEN

BOTTOM STOP RECESSED

Fig. 249

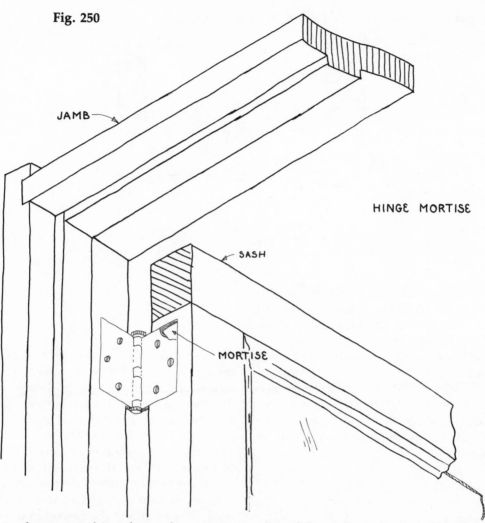

Fig. 250

JAMB

HINGE MORTISE

SASH

MORTISE

the screen can be mounted in a frame that screws to the outside of the outside casing. You can remove the screen every year to substitute a matching storm window (see page 148).

The drawback of the inward opening window is that the sash may be in the way when open. You can mount the hinges in either of the positions shown in Figure 247. But since the hinge will be visible from inside, you might want to mortise the hinges, as shown in Figure 250. This is a more trim way to mount hinges, since the crack between the sash and the jamb is small and only the barrel of the hinge is visible (see page 152 for instructions).

Recess the bottom outer stop into the bottom

edge of the sash as shown in Figure 251 to avoid trapping rainwater behind the stop.

If you want to mount the screen permanently, staple it to the outside of the stops the sash closes against. These stops will have to be flush with each other on the outside, even though the bottom one is a different shape. Cover the screening with a second outer row of stops, but omit the bottom stop, which would trap water. This can be done neatly if you put the hemmed edge of the screening *down*.

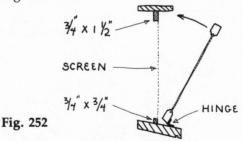

$\frac{3}{4}" \times 1\frac{1}{2}"$

SCREEN

$\frac{3}{4}" \times \frac{3}{4}"$

HINGE

Fig. 252

OUTWARD OPENING HOPPER. The main advantage of an outward opening hopper window is that it needs no crank. It will open by the force of gravity and can be closed with a nylon rope

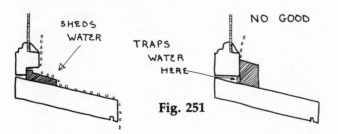

RECESS BOTTOM STOP

SHEDS WATER

NO GOOD

TRAPS WATER HERE

Fig. 251

HOPPER MECHANISM

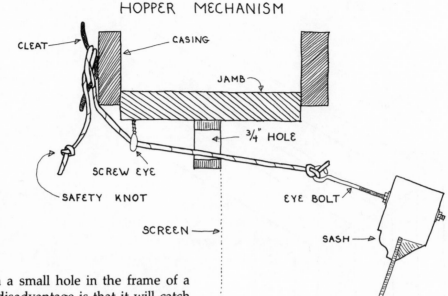

Fig. 253

threaded through a small hole in the frame of a screen. Its main disadvantage is that it will catch some water if left open in the rain. But it is the simplest type of homemade opening window.

Figure 253 shows the details of the mechanism. The top stop is 1½ inches wide instead of ¾ of an inch wide, so that you can drill a ¾-inch hole through it for the eyebolt. The eyebolt gives you something to attach the ⅛-inch nylon rope to, and you can also push against it to start the window opening.

SLIDING WINDOW DETAILS

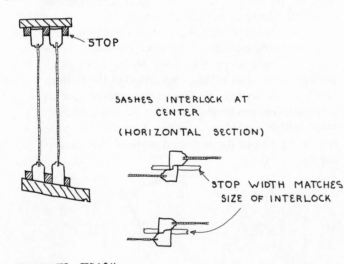

VERTICAL SECTION

STOP

SASHES INTERLOCK AT CENTER

(HORIZONTAL SECTION)

STOP WIDTH MATCHES SIZE OF INTERLOCK

ALTERNATE TRACK SYSTEM

Fig. 254

The sash will close directly against the screening and is installed after the screening. Mount the hinges after the screening and stops are in. Lay the frame down flat on sawhorses with the outer side facing up. Lay the sash and the hinges in place, and screw them to the sash and sill.

When the window is installed and cased (maybe several weeks later), install a small screw eye in the inside center of the top jamb and a small cleat to the top casing. Get some ⅛-inch nylon cord. Tie one end to the eyebolt in the sash. Then thread it through the ¾-inch hole and the screw eye. Cut the cord about 20 inches long, and tie a knot in the end. This knot prevents the window from flying too far open and breaking. The cord can be tied off to the cleat to position or close the window.

SLIDING WINDOWS. The most common sliding window is the regular double-hung window, which you should not try to build yourself. But a pair of sliders that slide horizontally is fairly easy to build. This type of window is tight and does not catch water. The screen can be on the outside without obstructing the sash. The only problem is that a sash taller than it is wide will not slide well. Sliders are best used with sash wider than they are tall.

The sash will slide in 2 adjacent tracks consisting of 3 rows of stops as shown in Figure 254. It will be easiest to understand exactly how this works if you examine an old wooden double-hung window. There must be some sort of interlock detail to close off the space between the two sash when the window is closed. The middle stop must be the same width as this interlock (Figure 254).

Fig. 255 DOUBLE GLAZING - HORIZONTAL SECTION

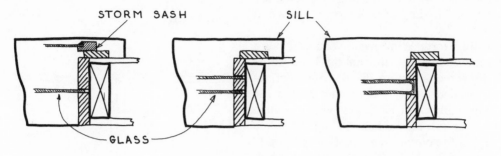

STORM SASH   TWO PANES   THERMAL GLASS

The outer bottom stops — the ones that might get rained on — should be shimmed up on neoprene washers for drainage. Nail the stops down through the hole in the washer.

The best sash for sliders are pairs of old double-hung windows turned sideways, which have the interlock mechanism built in. Some newer double-hung sash are made with a groove all the way down the edge. If you have these, use the alternate track system shown in Figure 254. Design the screen to be removable so the windows can be washed.

Double Glazing. Figure 255 shows three kinds of double glazing. The first is an ordinary storm window. The second is a second piece of glass mounted about ³⁄₄ of an inch or 1 inch away from the main piece of glass. This solution particularly applies to fixed windows. The third is insulated or thermal glass that has an airspace permanently sealed in. Glass companies can make thermal glass panels for you in any size.

With used sash, the simplest double glazing often consists of a storm window made from a used sash or which you make yourself with new glass. With fixed windows between the studs, 2 panes of glass will work well, but they tend to fog slightly.

If you are building fixed windows or openers with new sash, I suggest you find out what thermal glass will cost. Often it will not be much more than 2 panes of ordinary glass, particularly if you have several panels of the same size. Insulated glass also saves work because only one pane need be installed.

How to Build Screens. Good screens can be made out of some 1 × 2 boards. Figure 256A shows a screen design that can be used when the screen will be screwed or fastened in place rather than hinged. It consists of a 1 × 2 frame with 45-degree joints at the corners, fastened with Skotch fasteners, which are large staples you pound in with a hammer. They don't look like much, but are very strong. Put one on each side of each joint.

A hinged screen, or one that you want to look more finished, can be joined at the corners with a halflap joint and glued with Elmer's Waterproof Glue. The notch for the halflap can be made with a table saw, router, or a hand saw.

SCREENS

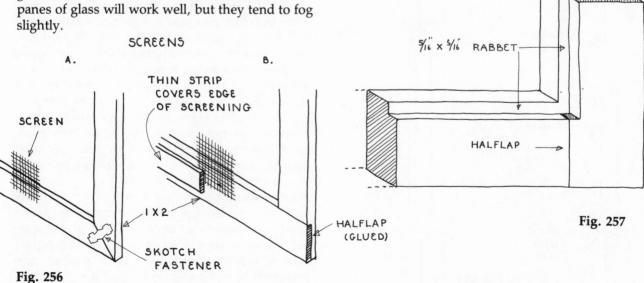

Fig. 256

Fig. 257

Attach the screening with a staple gun. Cover the edge of the screen by turning the screened side toward the building or by tacking thin wood strips over it.

How to Build Storm Windows.   You can build storm windows using the same halflap 1 × 2 frame described for screens (Figure 256–B). However, an extra notch, called a *rabbet*, is needed to bed the glass in. The rabbet can be made with the table saw, but be careful: the rabbets do not extend to the very end of the piece. They must be "stopped" at the corner and finished with hammer and chisel. The rabbet can be more easily made with a router fitted with a special rabbeting bit. If you use a router, cut the rabbet *after* the frame is glued together. The router will leave a small place in each corner that must be cut out by hand with a chisel. Mount single-strength glass in the frame with glazing compound (Figure 257).

You can attach your storm windows in a variety of ways. They can fit flush with the inside or outside casings and be held with a rotating butterfly catch, or they can overlap the inside or outside casings and be held on with screws.

How to Build Insulated Shutters.   Even with double glazing, a window will let out about ten times as much heat per square foot as an insulated wall. Heavy curtains will improve this situation if they are carefully closed when the room is not in use and at night. As Figure 258 shows, they will be more effective if they are boxed at the top to prevent circulation of air between the room and the space behind the curtain.

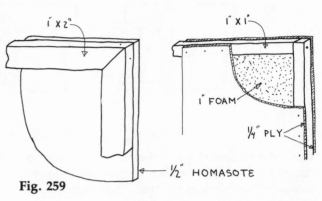

SHUTTERS

A. HOMASOTE   B. STYROFOAM

Fig. 259

Even more effective than curtains is an actual shutter. Figure 259 shows two constructions. The first has ½-inch Homasote nailed to a mitered frame of 1 × 2s. The second, which is more expensive but more effective, consists of 1 × 1 frame with 1-inch foam in the middle, covered by a layer of ¼-inch plywood on either side. You can make a thicker panel for 1½-inch or 2-inch foam the same way. Shutters go on the inside since they will be opened and closed frequently. They can be hinged to swing sideways or upward. They can slide sideways if there is wall space. Or they can clip into place and be stored on a rack or in a closet nearby when not in use (Figure 260).

Vents.   Vents used as supplementary ventilation are often built with louvers. A simpler and equally effective design is the awning vent illustrated in Figure 261.

The vent has a frame consisting of jambs and a sill like an opening window. An insulated panel with a 2-inch foam core sandwiched between two pieces of ¼-inch plywood is hinged at the top to open out. The plywood is nailed to a light 1 × 2 or 2 × 2 frame surrounding the foam. The shutter, which must be operated from outside, is held open with a ⅛-inch nylon rope hooked to the wall at the top. This door stays open all during the hot season. It closes against a set of stops just as a hopper window does, except it is upside-down. Screening is permanently stapled to the inside edge of these stops. There is an inner plywood door for cold nights. This basic idea can be varied to suit your particular situation.

Weatherstripping.   Weatherstripping is important because leakage around opening windows and doors is a major source of heat loss. Figure 262 shows a good kind of weatherstripping for most situations, which consists of a fabric strip protected by a wooden strip. Nail it up after the

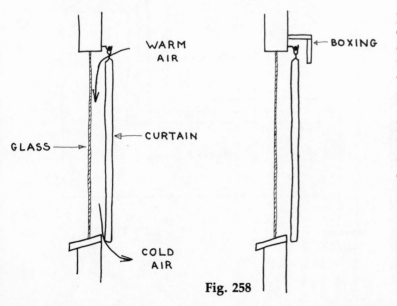

BOXING MAKES CURTAINS WORK BETTER BY REDUCING DRAFTS

Fig. 258

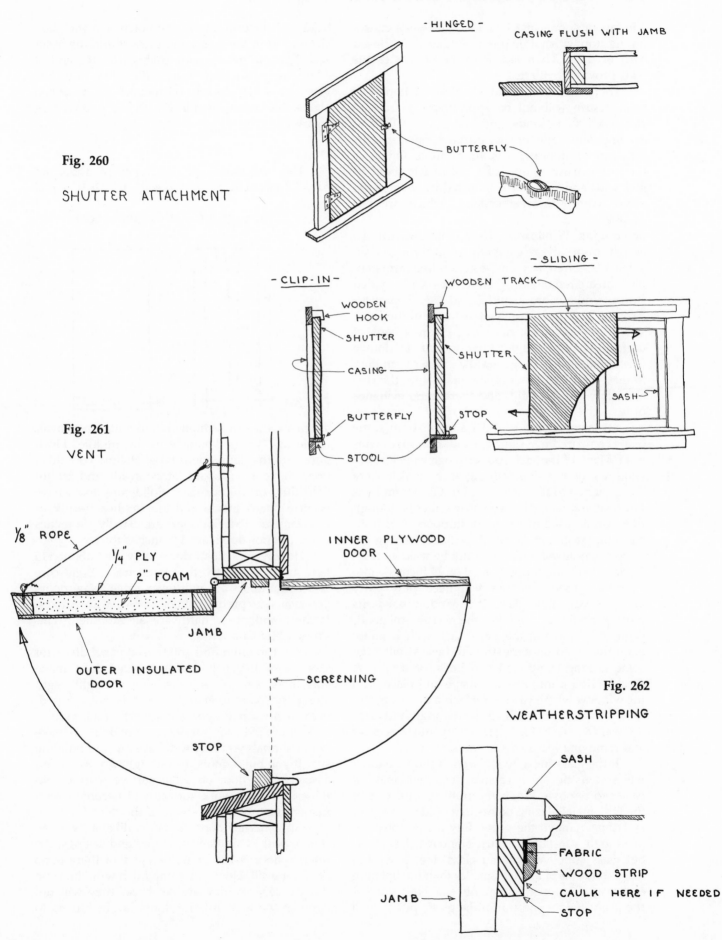

Fig. 260

SHUTTER ATTACHMENT

- HINGED -

CASING FLUSH WITH JAMB

BUTTERFLY

- CLIP-IN -

WOODEN HOOK

SHUTTER

CASING

BUTTERFLY

STOOL

- SLIDING -

WOODEN TRACK

SHUTTER

SASH

STOP

Fig. 261

VENT

⅛" ROPE

¼" PLY

2" FOAM

JAMB

OUTER INSULATED DOOR

INNER PLYWOOD DOOR

SCREENING

STOP

Fig. 262

WEATHERSTRIPPING

SASH

FABRIC

WOOD STRIP

CAULK HERE IF NEEDED

STOP

JAMB

window or door is installed. Place the weatherstrip on the stop with a little pressure against the closed sash or door. Then tack it to the stop with the nails provided with it.

There will be certain situations where this weatherstrip will not be appropriate. Hardware stores sell many kinds, and you can usually find one specially made for your purpose. Special strips are made for door bottoms, for example. One useful type consists simply of a roll of felt about 1/2 inch wide and about 1/8 of an inch thick. In general, avoid foam-type weatherstrips, which are not durable.

Scrounging Windows. Used windows can be bought from salvage companies and through classified ads. Often they can be gotten free from people who are remodeling their houses. Old wooden storm windows are plentiful and useful, particularly for fixed windows. Get as many of the same size as you can. You can either create a bank of uniform windows or use them in pairs as double glass. When possible, get used windows with their frames. Check them carefully: make sure the corner joints are still tight, and there is no evidence of rot.

A casement sash is under a lot of strain at the joints compared to a sliding, fixed, or hopper window. Many of the sash you scrounge will be storm windows or old double-hung sash, which were not designed to take much strain. Old storm windows should never be used as casements, though they can be used as sliders or hoppers. Old double-hung sash can be used as fixed, sliding, or hopper windows, but should not be used as casements if they are more than 20 or 24 inches wide.

Often used windows will need new putty and, perhaps, new glass. If a window needs its putty partially replaced, but the glass is still good, begin by removing the bad putty with a knife. Paint the wood underneath with linseed oil. Take some glazing compound and knead it until it is flexible. Roll it into a snake shape and place it on the window where you are replacing the old putty. Hold the putty knife at a 45-degree angle and draw it toward yourself, forcing the putty into the corner and removing the excess at the same time.

If the glass must be replaced, a propane torch will soften the old hardened putty and make it easier to remove. When the putty is out, extract the little metal glazing points that hold in the glass and then remove the glass. Buy a new piece of glass to fit. Most old sash use standard glass sizes, but glass suppliers will cut glass free. Make the glass about 1/16 of an inch smaller than the opening each way. For a permanent job, seal both sides of the glass. Before you put in the glass, put a small bead of latex caulking in the notch that the glass sits in. Put in the glass, and press it into the inner seal. Force in new glazing points with the end of a large screwdriver or putty knife. Then putty the glass in with glazing compound as described above. Mount the window with the puttied side facing out.

DOORS

The two most common types of doors are panel doors and flush doors (Figure 263). Panel

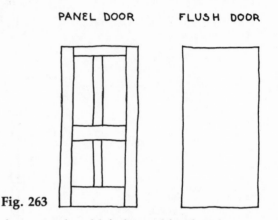

PANEL DOOR   FLUSH DOOR

Fig. 263

doors are the old-fashioned kind with a perimeter frame and molded panels in the middle. Flush doors are the flat modern type. Hollow-core flush doors have a cardboard lattice inside and are for light duty or interior uses. Solid-core doors have particle board inside and are for heavy-duty or exterior uses. Exterior doors are usually 1 3/4 inches thick; interior doors are 1 3/8 inches thick.

Hollow-core flush doors only cost about $15 new and are not worth buying used. Solid-core and panel doors are more expensive. New doors are available prehung in a frame, with hinges, latches, and other hardware all mounted. This saves a huge amount of work.

You can often find good, used panel doors for low prices. If you buy a used panel door, make sure there is no rot and the joints are tight. Sight along the door to make sure it is not warped, because a warped door is not worth anything.

Figure 264 shows three types of doors to make with materials you may well have on your building site. If you build doors, use straight dry wood and assemble the door on a flat surface. Any crookedness in your work surface will become a permanent feature of the shape of the door.

An exterior door frame is like a window frame, with a sill, jambs, stops, and casings. An interior door is the same, except that there is no need for a sill. Doors are hung flush with the jamb (Figure 265). If they are set back, they will not open all the way. Interior doors can be hinged to

Fig. 264 HOMEMADE DOORS

- INTERIOR Z-BRACE DOOR -   - EXTERIOR Z-BRACE DOOR -

TONGUE AND GROOVE
OR VERY WIDE (14"
MIN.) BOARDS,
ATTACHED TO Z-BRACE
WITH SCREWS

½" HOMASOTE

- PLYWOOD DOOR -

Fig. 265

HANG DOORS FLUSH WITH
JAMB

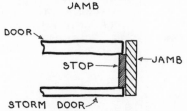

DOOR
STOP — JAMB
STORM DOOR

¼" PLY

2" FOAM

2" X 2"

open in the direction that is least obstructive. Exterior doors usually open in so a storm or screen door can open out.

Cut the jambs from straight, dry, relatively knot-free 1-inch or 2-inch lumber, or buy special jamb stock from the lumber yard. Ready-made jamb stock has no separate stops. The stop is

formed by notches taken out of the corners of the jamb (Figure 266).

You can make sills yourself out of dry, knot-free, 2 × 8s or 2 × 10s or you can buy special oak

Fig. 266 TYPICAL JAMB DIMENSIONS

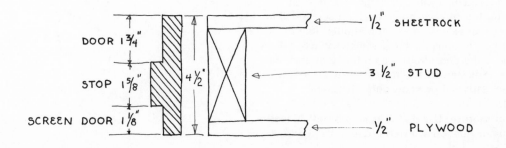

DOOR 1¾"

STOP 1⅝"

SCREEN DOOR 1⅛"

4½"

½" SHEETROCK

3½" STUD

½" PLYWOOD

Fig. 267

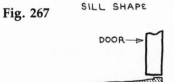

SILL SHAPE

DOOR→

sill stock, which has the shape shown in Figure 267. The little hump at the top makes water that runs under the door run out again. The sill and jamb stock you use must match the size of the door, the thickness of the door (or doors), and the thickness of the wall. The jamb should be as wide as the studs, plus the sheathing, plus the interior wall surface. Figure 266 shows a jamb made to fit a wall 4½ inches thick, with a 1¾-inch exterior door, and a 1⅛-inch screen door. Jamb stock from lumber yards is made to match these and other typical dimensions.

Most doors are hung on butt hinges notched into the door and the jamb. This notch is called a mortise (Figure 250).

How to Hang Doors on Butt Hinges

Step 1.

Build the door frame, consisting of jambs, stops, and (for exterior doors) a sill. Follow Steps 1 through 5 for windows, pages 142–43. The notch in the jamb for the sill is shown in Figure 268. Make

NOTCH IN JAMB FOR SILL

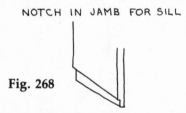

Fig. 268

the frame ³/₁₆ of an inch wider and ¼ of an inch higher than the door for clearance (Figure 269). If you are using an old door, square up the door with a skill saw or a sharp plane before making the frame.

Step 2.

When the frame is assembled and the stops in, lay the frame on the floor, hinge side up. Place the door in the frame, with a ⅛-inch crack at the top, and a ¹/₁₆-inch crack on the hinge side.

Step 3.

Mark the door and the jamb simultaneously for the hinge location, using a sharp pencil or knife and holding a square against the jamb. The line represents the top of each hinge on the door and the jamb. For an exterior door, add another line for a third hinge, locating the hinge somewhat above the middle of the door. Mark x's on the door and the jamb to indicate which side of the line each hinge goes on. This will prevent confusion later.

Step 4.

Lay out mortise. Use 3 × 3 loose-pin butt hinges for interior doors. For exterior doors use 3 3½" ×

3½" loose-pin butt hinges. Remove the door from the frame and draw each mortise on both the jamb and the door. Each mortise will be as wide as the hinge is wide and as deep as the hinge leaf is thick. The hinge itself can be used as a template for marking the door and jamb. Plan the mortise so that the hinge will stick out beyond the jamb by about ½ inch. This overhang makes room for the pin and provides clearance so that the door can open without hitting the casing (Figure 269).

Step 5.

With a sharp knife or a hammer and chisel, cut around the perimeter of the mortise, as shown in Figure 270. After cutting down on all 3 sides, remove the scrap as shown in Figure 270. A sharp chisel is the key to this procedure.

Step 6.

Remove the hinge pins and screw each leaf into its mortise with only 1 screw in each hinge.

Step 7.

Test-fit the door in the jamb by replacing the pins in the hinges and making any needed adjustments. Then put in the other screws.

Fig. 269

LAYOUT FOR HINGE MORTISING

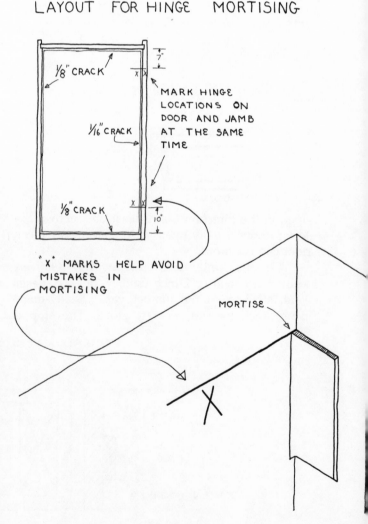

⅛" CRACK

¹/₁₆" CRACK

⅛" CRACK

MARK HINGE LOCATIONS ON DOOR AND JAMB AT THE SAME TIME

"X" MARKS HELP AVOID MISTAKES IN MORTISING

MORTISE

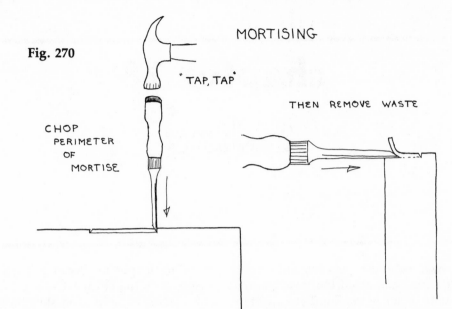

MORTISING

Fig. 270

CHOP PERIMETER OF MORTISE

"TAP, TAP"

THEN REMOVE WASTE

Step 8.

Mount the door frame in its rough opening with the door on its hinges. Adjust the door plumb and straight with shingles, using Step 8 for windows as shown on page 143. Make sure the door opens and closes correctly before you nail the frame to the studs permanently.

Doors are also occasionally hung on strap or T-hinges (Figure 271). They are not mortised in

STRAP HINGE   T HINGE

Fig. 271

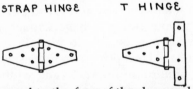

but simply screwed to the face of the door and the door casing. They can be used with homemade Z-brace doors or panel doors, but flush doors are not designed to be used with them.

SAMPLE MATERIALS LIST

You do not need elaborate drawings of window or door constructions. Make a horizontal and vertical cross section of each type you build to clarify the design and avoid errors (Figure 249). It is also a good idea to make a detailed exterior elevation of your house, showing siding, windows, casings, and other details in scale. It will help you find the width of casing that will look best.

Prices for new windows and doors can be obtained from a lumber yard or from a company that manufactures or distributes windows or doors. These millwork companies will usually give a better price than lumber yards. Get prices for sheet glass from a glass company. It pays to shop around for these items.

Homemade window and door frames can be built with lumber bought specially for the purpose. But if you are using any quantity of dry, planed boards for other parts of your house, it is a good plan to order a few hundred extra feet for window making and other fine work. As you build, choose the straightest and most knot-free boards and carefully sticker them up in a dry, clean place to be used for windows and similar projects.

Materials for Homemade Windows

Item	Quantity	Price/Unit	Total Cost
Sill stock (2 × 8 or 2 × 10, knot-free, planed, dry wood)	_____	$ _____ /bd. ft.	$ _____
Wood preservative for sills	2 gal.	$ _____ /gal.	$ _____
Lumber for jambs, casings, and stops About 25 bd. ft./window	_____	$ _____ /bd. ft.	$ _____
Glass	_____	$ _____ /	$ _____
Latex caulk for stops, 1 tube per every 6 windows	_____	$ _____ /tube	$ _____
Silicon caulk for bottom outer stops	1 tube	$ _____ /tube	$ _____
Casement window operators, if any	_____	$ _____ /each	$ _____
Hinges (2 × 2 loose pins galvanized butts)	_____	$ _____ /pair	$ _____
Other hardware (eye bolts, latches, etc.)	_____	$ _____ /	$ _____
Aluminum screening	_____	$ _____ /	$ _____
Weatherstripping	_____	$ _____ /	$ _____

chapter 18
Siding

If your work schedule permits, side your house after you roof it and put the windows in, and before you do inside work. But if you need to move into your house soon, siding can be delayed and you can proceed to the inside work. Plywood sheathing may be left uncovered indefinitely if you caulk the joints, particularly those above the windows. Board sheathing may be left unsided if you put flashings over the top windows and door casings and then cover the sheathing with 15-pound felt paper (tarpaper). Batten the felt down with scraps to keep the wind from carrying it away.

Figure 272 shows several common sidings. The top row shows boards used in various ways. These options, which are discussed in more detail later in this chapter, are economical and quick. Clapboards and shingles cost more and take longer to install. An option pictured in Figure 283 is textured plywood, such as T–111. This consists of plywood grooved on the outside to resemble vertical boards. Textured plywood is the fastest type of siding to put up because it goes up in large sheets. It is the cheapest siding because a single layer serves as siding and sheathing combined.

VERTICAL BOARDS

Vertical boarding is one of the simplest sidings. If you live in an area where there are sawmills, it will probably be one of the most economical as well. Siding boards should be air-dried or kiln-dried, unless the cracks will be covered with battens. Siding boards should also be planed if possible, because rough boards are not uniform in width and will take forever to put up well. If you want your siding to have a rough texture, a local sawmill may be able to provide you with boards that have been planed on three sides. Such boards are uniform in thickness and width, but one face is rough for appearance.

Sheathing under vertical boards can be 1-inch boards or exterior-grade plywood at least 1/2 inch

SIDING

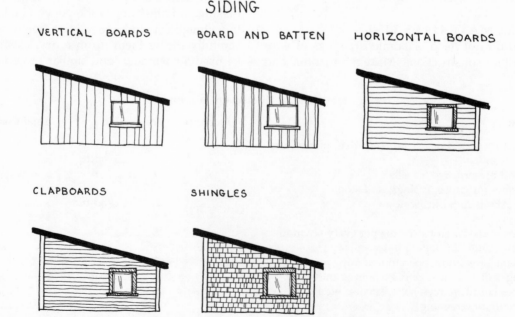

VERTICAL BOARDS   BOARD AND BATTEN   HORIZONTAL BOARDS

CLAPBOARDS   SHINGLES

Fig. 272

Fig. 273   VERTICAL SIDING VARIATIONS

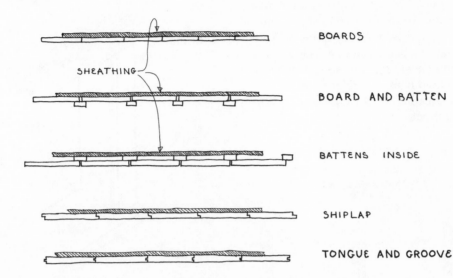

thick. Half-inch insulation boards will not hold nails well enough to keep vertical boards in place. Figure 273 shows typical vertical siding details. Notice that there are no casings: the siding itself will cover the cracks around windows neatly.

How to Apply Vertical Siding.

Step 1.
Scaffolding: Make some kind of staging or scaffolding to work from. If your house is low you can work easily from a stepladder or a plank across two sawhorses. But on a high wall, build a scaffolding (see chapter twenty-three).

Step 2.
15-pound felt: Put up tarpaper, which is more properly called 15-pound felt. On low, relatively accessible walls apply the felt horizontally, working from the bottom up and lapping the sheets about 6 inches. On high walls, it will be easier to install the paper vertically as you put up the siding, one or two sheets at a time. Attach the felt with short roofing nails or staples. The wind can rip the paper off, so hold it down with scrap lumber if it will be left exposed for long.

Step 3.
Siding: Start from one side and work toward the other. Make sure the first row is very straight and plumb, and nail it with 2 8d galvanized common nails every 2 or 3 feet. Board siding has a tendency to work loose in time, especially on the sunny side of the house. This is not too severe a problem over board sheathing, and you can secure the boards by driving the nails at various angles. But with ½-inch plywood sheathing, simply driving the nails at angles will not be enough. If the walls are not yet insulated, go inside the house and bend the nails over with your hammer. Should this be impossible because the walls are covered inside, use more

angled nails. Whatever nailing method you use, line the nails up neatly for a good-looking job.

If the house is so tall that one board will not make it from bottom to top, join the boards at a 45-degree angle as shown in Figure 274. This will make the joint shed water. Any two boards in the

Fig. 274

VERTICAL SIDING

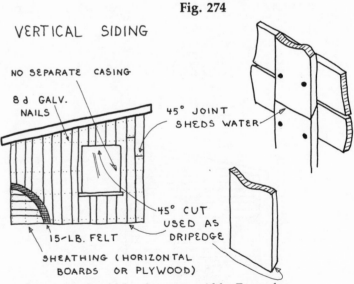

same row should be the same width. Every few rows, use a level to make sure the boards are plumb. If they are not, you can correct by leaving slight cracks between the next few boards at one end only, making the other end as tight as possible. No casing is needed around window and door openings. Above windows and doors, cut the boards at a 45-degree angle to create a dripedge, as in Figure 274. Do the same at the bottom of each row. If you have two power saws available, set one square and one at 45 degrees to avoid constant resetting.

HORIZONTAL BOARD SIDING

Figure 275 shows various types of horizontal board sidings. Any horizontal board siding must be tongue and groove or shiplapped to shed water, and the boards should be well air-dried or kiln-dried. Since horizontal boards can be nailed to the studs through the sheathing, the sheathing itself does not have to hold nails. Therefore you can use insulation board sheathing. Figure 276 shows horizontal siding methods.

Fig. 275

HORIZONTAL SIDING VARIATIONS

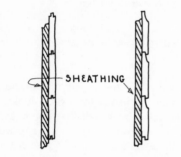

SHEATHING

SHIPLAP BOARDS   TONGUE AND GROOVE BOARDS   DROP SIDING   NOVELTY SIDING

HORIZONTAL SIDING

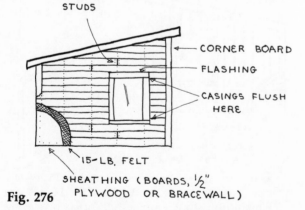

ALL JOINTS OVER STUDS

CORNER BOARD

FLASHING

CASINGS FLUSH HERE

15-LB. FELT

SHEATHING (BOARDS, ½" PLYWOOD OR BRACEWALL)

Fig. 276

How to Apply Horizontal Board Siding

Step 1.
15-lb. felt: Put up 15-pound felt over the sheathing in horizontal rows, working from the bottom up and lapping the sheets about 6 inches.

Step 2.
Window and door casings: Plain shiplap or tongue

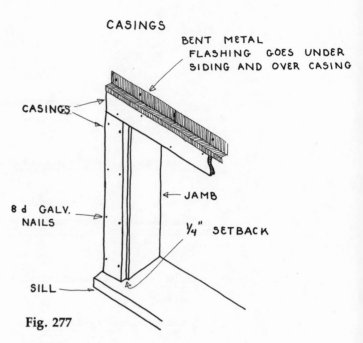

CASINGS

BENT METAL FLASHING GOES UNDER SIDING AND OVER CASING

CASINGS

8 d GALV. NAILS

JAMB

¼" SETBACK

SILL

Fig. 277

and groove boards may be put up with no casings if you want. But novelty siding, drop siding, and similar types of siding will not look or fit right without casings. Casings go up before the siding. As Figure 277 shows, the side casing should be flush at the top with the top casing and at the bottom with the sill. This will avoid notching the siding. If possible, make the casings out of wood somewhat thicker than the siding. If the siding is ³/4 of an inch, the casing can be about 1 inch. If the thicknesses are the same, you may have trouble getting a neat fit.

The width of casing you choose will affect the looks of the house. You can choose a casing width by making scale elevation drawings showing various possibilities or by casing a window with a particular size and seeing how it looks.

You will be putting up the casings so as to leave a ¼-inch setback, or *reveal*, all the way around the jamb (Figure 277). This will look better than if you try to make the casings flush with the jambs.

Put up the side casings first. Cut a 15-degree angle at the bottom to fit the sill. Then cut the side casings to length so that they run from the sill up to the top jamb, lapping over the top jamb by ¼ inch to create the ¼-inch setback. Set the side casings back ¼ inch on the side jamb and nail them on with 8d galvanized common nails. Cut the top casing to come flush with the outside edges of the side casings, and nail it on as you did the sides.
Step 3.
Flashing: A bent metal flashing goes above every top casing that might get rained on. You can make these yourself, by bending strips of aluminum, but they are sold by lumber yards ready-made to fit common thicknesses of casing.
Step 4.
Corner boards: Corner boards are shown in Figure

276. You can put up horizontal sidings with miter joints at the corners, but the corners will be easier if you use corner boards. As with casings, the width of the corner board will effect how the house looks, so choose it carefully. If you use drop siding or some other siding that is not flat on the outside, nail the corner boards up before the siding, just as you did the casings. Like the casings, the corner boards should be 1/4 of an inch thicker than the siding if possible, because the siding will butt to them. Before you install the corner boards, wrap the corners tightly with 15-pound felt. With sidings that are flat on the outside, such as plain shiplap boards, the corner boards can be put on after and on top of the siding. In that case, the corner boards need not be of thicker wood.

Step 5.

Siding: Horizontal siding can go up much like vertical siding. Start at the bottom, get the first row straight, and work up row by row. Put 2 8d galvanized common nails into each stud, driving them at varying angles. Fit the boards as tightly as possible, and check periodically to make sure they are parallel with the house frame. If not, make adjustments as you would with vertical boards.

The lower rows can be put up from the ground. Then you work on planks stretched across two or more sawhorses. Eventually you will need a scaffold (see chapter twenty-three).

CLAPBOARDS

Clapboards are one of the nicest kinds of sidings. The following instructions are for the standard 6-inch clapboards, but you can use the same methods to put up wider sizes, sometimes called bevel siding, except as noted below. You can buy redwood clapboards from a local lumber yard. They will be expensive. Sometimes small sawmills will saw out less expensive clapboards using native woods. Clapboards can be used over a sheathing of boards or 1/2-inch plywood. Bevel siding can be put up over insulation board because, being thicker, it can be nailed through to the studs with bigger nails. Figure 278 shows typical clapboard details.

CLAPBOARDS

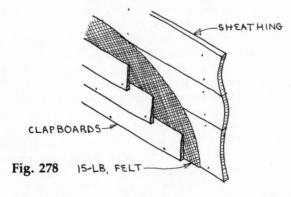

Fig. 278 15-LB. FELT SHEATHING CLAPBOARDS

How to Apply Clapboards

Step 1.
Paper: Staple up 15-pound felt paper horizontally, lapping the courses about 6 inches.

Step 2.
Casing and corner boards: Case the windows and put up corner boards as in Steps 2 through 4 beginning on page 156. Like other horizontal sidings, clapboards can be put up without them by mitering the corner joints, but this will take much longer.

Step 3.
Layout: Clapboards come in a variety of sizes, but the common size is 1/2 inch thick at the butt by 5 1/2 inches wide. This is nominally a 6-inch clapboard. Clapboards must overlap at least 1/2 inch. So with 6-inch clapboards there will be an exposure of from 3 inches (very uncommon) to 5 inches. I like a 4-inch exposure.

After you decide what exposure you like, figure out where the rows will be and mark the location of each row on the corner boards and casings. Try to make the bottom edge of a row come out even with, or slightly above, the top casing of windows and doors, and even with the bottom of the window sills (Figure 278). This will make the work quicker, easier, and neater. Your chosen weather exposure will usually not fit in perfectly with this objective, but often a small adjustment will make things come out right. For example, suppose you have chosen a 4-inch exposure and your layout comes out even with the sill of a window 46 1/2 inches high. Twelve rows of 4-inch exposure will come out at 48 inches, which is too high. But if the interval is adjusted to 3 7/8 inches, the top row will come out just right. Even an adjustment of 1/4 inch is almost unnoticeable. If a choice must be made, it is more important to make the rows come out right at the top than the bottom.

Step 4.
Nailing strip: Nail a narrow strip as thick as the thin end of the clapboards to the bottom edge of the wall. The first row will be shimmed up on this strip.

Step 5.
Nailing: Different ways of nailing up clapboards are used in different places. This is the way I know. Use a chalk line to locate the bottom of each row. Nail the clapboards with 5d galvanized box nails every 10 inches (more or less) nailing about 1/2 inch above the bottom of the clapboard (Figure 279). Stagger the joints at least 12 inches. The clapboards should fit tight at the ends. Use a small, fine-toothed hand saw, a backsaw, or a saber saw to cut them. Nail neatly, trying to establish an attractive nailing pattern. As in most finish work, the difference between a good job and a sloppy job is the care taken nailing.

If you are using bevel siding, which is 3/4 of an inch thick at the butt and wider than regular clapboards, nail 8d galvanized nails into each stud, and make all joints occur over the studs.

CLAPBOARD DETAILS   **Fig. 279**

CORNER BOARD

FLASHING

LINE UP COURSES
WITH WINDOW

5 d GALV.
BOX NAILS
10" O.C.

STAGGER JOINTS

Step 6.
Molding: Often there will be a molding to cover the joint between the top row of clapboards and the overhang of the roof. This is usually a complicated-shape molding, but a simple 1 × 1 will do as well. If the clapboard fits perfectly no molding is needed.

SHINGLES

Number 1 or number 2 grade cedar shingles (Figure 280) are perhaps the best-looking and most durable wooden siding. Unfortunately, they are expensive and take a long time to put up. Figure 281 shows typical shingle details, many of which are the same for clapboards. Shingles can be put up over a sheathing of 1-inch boards or ½-inch exterior-grade plywood.

SHINGLE

Fig. 280

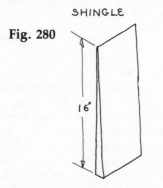

16"

How to Apply Shingle Siding.

Step 1.
15-pound felt: Put up 15-pound felt, lapping the courses about 6 inches.
Step 2.
Casing and corner boards: Case windows and doors, and install corner boards as for horizontal board siding (see Steps 2 through 4, pages 156–57).
Step 3.
Layout: Lay out the shingle courses as you would with clapboards (see Step 3 on page 157). Sixteen-inch shingles can be put up with 4 to 7½-inch exposure.
Step 4.
Start shingling by putting up a doubled bottom row, overhanging the sheathing at the bottom by ½ inch (Figure 281). Make sure the vertical joints are staggered. Shingles are blind-nailed with 5d galvanized box nails. (*Blind nailing* means that each row covers up the nails used to secure the previous row.) The nails should be about ¾ of an inch above where the bottom edge of the next row will be and about ¾ of an inch in from the edge of the shingle. Shingles up to 8 inches wide get 2 nails each, and shingles over 8 inches get 3 nails. The only visible nails will be in the topmost row.

Leave a ⅛-inch crack between shingles. When shingles get wet, they expand sideways. If the crack is not there, the shingles can buckle. However, do not leave any cracks at all where the shingles meet the corner boards or casings.

The shingles may be located with a chalk line. However, it is easiest to make a chalk line and then nail a straight board such as a 1 × 3 directly below the line for the shingles to sit on while they are positioned and nailed.

The vertical joints must be well staggered. If you look at Figure 282, each joint in Row B should be at least 1 inch away from any joint in Row A, and any joint in Row C should be at least 1 inch away from any joint in either Row B or Row A.

Shingles can be cut with a hand saw or saber saw, or neatly split with a hatchet or knife, and trimmed to exact size with a small 6-inch block plane. Choose a method of cutting that you can do quickly without too much climbing up and down.

Fig. 281

SHINGLE DETAILS

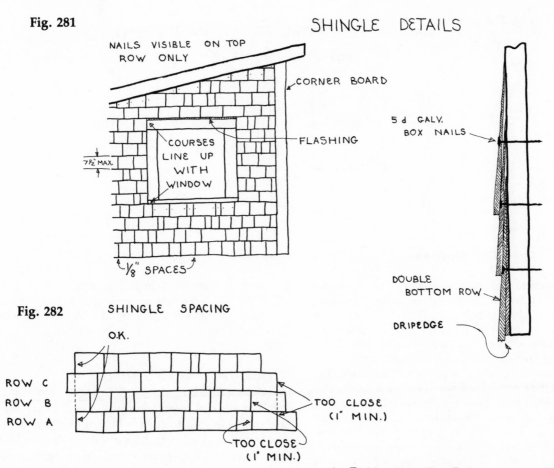

NAILS VISIBLE ON TOP
ROW ONLY

CORNER BOARD

COURSES
LINE UP
WITH
WINDOW

7½ MAX.

FLASHING

⅛" SPACES

5 d GALV.
BOX NAILS

DOUBLE
BOTTOM ROW

DRIPEDGE

Fig. 282   SHINGLE SPACING

O.K.

ROW C
ROW B
ROW A

TOO CLOSE
(1" MIN.)

TOO CLOSE
(1" MIN.)

Step 5.
Molding: A molding can be used to neaten the joint
between the top row of shingles and the roof overhang.

TEXTURED PLYWOOD

Textured plywood comes in a variety of designs. If you want to use it, see what local suppliers have to offer. It can be nailed directly to the
studs with no felt paper underneath.

How to Apply Textured Plywood

Step 1.
Planning: Before you buy siding first figure out
what length sheets will minimize horizontal joints.
Sometimes textured plywood will be available in
extra-long sheets. Second, figure out how you will
flash the tops of windows and doors. With other
sidings, the flashing goes on top of the sheathing
after the window is installed and the siding covers
the upper part of the flashing. You can't do this
with a single layer of plywood because the windows go in *after* the siding. If the top casing is well
covered by the roof overhang, you can perhaps
dispense with the flashing and simply caulk the
top casing with Phenoseal, butyl, silicon, or other
quality caulking. Otherwise you will have to figure
out a method for getting the flashing into the position shown in Figure 283, namely, lapping under

FLASHING TEXTURED PLYWOOD
SIDING

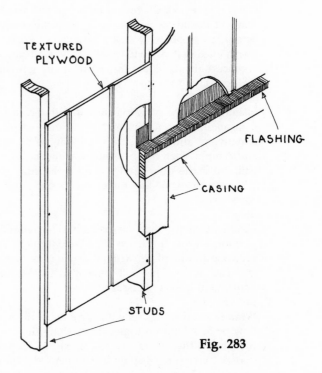

TEXTURED
PLYWOOD

FLASHING

CASING

STUDS

Fig. 283

Fig. 284

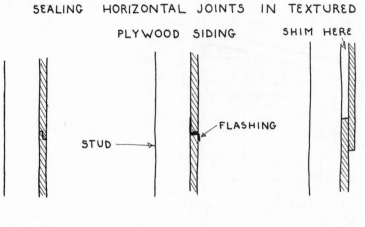

SEALING HORIZONTAL JOINTS IN TEXTURED

PLYWOOD SIDING

SHIM HERE

FLASHING

STUD

SHIPLAP   FLASHING   SHIM AND LAP

the plywood and over the casing. One way to do this is to leave the plywood directly above the windows un-nailed temporarily. Slide the flashing up under the plywood — again without nailing it. Install the window, slipping it up under the flashing. Finally, adjust the flashing down tight to the window casing, and then nail everything together.

If the plywood will have horizontal joints, you must plan how they will be sealed. Figure 284 shows three ways this can be done, depending on how you want the siding to look and how the brand of siding you buy is designed: (1) the joint can be shiplapped if the siding comes that way; (2) the joint can be flashed with a special flashing; (3) the top layer can be shimmed out so that it laps the bottom layer.

Step 2.

Cutting plywood: Chapter twenty-four shows a jig that will enable you to make long, perfectly straight cuts in plywood with a skill saw. This gadget is worth making if you will be using plywood siding, because tight joints are important if the job is to look good.

Step 3.

Nailing: Nail the plywood up with 6d galvanized nails about every 10 inches. Nail up the first piece tentatively, and make sure everything is straight and plumb. Then finish nailing the sheet. Do not nail above the doors and windows, because you will soon need to slide the casing flashing in the crack.

Step 4.

Casing flashings: Slide the casing flashings into the position shown in Figure 283. Tack through the plywood in one place, without driving the nail all the way down. This will allow you to make an adjustment later if necessary.

Step 5.

Windows and doors: Slide the top edge of the window or door unit up under the flashing first, and then bring the bottom in. Check the window or door to make sure it is plumb and opens and closes properly. Make any necessary adjustments in the

flashing in the top to make it fit right. Nail the unit in place through the casing with 10d galvanized box nails. Caulk the unit all around with a good grade of caulking.

FINISHING WOOD SIDING

Wooden siding does not have to have any finish at all. If it is put up right, it will never rot. The sun will tend to turn it brown and the parts that get rained on will become gray. If you like this weathered appearance, as I do, a finish may be just an unnecessary expense. But there is one problem that a finish can help. Sometimes, on the sunny side of a house, the alternate wetting and drying of the siding by rain and sun will tend to work some of the nails out, enabling the siding to warp. This is less of a problem if the boards are quite dry to begin with and if they are well nailed. But when the nailing is not ideal and the boards perhaps a little green, the siding can look quite bad a few months after installation.

Good nailing will reduce warping. So will using a finish that prevents the wood from repeatedly absorbing water, such as a paint or water-repellent wood preservative. Water-repellent preservatives are penetrating finishes that soak in rather than coat the surface. These finishes are available clear or mixed with various pigments, so they can double as stains (see Appendix G, on Wood Preserving).

SAMPLE MATERIALS LIST

For planning purposes you do not need any special drawings. However, if you are unsure what kind of siding to use, one way to study the question is to make scale elevations with various kinds of siding materials drawn in. This will show you to some extent how each might look.

Before making a materials list, find the area of wall in square feet to be covered by looking at your elevation drawings. If you are using boards, 125 percent of the area gives the number of board feet you need. Clapboards are also sold by the board foot. For a 4-inch exposure, 170 percent of the area gives the board feet needed. Shingles are sold by the bundle. Their number can be estimated according to the following chart:

Shingle Exposure	# of bundles per 100 sq.ft. area
4″	5
5″	4
6″	$3\frac{1}{3}$
7″	$2\frac{9}{10}$

Your lumber dealer can help you figure out what you need for other types of siding. It's a good idea to estimate the amount of nails you will need for siding, because you use them up so fast. For board siding, order 2 pounds of 8d galvanized common nails per 100 square feet of area. For clapboards, order 2 pounds of 5d galvanized box nails per 100 square feet. For shingles, order 4 pounds of 5d galvanized box nails per 100 square feet.

Sample Materials List

Item	Quantity	Price/Unit	Total Cost
Siding	_____	$ _____ /	$ _____
Nails	_____	$ _____ /lb.	$ _____
Felt paper	_____	$ _____ /roll	$ _____
Flashings	_____	$ _____ /	$ _____
Corner boards (full inch, if possible)	_____	$ _____ /bd.ft.	$ _____
Casings (full inch, if possible)	_____	$ _____ /bd.ft.	$ _____
Molding at top, if any	_____	$ _____ /	$ _____

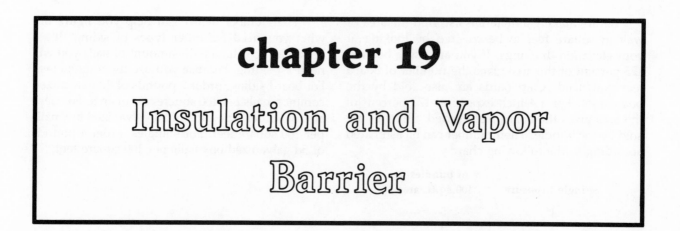

chapter 19
Insulation and Vapor Barrier

In winter, insulation slows down the rate at which the heat of the house is lost to the cooler air outside. In summer it keeps the hotter outside air from heating up the inside of the house. Every material insulates to some extent, but some are far better than others. Good insulators have a maximum of *dead-air spaces*; small pores or cavities within the structure of the material that provide the obstacle to heat transfer. Good insulators, like warm clothes, are lightweight and porous. Wood and carpeting are effective insulators. Dense materials like glass, metal, and masonry are poor. Materials sold as commercial insulation (foam, fiberglass) are even better insulators than wood because they have many times more dead-air spaces.

WHERE TO INSULATE

Insulation should surround the heated part of the house. Usually all exterior walls will be insulated. If a cellar is unheated, the first floor will be insulated. If the cellar is heated, the first floor will be uninsulated. Similarly, if an attic is unheated, the attic floor will be insulated but not the roof. If the attic is heated, the floor is not insulated, but the roof is.

WHAT KIND OF INSULATION AND HOW MUCH

When you think about what kind of insulation to use, and how much, you must weigh various factors. First, the insulation value of any insulator depends on the thickness. Two inches are twice as good as 1 inch of the same insulation. Thus, you want to have as much thickness as is practical. This will usually be limited by how the house is being built. If your wall is 4 inches thick, for example, you can only fit 4 inches of insulation into it. Second, some insulators are more effective than others, per inch of thickness. Two inches of one kind might be as good as 4 inches of another. Third, sometimes one type of insulation will be much more simple and convenient to install than another. Choose a kind of insulation that fits the way you are building your house. Finally, think about what a particular insulation will cost for the thickness you need.

Appendix E gives relative insulating value of insulations and building materials and explains how to use these figures to compute your heat loss with different designs. These computations will be particularly useful to people interested in solar heat or other experimental design ideas. But even if you are building a conventional house, Appendix E will help you understand how heat loss works, which will help you build a better house. These things might become clearer if we look at the three types of insulation commonly used in building: fiberglass, rigid foam, and insulation board.

Fiberglass. In most cases the easiest, fastest, and most economical insulation is fiberglass blanket insulation. It is stapled (or sometimes just stuffed) between the framing members of the building before the inside finish surface is put on. It comes in 2-, 3-, and 6-inch thicknesses and in widths to match the common 16- and 24-inch spacing of house frames. Usually fiberglass comes with an aluminum foil backing, which is faced toward the inside of the house to reflect radiant heat back into the house and serve as a vapor barrier (Figure 285).

FIBERGLASS

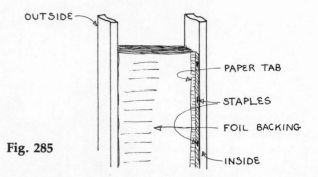

Fig. 285

Until recently, it has been standard practice to use 3 inches of fiberglass in walls and 6 inches in ceilings and floors. Some designers now recommend 6 inches in the walls, and 8 or 10 inches in the roof. This means framing walls with 2 × 6s, since a 2 × 4 wall does not have room for 6 inches of insulation. With fuel costs going up, the added building costs will be offset by eventual savings in heating costs. Even if you have wood heat and your own supply of wood, you will save on the work of cutting firewood. For a typical house of about 1000 square feet, the extra cost would be in the neighborhood of $400.

Rigid Foam Insulation. Foam insulation is sometimes sprayed in place, but for the owner-builder the practical foams will usually be foam board in large 2′ × 8′ or 4′ × 8′ sheets. Common thicknesses are ½, 1, 1½, and 2 inches. There are three types of foam board in common use. The most common type is expanded polystyrene, often called *beadboard*. It consists of molded beads of styrene insulation. Beadboard is always white and is the same material foam coffee cups are made of. Per inch of thickness, it insulates about 25 percent better than ordinary fiberglass. One inch of beadboard costs about as much as 3 inches of ordinary fiberglass, which makes beadboard significantly more expensive per unit of insulating value. Beadboard is sometimes erroneously referred to as Styrofoam.

Real Styrofoam is bluish in color and is only made by Dow Chemical Company. Per inch of thickness it insulates about 60 percent better than fiberglass, which makes it a lot more effective than beadboard. However, it costs roughly twice what beadboard costs.

The third common foam is urethane foam, which is greenish yellow in color. Per inch of thickness, it is about twice as effective as fiberglass, but it costs even more than Styrofoam.

Check the color of any foam you buy to make sure you are getting what you want.

Though foams are more effective than fiberglass per inch of thickness, they are rarely used as the primary wall or roof insulation because their high cost makes them less effective per dollar. Foam is primarily used where its rigidity and compactness provide special design economies and advantages. Though you could crush foam if you stepped on it firmly with your heel, it has enough strength to support a well-distributed load. For example, foam is often put under or next to concrete foundations to insulate a basement or concrete slab floor. Though the foam is being pressed between the earth and the concrete, it is stiff enough to keep its shape because the pressure is even. Fiberglass would collapse immediately under the slightest pressure. Foam is also used with special building systems, such as the exposed-beam roof design described in chapter fifteen. In such systems the savings in labor and lumber can outweigh the added cost of foam itself. If you want to use foam in your design, discuss your plans with an experienced person who can help you make sure your system will work well and can be built easily.

Insulation Board. Insulation board is the general name for a variety of light, soft, but fairly strong materials with a consistency somewhat like shirt cardboard. It comes in a 4′ × 8′ and larger sheets. The most common thickness is ½ inch. Homasote (beaverboard), which is often used for bulletin boards, and Bracewall, a black sheathing board, are examples. Insulation board is soft and light enough to be good insulation (though inferior to fiberglass or foam) yet heavy enough to have some strength (though weaker than wood). It is rarely used as a primary structural or insulating element, but it is very useful where the structural needs are not too great, and the insulation value or lightness is an advantage. For example, Homasote is used to cover ceilings or walls in rooms where the surfaces will not be subject to much abuse. Bracewall is used as sheathing under certain types of siding. Even though it is not as strong as plywood or boards, the fact that Bracewall comes in large sheets means that it gives good diagonal bracing to the house. Its insulating value and lightness are further benefits. These materials are usually less expensive than wood and are used in place of wood where moderate strength will do the job.

VAPOR BARRIERS AND VENTING

Any insulated wall, floor, or roof should have a vapor barrier to prevent condensation of water inside the wall, floor, or roof. Condensation occurs when moisture-laden warm air cools, because warm air can hold more moisture than cold air. Your own breath on a cold morning is a good example of this. The warm air in your lungs is very humid. When you exhale, the air cools, and some of this moisture immediately condenses, forming the cloud of mist you see. The temperature at which this condensation occurs is called the dew point. The dew point will vary depending on how hot and humid a body of air is.

To understand how condensation works inside a wall, we have to look at how moisture migrates through a wall. In winter, the air in your house is warm. Because of cooking, perspiration, respiration, showers, and such, it is also moist. You might wonder how moisture gets into the wall cavities and condenses, since air does not seem to pass through the wall surfaces. But in fact, moisture vapor flows through your wall. A wall surface can be permeable to *moisture vapor*, even though it is not permeable to either air or water as such. Moisture will migrate through most surfaces as long as the humidity on one side of the surface is higher than on the other. This is called vapor pressure.

In winter, the moisture inside a warm house is always flowing through the wall surface into the cooler cavities inside the wall. At some point in the migration, it will reach the dew point and condensation will take place. If the condensation is great, the insulation can become soaked and the framing can start to rot. How bad the condensation will be depends on exactly how the wall is constructed. Some materials are highly permeable to moisture migration and some are almost impermeable. Relatively impermeable materials are called *vapor barriers*.

When you design a wall or other surface, you have two goals. The first is to make the inner surface — the warm, moist side — as impermeable as possible to minimize the moisture that migrates into a wall. The second goal is to make the outer surface — the sheathing and siding — fairly permeable, so that the moisture that does find its way into the wall can eventually flow to the outside. This does not mean that the sheathing and siding are drafty. They can be relatively airtight but be made of materials permeable to moisture vapor.

In practice, these goals are readily achieved. To keep the inside surface impermeable, staple a vapor barrier behind the finish surface. In a floor, the vapor barrier will go under the flooring. In a wall or ceiling, it will go just under the wallboard or paneling material. Two materials are commonly used. Fiberglass insulation comes with a foil backing, which, when installed smooth and tight, is a sufficient vapor barrier. The aluminum foil itself is almost a 100 percent barrier, and any moisture that does get through must get in around the edges. When there is no foil backing (or sometimes as a supplement to the foil) you can use large sheets of 4 mil (.004") plastic. Plastic is probably more effective because there are fewer holes and joints.

The next problem is to provide a way out for the moisture that does find its way into wall, floor, or roof. Walls and floors are usually covered on the outside by some combination of wood, 15-pound felt, and sometimes 1/2-inch insulation board. These materials are sufficiently permeable to let excess moisture out, as long as there is a vapor barrier on the inside.

Roofs are often subject to more moisture penetration since the heat in the house tends to make them hotter. Also, many roofing materials, particularly metal and asphalt roofs, are effective vapor barriers that may not let excess moisture out. Therefore, it is common practice in building to ventilate the roof. This means providing a flow of outside air between the roofing and the insulation to carry off the excess moisture. Figure 286 shows the basic idea. (Chapter fifteen discusses this kind of ventilation in more detail, since venting is provided when the roof is framed and covered.) Usually there will be a screened inlet vent at the eave and an outlet at the peak or ridge of the roof. The air flows in the lower vent, rises in the cavity between the insulation and the sheathing, and exits at the top. This will not work if the entire cavity is stuffed with insulation, because there will be no path for the air to flow along.

VENTING A SHED ROOF

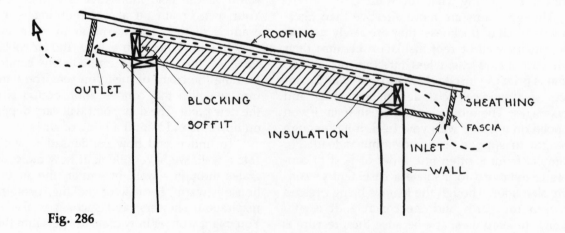

Fig. 286

INSTALLING FIBERGLASS INSULATION

Fiberglass is an incredibly itchy and unpleasant material to work with. Wear gloves, a long-sleeved shirt, goggles, and some sort of respirator over your mouth. A good place to start is to put a square of 1-inch rigid foam about 6" × 6" behind each electric box in the exterior walls. If you don't have any foam, stuff scraps of fiberglass there.

The walls will be insulated with 3-inch (sometimes 6-inch) insulation made in widths to fit the space between the studs. Fiberglass insulation comes in rolls or short 4-foot batts. To cut it to length, turn the roll or batt on its back, paper side down, and lay it on a scrap board to protect the floor. Cut across it with a utility knife, compressing the fiberglass as you cut and slicing through the paper. Measure for a snug fit. Staple the pieces as shown in Figure 285. The foil always faces inside. Cut notches to fit around the electric boxes. Stuff all cracks with scrap, particularly the cracks between window and door jambs and the adjacent studs. Your objective should be a tight, draft-free job.

Fiberglass sometimes comes without foil or paper backing. With this type, which is nearly as effective as the foil-backed type, you can stuff it gently into place and it will stay put with no stapling. Fiberglass without backing should definitely be covered with plastic.

Use the same method to insulate the roof, but use insulation 6 inches or more thick. If you are using more than 6 inches of insulation, you will have to put in two layers, because 6 inches is the thickest common size. Make sure the outer layer has no vapor barrier and that there is a path for the air to flow along just outside the insulation. If you have a vent at the eave and a vent at the ridge, but the air path is stuffed full of fiberglass, venting will not be very effective.

Insulate floors the same way, but you do not need any venting. Over an open space, make sure the fiberglass is supported by some sort of soffit so it will not fall out.

For methods of installing foam insulation, see chapter fifteen.

INSTALLING A PLASTIC VAPOR BARRIER

Plastic film comes in rolls of various sizes. Pick a size that will give you a minimum of joints but will be convenient to handle. Staple the plastic on the inside of the framing after insulating is completed. Join sheets over framing members, overlapping the pieces at least 6 inches. This is easier with 2 people.

SAMPLE MATERIALS LIST

Insulation: Order the number of square feet that you must cover.

Plastic: Buy a convenient size roll, and order extra for various miscellaneous jobs around the building site.

Item	Quantity	Price/Unit	Total Cost
Fiberglass for walls	_____	$ _____ /sq.ft.	$ _____
Fiberglass for roofs and floors	_____	$ _____ /sq.ft.	$ _____
Work gloves	_____	$ _____ /pair	$ _____
5000 staples	_____	$ _____ /box	$ _____
1" foam for behind electric boxes	_____	$ _____ /sq.ft.	$ _____
Four mil plastic film	_____	$ _____ /sq.ft.	$ _____

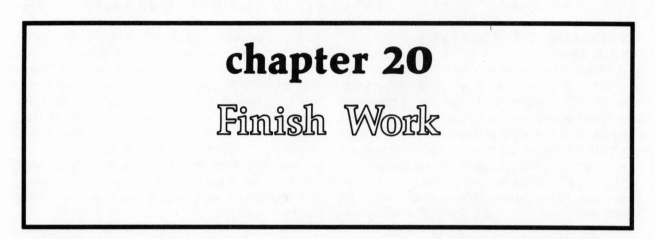

chapter 20

Finish Work

Finish work means all the parts of the house that show from the inside. It includes the floor, wall, and ceiling surfaces and all the trim such as casings, baseboards, and moldings. Figure 287 shows these basic elements. Finish work represents the last and most visible stage in building. Its success depends on doing a neat, careful job. The cheapest materials, used carefully, can look

terrific. The best materials put up carelessly will not look good. The finish-work stage is the time to slow down the pace, take pains, and work carefully.

Fortunately, this is not quite as hard as it seems. If you look at a well-built house inside, everything will look as though it fits perfectly. In fact, many of the joints in finish work are covered

ORDER OF FINISH WORK

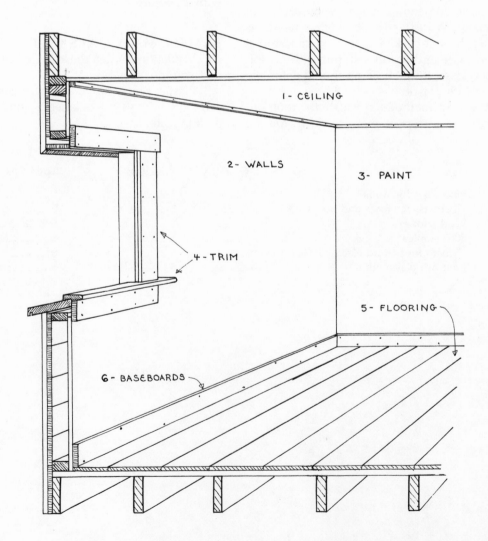

1- CEILING

2- WALLS

3- PAINT

4- TRIM

5- FLOORING

6- BASEBOARDS

Fig. 287

up by window casings, baseboards, or other trim, so they do not have to fit that well. For example, the baseboard covers the joint between the wall and the ends of the flooring. As long as the flooring comes to within ½ inch or so of the wall, it will look perfect once the baseboard is installed (Figure 288). In doing finish work, concentrate on

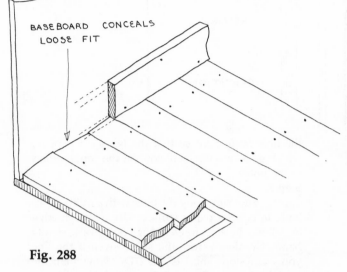

BASEBOARD CONCEALS
LOOSE FIT

Fig. 288

the joints that will ultimately be exposed. The hidden ones can be a loose or sloppy fit.

To take advantage of this principle, you must do things in the right order. If you put the baseboard down before the flooring, you would have to laboriously measure every piece of flooring and the fit would never be as good. Or if you tried to install sheetrock *around* the window trim instead of letting the trim cover the edges of the sheetrock, you would have a hopeless time fitting it properly.

The ideal sequence for the finish work pictured in Figure 287 is:

1. Sheetrock the ceiling.
2. Sheetrock the walls. The top edge of the wall masks minor inaccuracies at the edges of the ceiling. The sheetrock is fitted roughly around windows and doors, and at the floor, since these joints will be covered later.
3. Paint the ceiling and walls. Since the flooring, window trim, and baseboards aren't up yet, you don't need to mask anything, and you don't need dropcloths.
4. Put on the window and door trim, hiding the rough edges of the sheetrock around these openings.
5. Lay the floor.
6. Finally, the baseboards are put down, covering the joints between wall and floor.

Of course, it is not always possible to follow this order, and differences in design may make your work sequence vary.

WALLS AND CEILINGS

The same materials can be used on walls and ceilings, so both are discussed together. Sheetrock, Homasote, and wooden boards of various kinds are attached to the inside of the house frame after plumbing, wiring, and insulating are completed.

Sheetrock.   Sheetrock or wallboard consists of a core of gypsum — a powdery white mineral — with a coating of paper on either side. It comes in ⅜-, ½-, and ⅝-inch thicknesses, and in sheets 4' × 8', 4' × 10', 4' × 12', and 4' × 16'. Usually ½-inch is used on walls and ⅜-inch on ceilings. Joints between sheets are invisible when properly covered with paper tape and a special plaster called *sheetrock compound.* Sheetrock is the least expensive surface you can use, with the possible exception of the cheapest grades of prefinished plywood wall paneling. It is a relatively quick way to put up an economical ceiling or wall.

Step 1.

Planning: Even though sheetrock is heavy and clumsy, use the largest possible sheet to minimize the number of joints. Covering the joints is the most time-consuming part of sheetrocking. Never piece together small scraps if you can help it. It may save you the $3 another sheet costs, but the added labor of taping will offset the savings many times. Buy a few extra sheets in case one or two get ruined.

Before you start to hang the sheetrock, make sure all insulation, vapor barriers, plumbing, and wiring are in place. Also make sure you have provided sufficient support for the edges of the sheets. Joints that are perpendicular to the framing can be unsupported because sheetrock will span the 16 inches or 24 inches between framing members. But joints parallel to the framing or at the ends of the sheets must be supported. Usually the sheets will be nailed or screwed right to the framing, but occasionally there will be no framing where you need it. This often occurs at gable ends or near partitions. Nail in scraps to provide the necessary support. These added supports are called *returns* (Figure 289).

It is best to support sheetrock ceilings on 16-inch centers, because with a wider spacing the joints may not be as durable and the ceiling may sag somewhat. If your ceiling framing is 16 inches o.c., you can run the sheets whichever way will result in the fewest joints to tape. If the framing is 24 inches o.c., run the sheets parallel to the framing and use long sheets to reduce the number of unsupported joints. On walls you can run the sheets either way. Professional sheetrockers tend to use long sheets and run them horizontally to minimize joints.

Step 2.

Measuring and Marking: Though some sheets will

Fig. 289   SHEETROCK   RETURNS

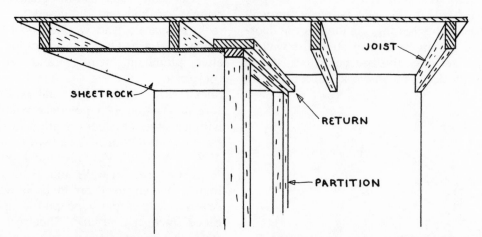

go up full size, many will have to be measured and cut. If the space is rectangular, you can simply measure the space and transfer these measurements to the sheet. Long lines for cutting can most easily be made by snapping a chalk line (see page 199). If one edge of the sheet must be cut at an angle, you can find the angle by measuring all 4 sides of the area empirically and transferring the measurements to the sheet. As long as 2 corners of the area are square, you will have an accurate shape. You can also measure angles with a rafter square. Place the rafter square in the corner that isn't square. See how much the line deviates from 90 degrees by the time it gets out to the end of the square. Then reproduce this deviation on the piece of sheetrock (Figure 290).

Locate the holes for electrical outlets by measuring up and over to the box from established lines. This can also be done empirically. Rub some carpenter's chalk along the edges of the box. When the sheetrock has been cut to size, hold it up in place and push it firmly against the chalked edges. The outline of the box will be marked on the back of the sheetrock. Whichever method you use, fit the hole fairly tight so that the box's cover plate, which goes on later, will conceal the rough edges of the hole.

Step 3.

Cutting: First run along the lines with a utility (mat) knife to cut the paper surface. Use a straightedge or follow the line freehand if you have a steady hand. Go clear across the sheet, even if the line you want stops short of the edge. Now snap the joint back as in Figure 291 to break the gypsum core. Keeping the sheetrock folded back, cut the paper backing at the crease with the utility knife. Notches, holes for electrical boxes, and curves can be cut with a keyhole saw, which is also handy for minor trimming.

Often when you try to fit a piece you have cut, it will be slightly too large in spots. Since a supertight fit is not necessary, you can avoid this by making your cuts on the light side. If a piece needs to be trimmed along an edge, you can shave it down with a rasp-type plane called a *Surform* or with the knife.

Step 4.

Hanging: Attach the sheetrock to the framing with

MEASURING   ANGLES

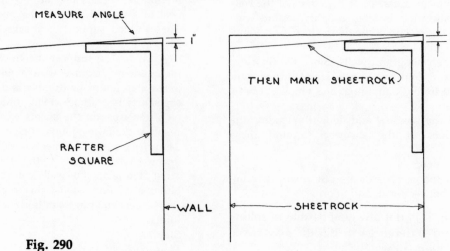

Fig. 290

CUTTING SHEETROCK

Fig. 291

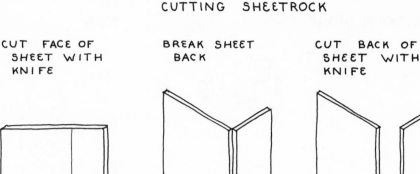

CUT FACE OF SHEET WITH KNIFE   BREAK SHEET BACK   CUT BACK OF SHEET WITH KNIFE

FACE

1¼-inch sheetrock nails or sheetrock screws. The latter are special Phillips head screws that are *self-tapping*, which means that no pilot hole is needed. They will dig their own way right into the wood. You can drive these screws with a ³⁄₈-inch variable speed electric drill fitted with a special screwdriving bit or with a special electric screw gun you rent. You can also drive them in with a large-size Yankee spiral ratchet screwdriver.

Space nails and screws about 8 inches apart, sinking them a little below the surface of the sheetrock, just enough to create a slight dimple, but not enough to break the paper surface (Figure 292).

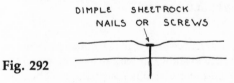

DIMPLE SHEETROCK NAILS OR SCREWS

Fig. 292

Later you will fill the dimple with sheetrock compound to make the nail invisible. You can hang the sheetrock on walls fairly easily with nails. But on ceilings, screws are better, since nailing from below is awkward.

To do the ceiling you will need at least 3 people. Two can hold the sheet in place while a third nails or screws it into the joists or rafters. This will be easier if you make a T-shaped prop to help support the sheet while it is being nailed (Figure 293). This should be a little longer than the distance from floor to ceiling, so you can jam it between the floor and ceiling.

When hanging sheetrock on walls, a tight fit is more important at the top than at the bottom, where the sheetrock will be covered by baseboards. When a single piece runs from floor to ceiling, cut it a little short. Using a flat bar or other tool as a lever, lift the piece up tight against the ceiling. This is easier as a two-person job, one lifting, one nailing. Align the edges of the sheet along the centers

of studs. Overlap the stud enough so that it can be nailed or screwed in all along, but leave enough of it exposed so that the next piece can also be attached. Tack each piece with 1 or 2 nails or screws, then examine the fit before driving the rest of the nails home.

The studs that don't come at joints will be hidden behind the sheets, so mark the stud location on the floor and ceiling in advance to find where the nails for these studs will go.

It may seem impossible to install sheetrock over a pipe coming through a wall. Cut the whole sheet to size, and cut the hole for the pipe. Cut a corner of the sheet off as shown in Figure 294. Install the larger part of the sheet in the usual way. The problem may now be that there is no framing to which to attach the second piece. If so, attach some 1 × 2 scraps to the back of the large part of the sheet with sheetrock screws (not nails). The small part of the sheet can then be screwed to these wooden tabs.

Step 5.

Installing beads: Sheetrock edges will usually be

2 X 4 PROP FOR SHEETROCKING CEILINGS

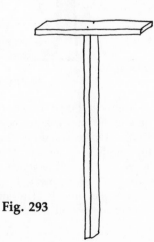

Fig. 293

FITTING SHEETROCK AROUND PIPE

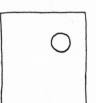

CUT HOLE

REMOVE CORNER

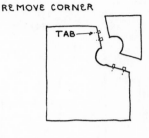

TAB

INSTALL 1"x2"x 6" TABS

FIT PIECES AROUND PIPE

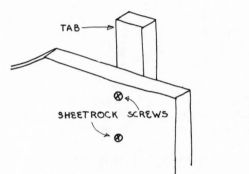

TAB

SHEETROCK SCREWS

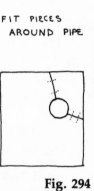

Fig. 294

concealed by joint compound or trim. But in some cases the edges need to be covered by special metal moldings, or *beads*, which are in turn covered with joint compound. One such situation is when 2 planes of sheetrock form an outside corner. Figure 295 shows an outside corner bead, sometimes known by the trade name Durabead. It is nailed over the outside corners with sheetrock nails approximately every 10 inches.

DURABEAD

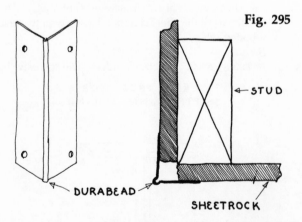

Fig. 295

STUD

DURABEAD

SHEETROCK

Where sheetrock butts into an exposed wooden piece and the joint will not be covered by molding or trim, a stop bead is used. There are two kinds of stop beads, J-bead and L-bead, both shown in Figure 296. L-bead is attached after the sheetrock is up, while J-bead has to be put up first and the sheetrock slid into it. The joint is later covered with joint compound.

L-BEAD   Fig. 296

L-BEAD

STUD

SHEETROCK

EXPOSED WOOD

L-BEAD

J-BEAD

J-BEAD

STUD

SHEETROCK

EXPOSED WOOD

J-BEAD

Step 6.

Taping sheetrock joints: Taping joints, like tying shoes, is easy to show but hard to explain in words. A little expert instruction is essential. Don't be surprised if different people have different methods, because everyone has his or her own way. Here I will summarize my method to give you the general idea of how it's done.

The compound is applied with a 6-inch-wide and a 10-inch-wide sheetrock trowel, which you can buy at any hardware store. Buy Hyde trowels if possible. You use these two trowels together. When you apply the compound with one, use the other as a palette to carry compound on. The compound comes ready-mixed in five-gallon pails. Buy USG nonasbestos joint compound if available.

Figure 297 shows, in somewhat exaggerated form, how I build up a sheetrock joint.

Day 1:

Lay a bed of sheetrock compound on the joint with the 6-inch trowel. Make sure this coat has no gaps, which will result in bubbles under the tape. Rip off a piece of tape the right length, and lay it along the joint over the compound. Use the 6-inch trowel to embed the tape firmly into the compound with one

Fig. 297

TAPING SHEETROCK JOINTS

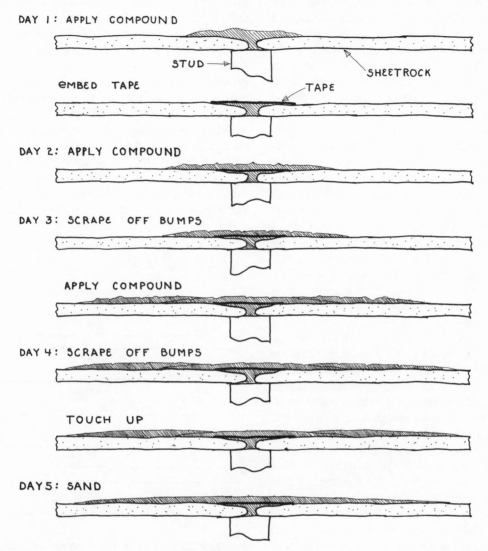

DAY 1: APPLY COMPOUND

STUD → ← TAPE

SHEETROCK

EMBED TAPE

DAY 2: APPLY COMPOUND

DAY 3: SCRAPE OFF BUMPS

APPLY COMPOUND

DAY 4: SCRAPE OFF BUMPS

TOUCH UP

DAY 5: SAND

long, firm, steady, downward stroke. This will clean off the excess compound, which you can reuse. Let this dry overnight.

Day 2:
Use the 6-inch trowel to spread a bed of compound over the tape, perhaps 6 or 8 inches wide and $1/8$ to $3/16$ of an inch thick. Then use the 10-inch trowel to smooth it. Hold the trowel at a 30-degree angle, use moderate pressure, and go over the joint in one steady stroke. Do not dab at the joint, because each time you do, your trowel will leave a mark. Do your best with one or two long strokes, and then leave the joint alone. It can be scraped down later. Where you have intersecting joints, do the verticals one day and the horizontals the next. Let this coat dry.

Day 3:
Use the 6-inch trowel as a scraper to remove any bumps sticking up. Then apply another 6- to 8-inch bed of compound on either side of the centered coat using the 6-inch trowel. Smooth these beds individually with the 10-inch trowel as you did the central coat, using a little more pressure. One end

of the trowel should be riding right on the sheetrock, and the other end should be riding down the center of the joint, which you have scraped smooth. Since this track theoretically will be quite straight, the joint should be looking quite good overall, but pockmarked with small imperfections. Let this dry overnight.

Day 4:
Use the 6-inch trowel to scrape the bumps off again. Then use either the 6- or 10-inch trowel to smooth in all the holes and dips and uneven places. Put a dab of compound over the hole, then wipe over the hole with a strong squeegee stroke, holding the trowel at about 45 degrees. This should clean off the compound except where the hole is. You can touch up several times in one day, since each coat will be thin and will dry quickly.

Day 5:
Keep touching up until the joint looks very flat. Sand lightly with 100-grit sandpaper. Wear a respirator because the dust is noxious, even if the brand of compound you buy does not have asbestos in it.

The nail holes can be filled using the same method as for touchups. Put a dab of compound over the hole, and then swipe over the hole with the 6-inch trowel. Use the trowel like a squeegee, cleaning off all the compound except what is in the nail hole. Since the compound shrinks as it dries, each nail hole should be gone over 3 times, with drying time in between.

Inside corners are filled with tape, as are regular joints, except that the tape is folded lengthwise to fit the corner. There is a special corner trowel that will make corners a lot easier. Corner bead and stop bead are covered with compound only. No tape is needed. First use the 6-inch trowel to cover the bead with a bed of compound about 4 inches wide. Then use the 6-inch trowel to clean off the excess in one long stroke, with firm pressure, holding the trowel at about 45 degrees. One side of the trowel should ride right on the sheetrock, and the other side should ride on the ridge of the bead. This ridge is there to give you a smooth, straight guide to slide your trowel along. These beads will need at least 3 coats. Scrape the bumps off between coats.

When the sheetrock is hung, beaded, taped, and sanded, put a primer coat of latex paint on it. You can't really tell how smooth and invisible the joints are until you look at them painted. Set up lights that approximate the lighting you will have when your house is done. If the joints are invisible under these circumstances. the sheetrocking is done. If some joints seem too noticeable, you can touch them up on top of the primer coat.

Molding and Battens.　It is not always easy to get good sheetrock joints when you are inexperienced. Some people seem to pick it up very quickly with a little instruction. Others find the joints taking forever to complete. One way to get around the problem is to reduce the number of joints you will tape. The first step in this direction is to put molding strips in the inside corners instead of taping them. You can do this between ceiling and wall or between two walls (Figure 287). The molding strip can be a 1″ × 1″ strip nailed to the studs with occasional 6d finish nails.

Sometimes noncorner joints are molded too. This is called *battening*. For example, in a ceiling the joints perpendicular to the sheets can be taped, but the parallel joints are covered with 1 × 3 battens applied after the ceiling is painted. Battening can look good if it is carefully planned.

Homasote.　Homasote is a soft gray insulation board. It has a softer appearance than sheetrock and provides better sound and heat insulation. It makes a good ceiling and can be used on walls in rooms where it will not get rough use. If it is put up neatly, the joints can be left alone or covered with battens. Use 6d nails every 8 inches to hold the Homasote to the framing. The plywood cutting jig described on page 202 will enable you to make perfectly straight cuts.

Wood Paneling.　Paneling made with real boards can never be as cheap or as fast as sheetrock. But if you live in an area where sawmills sell local wood, paneling will not be too expensive. If you plan your work carefully, wood paneling need not be much more time-consuming than sheetrock, especially if you have never done sheetrock before.

Figure 298 shows cross sections of different kinds of boards used for paneling. Theoretically

Fig. 298

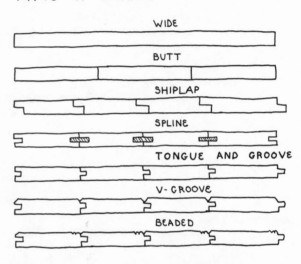

TYPES OF BOARDS

WIDE

BUTT

SHIPLAP

SPLINE

TONGUE AND GROOVE

V-GROOVE

BEADED

wood paneling can be used on either walls or ceilings, but in practice nailing boards up to a ceiling is incredibly time-consuming and awkward. If you want a wooden ceiling, it is better to build the exposed-frame type of ceiling or roof, in which the ceiling boards are nailed on top of exposed second-floor joists or roof rafters (see chapter fifteen).

You can put boards up in many ways. They can cover all the walls in a room, or just one or two; they can be vertical, horizontal, or diagonal; they can be rough or planed, sanded or unsanded, varnished, oiled, or completely unfinished. One of my favorite variations is the wainscoting shown in Figure 299, where the lower 3 feet of a wall is covered with boards and the upper part sheetrocked and painted.

Paneling boards should be well planed, clean, very dry, and good-looking. They will probably come from a local sawmill rather than from a lumber yard, because paneling from a lumber yard is expensive. To avoid big cracks during the winter, the boards must be very dry. This means finding

Fig. 299

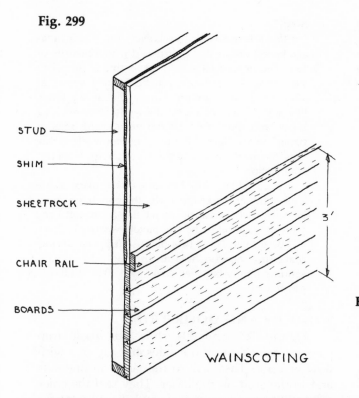

WAINSCOTING

boards with the heart side facing out, as in Figure 300, for a smoother wall. Also position boards to hide splits, bad knots, or other defects.

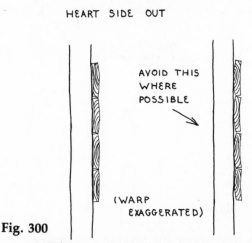

Fig. 300

a source of air-dried boards or air-drying the boards yourself. You must dry the boards even more by stacking them in a heated place for about 6 weeks before use. Even supposedly kiln-dried paneling from the lumber yard may need this final treatment. Chapter seven discusses these drying procedures in detail.

Boards can be milled for paneling in many ways. The patterns in Figure 298 are the most common. Shiplapping or tongue and grooving makes the wall tighter and conceals the insulation or plastic behind the boards if some shrinkage does occur in winter. Not all of the patterns shown are available everywhere. Sawmills usually sell only one or two types.

Step 1.

Blocking: If you are putting up boards vertically, you need horizontal blocking between the studs as a nailing surface. Tongue and groove boards can be supported every 4 feet, but square-edged or shiplapped boards need support at least every 3 feet. Any blocking you do should of course be done before you do the insulation and vapor barrier. If you are putting up boards horizontally, no blocking is necessary.

Step 2.

Measuring and cutting: You will be putting the boards up 1 row at a time. Select the boards that will make up a row, making sure all the boards in the same row are of the same width. Lay these out, or measure them roughly, to determine which studs the joints between boards will fall on. Stagger the joints from row to row. If possible, position the

When you have planned the row of boards and measured the pieces for cutting, you can cut them with a table saw, a radial arm saw, a skill saw, or a fine-toothed hand saw. See chapter twenty-four and pages 204–05 for cutting techniques.

Step 3.

Sanding: Usually you can avoid sanding almost completely if the boards are kept clean and have been smoothly planed by the sawmill. You can use 80-grit (medium) or 100-grit paper to touch up occasional rough or dirty spots. You can sand the wood more thoroughly by buying or renting a 3" × 21" size belt sander. Using an 80-grit sanding belt on this machine, you can sand a typical board completely in 2 or 3 minutes.

Step 4.

Nailing: If your boards are horizontal, start from the bottom and work up. Nail square-edge boards to the studs with 8d finish nails. Sink the nail heads about ⅛ of an inch below the surface using a nail set (Figure 301). Install shiplap boards the same

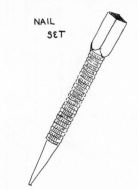

Fig. 301

way, making sure the row above laps *over* the row below. Tongue and groove boards have a special nailing procedure. Face-nail the first row with the tongue up. Fit the groove on the second row over the tongue of the first row. The bottom or grooved edge of the second row will be held in place by the tongue of the first row. Then blind-nail the top edge of the second row diagonally through the tongue, using a 6d finish nail (Figure 302). If the

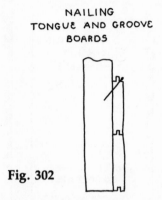

NAILING
TONGUE AND GROOVE
BOARDS

Fig. 302

nails tend to split the wood, predrill with a bit a little smaller than the nail. If a tongue and groove or shiplap board must be pounded into place, protect the edge with a scrap of the same type of board, fitted over the tongue you are pounding against. The top row of boards will have to be ripped to width and face-nailed.

Step 5.
Finishing: Board walls in relatively low traffic areas can be left unfinished or brushed with a mixture of 1/2 boiled linseed oil and 1/2 turpentine to bring out the grain. An oil finish can be applied before or after the boards go up. Apply the liquid finish liberally to the wood until the wood stops soaking it up, and then wipe off the excess with rags or paper towels. Burn these rags because a pile of oily rags can heat up and ignite through spontaneous combustion.

In a kitchen, a child's room, or any place where a lot of finger marks are likely, the paneling should be varnished, because an oil finish on softwood paneling will never be completely washable. A vinyl-based varnish is best because it is fast-drying. Make sure the wood is clean and apply 2 or 3 coats, sanding lightly between coats with 100- or 120-grit sandpaper.

WINDOW AND DOOR TRIM

Figures 303 and 304 show the basic trim pieces. Casings go on the sides and top of a window or door. They nail to the jamb on one side and to the stud on the other. They seal the crack around the window and conceal the edge of the

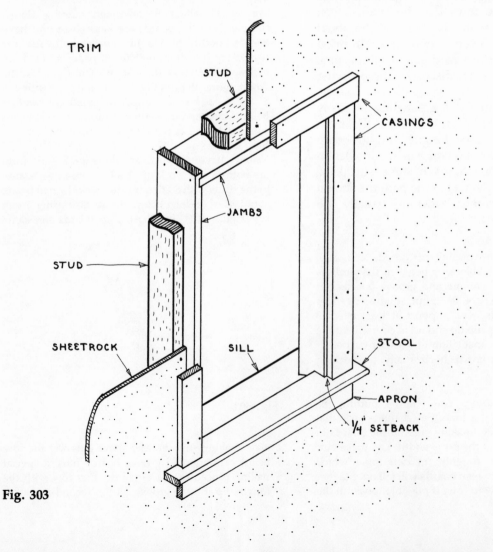

TRIM

Fig. 303

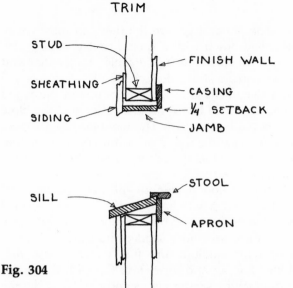

STUD — FINISH WALL

SHEATHING — CASING

SIDING — ¼" SETBACK

JAMB

SILL — STOOL

APRON

Fig. 304

¼ inch shy, nail on ¼-inch strips to make up the difference. If the discrepancy varies, nail up wide jamb extenders, countersink the nail heads with a nail set, and plane the extenders in place to the correct taper.

Step 2.

Stool: Figures 303 and 304 show a typical stool, which is the first piece of window trim to put up. Carefully cut and notch the stool to fit. It should stick past the casings about 1 inch. The inmost edge can be rounded off with a hand plane or a router, and then the whole piece can be sanded smooth. Nail the stool to the windowsill with 6d finish nails.

Step 3.

Interior stops for fixed windows between studs: If you have installed fixed glass directly between the studs with no jamb or frame, now is the time to install interior stops. They should come flush with the wall surface, as jambs do. Nail them to the studs with 4d finish nails. The stool can serve as the bottom stop.

Step 4.

Casings: The casings can be ³/₄ or ⁷/₈ inches thick, and 3 to 6 inches wide. The width is largely a question of looks. Usually there is a ¼-inch "reveal" on the jambs, which means that both top and side casings are set back ¼ inch from the inner edge of the jamb. This hides any irregularity and provides a space for hinge pins if there is sash or screen opening in. Therefore, the length of the side casings will be the distance from the stool to the bottom of the top jamb, plus ¼ inch. Cut the two side casings to this length, as square as possible. Using one 4d finish nail, temporarily tack the side casings to the jambs to hold them in position ¼ inch back from the edge of the jamb.

Often the top casing will overhang the side casings by ¼ to ³/₄ of an inch. Measure the length you want your top casing to be, and cut it. Set the piece in place to see how it fits. Perhaps it will fit perfectly, but if it doesn't, trim it with a very sharp block plane. You can plane either the tops of the side casings, or the bottom edge of the top casing.

When the fit is perfect, nail the side casings permanently. If the window in question is fixed glass between the studs, with no separate jamb, use small nails, because they must be removed to replace broken glass. Hammer 4d finish nails into the stops and 6d finish nails into the studs. With a regular window, nail to the jamb with 6d finish

finish-wall material. Casings are the same for both doors and windows, except windows also have a *stool* and an *apron* on the bottom. The stool is the protruding piece that hooks over the outside sill, and the apron is the piece underneath that supports it. The stool serves as a window stop and as a support for the casings. The apron reinforces the stool and covers the crack under the window. An alternative plan is to eliminate the stool and put casings on all four sides.

The width of trim pieces is arbitrary, as long as the pieces cover the cracks and can be nailed through into the studs. Pick a size that looks good to you. One by four is often used.

Procedures:

Step 1.

Jamb extenders: Theoretically, the jambs come exactly flush with the inside finish-wall surface, or perhaps stick into the room ¹/₁₆th of an inch. The casing will span the gap between these two flush surfaces. But it sometimes happens that they will not be flush. If the jambs stick out too far into the room, they can be planed down to size with a sharp hand plane. However, it is more likely that the jambs will not stick out far enough, because the window was originally made for a thinner wall or because of errors in building. If so, jamb extenders should be nailed on with 1 4d finish nail every 6 inches (Figure 305). For example, if the jambs are

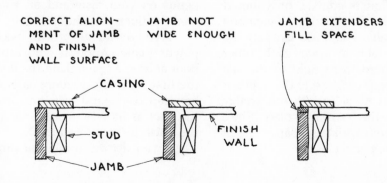

CORRECT ALIGN-
MENT OF JAMB
AND FINISH
WALL SURFACE

JAMB NOT
WIDE ENOUGH

JAMB EXTENDERS
FILL SPACE

CASING

STUD

FINISH
WALL

Fig. 305

JAMB

and to the stud with 8d finish. Make the nailing pattern neat, and try not to mash the wood with the head of the hammer.

Do not nail the top casing now. If you do, it will shrink just a hair, even if it has been carefully dried. You will lose your good fit between side and top casings. Instead, just let it sit there until the room has been heated for a week. Then nail it down as you did the others.

Step 5.

Apron: Line the apron up with the casings. Push it up as you nail it so it will give good support to the stool. Recess all nails about $1/8$ of an inch with a $2/32$ nail set.

Step 6.

Sand: Sand roughness and dirt from the casing with 80-grit sandpaper. Round off the sharp edges. These little touchups make a lot of difference in the appearance of the work.

Step 7.

Remove accidental hammer marks: If you have left an occasional hammer mark on the wood, take a sewing needle and puncture the spot about twenty times and wet it. The water will seep in, swell the wood, and presto! With a little light sanding, the mark will (usually) disappear completely.

Step 8.

Finish: Finish the trim before it gets dirty. See page 174 for finishing instructions.

FLOORING

Wood Flooring.   Many kinds of boards are used for flooring. Narrow 1×3 tongue and groove hardwood flooring comes in oak, birch, and other woods and is durable, beautiful, and expensive. Softwood boards can also be used, either tongue and groove or square edge. They will be less expensive and more subject to wear but beautiful in their own way. Pine boards 14 to 20 inches wide are available from some sawmills and make a very nice floor.

Whatever boards you use should be well-planed, straight, good-looking, and very dry. If you are using native boards from a sawmill, chapter seven explains how to dry the boards well enough to avoid cracks.

Begin by stapling a layer of 15-pound felt paper down on the subfloor. This will reduce drafts and prevent squeaks. Square-edged boards should be nailed down with 8d finish nails, 8d common nails, or 7d flooring nails. The finish nails are the least obtrusive but do not hold as well as the other kinds. If a board is hard to fit tight to the last board nailed, nail a scrap of 2×4 to the subfloor right next to the warped piece. Drive a wedge between them to force the board into place. Since the edges will be covered with baseboards, the fit at the wall need not be perfect.

Tongue and groove flooring can most easily be nailed down with a special rented nailing machine, which is much like a big stapler that you drive with a short sledgehammer. It drives the nails diagonally through the tongue of the wood so no nails will be exposed. The force of the blow draws the board tight. The hammer has a rubber face for beating the boards into position before nailing and a metal face for driving the plunger of the machine.

If your floor is smooth and flat, you can simply touch it up with hand sanding, or with a small portable belt sander, but usually it is worthwhile to rent a power floor sander and sand the whole floor with medium and fine paper. These machines are big and unwieldy. Go with the grain, and move the sander very smoothly. Never let the sander stop in one place for even a second; it will gouge the floor. A special edger is used around the edges of the room. If possible, get an experienced person to show you how to run these machines.

It is hard to make a clear recommendation here about floor finishing. Probably you should look at finishes in friends' houses and see what looks good to you. You can go in two directions. If you want a finish that will stay new-looking, you can use several coats of polyurethane varnish and wax the finish periodically to protect the varnish. This approach will work quite well on hardwood, but a softwood floor — especially a pine floor — will eventually get somewhat beat up and dented-looking in high traffic areas, just because the wood is so soft. To me, this worn appearance looks good but if you want the floor new-looking, you will probably not like it.

An alternative is to give up the idea of keeping the floor new-looking and develop a nice patina. For this, you apply many coats of oil finish at first and reoil periodically, perhaps every 3 months. No oil finish can seal the wood like a varnish. So everything that happens on the floor — all the dirt, food, and whatever, will become part of the finish. At first the floor may just look stained and uneven. But eventually it will get a nice, dark, fairly even patina. How beautiful this will be depends on your taste and on your willingness to reoil the floor periodically.

If you decide to varnish, use the best grade of polyurethane. Apply it with a brush, giving the floor at least 3 coats. Sand the floor smooth before the first coat, and vacuum carefully. Sand lightly between coats, and vacuum carefully again. Use the floor as little as possible for a few days, to let the finish get good and hard.

If you decide to oil, you can use a synthetic

Danish oil, such as Watco, or boiled linseed oil mixed 50-50 with turpentine. The Danish oil–type of finish will dry a little faster and is supposed to be somewhat harder. Flood the floor generously, and keep it wet for about an hour. Then wipe the excess off with rags. (Burn the rags immediately to prevent spontaneous combustion.) Reoil daily for a week. You may need fewer coats with the synthetic oils. After the first week, oil the floor every week or so for a month or two, and then whenever the floor seems to need it.

Other Flooring Materials.   Vinyl tile, ceramic tile, or carpet can also be used as a finish floor over a subfloor of 3/4-inch plywood or particle board if all the joints in the subfloor are supported by framing. Particle board subfloor needs a joist spacing of 16 inches o.c.; 3/4-inch plywood can span 2 feet.

A single layer of dense, 3/4-inch particle board can make a good finish floor by itself if it is painted. Particle board consists of wood particles glued together into sheets under great pressure. It has no grain, so it has very little tensile strength. But it is very hard and makes a rugged floor. If a single layer of 3/4-inch particle board is used with no subfloor, all joints must be supported with framing.

BASEBOARDS

Baseboards are 3/4-inch boards 3 1/2 inches or wider used to cover the edge of the flooring and protect the bottom of the wall surface. Install them after the trim is done, the walls are painted, and the floor is finished. Start at one corner and work around the room. I usually nail them in temporarily with 1 or 2 nails, leaving the heads up so I can remove the boards later. When they are all fitted, I remove them for painting or varnishing and then reinstall them permanently. Nail them to the wall studs with 8d finish nails, and countersink the nails with your nail set.

FINISH CARPENTRY TECHNIQUES

The techniques of doing window and door trim, baseboards, paneling, and other visible woodwork belong to what is known as *finish carpentry*. Finish carpentry techniques are, in a way, techniques of deception. When you look at a room that has been well finished, the woodwork will look as if every cut is square, every board straight, and every cut carefully made. But in reality, few houses are really quite square or level, and few boards are quite straight, square, or flat. The art of finish carpentry consists first of knowing how to fit things tight so that minor variations are not noticeable; second, of planning work to minimize the *number* of perfect fits that have to be made;

and third, of concealing building faults through visual deception. Finish carpentry is a whole art or trade in itself, and it is not possible to provide a complete description here. I will just list some practical hints that I have found useful:

Plan your sequence to minimize tight joints. This is the idea behind a molding. A single piece put on later covers several loose joints made earlier. The crack between the flooring and the wall is left sloppy; then a baseboard covers this joint to make it invisible.

Avoid flush edges where possible. You can keep from having to make edges line up perfectly by using a setback, or *reveal*. In Figure 303, the casing is set back on the jamb 1/4 of an inch to leave a 1/4-inch reveal. This looks good and leaves a place for hinges; it also saves a lot of work. If the casing and jamb were flush, the slightest discrepancy between them would be noticeable. You would have to fit them very laboriously to make the joint look right. With the reveal, even a 1/16-inch error would be unnoticeable.

Figure 306 shows another example. Top window casings can be made flush with the side casings. But if they are, the slightest error in cutting will mean a sloppy job or a wasted piece, because even 1/16-inch errors will show. If the top casings are allowed to overhang the side ones 1/4 inch or so, such cutting errors become completely unnoticeable.

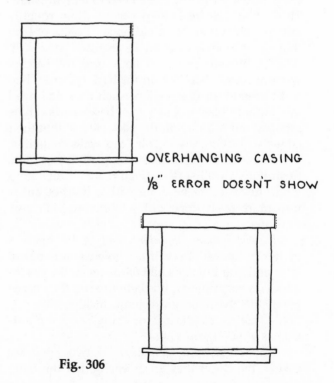

FLUSH CASING

1/8" ERROR LOOKS BAD

OVERHANGING CASING

1/8" ERROR DOESN'T SHOW

Fig. 306

Fig. 307   SIDE STOPS INSTALLED   TOP STOP INSTALLED
FIRST   FIRST

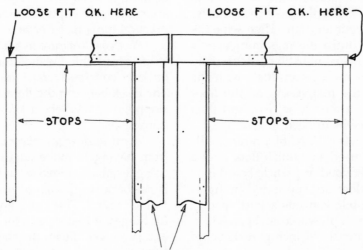

LOOSE FIT O.K. HERE   LOOSE FIT O.K. HERE

STOPS   STOPS

CASING

Minimize double-ended cuts. It is much easier to cut a piece to fit perfectly at 1 end only than to cut it to fit perfectly at both ends. Figure 307 shows the 2 ways to cut stops. Note that most of the joint between the side and top stops will be covered by the casing. Thus it will be faster to cut the sides first, because only 1 piece, the top stop, will have to fit perfectly on both ends. If you cut the top first, both side stops would have to be cut perfectly to length. This may seem trivial in a particular case; over the course of a whole house it will save a lot of time and aggravation.

Don't be fussy where you don't have to be. Only the exposed parts of a piece need to look finished. Those that will be hidden can be done roughly and quickly. Often in an old house a piece of trim that looks immaculate on its exposed side will, when removed, prove to be a mass of hatchet work or rough chiseling on the back, where it had to fit around an obstruction, such as a nail head or a lump of plaster. Casings or baseboards can be scooped out roughly on the back side so that their edges will fit tightly against the walls or jambs. This is especially useful when a jamb is not quite flush with a wall surface (Figure 308). This "hogging out" used to be done with a hatchet but is now more easily done with a table saw, skill saw, or router.

Parallel is more important than level. This is a matter of optical effect. If a whole room is out of level and you put up wall boards level, the crookedness is accentuated. It is better to run the boards parallel to the floor and ceiling. Incidentally, this holds true for clapboards or shingles on the outside as well (Figure 309).

Keep discrepancies far apart. If two lines are askew, the closer they are to each other the more

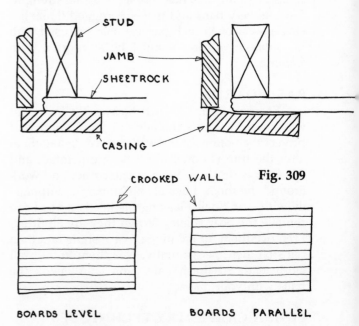

HOGGING OUT CASING CONCEALS   **Fig. 308**
MISALIGNMENT OF JAMB

STUD

JAMB

SHEETROCK

CASING

CROOKED WALL   **Fig. 309**

BOARDS LEVEL   BOARDS PARALLEL

crooked they will look. If you have a sloping floor but a level chair rail above it, the farther up the chair rail is on the wall, the harder it will be to tell that the two are out of line. As another example, Figure 310 shows the right and wrong way to panel a wall where the top is slightly out of parallel with the bottom. If you run the boards parallel to the bottom, they will look crooked in relation to the top. But if as you work up you taper each board slightly, the discrepancy will be averaged out over many boards. No two adjacent lines will be noticeably out of parallel, and the overall crookedness will not be seen. This is called *splitting the difference.*

BOARDS PARALLEL
TO BOTTOM OF
WALL

BOARDS TAPERED
TO CONCEAL
CROOKEDNESS

Fig. 310

See chapter twenty-four for instructions on how to make accurate cuts.

SAMPLE MATERIALS LIST

The rule of thumb for ordering tongue and groove boards is: the area to be covered plus $1/3$ equals the number of board feet needed.

For tongue and groove wall paneling, order 2 pounds of nails per 100 feet of surface.

Order 1 pound of sheetrock nails for every 6 sheets of 4 × 8 sheetrock.

Item	Quantity	Price/Unit	Total Cost
Ceiling Materials:			
Sheetrock (or other)	_____	$ _____ /	$ _____
1¼″ sheetrock nails or screws	_____	$ _____ /	$ _____
large roll sheetrock tape	_____	$ _____ /roll	$ _____
nonasbestos sheetrock compound	5 gals.	$ _____ /5-gal. pail	$ _____
120-grit sandpaper	5 sheets	$ _____ /sheet	$ _____
Durabead	_____	$ _____ /	$ _____
L-bead	_____	$ _____ /	$ _____
paint and painting materials	_____	$ _____ /	$ _____
Wall Materials:			
For board walls:			
boards	_____	$ _____ /	$ _____
nails	_____	$ _____ /lb.	$ _____
sandpaper	_____	$ _____ /sheet	$ _____
finishing materials (varnish, oil, turpentine)	_____	$ _____ /	$ _____
For sheetrock walls:			
as above under *Ceiling Materials*			
Trim Materials:			
casings, stools, stops, apron material (¾″ boards)	_____	$ _____ /bd.ft.	$ _____
baseboard material	_____	$ _____ /bd.ft.	$ _____
4d finish nails	5 lbs.	$ _____ /lb.	$ _____
6d finish nails	5 lbs.	$ _____ /lb.	$ _____
8d finish nails	5 lbs.	$ _____ /lb.	$ _____
Flooring Materials:			
15-lb. felt	_____	$ _____ /roll	$ _____
flooring	_____	$ _____ /bd.ft.	$ _____
nails	_____	$ _____ /lb.	$ _____
sanding equipment and paper	_____	$ _____ /	$ _____
finishing materials	_____	$ _____ /	$ _____

chapter 21

Stairs

Building a staircase is one of the most difficult parts of building: the geometry is hard to visualize, and the carpentry must be precise. But building a staircase is satisfying because the staircase has a large impact on how a house looks. A well-thought-out and well-made staircase makes the whole house more interesting and beautiful. A main reason many older houses are so appealing is that the stairs are more than just a way to get to the second floor.

PLANNING

Locating the Stairs. Building a staircase will be easier if you plan it while making floor plans and elevation drawings. Find a general location on your first- and second-floor plans that fits the overall plan. That means the stairs will start and end in locations that fit with the traffic pattern you want. People should be able to get upstairs and down without disrupting parts of the house that are supposed to be private or quiet.

In short, make the staircase an integral part of the house plan. Often in a big, old house an elaborate staircase will be in a central hall, right inside the front door (Figure 311–A). When you enter you can go directly to any area of the house. Such

a staircase ties the house together visually, while preserving the privacy a family needs. The same layout with the stairs moved would be less practical and more disruptive (Figure 311–B).

The staircase in a house you build can be in harmony with the design you have. Figure 312 shows an arrangement for a house in which the kitchen is the center of activity for the family.

A MORE MODERN LAYOUT

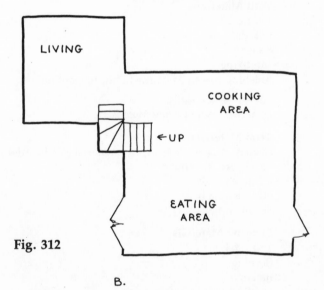

Fig. 312

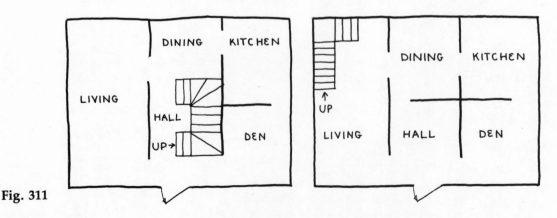

A.
TYPICAL OLD-FASHIONED LAYOUT

B.
BAD STAIR LOCATION

Fig. 311

STAIRCASE LAYOUT

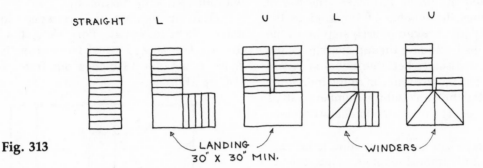

Fig. 313

There is no hall, but traffic flows through the large kitchen along paths that divide the eating and cooking areas.

Chapters two and four on design will help you find the best place for your stairs. Look for a plan in which the traffic areas do not use up a disproportionate amount of your floor area. In most good plans the stairs will be found fairly near the most commonly used entrance.

Layout. When you know roughly where the stairs will go, figure out a tentative layout. Figure 313 shows the most common stair layouts. A straight staircase is the most economical and easiest to build. Build a straight staircase if possible if you have never built a staircase before. But often, particularly in a small house, the floor plan will not accommodate a straight layout. You may have to build an L-shaped or U-shaped stairs with a landing. This is like building two staircases that meet at a platform. Sometimes even a landing staircase will not fit. The landing will have to be replaced with two or more triangular winding stairs, called *winders*, to compress the staircase. The trouble, however, is that a winding staircase

is harder to build and more dangerous to use.

The layout you choose has to fit in with the floor framing as well as the floor plan, because you have to make a very large hole in the second floor for the staircase. If the hole is parallel with the floor joists, it is fairly easy to leave 1 or 2 joists out to make room for the stairs. But if the staircase is perpendicular to the floor joists, you might have to cut 6 or 8 joists off in midspan to make the hole. Try to minimize the disruption of the framing. (Chapter thirteen, on floors, shows how stairwells are framed.)

Scale Drawings. Once you have a tentative idea of the general shape and location of the stairs, make scale floor plans for elevations or cross sections. Show each step in scale so that you can make sure everything will work.

Staircase angles, like rafter angles, are not expressed in degrees, but in *rise* and *run*. In Figure 314, the distance from the finish floor downstairs to the finish floor upstairs is 8 feet. This is the total rise. The floor area used up by the stairs is 10 feet. This is the total run. So this is a staircase with an angle of 8:10. Each step is a triangle that is a small

STAIR DETAILS

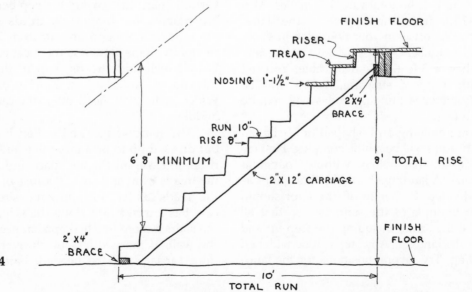

Fig. 314

version of this large triangle. The rise of each step is 8 inches, and the run is 10 inches. The rise of each step, times the number of steps, gives the total rise. Similarly, the run of each step times the number of steps (including the top step) gives the total run. If the distance between floors in Figure 314 were greater, the rise and run of the individual steps might stay the same but the number of steps would be greater. The numbers don't always come out so even.

Certain step sizes have been found to be safe, comfortable, and gradual enough. One rule of thumb is that the rise plus the run should be a number between 17 and 18. Aim for a rise of 7 or 8 inches and a run of 9 to 11 inches. This will yield a fairly gentle pitch, a good wide tread, and a reasonable step height.

Start with the total rise, which is a given. Find a figure between 7 and 8 inches that divides evenly into the total rise. In Figure 314, 8 inches goes into 8 feet exactly 12 times. This would give 12 steps, each with a rise of 8 inches. Suppose your total rise was 126 inches:

$$\frac{126}{15} = 8.4''$$

$$\frac{126}{16} = 7.8''$$

$$\frac{126}{17} = 7.4''$$

You have a choice between 15, 16, or 17 steps. If you had 15 steps 8.4″ high, the steps would definitely feel a little tall. Either 16 or 17 will give a more comfortable rise.

To find a good run to match the rise, subtract the rise from 17½ inches. In the example above, subtracting 7.4 from 17.5 inches would give 10.1 inches. This could be fixed in practice at 10 or maybe 10¼ inches. Now that you have the run (say it is 10 inches), multiply it times the number of steps (17) to get the total run, 170 inches. You will need 170 inches of floor space for the stairs.

Draw the staircase on your floor plan in scale, with the right number of steps. Make a main staircase 30 inches or 3 feet wide if possible. You can get by with a 2-foot staircase, but it will be cramped. Sometimes building codes will require a width of 3 feet.

If you are building an L-shaped or U-shaped stairs, this process will be a little complex. First try to find a design that will fit without triangular winding stairs. A landing should be thought of as an extrawide step. Its height off the floor should be an even multiple of the stair rise, so that all steps will be the same, including the step up and down from the landing. Any step can be widened into a landing. Try several positions for the land-

ing to find the one that gives the best floor plan without sacrificing headroom.

Draw in winders if a cramped floor space makes them necessary. For safety, the width of the winders should equal the run of the regular stairs at a point 18 inches out from the corner (Figure 315).

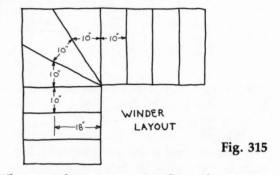

WINDER LAYOUT

Fig. 315

When you have a tentative floor plan, use it to add your staircase to the elevation or cross section drawings you have made of your design. For turning staircases, you may need a drawing from two different angles. Probably the easiest way to make these drawings is to lay a tracing of the appropriate elevation over the stair plan. These drawings will help you visualize how the stairs will be built and enable you to make sure there is sufficient headroom below and above the stairs. As Figure 314 shows, the minimum headroom in building codes is 6 feet, 8 inches, although 6 feet, 4 inches will provide fairly ample headroom. Six feet even is tight but usable.

When you have made sure the staircase will fit and the floor framing can make way for the stairwell, you are ready to consider how the staircase will be built.

Figure 316 shows the most common ways to build stairs. Part A is an open-riser type, which means it has treads but no risers (the riser is the vertical board that covers the gap between steps). The timbers that support the treads are called *carriages* or *stringers* and are cut from 2 × 12s. The sawtooth-shape shown is the most common type. With 2-inch-thick treads, two of these carriages can support treads 3 feet, 6 inches or 4 feet wide. Wider stairs will need an extra carriage in the middle.

The staircase pictured in Part B is like Part A but dressed up to be a more finished stairs. It has risers to close off the toe space and help support the treads front and back. Because of this support, the treads can be 1 inch thick if desired. This staircase has a trim board along the side, which gives the stairs a more finished appearance and protects the wall. If the width is much over 30 inches, a third carriage will be needed. Part C is a more

Fig. 316   TYPES   OF   STAIRS

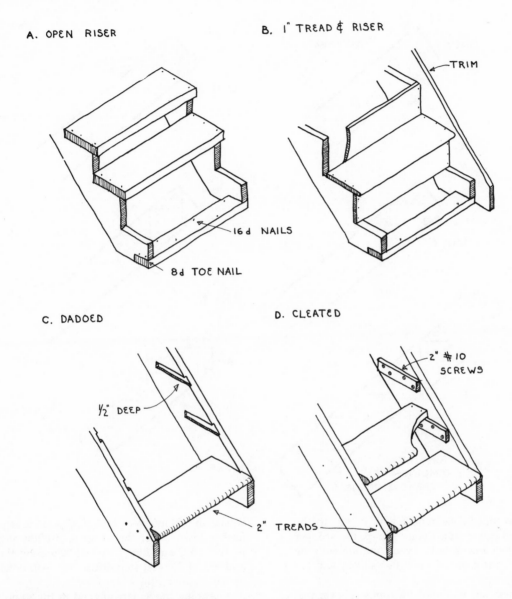

A. OPEN RISER

B. 1" TREAD & RISER

—TRIM

16d NAILS

8d TOE NAIL

C. DADOED

D. CLEATED

2" #10 SCREWS

½" DEEP

2" TREADS

finished open-riser staircase in which the carriage is notched or dadoed out for each tread.

The cleated carriage in Part D is perhaps the easiest type to build of all the stairs shown.

This chapter describes how to build this kind of staircase with sawtoothed carriage. Adapt the directions as needed if you are building any of the other types.

HOW TO BUILD STAIRS

The basic parts of the staircases are the carriages, treads, risers (if any), and 2 2 × 4 cleats or braces, notched into the stringers to hold the ends of the carriages in position. Building a staircase will be easier if you have a drawing, such as Figure 314, which clearly pictures all these parts in scale.

Step 1.

Lay out carriages: Make the carriage from the best 2 × 12s you have. You will mark these using a rafter square and a sharp pencil. Figure 317 shows the procedures for laying out a stringer for a staircase with a rise of 8 inches and a run of 10 inches. You can substitute the rise-and-run numbers from your own design. Put a 2 × 12 on a pair of sawhorses. Measure down from the top end about 8 or 10 inches along its *bottom* edge and make a mark. Line up the square on the stringer as shown in Figure 317, Part A. Here the 8 on the long side of the square is on the mark you just made. The 10 on the short side of the square is lined up with the bottom edge of the 2 × 12. With the square in this position, mark line A, which represents the topmost vertical cut on the stringer.

Fig. 317   MARKING THE CARRIAGE

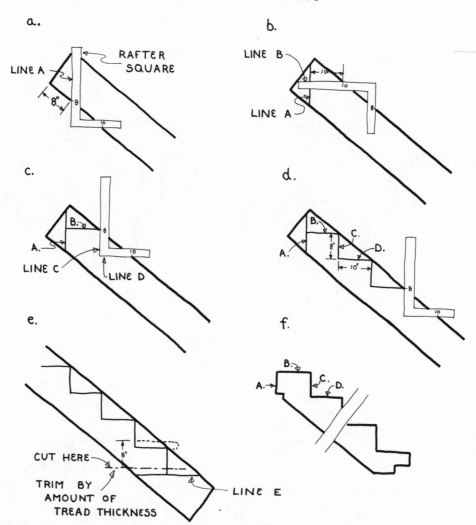

It may not be clear now why lining up the square this way enables you to mark the stringer at the correct angles, but as you continue with the procedure, the logic of the rafter square will become clearer.

The next step is to mark the topmost horizontal line of the stringer, line B, Figure 317–B. Flip the rafter square into the position shown. The 10 on the long side and the 8 on the short side are lined up with the *top* edge of the 2 × 12. Now slide the square along the top edge of the 2 × 12 until the distance from Line A to the top edge of the 2 × 12, where the long side of the square crosses it, equals the run of the stairs. In the example shown, this is 10 inches. Then mark Line B as shown. This is the top step.

You next mark the first notch to be taken out of the stringer, which represents the first step down. Place the square as shown in Part C, again aligning the rise and run along the top edge of the 2 × 12. The 8-inch mark on the long side of the square should just intersect the right-hand end of Line B. The 10-inch mark in the short side of the

square should intersect the top edge of the stringer, farther down. When the square is carefully aligned, mark Line C and Line D, which represent the rise and run of the first step down. You will notch out by cutting along these lines.

Keeping the square aligned in the same way, slide it down the 2 × 12 one full step, that is, until the long side of the square lines up with the right-hand end of Line D. You can now mark the second step down. Continue sliding the square down, laying out the steps one at a time, as in Part D.

The marking procedure will be easier if you buy a set of stair fixtures, little brass clamps that tighten down onto the square and act as stops to align the square. Finish off at the bottom by drawing Line E, the horizontal line at the bottom of the last rise line (Part E). Your carriage is laid out. Check your elevation drawing to make sure you have marked the right number of steps.

The next step is called *dropping the carriage*. If you cut the bottom of the carriage along Line E and used it that way, you would have a problem. Once the treads were nailed on, the bottom step would be higher than the others by the thickness of 1 tread. Therefore you have to trim off the bottom of the carriage by an amount equal to the tread thickness. Measure up from Line E that distance and draw a line parallel to it. This is where your carriage will be cut off. However, if you are installing the staircase on the subfloor — that is, if your finish floor is not yet laid when you do your staircase — you have a further complication. You must draw a new cutoff line *below* the old one by a distance equal to the anticipated thickness of the finish floor in order to bring the carriage all the way down to the subfloor.

Finally, mark the notches for the 2 × 4 braces that will hold the carriage to your house framing, as shown in Part F. Sometimes these braces are omitted at the bottom, and the carriage just sits on the floor. This will be adequate only as long as the carriages remain firmly attached at the top, so the staircase cannot slide downward and outward.

Step 2.

Cut stringer: Cut out the stringer on the lines you have made. The cuts for the steps can be started with a skill saw but will have to be finished with a hand saw or saber saw. Sometimes you will have to use a sharp chisel to neaten the inside corners.

Step 3.

Check carriage: Take the stringer over to the opening in the floor for the stairs and position it in place. Put a level on a few of the cuts for the treads. Usually if the level reads level here, you have done everything right. If the level is off by much, make what adjustment you can to correct the situation. Check that the carriage is sitting at the level of the finish floor (if it is planned that way) and not on the subfloor. Take a scrap of the material you will use for treads (or any lumber of the same thickness) and stick it on the top and bottom step. At the top, the tread should come flush with the finish flooring. At the bottom, the tread should be exactly 1 rise above the finish flooring level. Sometimes a little trimming or shimming at the top or bottom will make the carriage line up right.

Step 4.

Cut other carriages: When you are sure the first carriage is right, use it as a template to mark the other carriage or carriages. If you have three, use the first as the template for both of the others.

Step 5.

Test carriages: Put all the carriages up to make sure they are right. Put a level across from one to the other to make sure the treads will be level. If there are three, use a straightedge to make sure all three are lined up in the same plane. Make any adjustments needed.

Step 6.

2 × 4 braces: When everything is checked, and before you take the carriage down, mark the floor at the bottom and the framing at the top to indicate exactly where the 2 × 4 braces should be located. Take the stringers down, cut the 2 × 4s, and nail

them with 16d nails on the marks you have just made.

Step 7.

Treads and risers: The nosing on the treads should overhang the risers (if any) by 1 to 1½ inches. If there are no risers, the treads should overhang the notches in the carriages by that amount. Risers should run past the treads at the bottom and butt up to the treads at the top. You can put screws through each riser into the back of the tread for strength. One-inch treads and risers can be nailed to the carriages with 8d finish nails. Two-inch treads will need 16d finish nails. If the nails split the wood, predrill with a bit slightly smaller than the nails.

Step 8.

Protecting and finishing the stairs: A staircase can be left unfinished, but you may want to oil or varnish it to match the floors. This should be done as soon as possible after the treads go on so dirt is not ground into the wood. If the staircase goes in while heavy building is still going on, tack or tie protective masonite or plywood covers over the freshly finished stairs. You may also install temporary treads made from scrap lumber that can be replaced with good treads after the heavy building is over.

Landings and Winders. Structurally, think of a landing as a floor, framed like a regular floor, with 2 staircases attached. Figure 318 shows a typical landing. It consists of a box of 2 × 6s (joists), which can be supported by doubled 2 × 4 posts to the floor or nailed to adjacent walls with numerous 20d common nails. This can be topped with a plywood subfloor and then a flooring that matches your treads. Run this flooring parallel with the lower stairs to provide a nosing where you step up on the landing. Notice that the landing is wider than the bottom stairs so that it can fully support the upper staircase.

This same approach can be adapted to building a set of winders, as shown in Figure 319. First, build a full-size rectangular landing as just described. This will be the first winder. Then build a stout platform with a 2-inch-thick frame on top of the landing, with a plywood subfloor and then a flooring of your tread material. Run the flooring parallel to the leading edge or riser of the winder. If there is a third winder, it can be built the same way on top of the second. Notice that the landing and both winders go under the upper run of stairs to give it good support. Then the upper staircases can be built on the winders just as though on a floor.

Winding staircases that are right up against walls (as most winding stairs are) are often built with a lighter framework of cleats nailed to the adjacent walls. Instead of the steps being stacked like blocks, each winder is supported at the ends

Fig. 318   LANDING

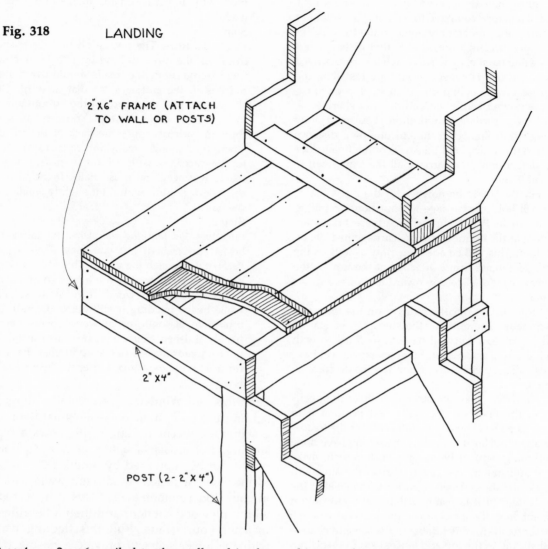

2"X6" FRAME (ATTACH
TO WALL OR POSTS)

2"X4"

POST (2- 2"X4")

by 2 × 4s or 2 × 6s nailed to the wall and in the middle by the risers that connect the treads together. These frames are usually improvised in a somewhat haphazard way, since they will not be exposed to view in the main part of the house. In this case the upper staircase cannot be supported by the winders but must be nailed directly into the walls. If you want to build winders this way, study examples in existing houses and get some experienced help if possible.

Fig. 319

WINDERS

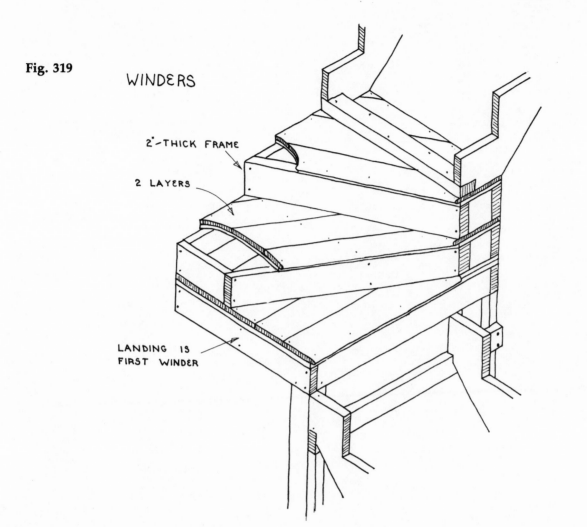

2"-THICK FRAME

2 LAYERS

LANDING IS
FIRST WINDER

SAMPLE MATERIALS LIST

Item	Quantity	Price/Unit	Total Cost
2 × 12 stringers	_____	$ _____ /bd.ft.	$ _____
stock for treads	_____	$ _____ /bd.ft.	$ _____
stock for risers	_____	$ _____ /bd.ft.	$ _____
urethane varnish or oil for finish	_____	$ _____ /gal.	$ _____
misc. 2 × 4, and 2 × 6 for cleats, braces, landing	_____	$ _____ /bd.ft.	$ _____
1/8" masonite to protect treads during building	1 sheet	$ _____ /sheet	$ _____

PART FOUR
ESTIMATING

chapter 22
Estimating

This section on estimating is short but important. To be in control of your building project, and have fun doing it, you need realistic expectations of what your house will cost and how much work it will take to make it livable. There are several things you can do to bring that about. First, make careful, detailed estimates according to the instructions in this chapter. Second, be skeptical and conservative about the estimates you make. People always tend to underestimate. Third, adopt the same skepticism to any estimates that plumbers, electricians, or other workers give you. Unless these subcontractors are offering you a fixed price for the job, or are known as accurate estimators, assume their work may cost more than they say it will. Fourth, plan what you will do if the money and time start to run out. Have a part of the work in mind that can be put off, simplified, or eliminated if necessary.

These precautions may seem excessive, but they are not. Probably half of the people who build their own houses find out that the job takes twice as much time and costs twice as much money as they expected. When this happens, the new house can become a burden instead of a pleasure. If your time and money are limited, estimate carefully.

Your estimate has three parts: a *cost estimate*, showing how much money you expect to spend; a *labor estimate*, showing how long the job should take; and a *schedule*, showing when and in what order events should happen. All three are needed for a well-coordinated, smooth-running operation.

COST ESTIMATE

Your estimate of costs will include:

a list of design and preliminary planning costs

a list of materials, showing actual costs from actual suppliers

a plumbing, wiring, and heating budget, which will either be your own, if you're doing the work yourself, or a bid or estimate from an electrician or plumber.

a list of any subcontracts, such as septic system, well drilling, etc.

a budget for any help you expect to pay for, such as a carpenter or mason

a list of tool costs

Design and Planning Costs. Include the costs of any permits or other legal expenses. The town clerk or building department can issue applications for these permits and tell you what they will cost. Include here any money you spend for design advice. This could mean hiring an architect to design your house. For the owner-builder it will probably mean hiring an architect, builder, or carpenter to work on the design and estimate, or simply to look over and criticize the design. You should offer to pay professional people for the advice they give you if they spend more than an hour or two at it. This advice is worth money to you, and it usually will be given to you during time when the person would otherwise be earning money.

Materials Cost. A complete list of materials should include all the un-obvious little items, as well as the obvious big expenses. I have tried in the sample materials lists at the end of chapters nine through nineteen to include every category of material that applies except the plumbing and wiring materials, which we will get to later. Make a separate list for each part of your house, based on these samples. Add or subtract items to adapt the lists to your design. Itemize what you need in each category. Usually your drawings will provide the best tool for figuring quantities. For example, you can figure out what studs you need by counting the studs in your framing plans. You can figure your siding by measuring the wall area with your architect's scale right on your elevation drawings. Most of the sample lists are preceded by tips to help you figure quantities. Model your lists after this form:

Item	Quantity	Price/Unit	Total Cost
Insulation:			
6″ × 23″ foil-backed fiberglass insulation	1100 sq.ft.	.21/sq.ft.	$231.00
Soffit:			
½″ × 4′ × 8′ bracewall	12 sheets	6.40/sheet	76.80
Joists:			
13 2 × 6 × 16	208 bd.ft.	.20/bd.ft.	41.60
11 2 × 6 × 12	132 bd.ft.	.20/bd.ft.	26.40

Under "Quantity," use the units the material is commonly sold in, as I have done in the sample lists. In the case of framing lumber, you will be listing the quantities two different ways. Under the heading "Item," write exactly how many of each size you need. But under the heading "Quantity," translate the units into board feet, which is how lumber is priced.

Some materials will not have found their way on to one of the materials lists you have made. Add a list of these essential extras, which may include the following items:

NAILS.   The selection below is a good supply to start building with.

50 lbs. 8d common nails
50 lbs. 8d galvanized common nails (if your siding consists of boards)
50 lbs. 5d galvanized box nails (if the siding consists of clapboards or shingles)
25 lbs. 10d common nails
50 lbs. 16d common nails
20 lbs. 20d common nails
5 lbs. 8d duplex (double-headed) nails, for scaffolding
5 lbs. 16d duplex nails, for scaffolding
5 lbs. 10d finish nails
5 lbs. 8d finish nails
5 lbs. 6d finish nails
5 lbs. 4d finish nails

EXTRA LUMBER.   Besides the wood that actually goes into the house, you will need lumber for a few special purposes.

For sawhorse tops:
1 — 2 × 6 × 12
For scaffolding:
6 — 2 × 6 × 8 (planed)
12 — 2 × 4 × 16
6 — 2 × 10 × 16 (rough, if possible)
For miscellaneous jobs:
300 bd.ft. extra boards, cheap grade from the sawmill
20 — 2 × 4 × 16
1 bundle shim shingles

MISCELLANEOUS

12 joist hangers for attaching scaffolding to the sheathing.
1 roll of 4 mil plastic, 20″ × 100″ for covering lumber and other uses

Next, reorganize these lists into a consolidated form for suppliers. First make a list of the things you expect to buy from the lumber yard. On this list group all the insulation together, all the nails together, all the framing lumber together, and so on. Consolidate items such as 2 × 4s that are found on more than one of your original lists.

Lumber Yard List

Date Needed	Item	Quantity	Price/Unit	Total Cost
	Insulation:			
7/15	6″ × 23″ fiberglass	2000 sq.ft.	.21/sq.ft.	$420.00
7/15	3½″ × 16″ fiberglass	1500 sq.ft.	.16/sq.ft.	240.00
8/15	2″ × 2′ × 8′ urethane	256 sq.ft.	.30/sq.ft.	76.80
7/1	½″ × 4′ × 8′ bracewall	26 sheets	6.40/sheet	166.40
	Framing:			
7/15	26 2 × 4 × 8	780 bd.ft.	.20/bd.ft.	156.00
	50 2 × 4 × 12			
	11 2 × 4 × 14			
	13 2 × 4 × 16			
7/1	12 2 × 6 × 12	144 bd.ft.	.21/bd.ft.	30.24
8/1	18 2 × 8 × 18	432 bd.ft.	.22/bd.ft.	95.04
8/1	1 2 × 12 × 16	32 bd.ft.	.22/bd.ft.	7.04

Make separate lists for sawmills, hardware stores, glass shops, and any other suppliers. These consolidated lists can follow the general form of the samples, but add an extra column to record the dates by which you will need each item.

Preceding is a sample Lumber Yard List. Note that the 2 × 4s are priced in one lump of 780 board feet for convenience. Framing lumber is often sold at a single board-foot price, even for pieces of different sizes. In that case, you consolidate all framing lumber under "Quantity" and "Price," even though you itemize it separately in the "Items" column.

Use the final lists when you visit suppliers. Add sales tax (if any) to totals.

Plumbing, Wiring, and Heating Budget.   If you are doing your own plumbing, wiring, or heating work, list materials just as you did others. The bibliography lists books that can help you. Check discount stores, Sears, Roebuck, etc., for good prices.

If you will be hiring someone to do this work, you can get comparative *bids* or *estimates*. A *bid* is a written or oral commitment to perform certain work for a specified total price. If you want to compare bids, specify the work clearly enough so that you are sure the bids from different contractors are for comparable work.

An *estimate* is very different from a bid. It is merely a worker's opinion about the cost of the job, and implies no legal responsibility. You will actually be paying for the work by the hour, plus materials costs. Some electricians, plumbers, and other workers are expert at their trade but poor at estimating, so you should find out whether the people you talk to have a reputation for good or poor estimating. The person who gives the lowest estimate will not necessarily end up doing the work for the lowest price. If you are unsure about the accuracy of an estimate, inflate it by 50 percent for planning purposes.

Much more important than estimates or bids is the person's reputation for good work, fair prices, and promptness. I would much rather hire someone reliable by the hour than accept a low bid from someone questionable.

When you have decided whom to hire, their bid or estimate can be included in your estimate of costs. Typical plumbing, wiring, and heating costs are given in chapter two on preliminary design.

Other Subcontractors.   Obtain bids or estimates on roadwork, excavation, well drilling, foundation, septic system, and so forth from other subcontractors. Also include the cost of the electrical service to be provided by the electric company.

Budget for Hired Help.   As I suggest in chapter two, inexperienced people will usually benefit from hiring a friendly experienced carpenter (or for stonework, a mason) to act as teacher and co-worker. Such a person can work full-time, part-time, or just be available for consultations. It helps to have this person around early to help with design and estimating. You may also want to hire other skilled or unskilled people to help you build.

After you have estimated how much work your house will require (see Labor Estimate, below), make a list showing whom you plan to hire, how long you want them to work, what the wages will be, and what the approximate total cost will be.

Tool Budget.   Chapter twenty-four lists essential tools and suggests possible places to buy them at reasonable costs.

Your Final Cost Estimate:

1. Design Costs
   Permits
   Design advice
2. Materials
   Lumber yard
   Sawmill
   Hardware store
   Glass supplier
   Other
   Plus 20% for unanticipated items
   Plus sales tax, if any
3. Plumbing, wiring, heating budget
   Plumbing
   Wiring
   Heating
   Note: Inflate unreliable estimates 50%; inflate reliable estimates 15%
4. Other subcontractors
   Well
   Excavation
   Septic system
   Roadwork
   Mason
   Electrical service
   Other
   Note: Inflate unreliable estimates 50%; inflate reliable estimates 15%
5. Budget for hired help
6. Tool costs
7. Miscellaneous

LABOR ESTIMATE

You can't predict precisely how long it will take to build your house, but you can make a projection for planning purposes. I suggest you make 2 kinds of time estimates. First, make your own estimate using the guidelines in this section. Then, if you are hiring someone to help you build, pay him or her to do another estimate, based on your actual design. Base planning on the higher of the two estimates.

Since every house and every crew are different, it would seem impossible to make an accurate estimate of labor time. I have found that there is at least a range of consistency from one owner-built project to another. Most owner-built houses take between 2 and 4 hours of work per square foot of living space (total usable floor area). Thus a 1000-square-foot house is likely to take from 2000 to 4000 hours to build more or less completely.

To help you figure out where you fit in this spectrum, I am going to introduce two arbitrary but useful measures: the *typical house* and the *mixed crew*.

By a *typical house* I mean a house that is fairly simple, fairly economical in materials but that has some special features or complications that will take some extra time to complete. Houses 1, 2, 4, 6, and 9 in the introduction are examples of what I mean. One house has a complex roof. One has an octagonal addition. One has a very simple plan but uses slow materials, like clapboards and real plaster walls. But all these houses are essentially straightforward, not tricky. None has a lot of stonework, uses recycled wood, or has a hard-to-build shape. If the shape of the house *seems* complex, the complexity was achieved by combining simple boxlike shapes.

By a *mixed crew*, I mean one in which there are both experienced and inexperienced workers. A mixed crew might consist of:

> one professional carpenter, plus two inexperienced people
> or, one somewhat experienced but nonprofessional builder, plus one inexperienced person
> or, two energetic and handy but inexperienced people, plus daily advice and supervision from a very experienced carpenter or builder
> or, a larger crew with the same basic proportions as those above

These crews are typical of owner-built projects and can be considered about equally productive. If you have what I call a typical design and a mixed crew, your house will take about 3 hours of labor to build per square foot of floor space. You can add up the floor area of the house and multiply by 3 to figure out how many hours you might need. Decks are much simpler to make than rooms, so when totaling floor area, take a third of the actual deck area as your deck figure.

If the house is 800 square feet, plus a deck of 300 square feet, your calculations might look like those in the following sample.

Floor area	800 sq.ft.
1/3 of deck area	100 sq.ft.
Total Area	900 sq.ft.
Times 3 hrs./sq.ft.	× 3
Total hrs. needed	2700 hrs.

Average crew size	4
Times average work week	× 40 hrs.
Weekly output of crew	160 hrs/wk.

$$\frac{\text{Hr. needed to finish}}{\text{Weekly output of crew}} = \frac{2700}{160} = 17 \text{ weeks of work to build house}$$

Factors that would make the job take longer to build than a typical house:

Complicated design. If the design has lots of cupolas, diagonal walls, bay windows, complex roof shapes, curved windows, 4 stories, or similar complications you can expect it to take you an extra hour per foot, at least. House 5 is a good example of what I mean by a complicated house.

Stonework. Any significant amount of stonework will add to labor time. If all the walls of a house are stone, for example, the extra work could easily add 2 hours per square foot to your labor time.

Recycled lumber. If you are building your house with recycled lumber, you can expect to spend an extra 1 hour or more per foot if you include the work of tearing down the old building. Houses 3 and 7 were built with used lumber.

Inaccessible site: If your site has a difficult access, or if you have no electricity for power tools, allow 1 extra hour per foot or more.

High degree of finish: If you are striving for a highly finished appearance throughout, with lots of trim, fancy joints, precise finish work, etc., expect to spend an extra hour per square foot, or more.

Factors that can make your house go up *faster* than a typical house:

Plywood: Plywood as subfloor, sheathing, or siding, is much quicker to put up than boards. If you use plywood extensively, expect to save about 1/2 hour per square foot. This will be particularly true if the materials you put *over* the plywood are fairly fast to put up. For example, if you use vertical board siding (or no siding) over plywood sheathing, you have a relatively fast design, but the extra work of shingling would offset the time saved using plywood.

Simplified design: Our typical, 3-hour-per square-foot house is not overcomplicated, but it does have some extras and complications. You can design a house with a *very* simple shape, a *very* simple roof, and *none* of the extras mentioned above and save about 1/2 hour of work per square foot, in addition to any time you save by using plywood. Houses 6 and 10 in the introduction are examples.

Total the factors that add to or subtract from building time, starting with the basic figure of 3 hours/sq.ft. If you build a stone house in an inaccessible place with a cupola, a bay window, and a curved wall, you may spend 6 hours/sq.ft. or more. If you build a simple pole house and use plywood extensively, your house may take only 2 hours/sq.ft.

All the foregoing calculations assume a *mixed crew*. Now adjust your calculations to account for the specific complexion of your work crew. A crew that consists entirely of or mostly of experienced people could get a house built much faster than a mixed crew — perhaps in 65 percent to 75 percent of the time. On the other hand, a completely inexperienced crew, with little or no support from skilled people, will require maybe half again as much time as a mixed crew. Some inexperienced people can work as productively as a professional, if the person supervising the day's work is good at supervising and if the inexperienced person is handy, energetic, and fairly confident. Even without supervision, some inexperienced people work very quickly because they have a knack for building or have experience in other areas of life they can apply to building. Others may work more slowly.

Many people will be moving in as soon as their house is livable and finishing the job at a much slower pace. They will need to know how long it will take to provide a livable shelter, even if some of the insulation is exposed, some of the windows are only sheets of plastic, and finish flooring is not down yet. You would probably not be too far wrong if you assumed that, with careful planning, you could move into your house with some degree of comfort after about two thirds of the work is done.

SCHEDULE

A good estimate of your costs and your time will enable you to make a schedule showing when things will happen. Your schedule coordinates both materials and people. If it is well planned, you will have the materials and help you need when you are ready for them. The plumber will be there when you are ready for the plumbing to be done; the forms will be built when the concrete truck arrives; dried boards will be on hand when it is time to put up sheathing; a big crew will be available when you are roofing.

Advance planning is particularly important when subcontractors and suppliers are concerned because they may run behind schedule during the warm-weather building season. If you know beforehand when you will need them, you can be near the top of their list, so you won't be repeatedly put off with promises to show up or deliver "by the first of next week."

Designs vary too much to say just how long each phase of building will take. But knowing approximately how long the project as a whole will take gives you a rough idea of how long the different stages will require. If a carpenter or builder will be helping you, he or she can help you make up a schedule. The sample schedule that follows will provide a rough guide.

Sample Schedule.

First Summer:
Look for land, check local laws governing building; buy the land
Winter before building:
November–February:
    Design house
    Look for new and used building materials; visit sawmills
    Look for and hire carpenter or builder to work with you (if any)
    Buy tools
    Make detailed estimates
March: Obtain all required permits
April:
    Hire well driller, plumber, electrician, and any other subcontractors
    Arrange for temporary electrical hookup
    Buy any boards from sawmills that you must air-dry yourself, and sticker them on your land
Second summer:
May:
    Prepare site
    Well drilling and excavation begin
    Build foundation
    Materials arrive for building floor, walls
June:
    Build floor and walls
    Materials arrive for roof
    Doors and windows arrive
July:
    Build roof, install windows, doors, siding
    Do rough electrical and plumbing work
    Prepare all materials for finish work
August:
    Put up interior walls and ceilings
    Finish plumbing, wiring
    Move in
September:
    Do finish work
    Sticker best boards inside
October–December:
    Take care of any final details

PART FIVE
ON THE JOB

chapter 23
Scaffolding

Scaffolding is usually built quickly, but it must be strong, because a fall from 20 feet is no joke. I have had scaffolding that looked strong collapse under me more than once, and only luck — in the form of something handy to jump to — prevented me from being hurt. Check a scaffolding carefully before you trust your life to it. Inspect it every day or two. Look for loose joints and nails pulling out. Never climb on a scaffolding you didn't build yourself until you have made sure it is safe.

HOW TO BUILD A SCAFFOLD

Figure 320 shows the most common scaffolding techniques. The point is to support the horizontal 2 × 10 or 2 × 12 planks that you will walk on with the minimum structure that is strong. Different structures apply to different situations. The middle section of the drawing shows the most stable and safe way to support planks in the middle of a wall. Crosspieces run between the house and a post sitting firmly on the ground. At the house, the

Fig. 320   SCAFFOLDING

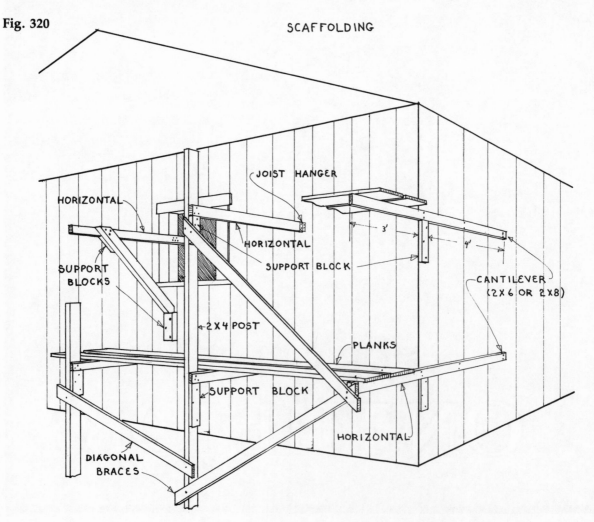

crosspiece sits in a joist hanger nailed to the sheathing. If joist hangers aren't handy, rest the crosspiece on a 2 × 4 cleat nailed firmly into the *wall studs*, not just the sheathing. At the outer end, nail the crosspiece into the post. It also has a support block underneath, so that the joint does not depend on just one set of nails.

The upper left-hand part of Figure 320 shows how to support the crosspiece with a diagonal brace. The 2 × 4 diagonal is supported at the bottom by a block or cleat nailed into the wall studs. The brace should not stick out from the house more than 45 degrees. You *cannot* simply attach the inner end of the crosspiece to the house with a joist hanger, as the outward thrust of the crosspiece will pull the joist hanger away from the wall. The solution shown is to nail the crosspiece solidly into the window frame. You can further strengthen the joint by nailing a support block to its inner side to hook on to the wall stud (Figure 321).

In the upper right-hand part of Figure 320, the crosspiece is cantilevered out from the adjacent wall of the building. You can do this with 2 × 6s or 2 × 8s but not with 2 × 4s. The crosspiece should extend at least 4 feet on the wall and into the air no more than 3 feet. This cantilevered crosspiece should be firmly nailed into each wall *stud* (not just sheathing), and there should be a well-nailed support block at the corner.

Once you have provided horizontal support,

lay 2 × 10 or 2 × 12 planks on the crosspieces. They can span 8 or 10 feet, depending on the quality of the planks. Inspect them for large knots, splits, or other defects. When they are in place, nail them down to the crosspieces.

To make the scaffold rigid, nail on diagonal bracing as shown in Figure 320. This can be any 1"- or 2"-board, nailed with 1 or 2 nails at each joint. Keep nailing on braces until the entire scaffold is rigid when you shake it from the ground.

When the scaffold is complete, climb on and see how it feels. Bounce on it gently. Make sure none of the nails is pulling loose. The planks can be somewhat springy, but if they feel too springy, provide more supports or stack another set of planks on top of the first. When in doubt, add more lumber, nails, crosspieces, or support blocks.

On a high scaffold, add a railing. The easiest railing is made by letting the 2 × 4 posts run up higher than the planks. Nail the railing to the insides of the posts.

How you nail a scaffold will affect its strength. Large nails have more holding power. When nailing 2 pieces together, drive the nails in at various angles to strengthen the joint. It often helps to clamp the pieces together before nailing. The scaffold will be easier to take apart later if you use duplex nails. These have 2 heads so the nail can be driven home but still extracted by the second head.

Fig. 321   SCAFFOLDING DETAIL
(HORIZONTAL SECTION)

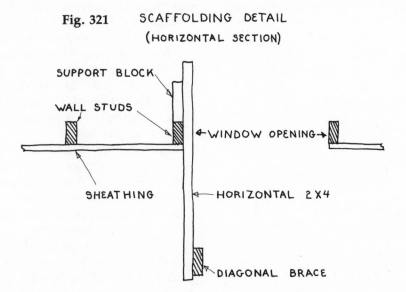

chapter 24
Using Tools

HAND TOOLS YOU WILL NEED

You can buy good, used hand tools through classified ads or from stores that specialize in secondhand tools. New tools can be purchased at hardware stores, discount houses, and Sears, Roebuck. The bibliography lists tool catalogues you can send for. Hand tools are sold in several qualities. Sears, for example, sells a top line called Craftsman, and a medium line called Companion. The less-expensive Stanley line is called Handyman. In general, buy top-grade hand tools. The medium grade will work, but not as well. Where possible I have indicated brands I have had good luck with.

Hand Saws. Figure 322 shows four kinds of hand saws. The hacksaw is for cutting metal. The 8 point crosscut saw (8 teeth per inch) is for framing and rough work. A 10 point or 12 point crosscut saw, sometimes called a finish saw or panel saw, is for

Fig. 322   HAND SAWS

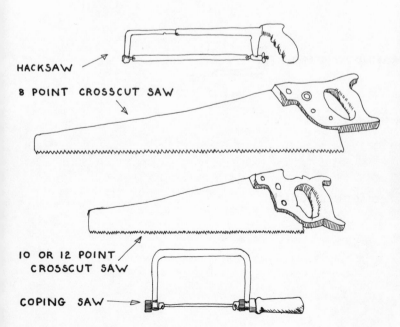

HACKSAW

8 POINT CROSSCUT SAW

10 OR 12 POINT
CROSSCUT SAW

COPING SAW

finish work because its smaller teeth make a finer cut. A coping saw is for cutting curves.

Measuring Tools

RAFTER SQUARE.   Figure 323 shows a rafter square, also known as a steel square, a handy tool for measuring and marking operations, especially during framing. It is also handy as a straightedge and for innumerable little tasks. Beyond this, the rafter square is the carpenter's computer. The tables and numbers on the square enable you to figure rafter lengths, find angles, and solve countless other carpentry problems. Stanley rafter squares come with a little book called *How to Use the Stanley Steel Square*, by L. Perth, which provides an excellent introduction to the use of this tool. This is not essential knowledge for someone building just one house, but if you enjoy geometry, it may be worth learning about the rafter square.

TWENTY-EIGHT INCH LEVEL.   The level is used to make sure surfaces are exactly level (horizontal) or plumb (vertical). Often there will be 2 vials for horizontal measurement and 2 for vertical measurement. I like the 24-inch or 28-inch size. When the bubble in the vial is centered between the lines, the surface the level is resting on is level or plumb, as the case may be.

COMBINATION SQUARE.   The combination square is a good tool to carry while working, because it is so versatile. It measures 90-degree and 45-degree angles, which you have to do continually. By sliding the 12-inch ruler back and forth in the cast-iron frame, you can use the combination square to make many identical measurements quickly. If you want to make a series of marks 6 inches in from the edge of a board, set the ruler to protrude from the frame by 6 inches. Then slide the square along the board, and make your series of measurements quickly and accurately.

BEVEL GAUGE.   Also known as an angle bevel, the bevel gauge pivots at the joint to measure and mark any angle.

Fig. 323   MEASURING   TOOLS

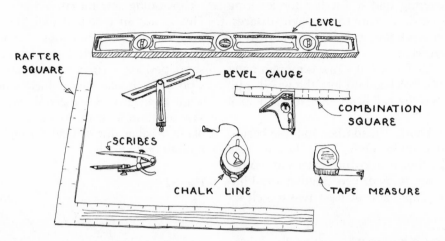

TAPE MEASURE.   Always carry a tape measure with you. The best ones (in my opinion) are Powerlock tapes by Stanley. Probably the most versatile size is the ³/₄″ × 16′ model (PL 316). You also will need a 50-foot tape for laying out your foundation, but this is a good tool to borrow since you will only need it for a few days.

CHALK LINE.   This is a reel of string inside a case filled with powdered chalk used to make long, straight lines. Stretch the string tight between two points and snap the line in the middle. This will leave a line of chalk on the work.

SCRIBES.   A set of scribes is like a compass, except that there is a lock to hold the setting. Scribes are used to transfer shapes for curved or irregular cuts.

MITER GAUGE.   A miter gauge, or protractor guide, is an adjustable T-square used as a guide or fence with skill saws. Figure 335 shows a protractor guide being used.

Edge Tools (Figure 324)

PLANES.   You need a large plane for smoothing or trimming the edges of boards and a small one for rounding edges and trimming end-grain. The large plane can be either a smoothing plane (8–10 inches) or a jack plane (13–14 inches). The short plane should be a block plane (about 6 inches).

CHISELS.   I suggest buying a ¹/₂, a 1, and a 2-inch chisel. Stanley and Millers Falls are good brands, but also keep your eye out for Buck, Greenley, Marples, and Witherby.

COMBINATION STONE.   To sharpen your edge tools, you will need a combination sharpening stone with a coarse and a medium side. Finer stones can be obtained through the tool catalogues listed in the bibliography.

Hammers and Bars (Figure 325)

Fig. 325   HAMMERS   AND   BARS

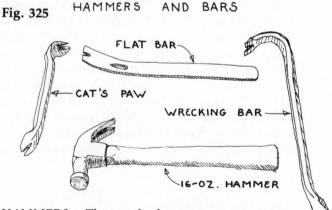

HAMMERS.   The regular hammer you see everywhere is called a 16-ounce claw hammer. I think most people will have the best luck with this size hammer, but some people may prefer the larger 20-ounce framing hammer. Buy a top-quality hammer, because cheaper hammers may break and will be more fatiguing to use. Stanley, Plumb, Trustworthy, and True Temper make good hammers. Heft several brands and pick the one that feels most comfortable in your hand. You may also want to invest in a medium-weight sledgehammer.

EDGE   TOOLS   **Fig. 324**

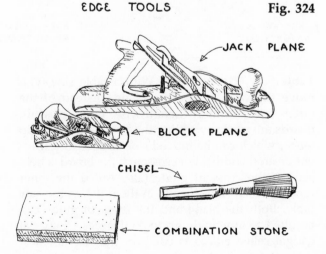

BARS. You need a hook-shaped wrecking bar for heavy-duty levering and a flat bar for levering objects when you don't want to mar their surfaces. For foundation work you may want to borrow or rent a 5-foot crowbar.

CAT'S PAW. The Drew Cat's Paw is for removing nails. Pound the notched end into the wood until the notch catches the nail head, then lever the nail out.

Miscellaneous Tools. In addition to these basics, you will need a utility knife, a staple gun, nail aprons, two 25-foot heavy-duty extension cords, a $2/32$-inch nail set, screwdrivers (regular and Phillips head), tin snips, and at least two 6-inch C-clamps.

POWER TOOLS TO BUY

Though you should buy top-quality hand tools, I think with power tools it is best to buy the cheaper models of the better brands, such as Skil, Rockwell, Black & Decker, Stanley, or Sears's Craftsman. Such tools will be powerful and durable enough for your purposes and sometimes lighter and easier to handle than more expensive models. These tools can be bought at discount houses or on sale.

$7^1/4$-inch Portable Circular Saw (Figure 333). This is the indispensable power tool. It is often called a skill saw, which is actually a trade name of the Skil Company. Good saws are made by Rockwell, Black & Decker, Stanley and Sears, but I recommend the Skil 574 or 559. These saws are light, have good visibility, and in general are easier to use than most. You will need a few $7^1/4$-inch rough-cut combination blades and one smooth-cut combination blade. A combination blade can cut both with and across the grain. A single carbide-tipped combination blade, which will stay sharp all summer, can do the job of several regular-tipped blades. A carbide blade costs about $30, but the savings in convenience and sharpening costs are worth it in the end.

SABER SAW

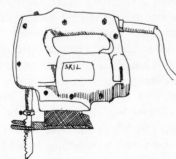

Fig. 326

Saber Saw (Figure 326). A saber saw is a portable reciprocating saw for curved cuts and scrollwork. This is not an essential tool, but it is cheap and very handy for small jobs. Some inexperienced people — particularly those who help you out for short periods — may have a hard time handling a portable circular saw, which is heavy and somewhat awkward. Such people will find the saber saw much more comfortable to use. With a sharp blade, a saber saw can cut through 2-inch framing lumber quite easily.

Fig. 327

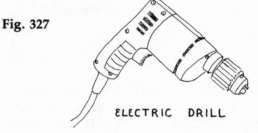

ELECTRIC DRILL

Electric Drill (Figure 327). Any electric drill will drill holes, but if you can afford it, a $3/8$-inch variable-speed reversing drill will give you more power than the cheaper $1/4$-inch models and can also drive screws. A $3/8$-inch drill will be particularly useful for sheetrocking. You will also need a small set of twist-type drill bits ($1/16$ inch to $1/4$ inch) and a set of the flat-type high-speed bits (sometimes called spade bits) going from $1/4$ inch to 1 inch.

TABLE SAW   **Fig. 328**

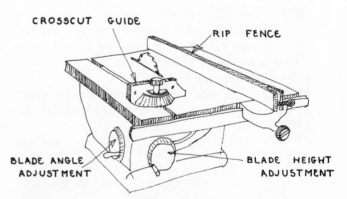

CROSSCUT GUIDE
RIP FENCE
BLADE ANGLE ADJUSTMENT
BLADE HEIGHT ADJUSTMENT

Table Saw (Figure 328). With a table saw, you move the work across the blade, instead of the other way around. Lengthwise cuts (rips) in boards are made by sliding the board along the rip fence, which can be moved side to side for different desired widths. For crosscuts, the board is held against the crosscut guide (also called the miter fence), which slides neatly in the notch of the saw table. Both the blade and the crosscut guide can be tilted to any angle up to 45 degrees. A special gadget called a *dado* is used for making notches.

It consists of several blades that stack together in various combinations for cuts of various widths. If you buy a dado, buy the stacking kind, rather than the adjustable one-piece kind, which are *very* unsafe.

I strongly recommend buying a table saw. It permits you to cut boards accurately both with and against the grain and to make cuts at almost any angle, and it makes notches and joints of many kinds. All this can be done with hand saws or a portable circular saw, but the table saw will do them more quickly, easily, and accurately. The savings in time will be particularly great for finish work, window making, cabinet making, and other fine work. You can buy a used saw for $100 to $200 and resell it later at the same price. Look for an old Craftsman 10-inch model, such as is shown in Figure 328, or a Rockwell or Delta 8-inch saw. When you buy a used saw, have a knowledgeable person look it over to make sure it is all there and in good shape.

You will see many professional woodworkers (including myself) walking around with missing or shortened fingers; most of these people got those injuries on the table saw. A table saw is safe only when used properly. Its hazards are not obvious, and you can risk injury without being aware of it. For each type of cut there are one or two safe techniques and two or three techniques that *appear* safe. There are good books on using table saws, but I think you should have someone who knows how to use one correctly teach you safe cutting methods and watch you use the machine at first.

While you are shopping for tools, someone may recommend that you buy a radial arm saw. This is a type of saw in which the blade and motor move back and forth above the saw table on a track. A radial arm saw does the same work that a table saw does and is strongly promoted by stores and home hobby books. Its advantage is that the work is stationary and the saw moves, so long pieces, which would be unwieldy on a table saw, can be crosscut easily.

If you value your fingers, do not buy a radial saw. This saw is dangerous for crosscutting because so much of the blade is exposed that a slight inattention can result in an accident. For rip cuts, the radial saw is intrinsically dangerous even if you give full attention to what you're doing.

Router (Figure 329). A router is a motor mounted on a circular base. A chuck called a *collet* on the end of the motor shaft holds bits of many shapes to make various cuts. A router is not an essential tool, but it is handy for notches, grooves, and molding shapes. I use mine to make hinge mor-

Fig. 329 STANLEY ROUTER

TYPICAL ROUTER CUTS

tises, notches in window and door jambs, and for similar work.

Belt Sander (Figure 330). With a belt sander, you can sand your woodwork 10 or 20 times as fast as you can by hand. While a belt sander is not essential, it will be a big help if you plan to sand much of your finish work. Get the 3″ × 21″ belt size.

BELT SANDER

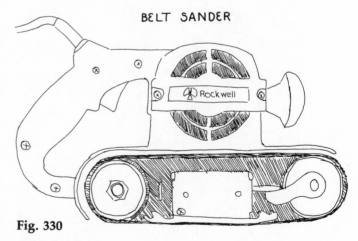

Fig. 330

TOOLS TO MAKE
Sawhorses. Amateur builders almost never build sawhorses, but they are worth the effort. Sawhorses serve as chair, table, workbench, scaffold,

and in general make it possible for you to work at a comfortable height. You can do everything working on the floor, but it is more fatiguing and takes longer.

You will need 4, preferably 6, sawhorses. Figure 331 shows a design that I have found quick to build and fairly strong. It will be relatively easy to figure out the angles if you make a full-scale drawing of the sawhorse on a piece of plywood.

SAWHORSE

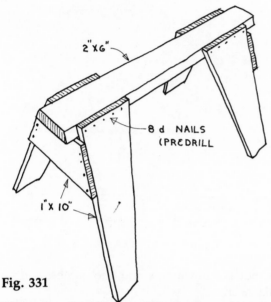

Fig. 331

Water Level.   Figure 332 shows a homemade water level, a cheap, little used but essential tool for leveling foundations and other large-scale leveling operations. It consists of a jug and 15 to 30 feet of ¼-inch (inside diameter) clear plastic tubing from a hardware store.

WATER   LEVEL   **Fig. 332**

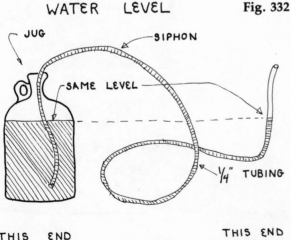

THIS END
STATIONARY

THIS END
MOVES

To set up the level, fill the jug with water. Then stick one end of the tube in the jug. It helps to use string or a coathanger to secure the tubing

to the jug. Suck on the free end of the tube to fill the tube with water.

The first time you are likely to use your water level is when you put up batter boards for the foundation. These boards have to be the same height, so you have to mark the stakes all at the same level, namely, the foundation height. Here is the procedure for making such a measurement with the water level. You can use the same method with any similar problem.

Set the jug securely somewhere so that the water inside is even with the proposed foundation height. You can make minor adjustments by letting a little water out of the jug through the tube or by pouring a little more into the jug. Carry the far end of the tube to each stake and hold the tube against the stake. When the water settles down, mark the stake opposite the water level in the tube. Always take measurements within 6 inches of the end of the tube. Keep your finger over the end of the tube while carrying it around to keep water from leaking out and changing the setting.

If the level is not working right, there may be a kink in the tube or air may have gotten into the line back at the jug. Remove the bubbles by letting water run out of the far end of the tube, and start again.

When it is inconvenient to place the jug at the level you want to find, put the reservoir at an arbitrary level and take readings at the various locations. Then measure up or down a uniform amount to the final level you need.

Plywood Cutting Jig.   If you will use a lot of plywood in your design, the jig shown in Figure 333 is worth making. It is a straight track 8 feet long that your circular saw rides along to make long straight cuts. The jig is made from 2 strips of straight, unwarped ½-inch plywood, one 6″ × 8′ and the other approximately 12″ × 8′. The saw rides on top of the wide piece, with the base sliding against the edge of the narrow piece. This edge — Edge A in Figure 333 — must be perfectly straight, so it should consist of one of the factory-cut plywood edges, which will be perfectly straight. Edge B is precisely as far away from Edge A as the saw blade is from the left edge of the saw base. Thus Edge B shows exactly where the saw will cut.

The accuracy of the jig depends on the precision of the distance between Edge A and Edge B. Do not try to align these two edges by measurement. Instead, build the jig with the bottom piece oversize an inch or two on the right. The first time you run the saw down the track — being careful to keep the saw smoothly against Edge A — the saw itself will cut Edge B perfectly.

Fig. 333

PLYWOOD CUTTING JIG

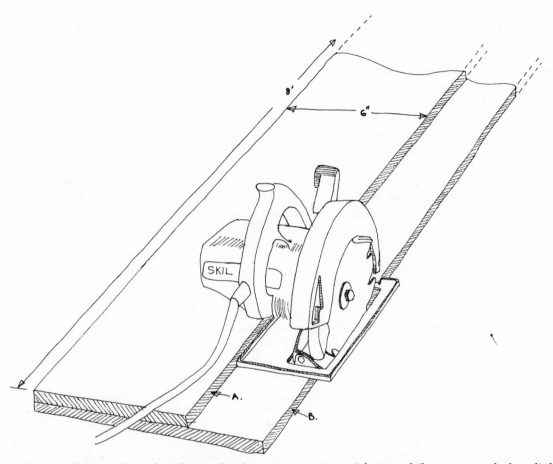

To use the jig, place the plywood to be cut on sawhorses, and mark it. Place Edge B on your marks, and clamp or tack the jig to the work. Set the saw blade just deep enough to cut through the plywood, and carefully run the portable circular saw down the track.

USING TOOLS

Sharpening. A sharp saw or chisel will work ten times faster than a dull one. Often the difference between the results an experienced person gets and an inexperienced person gets is the difference in the sharpness of their tools.

Lumber yards, hardware stores, and saw shops will sharpen saw blades for you on short notice.

You can sharpen chisels and planes yourself with a combination stone, which has a medium and a coarse side (Figure 324). Start on the coarse side. Wet the stone thoroughly with light oil, such as 3-in-1 or kerosene, and keep it wet. Grind the bevel side only and grind the whole bevel surface at once, holding the blade as in Part A of Figure 334. Move the blade in a broad figure eight pat-

tern. After a while, you can feel a slight burr on the back side of the sharpened edge. When you feel this burr all along the edge, remove it by turning the stone to the medium side and rubbing the chisel a few times, holding the chisel flat as

SHARPENING **Fig. 334**

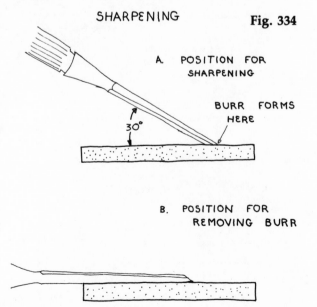

A. POSITION FOR SHARPENING

BURR FORMS HERE

30°

B. POSITION FOR REMOVING BURR

shown in Part B. Then grind the beveled side again, this time using the fine side of the stone until another burr forms. Remove the burr as before.

This sharpening method will give a sharp, usable edge. If nicks are avoided, you will not need to use the coarse side again. Just touch up with the medium side. If a blade gets nicked, it can be taken down on a grinder and then sharpened with a stone. A razor-sharp edge can be obtained with finer sharpening stones purchased through mail-order tool dealers. A really sharp plane is a joy to use, and any energy or money spent on sharpening will be returned to you amply.

Safety.   Both hand and power tools can injure you seriously. Some safety rules apply equally to both:

> No part of your body should be in the line of action of a tool; cut away from yourself

> Secure the work with nails, clamps, or a firm knee before you cut

> Make sure you have a sure footing

> Don't work in an awkward position

Some rules are particularly important with power tools.

> Do not wear loose clothing, which can get tangled in the tool

> Keep long hair from dangling loose

> Learn how to use a new power tool from someone experienced

How to Saw.

POSITIONING.   Position a piece of wood where you can work on it comfortably. Sometimes this will be on your lumber pile or a low table. Sawhorses often provide the best support. Position the piece so that the part you will be using is supported but the part that will be cut off — the scrap — is free to drop to the ground. Otherwise

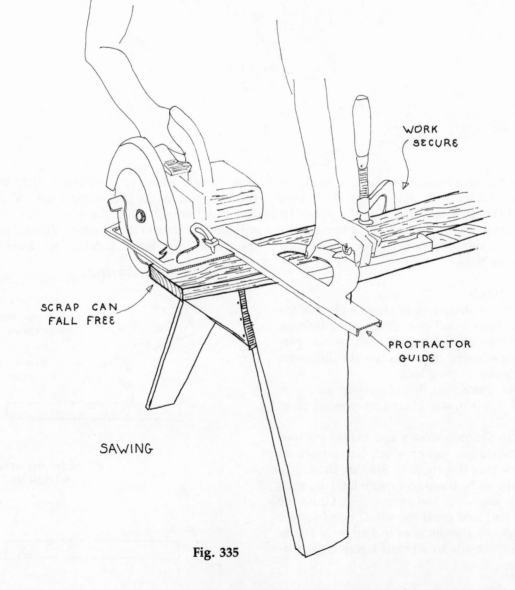

WORK SECURE

SCRAP CAN FALL FREE

PROTRACTOR GUIDE

SAWING

Fig. 335

MARKING

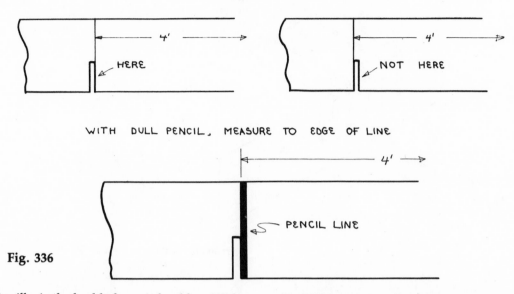

SAW ON WASTE SIDE OF LINE

WITH DULL PENCIL, MEASURE TO EDGE OF LINE

Fig. 336

the wood will pinch the blade as it buckles. With a short piece, you can position the wood on a single sawhorse, as shown in Figure 335. Long pieces can be supported by two horses. In that case do not saw between the horses. Cut at one end, so that the scrap can fall free.

Secure the work. Heavy pieces will stay put by their own weight. Some people can comfortably hold down medium-sized pieces with one knee. The most reliable method is to clamp the piece down with a large clamp, particularly if the piece is small.

MARKING FOR A CUT.   Cut on the waste side of the line. Suppose you want a piece 4 feet long. In Figure 336, if you measured 4 feet from the right-hand end of the piece, made a line, and then sawed to the *right* of the line, you would be cutting the piece too short by the width of the saw blade. With a dull pencil, even sawing on the correct side of the line may leave you with some inaccuracy, because the line itself has thickness. The method I use is quite accurate even with a dull pencil. The line is drawn so that its left-hand *edge* is at 4 feet. The saw cuts to the left of the mark, leaving the line on the piece.

CUTTING.   Take a wide, stable, and secure stance, with firm control. With a hand saw, follow the line by eye and use long, strong, angled strokes of the saw. Keep the saw vertical by feel or by eye. If you are using a power saw, you can also follow the line by eye. However, for an automatically straight and smooth cut that does not depend as much on your skill, use a mitre gauge (Figure 335). This large T-square can be set at any

angle. Hold it against the edge of the wood, then run the metal base of the saw against it.

Some cuts are not so simple. In an angle cut, the blade passes through the wood at an angle rather than straight up and down (Figure 337). If

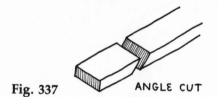

Fig. 337   ANGLE CUT

you are using a portable circular saw, you adjust the base of the saw to the correct angle (measuring with a bevel gauge) and saw as before. With a hand saw, draw the angle on the edge of the piece to guide you in holding the hand saw at the proper angle.

How to Make Notches.   Even big notches can be made quickly with a power saw and chisel. To make a through notch, one going all the way across a piece, set the circular saw to the same depth as the notch should be and make a series of cuts 1/4 inch to 1/2 inch apart in the area to be notched out. Then chisel out the waste, beginning with the chisel in the position shown in Figure 338. Position the chisel bevel up. The saw cuts guide the chisel along the right line and make the work easier for the chisel. Chisel out the visible part of the joint first, then knock out the rest more quickly. Usually a firm hand and sharp blows will give better results than a hesitant approach.

The blade of a chisel tends to follow the grain of the wood, and sometimes the chisel will follow

Fig. 338   NOTCHING

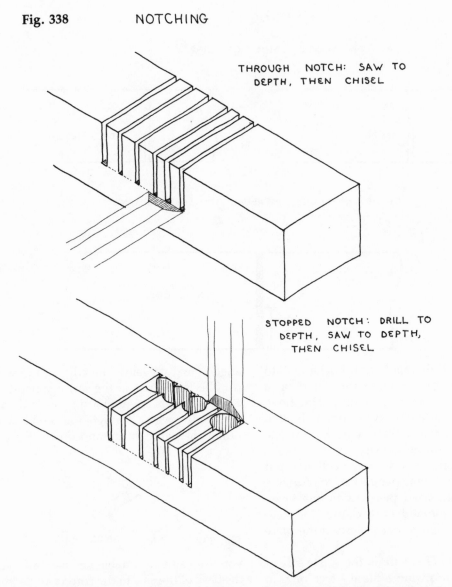

THROUGH NOTCH: SAW TO
DEPTH, THEN CHISEL

STOPPED NOTCH: DRILL TO
DEPTH, SAW TO DEPTH,
THEN CHISEL

the grain in the wrong direction and make a messy job. When this starts to happen, or you anticipate that it will, approach the cut from another direction or angle. Watch the grain as you work, and you will soon learn which angles work best.

If a notch stops partway across the piece, drill a series of holes, as shown in Figure 338. Use a convenient-size drill and drill to the right depth. A piece of tape on the bit will help mark the right depth to drill. Then saw and chisel out the notch as before. The drilling removes enough of the wood to make the chiseling easier and guides the chisel in the right direction. Notice that usually the beveled side of the chisel faces the wood to be removed.

Certain notches may call for variations on this method. Sometimes a hand saw will work better, because the power saw will not reach deep enough. Sometimes a saber saw will do the whole notch. The basic idea is to use saw cuts and drilled

holes to guide the chisel and reduce the amount of work the chisel must do.

Planing.   Planes are used for trimming and smoothing. Keep all planes sharp and adjusted properly. Hold a plane upside-down near a light to see if its blade is parallel to the sole of the plane where it sticks through. If not, the lever near the handle is for adjusting the blade side to side. The knob is for adjusting how much the blade sticks out. For a very smooth cut, or for trimming end-grain, you will need a fine cut. Keep adjusting between trial cuts until the plane cuts well.

Secure the board you are working on. Figure 337 shows a simple method. Nail a block to a sawhorse and clamp your board to the block. For longitudinal planing you will find that the plane usually cuts much better in one direction relative to the grain pattern. Figure 339 shows the right direction. When you begin the stroke, put a little more weight on the forward end of the plane to avoid rounding off the near end of the board. At the far end of the cut, put more weight on the rear end of the plane to avoid rounding off the far end of the board. Use a firm stroke.

When planing end-grain, avoid splitting the wood at the edge by planing from both sides toward the middle as shown in Figure 340.

Scribing. Scribes are for marking irregular or curved cuts (Figure 341). Put the piece you must mark as close as possible to its final location. Set the scribe to a convenient distance. In the illustration this is the maximum width of the crack. Then transfer the curve to the piece to be cut by running the metal point along the curve while the pencil marks the other piece.

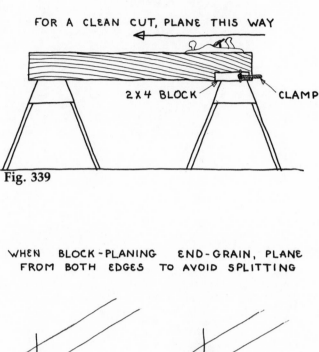

FOR A CLEAN CUT, PLANE THIS WAY

2 X 4 BLOCK   CLAMP

Fig. 339

WHEN BLOCK-PLANING END-GRAIN, PLANE FROM BOTH EDGES TO AVOID SPLITTING

SCRIBING

Fig. 340

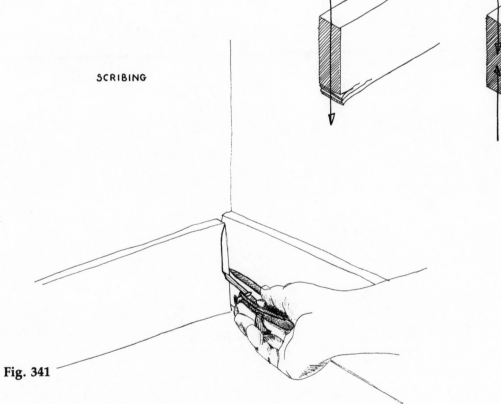

Fig. 341

APPENDICES

APPENDIX A
STRENGTH OF TIMBERS

Chapter six introduced some of the engineering ideas you can use to make sure your house structure is strong. This appendix explains how to use some of these ideas to figure out what sizes of wooden timbers to use in various situations.

HOW MUCH WILL A BEAM SUPPORT?

You can get an idea of how the strength of beams varies by experimenting with a few small pieces of wood, say an oak 1 × 1 × 4', a pine 1 × 1 × 4', and a pine 1 × 2 × 4'. Compare their strengths under different situations. Support them between two chairs. Orient them in different ways. Move the chairs closer together and further apart (span). Push down on them under different arrangements.

Species of wood vary greatly in strength. The oak 1 × 1 will be much stronger than the pine 1 × 1. The strength rating is called "fiber stress in bending" or F. Each kind and grade of wood has an F number (see Appendix B). Eastern spruce has an F of about 1000, and larch graded #1 or #2 has an F of 2050. That means the larch is twice as strong as the spruce.

Your comparisons will show that if the breadth (B) of a piece is doubled, keeping everything else constant, the strength also is doubled. Strength is proportional to breadth. A 2 × 4 on the flat will support twice what a 2 × 2 will. It's

the same as having two pieces instead of one (Figure 342).

If you double the size the other way, in depth (d), the strength increases 4 times. Strength is proportional to the square of the depth. On edge, a 2 × 4 will support 4 times what a 2 × 2 will (Figure 343).

This means a 2 × 4 is twice as strong on edge as lying flat (Figure 344).

If you double the span (L), you halve the strength. Strength is inversely proportional to the span. A 2 × 4 8 feet long supported at the ends will carry half what a 2 × 4 4 feet long will.

Adding these facts together we get the formula used for computing the strength of a beam.

$$\frac{FBd^2}{9L} = \text{Maximum load in lbs.}$$

where   F = the fiber stress (F) of the wood used
        B = the breadth of the beam, in inches
        d = the depth of the beam, in inches
        L = the span, in feet

This form of the formula applies to conditions of uniform distribution of weight, or load. That is, the load is spread approximately evenly over the length of the beam rather than concentrated in one place. Normally the span will be the distance between supports. With sloping rafters, however, the *span* is measured horizontally and will be different than the rafter *length* (Figure 345).

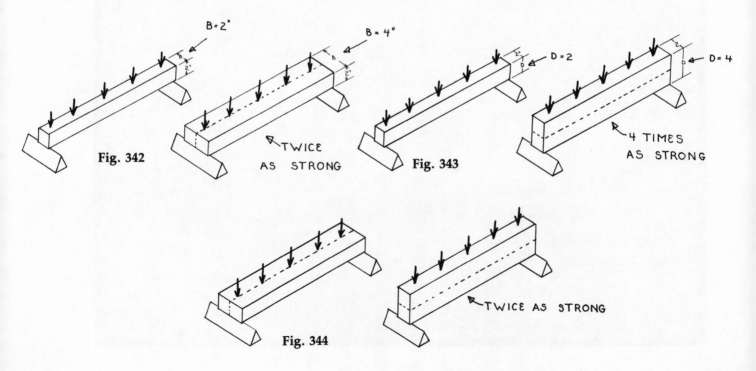

B = 2"   B = 4"   D = 2   D = 4

Fig. 342   TWICE AS STRONG   **Fig. 343**   4 TIMES AS STRONG

Fig. 344   TWICE AS STRONG

Fig. 345

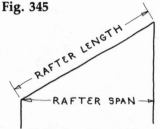

RAFTER LENGTH

RAFTER SPAN

Fig. 346   DEAD LOAD

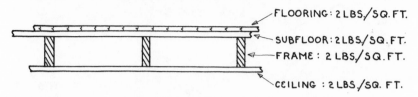

FLOORING: 2 LBS./SQ. FT.

SUBFLOOR: 2 LBS./SQ. FT.

FRAME: 2 LBS./SQ. FT.

CEILING : 2 LBS./SQ. FT.

If the load is concentrated in the middle of a beam, the formula is

$$\frac{FBd^2}{18L} = \text{Maximum load in lbs.}$$

For a cantilever with a uniformly distributed load, the formula is

$$\frac{FBd^2}{36L} = \text{Maximum load in lbs.}$$

For a cantilever with a load concentrated at the end, the formula is

$$\frac{FBd^2}{72L} = \text{Maximum load in lbs.}$$

I should mention here that cantilevers that have the maximum loads these formulas imply will be springy. For this reason it is best to limit the length of cantilevers to about two thirds of the theoretical maximum extension. (Cantilevers are discussed more extensively in chapter six).

Suppose you had a douglas fir 4 × 8, 12 feet long. How much weight would it hold loaded uniformly? From Appendix B you would find the F value of 1600. A nominal 4 × 8 is actually $3^1/_2$ × $7^1/_2$. So B = $3^1/_2$, and d = $7^1/_2$, d² (rounded off) = 56, and L is 12.

$$\frac{\overset{(F)\quad(B)\quad(d^2)}{1600 \times 3.5 \times 56}}{\underset{(L)}{9 \times 12}} = 2904 \text{ lbs.}$$

This does not mean it would break if you put 1 ounce of weight on the timber above the amount computed. A large safety factor is built into these formulas. Also, most beams are actually subjected to their loadings intermittently. The formulas are designed so that if you compute your timbers for the maximum loads they will be subjected to, they will be a good size for their routine and extra-large loadings.

ACTUAL LOADS AND LOAD ASSUMPTIONS

To use these formulas you must know the weight in pounds the timber will have to support. The timber will have to support itself plus part of the building structure. This is called the *dead load*

on the beam. The beam will also be supporting furniture, people, fixtures, snow, and other contents of the building. These weights taken together are called the *live load*.

Dead Loads.

You can find the dead load for a given beam by laboriously adding up the weight of the beam itself and of the other parts of the structure it will support. In Figure 346, the frame weighs about 2 lbs./sq.ft. The plywood subfloor, the oak flooring, and the sheetrock ceiling also weigh about 2 lbs./sq.ft. each. This is a total of 8 lbs./sq.ft. A more precise calculation could be made using densities given in Appendix K.

In fact, you do not need to figure dead loads piece by piece. Usually the total dead load of a floor, wall, or roof is assumed to be 10 lbs./sq.ft. in wood-frame construction. This assumption is conservative and avoids needless calculations. If the structure contains very heavy materials — such as a slate roof or a concrete slab on a floor — make a detailed calculation using the information in Appendix K.

Live Loads.   The snow, furniture, people, and other contents that constitute live load are continually changing, so it does not make sense to figure live loads piece by piece. Instead, calculations are based on assumed average loads. The first floor or living area live load can be assumed to be 40 lbs./sq.ft. The second floor or study areas get lighter use and can be designed for a live load of 30 lbs./sq.ft.

Any roof should be designed to bear a minimum live load of 25 lbs./sq.ft., because even if a roof normally carries nothing, it should be strong enough to support workers during construction or repair. Twenty-five pounds will be a good standard in areas of little or no snow, or for roofs in snow climates that will shed snow. How well a roof sheds snow will depend on conditions of wind and weather and on how slippery the roofing surface is, but usually a roof with a rise of 4 inches per foot (about 20 degrees) will shed deep snow.

Flatter roofs in snow areas can be designed by assuming accumulated snow to weigh about 10 lbs/sq.ft. per foot of depth. In Vermont, where the maximum accumulation on a roof would be about 5 feet, a low-slope roof could be designed to carry

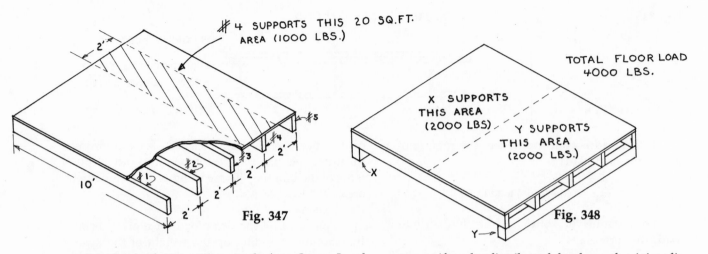

Fig. 347

Fig. 348

a live load of 40 or 50 pounds (see Snow Load map, Appendix J).

Examples of Load Computations. Computing the load a beam will carry proceeds in several steps. First, figure out how many square feet the piece supports. Then figure what each square foot weighs, live and dead loads combined. To take a simple example, imagine a series of floor beams (joists) spaced 2 feet apart, each one 10 feet long and supported at the ends (Figure 347).

Each one supports an area 10 feet long extending halfway to the next joist on the left and halfway to the next joist on the right. This is an area of 10′ × 2′ or 20 square feet. If this were a first floor, the dead load would be 10 lbs./sq.ft., the live load 40 lbs./sq.ft., and the total load 50 lbs./sq.ft. Since each beam supports 20 square feet, the total load per beam is 1000 pounds (20 sq.ft. × 50 lbs.). Note, however, that the first and last joist, #1 and #5, support half the area, hence carry only half the load, or 500 pounds. The total load of the entire floor is 4000 pounds.

Suppose this floor, in turn, was supported by two main beams, x and y, as in Figure 348. These two beams span 8 feet and share the weight of the 10-foot span equally. Each supports an area 5 feet wide and 8 feet long, or 40 square feet. At 50 lbs./sq.ft., the total load is 2000 pounds per beam.

Extra weights, such as partitions, on the floor could complicate your calculations further. Suppose there were a wall 8 feet high on the floor above Beam y, as in Figure 349 (Wall A). This wall has an area of 8′ × 8′ or 64 square feet. Since walls are assumed to weigh 10 lbs./sq.ft., this one can be seen as weighing 640 pounds, 700 pounds rounded off. We add this 700 pounds to the floor load on Beam y of 2000 pounds to get a total load on Beam y of 2700 pounds.

Concentrated loads would complicate things even more. In Figure 350 we have another wall, Wall B, over the middle joist. This wall exerts an

extra uniformly distributed load on the joist directly below it of 10′ × 8′ × 10 pounds or 800 pounds total. But this wall also imposes a concentrated load at midspan on main timbers x and y.

Wall B is carried equally by x and y, so this concentrated load is ½ of 800 pounds or 400 pounds on x and 400 pounds on y. For concentrated loads the formula is not $FBd^2/9L$ but $FBd^2/18L$. That in effect means that a concentrated load counts double. We can convert our concentrated load of 400 to its equivalent as a distributed load, or 800 pounds on x and 800 pounds on y. This enables us to express the total loads on x and y in a single number.

To summarize, Beam x carries:

2000 lbs. (half of the floor)
+ 800 lbs. (half of wall #B, expressed as a uniform load)
2800 lbs. Total load.

Beam Y carries:
2000 lbs. (half of the floor)
+ 700 lbs. (all of wall#A)
+ 800 lbs. (half of wall #B, expressed as a uniform load)
3500 lbs. Total load.

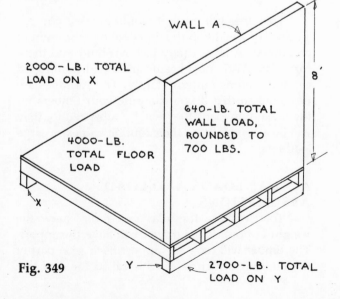

Fig. 349

Fig. 350

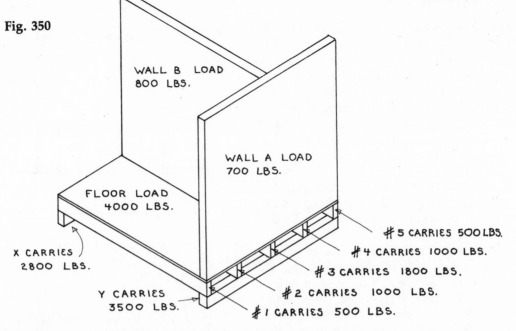

WALL B LOAD
800 LBS.

WALL A LOAD
700 LBS.

FLOOR LOAD
4000 LBS.

X CARRIES
2800 LBS.

Y CARRIES
3500 LBS.

#5 CARRIES 500 LBS.

#4 CARRIES 1000 LBS.

#3 CARRIES 1800 LBS.

#2 CARRIES 1000 LBS.

#1 CARRIES 500 LBS.

Examples of Timber Size Calculations. We can use the same imaginary structure to show how the formula is used to find the correct sizes of timber under different conditions. Suppose we were using rough-cut spruce from New England, sawn to full dimensions so that a 2 × 6 would actually be 2 inches by 6 inches. Such spruce has an F of about 1000. Let us compute what size to use for our 10-foot-long joists 2 feet apart. To make this calculation, guess what size timber would work and try it out in the formula. My guess is 2 × 8. The formula is FBd²/9L. Here F is 1000, B is 2, d² is 64, and L is 10.

$$\frac{\overset{(F)}{1000} \times \overset{(B)}{2} \times \overset{(d^2)}{64}}{\underset{(L)}{9 \times 10}} = 1422 \text{ lbs.}$$

As shown in Figure 350, joists #1 and #5 carry 500 pounds each, #2 and #4 carry 1000 each, and #3 carries 1800. Thus our 2 × 8 is more than strong enough for #1, #2, #4, and #5, but undersize for #3. In carpentry, a joist carrying a partition is reinforced simply by doubling up the joist, which will work here. So 2 × 8 would be an adequate joist size.

Since 2 × 8s actually give much more strength than needed, let's see if 2 × 6s would be sufficient.

$$\frac{\overset{(F)}{1000} \times \overset{(B)}{2} \times \overset{(d^2)}{36}}{\underset{(L)}{9 \times 10}} = 800 \text{ lbs.}$$

This is sufficient for #1 and #5, but insufficient for the #2 and #4 and also for #3 even if it is doubled up. The 2 × 6s are too small.

Of the beams that support the floor joists in our hypothetical structure, Beam x, 8 feet long, carries 2800 pounds. Again assuming wood with an F of 1000, let's see if a 6 × 6 is strong enough.

$$\frac{\overset{(F)}{1000} \times \overset{(B)}{6} \times \overset{(d^2)}{36}}{\underset{(L)}{9 \times 8}} = 3000, \text{ more than enough.}$$

The guess for Beam y is 6 × 8. Being 4/3 as wide (B), it should hold 4/3 of the load, or 4000 pounds. That is more than our design load of 3500. It should be noted that the 6 × 8 will do more work placed narrow side down.

DEFLECTION

Up till now we have been talking about calculations for strength. Sometimes you may also want to worry about stiffness or deflection. Any timber — even one that has been computed for strength — will deflect: it will sag to some extent and spring somewhat when subjected to an impact. Usually this is nothing to worry about because a timber computed for strength will not deflect noticeably. A 12-foot floor beam or sill could sag ½ inch without being noticed. But in a few specific instances, you may want to make sure the amount of deflection is within certain limits.

One, if there will be a real plaster ceiling the deflection should be limited to prevent the plaster from cracking over time.

Two, it is a good idea to limit the deflection of floor joists 14 feet long or more, so the floor does not feel springy.

Three, it is a good idea to limit the deflection of ceiling or roof timbers at or near eye level on spans over 12 feet. A timber way above your head could sag 1 inch without anyone being able to see it. The same sag in a timber you could sight along, though harmless, might be irritating or wrong-looking, particularly if you are fussy about such things (as I am). The timbers to worry about are beams or joists supporting low ceilings, or which can be viewed at eye level because of stairways.

In all of these examples a standard limit used in design is 1/360 of the span. The deflection in a 16-foot beam, for example, would be limited to slightly more than 1/2 inch.

The stiffness of a particular kind of wood is indicated by its *modulus of elasticity* or E rating. The stiffness of a timber varies with several factors. Some species are stiffer than others. Douglas fir is generally stiff, while cedar species are generally not. A knot-free piece will be stiffer than a piece with large knots or knots along its edges. A dry timber will be stiffer than a green one. In general, stiffness is related to the density of the seasoned timber. Within a species, a heavy piece will be stiffer than a lighter one and a heavy species will be stiffer overall than a light species.

E values for stress-graded lumber yard woods are given in Appendix B, Tables 3 and 4. E values for ungraded species — the lumber from local saw-mills — are given in Appendix B, Tables 1 and 2. In both cases, the ratings are actually averages. For stress-graded wood, the average covers a narrow range because of the grading process. You can use the values given with confidence as long as there is nothing obviously wrong with the specific pieces of lumber you are using. With ungraded sawmill lumber the average covers a much wider range, and you will have to temper your calculations by carefully looking over the pieces. For the long spans choose the pieces with the highest (dry) weight and the fewest knots.

The formula for computing deflection is too complicated for nonengineers, such as myself, to use. You can use Tables 4 and 5 in Appendix C to find the minimum E values needed to limit deflection to 1/360 of the span under different circumstances.

The Western Wood Products Association, a trade organization, makes a special little slide rule called a WWPA Span Computer that you can use to figure joist, rafter, and beam spans for both strength and stiffness (deflection). Its only drawback is that it only makes calculations for planed timber sizes. It is available for $1 from the Western Wood Products Association, Yeon Building, Portland, Oregon 97204.

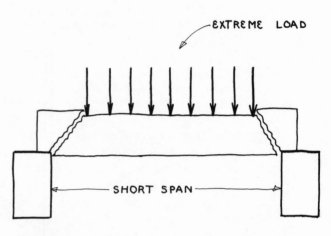

Fig. 351

SHEAR FAILURE

SHEAR

Figure 351 shows a beam failing as a result of shear forces. The timber is cut off at its bearings, much as a paper punch makes a hole in a piece of paper. This kind of failure almost never occurs in wooden buildings, because timbers computed for strength or deflection will be more than adequate against shear under most conditions. In general, you need not calculate beams for shear. Shear strength is only important when the load on a timber is abnormally large over an abnormally short span. Under these conditions, a slender timber may be adequate according to calculations for strength or stiffness, but not stout enough to take the shearing forces at the joint. If you have such a situation, have your design checked by a builder or designer to make sure there is no problem.

COLUMNS

Wooden timbers used as columns are incredibly strong, much stronger than they look. I don't think carpenters ever bother to compute posts in wooden houses. In general, a 4 × 4 up to 8 feet long can hold almost anything you can put on it in a one-story house, and a 6 × 6 or similar timber will do most jobs on a two-story house. Often a big post will be used to make the various joints strong and easy to fit, even when a smaller column would theoretically hold the weight. Often, also, a post will be large for appearances' sake. Generally, if a post looks strong enough, and the beams it supports are well fastened and supported, it will be big enough.

If in doubt, Appendix C, Table 8, gives maximum loads for timber posts. Just for fun, I will briefly explain the formulas upon which these tables are based.

Columns can fail two ways. Relatively slender columns will fail by bending sideways in the middle, like toothpicks you squeeze between your thumb and forefinger. Short stubby columns, however, will actually crush before they start to bend in the middle. Most columns in building are in the first category. The calculations for failure by bending in the middle are based on Euler's formula:

$$\text{Maximum load in lbs.} = \frac{.3 \times E \times \text{Area}}{(L/d)^2}$$

EULER'S FORMULA

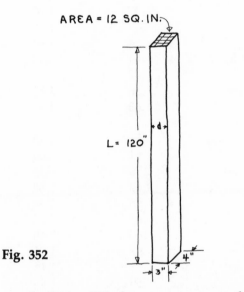

AREA = 12 SQ. IN.

L = 120"

d

4"

3"

Fig. 352

As Figure 352 shows, area means the area in cross section of the post, in square inches. L is the height of the post, in inches; if a post is firmly braced in the middle — in both directions — L will be the longest unsupported height. The narrowest dimension of the column in inches is d. In the figure, the area is 12 square inches, L is 120 inches, and d is 3 inches. E refers to the modulus of elasticity of the wood, which you can find in Appendix B.

A stiffer wood, or a larger cross-sectional area will reduce the possibility of a column bending out in the middle. In the formula, the load is directly proportional to these two factors (E and Area). The other factor that affects the loading capacity is the slenderness ratio — L/d in the formula — which is really the relative skinniness of the column. If the height is greater in comparison with the least dimension, the post will be weaker. Specifically, if you double the height of a column, it will hold only one fourth of the load.

That is why L/d is squared in the formula. This formula applies only to relatively slender columns that will fail first by bending out in the middle. If L/d for the column is less than about 20, you have a short column, and you should make sure it will not fail by crushing.

The compressive strength of a particular kind of wood (its resistance to crushing) is indicated by its "fiber stress in compression," or F_c. (This is a rating much like F in the beam formula.) Each wood has two F_c ratings, because wood can be crushed more easily when the force is applied perpendicular to the grain than it can when the force is applied parallel to the grain, as is the case in columns. In Appendix B, Table 4, "F_c parallel to grain" is the one we are interested in. The other is labeled $F_c\perp$, the upside-down T being a symbol for "perpendicular to grain."

F_c ratings are in pounds per square inch. Thus, #1 hemfir has an F_c parallel to grain of 775 pounds per square inch. If you multiply the cross-sectional area in square inches of a short column by its F_c parallel to grain, you get the maximum capacity of the post in pounds. For example, a short hemfir post $3\frac{1}{2}'' \times 3\frac{1}{2}''$ has an area in cross section of 12.25 square inches. F_c parallel to grain is 775 lbs./sq.in. The capacity is 775×12.25 or 9494 pounds.

Here are 2 sample computations:

First, what will a #1 grade hemfir column $5\frac{1}{2} \times 3\frac{1}{2} \times 120''$ carry?

L/d is 120/3.5 or about 34. Since 34 is way over 20, the column will fail by bending out, so its capacity should be figured using Euler's formula. From Appendix B, Table 4, we get the E value of 1,300,000.

$$\frac{.3 \times 1,300,000 \times 3.5 \times 5.5}{(120/3.5)^2} = 6500 \text{ lbs.}$$

Second, consider the same column, but 48 inches tall. L/d is 48/3.5 or about 13.7. Since this is quite a lot below 20, it is a short column and its capacity will be limited by the compressive strength of the wood itself rather than by its tendency to bend out. F_c parallel to grain is 775 lbs./sq. in. The area is $3.5 \times 5.5 = 19.25$.

775 lbs. × 19.25 sq.in. = 14,919 lbs. capacity

If L/d is close to 20 — say between 18 and 22 — calculate the column capacity using both methods, and use the lower rating.

APPENDIX B
F AND E VALUES FOR TIMBER CALCULATIONS

To use the formulas in Appendix A, you need to know the F value or fiber stress rating of the wood you are using. E (modulus of elasticity) ratings are needed for computing timber sizes for stiffness (deflection) as opposed to strength and are needed for Tables 4 and 5 in Appendix C.

E values for ungraded hardwoods are given in Table 1. E values for ungraded softwoods are in Table 2.

Most lumber yards sell stress-graded Western lumber, each piece of which is stamped with a special label that shows the species, grade, dryness at the time of planing, and other information. When you know the grade and species, you can look up the F and E values on a chart in a pamphlet that is available from the Western Wood Products Association (Yeon Building, Portland, Oregon 97204), which is the major trade association of the lumber industry. This is known as Product Use Manual #6d. Tables 3 and 4 and the explanation of lumber grade stamps are reprinted by permission of the WWPA.

The charts refer to the F we are concerned with as "F_b" to distinguish it from other mechanical properties used for other calculations. Table 3 gives the values to use for joists, rafters, and planks. Notice that two values of F_b are given, one marked "single" and one marked "repetitive." When joists or rafters are spaced 24 inches or less on center or closer they lend each other strength, so the F_b repetitive values can be used. Table 4 gives the values to use for sills and posts and timbers over 4 inches thick.

Native lumber you buy from a sawmill will not be officially graded. In my experience the common softwoods used for framing in the Northeast, such as spruce, hemlock, or fir, can be assumed to have an F of 1000. Pine would be around 800, although some pieces will be much weaker because of large knots, and others may be stronger — more like spruce, hemlock, and fir — if relatively free of knots.

In other regions you can probably find the relative strengths of local woods by talking to carpenters or sawmill operators. They may not know about F values, but they can tell you how sawmill lumber compares to lumber yard lumber, and you can approximate F values from that.

TABLE 1.
Modulus of Elasticity (E)
for Ungraded Hardwoods

Common name of species	Specific gravity	Modulus of Elasticity (× 1,000,000)
Hardwoods:		
Black maple	.52	1.33
	.57	1.62
Red maple	.49	1.39
	.54	1.64
Silver maple	.44	.94
	.47	1.14
Sugar maple	.56	1.55
	.63	1.83
Oak, red		
Black	.56	1.18
	.61	1.64
Northern red	.56	1.35
	.63	1.82
Pin	.58	1.32
	.63	7.73
Scarlet	.60	1.48
	.67	1.91
Southern red	.52	1.14
	.59	1.49
Water	.56	1.55
	.63	2.02
Willow	.56	1.29
	.69	1.90
Oak, white		
Bur	.58	.88
	.64	1.03
Chestnut	.57	1.37
	.66	1.59
Live	.80	1.58
	.88	1.98
Overcup	.57	1.15
	.63	1.42
Post	.60	1.09
	.67	1.51
Swamp chestnut	.60	1.35
	.67	1.77
Swampy white	.64	1.59
	.72	2.05
White	.60	1.25
	.68	1.75

TABLE 2.
Modulus of Elasticity (E)
of Ungraded Softwoods

Common name of species	Specific gravity	Modulus of Elasticity (× 1,000,000)
Softwoods:		
Bald cypress	.42	1.18
	.46	1.44
Cedar		
Alaska	.42	1.14
	.44	1.42
Atlantic white	.31	.75
	.32	.93
Eastern red cedar	.44	.65
	.47	.88
Incense	.35	.84
	.37	1.04
Northern white	.29	.64
	.31	.80
Western red cedar	.31	.94
		1.11
Fir		
Balsam	.34	.96
	.36	1.23
California red	.36	1.17
	.38	1.49
Grand	.35	1.25
	.37	1.57
Noble	.37	1.38
	.39	1.73
Pacific silver	.40	1.42
	.43	1.72
Subalpine	.31	1.05
	.32	1.29
White	.37	1.16
	.39	1.49
Hemlock		
Eastern	.38	1.07
	.40	1.20
Mountain	.42	1.04
	.45	1.33
Western	.42	1.31
	.45	1.64
Larch, western	.48	.96
	.52	1.87
Pine		
Eastern white	.34	.99
	.35	1.24
Jack	.40	1.07
	.43	1.35
Loblolly	.47	1.40
	.51	1.79
Lodgepole	.38	1.08
	.41	1.34

Common name of species	Specific gravity	Modulus of Elasticity (× 1,000,000)
Longleaf	.54	1.59
	.59	1.98
Pitch	.47	1.20
	.52	1.43
Pond	.51	1.28
	.56	1.75
Ponderosa	.38	1.00
	.40	1.29
Red	.41	1.28
	.46	1.63
Sand	.46	1.02
	.48	1.41
Shortleaf	.47	1.39
	.51	1.75
Slash	.54	1.53
	.59	1.98
Spruce	.41	1.00
	.44	1.23
Sugar	.34	1.03
	.36	1.19
Virginia	.45	1.22
	.48	1.52
Western white	.35	1.19
	.38	1.46
Spruce		
Black	.38	1.06
	.40	1.53
Engelmann	.33	1.03
	.35	1.30
Red	.38	1.19
	.41	1.52
Sitka	.37	1.23
	.40	1.57
White	.37	1.07
	.40	1.34
Tamarack	.49	1.24
	.53	1.64

Source of Tables 1 and 2: *Wood Handbook (Agriculture Handbook No. 72)* by U.S. Forest Products Laboratory, USDA, 1974, p. 4–7 ff.

LUMBER GRADES

Grading practices of WWPA member mills are closely supervised by the Association to assure uniformity. The resulting grades provide the specifier with a dependable measure for determining the value of lumber.

The many mills manufacturing lumber from the same or similar woods apply the grade stamp to indicate that they employ stringent quality control standards to achieve a better than 95 percent probability that an individual piece of lumber will equal the predicted average strength for the grade.

The official WWPA grade stamp on a piece of lumber is assurance of its assigned grade. It is recommended wherever possible that grade-marked stock be specified. This includes lumber manufactured from 12 commercially important species in the 12 Western states.

The official Association mark (a.) on WWPA Region lumber species indicates that standard grading rules of the Association have been applied under its supervision. Each mill is assigned a permanent number (b.) for grade stamp purposes. In lieu of the mill number the mill name is often used. The official grade name (c.) as defined by the Association is part of the stamp and gives positive identification to graded lumber. The species mark (d.) identifies the wood.

S-DRY MC 15 S-GRN

Any one of the above marks found in a grade-stamp denotes the moisture content of lumber at time of surfacing. "S-DRY" indicates a moisture content not exceeding 19 percent. "MC 15" indicates a moisture content not exceeding 15 percent. "S-GRN" indicates that the moisture content exceeded 19 percent.

DESIGN VALUES/WWPA STANDARD GRADING RULES

TABLE 3
Structural Joists and Planks and Appearance — 2" to 4" Thick, 5" and Wider
Design Values in Pounds Per Square Inch*

Species or Group	Grade	Extreme Fiber Stress in Bending "Fb" Single	Extreme Fiber Stress in Bending "Fb" Repetitive	Tension Parallel to Grain "Ft"**	Horizontal Shear "Fv"	Compression Perpendicular "Fc ⊥"	Compression Parallel to Grain "Fc"	Modulus of Elasticity "E"
DOUGLAS FIR-LARCH	Select Structural	1800	2050	1200	95	385	1400	1,800,000
	No. 1/Appearance	1500	1750	1000	95	385	1250/1500	1,800,000
	No. 2	1250	1450	650	95	385	1050	1,700,000
	No. 3	725	850	375	95	385	675	1,500,000
DOUGLAS FIR SOUTH	Select Structural	1700	1950	1150	90	335	1250	1,400,000
	No. 1/Appearance	1450	1650	975	90	335	1150/1350	1,400,000
	No. 2	1200	1350	625	90	335	950	1,300,000
	No. 3	700	800	350	90	335	600	1,100,000
HEM-FIR	Select Structural	1400	1650	950	75	245	1150	1,500,000
	No. 1/Appearance	1200	1400	800	75	245	1050/1250	1,500,000
	No. 2	1000	1150	525	75	245	875	1,400,000
	No. 3	575	675	300	75	245	550	1,200,000
MOUNTAIN HEMLOCK	Select Structural	1500	1700	1000	95	370	1100	1,300,000
	No. 1/Appearance	1250	1450	850	95	370	1000/1200	1,300,000
	No. 2	1050	1200	550	95	370	825	1,100,000
	No. 3	625	700	325	95	370	525	1,000,000
MOUNTAIN HEMLOCK- HEM-FIR	Select Structural	1400	1650	950	75	245	1100	1,300,000
	No. 1/Appearance	1200	1400	800	75	245	1000/1200	1,300,000
	No. 2	1000	1150	525	75	245	825	1,100,000
	No. 3	575	675	300	75	245	525	1,000,000
WESTERN HEMLOCK	Select Structural	1550	1800	1050	90	280	1300	1,600,000
	No. 1/Appearance	1350	1550	900	90	280	1150/1350	1,600,000
	No. 2	1100	1250	575	90	280	975	1,400,000
	No. 3	650	750	325	90	280	625	1,300,000

| Species or Group | Grade | Extreme Fiber Stress in Bending "Fb" | | Tension Parallel to Grain "Ft"** | Horizontal Shear "Fv" | Compression | | Modulus of Elasticity "E" |
		Single	Repetitive			Perpendicular "Fc ⊥"	Parallel to Grain "Fc"	
ENGEL-MANN SPRUCE-ALPINE FIR (Engelmann Spruce-Lodgepole Pine)	Select Structural	1200	1350	775	70	195	850	1,300,000
	No. 1/Appearance	1000	1150	675	70	195	750/900	1,300,000
	No. 2	825	950	425	70	195	625	1,100,000
	No. 3	475	550	250	70	195	400	1,000,000
LODGE-POLE PINE	Select Structural	1300	1500	875	70	250	1000	1,300,000
	No. 1/Appearance	1100	1300	750	70	250	900/1050	1,300,000
	No. 2	925	1050	475	70	250	750	1,200,000
	No. 3	525	625	275	70	250	475	1,000,000
PONDE-ROSA PINE-SUGAR PINE (Ponderosa Pine-Lodgepole Pine)	Select Structural	1200	1400	825	70	235	950	1,200,000
	No. 1/Appearance	1050	1200	700	70	235	850/1000	1,200,000
	No. 2	850	975	450	70	235	700	1,100,000
	No. 3	500	575	250	70	235	450	1,000,000
IDAHO WHITE PINE	Select Structural	1150	1300	775	70	190	950	1,400,000
	No. 1/Appearance	975	1100	650	70	190	875/1050	1,400,000
	No. 2	800	925	425	70	190	725	1,300,000
	No. 3	475	550	250	70	190	450	1,200,000
WESTERN CEDARS	Select Structural	1300	1500	875	75	265	1050	1,100,000
	No. 1/Appearance	1100	1300	750	75	265	950/1100	1,100,000
	No. 2	925	1050	475	75	265	800	1,000,000
	No. 3	525	625	275	75	265	500	900,000
WHITE WOODS (Western Woods)	Select Structural	1150	1300	775	70	190	850	1,100,000
	No. 1/Appearance	975	1100	650	70	190	750/900	1,100,000
	No. 2	800	925	425	70	190	625	1,000,000
	No. 3	475	550	250	70	190	400	900,000

* These design values are calculated in accordance with ASTM standards. For information about use of these values, see Sections 100.00 through 170.00 in WWPA Grading Rules.
** Tabulated values apply to 5″ and 6″ widths. For 8″ width, use 90% of tabulated tension parallel to grain value for Select Structural and 80% for all other grades. For 10″ and wider widths, use 80% of tabulated tension parallel to grain value for Select Structural and 60% for all other grades.

DESIGN VALUES/WWPA STANDARD GRADING RULES

TABLE 4
Beams and Stringers — 5" and Thicker
Width More Than 2" Greater Than Thickness
Design Values in Pounds Per Square Inch*
Grades Described in Section 70.00 WWPA Grading Rules

Species or Group	Grade	Extreme Fiber Stress in Bending "Fb" — Single Members	Tension Parallel to Grain "Ft"	Horizontal Shear "Fv"	Compression — Perpendicular "Fc ⊥"	Compression — Parallel to Grain "Fc"	Modulus of Elasticity "E"
DOUGLAS FIR-LARCH	Select Structural	1600	1050	85	385	1100	1,600,000
	No. 1	1350	900	85	385	925	1,600,000
DOUGLAS FIR SOUTH	Select Structural	1550	1050	85	335	1000	1,200,000
	No. 1	1300	850	85	335	850	1,200,000
HEM-FIR	Select Structural	1250	850	70	245	925	1,300,000
	No. 1	1050	725	70	245	775	1,300,000
MOUNTAIN HEMLOCK	Select Structural	1350	900	90	370	875	1,100,000
	No. 1	1100	750	90	370	750	1,100,000
MOUNTAIN HEMLOCK — HEM-FIR	Select Structural	1250	850	70	245	875	1,100,000
	No. 1	1050	725	70	245	750	1,100,000
WESTERN HEMLOCK	Select Structural	1400	950	85	280	1000	1,400,000
	No. 1	1150	775	85	280	850	1,400,000
ENGELMANN SPRUCE — AL-PINE FIR (Engelmann Spruce-Lodgepole Pine)	Select Structural	1050	700	65	195	675	1,100,000
	No. 1	875	600	65	195	550	1,100,000
LODGEPOLE PINE	Select Structural	1150	775	65	250	800	1,100,000
	No. 1	975	650	65	250	675	1,100,000
PONDEROSA PINE-SUGAR PINE (Ponderosa Pine-Lodgepole Pine)	Select Structural	1100	725	65	235	750	1,100,000
	No. 1	925	625	65	235	625	1,100,000
IDAHO WHITE PINE	Select Structural	1000	700	65	190	775	1,300,000
	No. 1	850	575	65	190	650	1,300,000
WESTERN CEDARS	Select Structural	1150	775	70	265	875	1,000,000
	No. 1	975	650	70	265	725	1,000,000
WHITE WOODS (Western Woods)	Select Structural	1000	700	65	190	675	1,000,000
	No. 1	850	575	65	190	550	1,000,000

* These design values were calculated in accordance with ASTM standards. For information about use of these values, see Sections 100.00 through 170.000 in WWPA Grading Rules.

APPENDIX C
JOIST, RAFTER, HEADER, SILL, AND COLUMN SIZE TABLES

List of Tables:

1. *Maximum spans for first-floor joists and for rafters supporting over 3 feet of snow*
2. *Maximum spans for second-floor joists and for rafters supporting 3 feet of snow or less*
3. *Sizes for heavy timber rafters*
4. *Maximum spans for joists and rafters when deflection is limited to 1/360 of span*
5. *Maximum spans for heavy timbers when deflection is limited to 1/360 of span*
6. *Header sizes*
7. *Sill sizes*
8. *Safe loads on solid wood columns*

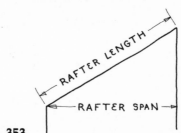

Fig. 353

TABLE 1
Maximum spans for first-floor joists and for rafters supporting over 3 feet of snow under worst conditions (total load 50 lbs./sq.ft.)

Spans can be used with typical lumber yard #1 and #2 timbers (F approximately 1200) or rough sawmill timbers (F approximately 1000). Note rafter spans are measured horizontally, not along rafter length (See Figure 353).

Size	Maximum span 24" o.c.	Maximum span 16" o.c.
2 × 4	4'11"	6'0"
2 × 6	7'9"	9'6"
2 × 8	10'3"	12'6"
2 × 10	13'1"	16'0"
2 × 12	15'11"	19'6"

Source: Table computed by author.

TABLE 2
Maximum spans for second-floor joists and for rafters supporting 3 feet of snow or less under worst conditions (total load 40 lbs./sq.ft.)

Spans can be used with typical lumber yard #1 or #2 timbers (F approximately 1200) or typical rough-sawn sawmill lumber (F approximately 1000). Note rafter spans are measured horizontally, not along rafter length (See Figure 353).

Size	Maximum span with 24" centers	Maximum Span with 16" centers
2 × 4	5'6"	6'9"
2 × 6	8'8"	10'8"
2 × 8	11'5"	14'0"
2 × 10	14'8"	17'11"
2 × 12	17'9"	21'9"

Source: Table computed by author.

TABLE 3
Sizes for heavy timber rafters

Rafter sizes for exposed frame, widely spaced roofs, using rough native lumber, F 1000. Notice that rafter sizes are based on span measured horizontally rather than rafter length (See Figure 353).

SPAN	Total load 35 lbs/sq.ft. Max. 30" snow accumulation			Total Load 50 lbs./sq.ft. 3–5' snow accumulation		
	2' o.c.	3' o.c.	4' o.c.	2' o.c.	3' o.c.	4' o.c.
7'	2 × 4	3 × 4 2 × 6	4 × 4 2 × 6	3 × 4 2 × 6	2 × 6	3 × 6 2 × 8
8'	3 × 4 2 × 6	4 × 4 2 × 6	3 × 6 2 × 8	4 × 4 2 × 6	3 × 6 2 × 8	2 × 8
10'	4 × 4 2 × 6	3 × 6 2 × 8	2 × 8	3 × 6 2 × 8	4 × 6 3 × 8 2 × 10	3 × 8 2 × 10
12'	3 × 6 2 × 8	4 × 6 3 × 8 2 × 10	3 × 8 2 × 10	4 × 6 3 × 8 2 × 10	2 × 10	2 × 12
14'	2 × 8	3 × 8 2 × 10	4 × 8 2 × 12	3 × 8 2 × 10	2 × 12	4 × 10 3 × 12
16'	3 × 8 2 × 10	4 × 8 2 × 12	4 × 10 3 × 12	4 × 8 2 × 12	4 × 10 3 × 12	4 × 12
18'	4 × 8 2 × 12	4 × 10 3 × 12	3 × 12	3 × 10	4 × 12	4 × 14

Source: Computed by author and Jim Rader from formulas in Appendix A.

TABLE 4
Maximum spans for joists and rafters when deflection is limited to 1/360 of span

In Table 4, E values (modulus of elasticity, see Appendix B) are expressed in scientific notation. For example, if E is 1,600,000, it will be shown in the chart as 1.6, meaning 1.6×10^6. This chart was computed by the author for planed timber sizes.

The maximum spans given will therefore be conservative for full-size, rough-cut timbers. Note that these figures depend on live load alone, not total load.

TIMBER	Live Load = 30 lbs/sq.ft.		Live Load = 40 lbs/sq.ft.		TIMBER	Live Load = 30 lbs/sq.ft.		Live Load = 40 lbs/sq.ft.	
	($E \times 10^6$)	max Span	($E \times 10^6$)	max Span		($E \times 10^6$)	max Span	($E \times 10^6$)	max Span
2 × 4, 24″ o.c.	.8	4′8″	.8	4′3″	2 × 8 16″ o.c.	.8	11′2″	.8	10′2″
	1.0	5′1″	1.0	4′7″		1.0	12′0″	1.0	11′0″
	1.2	5′5″	1.2	4′11″		1.2	12′10″	1.2	11′8″
	1.4	5′8″	1.4	5′2″		1.4	13′6″	1.4	12′3″
	1.6	5′11″	1.6	5′5″		1.6	14′1″	1.6	12′10″
	1.8	6′2″	1.8	5′7″		1.8	14′8″	1.8	13′4″
2 × 4, 16″ o.c.	.8	5′5″	.8	4′11″	2 × 10 24″ o.c.	.8	12′6″	.8	11′4″
	1.0	5′10″	1.0	5′3″		1.0	13′6″	1.0	12′3″
	1.2	6′2″	1.2	5′7″		1.2	14′3″	1.2	13′0″
	1.4	6′6″	1.4	5′11″		1.4	15′0″	1.4	13′8″
	1.6	6′10″	1.6	6′2″		1.6	15′9″	1.6	14′4″
	1.8	7′1″	1.8	6′5″		1.8	16′4″	1.8	14′10″
2 × 6 24″ o.c.	.8	7′5″	.8	6′9″	2 × 10 16″ o.c.	.8	14′3″	.8	13′0″
	1.0	8′0″	1.0	7′3″		1.0	15′5″	1.0	14′0″
	1.2	8′6″	1.2	7′9″		1.2	16′4″	1.2	14′10″
	1.4	8′11″	1.4	8′2″		1.4	17′3″	1.4	15′7″
	1.6	9′4″	1.6	8′6″		1.6	18′0″	1.6	16′4″
	1.8	9′9″	1.8	8′10″		1.8	18′9″	1.8	17′0″
2 × 6 16″ o.c.	.8	8′6″	.8	7′8″	2 × 12 24″ o.c.	.8	15′2″	.8	13′10″
	1.0	9′2″	1.0	8′4″		1.0	16′4″	1.0	14′10″
	1.2	9′9″	1.2	8′10″		1.2	17′5″	1.2	15′9″
	1.4	10′3″	1.4	9′4″		1.4	18′3″	1.4	16′7″
	1.6	10′8″	1.6	9′9″		1.6	19′1″	1.6	17′5″
	1.8	11′1″	1.8	10′1″		1.8	19′11″	1.8	18′1″
2 × 8 24″ o.c.	.8	9′10″	.8	8′11″	2 × 12 16″ o.c.	.8	17′5″	.8	15′9″
	1.0	10′6″	1.0	9′7″		1.0	18′9″	1.0	17′0″
	1.2	11′3″	1.2	10′3″		1.2	19′11″	1.2	18′1″
	1.4	11′9″	1.4	10′9″		1.4	20′11″	1.4	19′0″
	1.6	12′4″	1.6	11′3″		1.6	21′10″	1.6	19′11″
	1.8	12′10″	1.8	11′8″		1.8	22′9″	1.8	20′8″

TABLE 5
Maximum spans for heavy timbers when deflection is limited to 1/360 of span

As in Table 4, E values are expressed in scientific notation for convenience. For example, an E of 1,600,000 is expressed as 1.6, meaning 1.6 × 10⁶. The figures given were computed by the author using the WWPA span computer for planed timber sizes, but the spans given will work also for rough timbers. Loads are expressed not in lbs./sq.ft. but in lbs./running foot, or more simply lbs./foot of beam. Thus a timber 10 feet long with a load of 200 lbs./ft. will carry a total of 2000 pounds.

The table gives 3-inch-wide and 4-inch-wide timbers only, but maximum spans for 6-inch-wide or 8-inch-wide timbers can be determined by dividing the load/ft. by 2 and finding the appropriate 3-inch-wide or 4-inch-wide timber. For example, to find the maximum span of a 6 × 8 of E 1.2 × 10⁶, when the load is 400 lbs./ft., look up the maximum span of a 3 × 8 of E 1.2 × 10⁶ with a load of 200 lbs./ft.

TIMBER	LIVE LOAD					
	200 lbs./ft.		300 lbs./ft.		400 lbs./ft.	
	$(E \times 10^6)$	max Span	$(E \times 10^6)$	max Span	$(E \times 10^6)$	max Span
3 × 6	.8	5'10"	.8	5'2"	.8	4'8"
	1.0	6'4"	1.0	5'6"	1.0	5'0"
	1.2	6'9"	1.2	5'10"	1.2	5'4"
	1.4	7'1"	1.4	6'2"	1.4	5'7"
	1.6	7'5"	1.6	6'6"	1.6	5'10"
	1.8	7'9"	1.8	6'9"	1.8	6'1"
4 × 6	.8	6'7"	.8	5'9"	.8	5'3"
	1.0	7'1"	1.0	6'2"	1.0	5'7"
	1.2	7'6"	1.2	6'7"	1.2	6'0"
	1.4	7'11"	1.4	6'11"	1.4	6'4"
	1.6	8'4"	1.6	7'3"	1.6	6'7"
	1.8	8'8"	1.8	7'6"	1.8	6'9"
3 × 8	.8	7'9"	.8	6'9"	.8	6'2"
	1.0	8'4"	1.0	7'4"	1.0	6'7"
	1.2	8'10"	1.2	7'9"	1.2	7'0"
	1.4	9'4"	1.4	8'2"	1.4	7'5"
	1.6	9'9"	1.6	8'6"	1.6	7'9"
	1.8	10'2"	1.8	8'10"	1.8	8'0"
4 × 8	.8	8'8"	.8	7'7"	.8	6'10"
	1.0	9'4"	1.0	8'2"	1.0	7'5"
	1.2	9'11"	1.2	8'8"	1.2	7'10"
	1.4	10'6"	1.4	9'2"	1.4	8'4"
	1.6	11'0"	1.6	9'6"	1.6	8'8"
	1.8	11'5"	1.8	9'11"	1.8	9'0"
3 × 10	.8	9'11"	.8	8'8"	.8	7'10"
	1.0	10'8"	1.0	9'4"	1.0	8'5"
	1.2	11'4"	1.2	9'10"	1.2	9'0"
	1.4	11'11"	1.4	10'5"	1.4	9'5"
	1.6	12'6"	1.6	10'11"	1.6	9'10"
	1.8	13'0"	1.8	11'4"	1.8	10'3"
4 × 10	.8	11'0"	.8	9'8"	.8	8'9"
	1.0	11'11"	1.0	10'5"	1.0	9'5"
	1.2	12'8"	1.2	11'1"	1.2	10'0"
	1.4	13'4"	1.4	11'8"	1.4	10'7"
	1.6	14'0"	1.6	12'2"	1.6	11'1"
	1.8	14'6"	1.8	12'8"	1.8	11'6"

TIMBER	LIVE LOAD					
	200 lbs./ft.		300 lbs./ft.		400 lbs./ft.	
	$(E \times 10^6)$	max Span	$(E \times 10^6)$	max Span	$(E \times 10^6)$	max Span
2 × 12	.8	10'2"	.8	8'10"	.8	8'0"
	1.0	10'11"	1.0	9'6"	1.0	8'8"
	1.2	11'7"	1.2	10'2"	1.2	9'2"
	1.4	12'3"	1.4	10'8"	1.4	9'8"
	1.6	12'9"	1.6	11'2"	1.6	10'2"
	1.8	13'4"	1.8	11'7"	1.8	10'6"
3 × 12	.8	12'0"	.8	10'6"	.8	9'6"
	1.0	13'0"	1.0	11'4"	1.0	10'3"
	1.2	13'9"	1.2	12'0"	1.2	10'11"
	1.4	14'6"	1.4	12'8"	1.4	11'6"
	1.6	15'2"	1.6	13'3"	1.6	12'0"
	1.8	15'9"	1.8	13'9"	1.8	12'6"
4 × 12	.8	13'6"	.8	11'9"	.8	10'8"
	1.0	14'6"	1.0	12'8"	1.0	11'6"
	1.2	15'5"	1.2	13'6"	1.2	12'3"
	1.4	16'3"	1.4	14'2"	1.4	12'10"
	1.6	17'0"	1.6	14'9"	1.6	13'6"
	1.8	17'8"	1.8	15'5"	1.8	14'0"

TABLE 6
Header Sizes

This table assumes #1 or #2 graded lumber or rough-sawn native lumber, F 1000, and that headers are supporting joists or rafters spanning approximately 10 feet.

Span	Size if supporting roof only	Size if supporting one floor plus roof	Size if supporting two floors plus roof
4'	2–2×4	2–2×6	2–2×8
6'	2–2×6	2–2×8	2–2×10
8'	2–2×8	2–2×10	2–2×12
10'	2–2×10	2–2×12	

Source: Massachusetts Building Code.

TABLE 7
Sill Sizes

Sill sizes can be taken from the table, but a computation for your exact design (Appendix A) might well enable you to use smaller timbers than those shown. The next size smaller sill may usually be used if the wall directly above is covered with 1/2-inch or thicker plywood sheathing, well-nailed, and the wall is not interrupted by doorways. The table assumes full-size native lumber, F 1000.

One-Story Houses

Sill Span	Distance Between Rows of Posts (Joist Span)				
	8'	10'	12'	14'	16'
8'	4 × 10 6 × 8	6 × 8	6 × 10 6 × 8	6 × 10 6 × 8	6 × 10
10'	4 × 12 8 × 8	8 × 8	8 × 10	10 × 10 6 × 12	10 × 10 6 × 12
12'	6 × 12 8 × 10	8 × 10 6 × 12	10 × 10 6 × 12	10 × 10	10 × 12

Two-Story Houses

Sill Span	Distance Between Rows of Posts (Joist Span)				
	8'	10'	12'	14'	16'
8'	6 × 10 8 × 8	6 × 10 8 × 8	6 × 10 8 × 10	8 × 10 6 × 12	8 × 10 6 × 12
10'	8 × 10 6 × 12	8 × 10 6 × 12	10 × 10	10 × 10	10 × 12
12'	10 × 10	10 × 12	10 × 12	10 × 12	12 × 12

Computed by Author from formula in Appendix A.

TABLE 8
Safe Loads on Solid Wood Columns (Thousands of Pounds)

The maximum loads in the table apply to either planed or rough timbers. The values given under A are for relatively strong woods; those under B are for relatively weak woods. A woods are those with an F_c parallel to grain of 1000 to 1600, and an E of 1.2 to 1.6 $\times$ 10^6. B woods have an F_c of about 800 and an E of about .8 $\times$ 10^6.

Nominal Column Size (inches)	Unsupported Length in Feet									
	6		8		10		12		14	
	A	B	A	B	A	B	A	B	A	B
4 × 4	13.5	9.7	7.5	5.4	4.8	3.4	3.5	2.5	2.5	1.8
4 × 6	21.2	15.2	11.7	8.4	7.5	5.4	5.3	3.8	3.9	2.8
4 × 8	28.0	20.0	15.6	11.1	9.9	7.1	7.0	5.0	5.1	3.6
6 × 6	39.4	30.3	46.0	32.8	29.2	20.9	20.5	14.6	14.9	10.6
6 × 8	51.0	39.7	55.0	39.3	38.1	27.2	26.4	18.9	19.3	13.8
6 × 10	66.0	50.3	71.0	50.7	49.0	35.0	34.2	24.4	25.0	17.8
6 × 12	80.6	60.9	80.5	62.0	60.0	42.7	41.8	29.8	30.6	21.8
8 × 8	68.5	52.5	68.2	52.5	58.2	52.5	61.5	43.8	44.8	32.0
8 × 10	87.0	67.0	87.0	67.0	87.5	67.0	78.5	56.0	65.8	47.0
8 × 12	106.5	83.0	105.5	81.7	105.5	81.7	105.5	81.7	70.0	50.0
10 × 10	111.5	86.6	111.0	86.6	111.0	86.6	111.0	86.6	111.0	84.5
10 × 12	135.5	105.0	135.0	105.0	135.0	105.0	135.0	105.0	135.0	103.0
12 × 12	164.0	127.0	164.0	127.0	164.0	127.0	164.0	127.0	164.0	127.0

Source: *Practical Farm Buildings*, by James S. Boyd. Danville, Ill.: The Interstate Printers and Publishers, Inc., 1973, p. 79. Used by permission of the publisher.

APPENDIX D
SUN PATHS

The sun doesn't exactly rise in the east and set in the west. In summer it rises in the northeast, describes a high arc across the southern sky, and sets in the northwest. In winter it rises in the southeast, describes a low arc across the southern sky, and sets in the southwest. The exact pattern depends on the latitude in which you live. In northerly areas, the arc will be lower in the sky. For example, in Canada (latitude 52°N) the sun never gets above 62° off the horizon, while in the Caribbean (latitude 24°N) it reaches almost 90°.

Similarly, in northerly areas the sunrise will move further into the north in summer and further into the south in winter than in more southerly areas.

In any latitude, December 21 is the shortest day, and the sunrise and sunset will be in their most southerly locations for the year. The altitude of the sun above the southern horizon at noon will be the minimum for the year. On June 21 the altitude will be maximum and the sunrise and sunset will be in their most northerly locations.

Halfway between — September 21 and March 21 — are the only two days when the sun actually rises in the east and sets in the west. These days are the fall and spring equinoxes.

Figure 354 shows how the sunrise and sunset vary with the seasons in each latitude. Figure 355 shows how the sun's altitude varies in different latitudes. In both cases, the diagram shows the range: the sun location will vary gradually between the extremes shown. Notice in Figure 354 that south is at the top of the page.

Use Figure 356 to find the latitude and the relationship of magnetic (or compass) north to true north where you live. Magnetic north matches true north along a line that is south of the North Pole on a line that goes through Indiana, across Appalachia, and follows the east coast of Florida. This line is marked "O" on the map. If you live east of

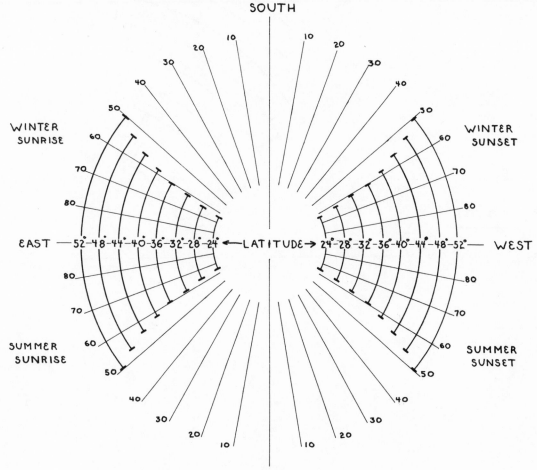

Fig. 354

the line, true north will be east of magnetic north by the number of degrees shown. If you live west of the line, true north will be west of the line by the number of degrees shown.

Find the band on Figures 354 and 355 for your latitude. For example, suppose you live in Central Wisconsin, latitude 44°N. Central Wisconsin is on the 3° line west of the O line, so true north will be 3° west of compass north. The sun, on December 21, will rise at a point 56° east of south and set at a point 56° west of south. On June 21, it will rise at a spot 56° east of north and set at 56° west of north. Between these dates the point will slowly move between those extremes. From Figure 355, you can see that on December 21 the sun will at midday only rise about 23° above the horizon. On June 21 the sun will reach its maximum height of about 70°.

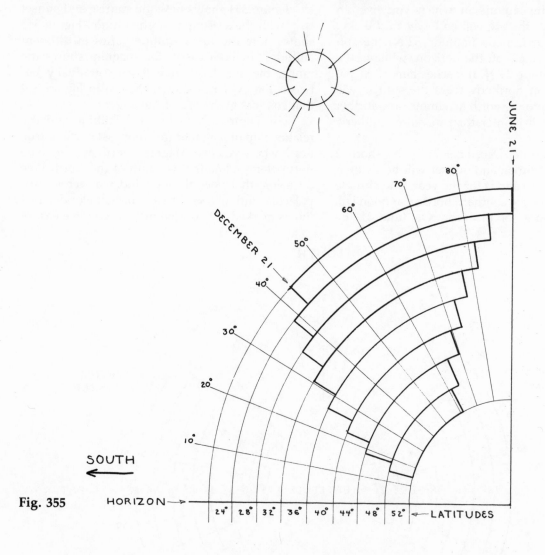

Fig. 355

LATITUDE

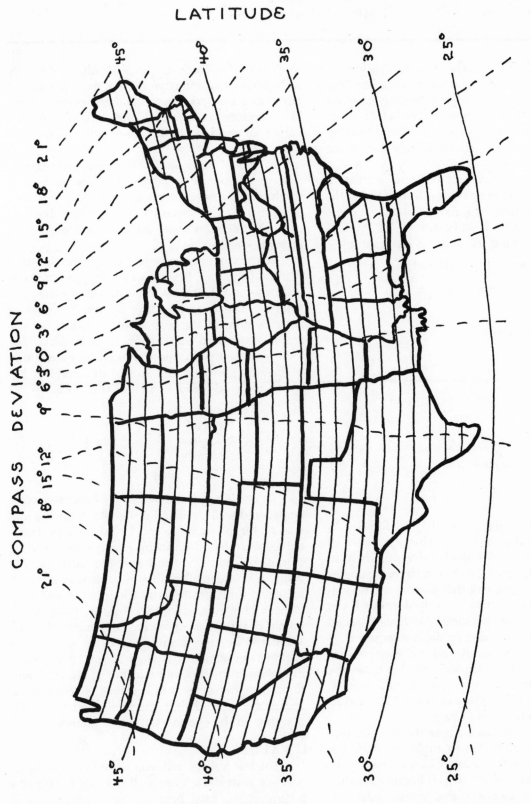

Isogonic Chart of the United States. From Coast and Geodetic Survey, U.S. Department of Commerce, 1965.

Fig. 356

APPENDIX E
COMPUTING HEAT LOSS

In a simplified form, this appendix shows (1) how to figure the hourly heat loss of your building design, which tells how much heating capacity you will need, and (2) how to predict approximately your annual fuel consumption and heating cost. The bibliography lists books that give more detailed calculations.

All building materials have some insulative value, but some are much more effective than others. The effectiveness of a given material or combination of materials is indicated by its thermal resistance or R rating. Here are a few examples:

Item	r(R/inch)	R
Fiberglass insulation	3.3	
3–3½"		11
5–6"		19
Urethane foam board	7.1	
1"		7.1
2"		14.2
3"		21.3
Hardwood	.91	
Softwood	1.25	
Sheetrock		
³⁄₈"		.32
½"		.45
Window, single glass		.89
Insulating glass,		
³⁄₁₆" space		1.44

For most building materials, the R value is proportional to the thickness. Thus, 2 inches of urethane foam has twice the R value of 1 inch. In Table 1 of this appendix, from which the examples above are taken, you will therefore see some materials rated for convenience in the form of R per inch of thickness. In this form, the value is called resistivity and is indicated by the lower-case r.

If you know that hardwood, for example, has an r of .91, you can easily multiply this times the thickness of hardwood you are using to find its R. Two inches of hardwood would be R 1.82, and ³⁄₄ inches of hardwood would be R .68.

There are a few cases where the R is not proportional to thickness. For example, ⅛-inch glass is only slightly better than ¹⁄₁₆-inch glass, even though it is twice as thick. This is because window glass is a poor insulator that resists heat loss mostly because it seals off the window, creating an insulating air film on the interior surface. Its ability to seal off the window is not improved by making it thicker. Airspaces within a wall are another example of the R value not being directly proportional to thickness. A wide airspace will be somewhat more effective than a narrow one but not in direct proportion to the thickness (see Table 2). Therefore, in Tables 1 and 2 there are no r values for windows or airspaces, only R's for each case.

In Table 1 you will find that, for convenience, sometimes specific R values are given instead of r values. You never need to know the resistance of a full 1 inch of sheetrock, for example, but you may often need to know the resistance of ³⁄₈ or ½ inch thicknesses.

When you evaluate your design, the first step is to find the total R values for the types of floor, wall, roof, and window construction you are considering. Do this by adding up the R values of each element of the wall, roof, or floor. For example, a standard wall section might consist of ³⁄₄-inch softwood siding on the outside, a sheathing of ½-inch plywood, 3½ inches of fiberglass between the studs, and ½ inch of sheetrock.

Siding	.79
Plywood	.62
Fiberglass	11.00
Sheetrock	.45
Total R	12.86

At one time, buildings in cold climates were considered well insulated if the total R for the roof was 24, for the walls 13, and for the floor 19. These values were based on using 6 inches of fiberglass in the roof and floor and 3 or 3½ inches in the walls. A house insulated to these standards is well insulated and can be quite comfortable and easy to heat. However, since fuel costs are going up so much, designers are now recommending that the standards be significantly raised. In the coldest regions the standard is now about 10 inches of fiberglass in the roof and 6 inches in the walls and floor. This translates into R values of about 36 for the roof and 19–22 for the walls and floor, depending on the exact construction method.

U VALUES.

Total R values tell you whether individual parts of your design are well insulated. To get a picture of the total heat loss of a design, the R values can be converted into another unit, U, the coefficient of thermal transmission. R tells you how well something insulates. U is the opposite side of the coin and tells you how much heat gets through, which in turn tells you how much fuel you will need to replace the heat lost. Mathematically, U is the reciprocal of R:

$$\frac{1}{R} = U \qquad \frac{1}{U} = R$$

U is expressed in a very specific unit, namely Btu/hr./sq.ft./degree difference. Btu stands for British Thermal Unit(s), which is the unit of heat used in this kind of engineering. Square foot means square foot of building surface. Degree differences refers to the difference in temperature inside and out, in degrees Fahrenheit. If a certain wall has an R value of 20, it will have a U value of 1/20 or .05. This means that .05 Btu of heat will pass through each square foot of the wall every hour, for each degree of temperature difference. If it is 20° F. outside and 70° F. inside, that is a temperature difference of 50° F. Thus, our U value of .05 times 50° temperature difference gives us 2.5, the Btu that will pass through each square foot of the wall. If the whole wall were 10 feet square (100 square feet) the heat loss through it would be 100 × 2.5, or 250 Btu/hr. To maintain the inside temperature of 70° F., you would need to replace these 250 Btu/hr. from your heating system, the sunlight, and other marginal sources of heat such as cooking and body heat.

HOW TO FIND THE HEAT LOSS FOR A SPECIFIC DESIGN:

1. Find the area in square feet for each part or section of the exterior surface of the building.

Section	Area
Floor	800 sq.ft.
Roof	1000
Walls, excluding windows and doors	1200
Windows	300
Doors	50

2. Find the total R value for each section. Then take 1/R to get the U value for that section. Make a chart as shown below.

3. Multiply the U value of each section times the area of the section, then multiply the product times the degree difference. The degree difference chosen will be the desired difference between the inside and outside temperatures on the coldest day. Choose a figure that

represents the maximum performance you will expect from your heating system. The final product is the Btu/hr. needed to replace the heat lost through that section of the building exterior, assuming the specified temperature difference.

4. Total the Btu figures for each section to find the heat loss for the building as a whole. In the example, the total is 19,745 Btu/hr.

5. This total does not take into account the heat loss due to infiltration, which is the heat loss due to leaks, drafts, and from opening and closing doors and windows. The infiltration should not be ignored, because it will often amount to 25 percent or more of the heat loss. There is no precise way of measuring infiltration, but you can use the air exchange method to make a good approximation. This method takes advantage of the fact that it takes .018 Btu to raise the temperature of 1 cubic foot of air 1 degree.

If you know approximately how much air will infiltrate per hour, you can compute the resultant heat loss easily. On the average, a reasonably tight house will have one air change per hour. In other words, if its volume is 8000 cubic feet, about 8000 cubic feet of air will infiltrate per hour. Each of these cubic feet of air will require .018 Btu, per degree of temperature difference. If the degree difference was 50°, the heat loss per hour due to infiltration would be:

8000 cu.ft. × .018 Btu × 50° = 7200 Btu/hr.
(Volume)   (Degree Difference)

A really tight house will have only about .7 air changes per hour. In our example, if the 8000-cubic-foot house was very tight, the Btu/hr. total would have to be adjusted accordingly.

7200 Btu/hr. × .7 = 5040 Btu/hr.

Similarly, if the house was drafty, there would be an average of 1.5, 2, or even more air changes per hour, and the Btu total would have to be adjusted upward.

7200 Btu/hr. × 1.5 = 10,800 Btu/hr.

In sum, the formulas for approximate infiltration are: Reasonably tight house:

volume × .018 × degree difference = Btu/hr needed.

Very tight house:

volume × .018 × degree difference × .7 = Btu/hr needed.

	Area	Total R	U	U × area	Degree diff.	U × area × deg. diff.
Floor	800	17	.059	47.2	50°F	2360 Btu/hr.
Roof	1000	22	.045	45	50°F	2250
Walls	1200	18	.056	67.2	50°F	3360
Windows	300	1.44	.69	207	50°F	10,350
Doors	50	1.75	.57	28.5	50°F	1425
					Total	19,745 Btu/hr.

Drafty house:

volume × .018 × degree difference × 1.5 = Btu/hr needed.

Add this amount to your previous total. In the example, the heat loss, not counting infiltration, was 19,745 Btu/hr. If the house volume was 8000 cubic feet, the degree difference 50° (the same figure used in computing R and U values) and we assume a reasonably tight house, the infiltration loss will be 7200:

19,745	Heat loss through walls, roof, etc.
7,200	Heat loss through infiltration
26,945 Btu/hr.	Total heat loss

You now have the total heat loss per hour for a given design under the coldest conditions. This tells you what the maximum output of your total heating system should be. Most gas, oil, and electric heating systems are rated in Btu output per hour, so you can find the right-size unit. To find the right size and type of wood stove, consult the books on wood stoves listed in the bibliography, as well as the experience of friends living in your locale. Most of the literature stove companies give out is only a vague guide to stove capacities.

Remember that it is the Btu output of your total heating system — not necessarily your furnace only — that should equal the maximum heat loss per hour. If you are using a gas, oil, or electric furnace in combination with a wood stove or fireplace, the furnace by itself will not need an output equal to the maximum Btu/hr. needed. Furnaces work most efficiently operated somewhere near their maximum output, and if you pick a furnace to match the most extreme weather, it may not work that efficiently under normal conditions. It is better to assume that under extreme cold the wood stove or fireplace will be supplying some fraction of the needed heat and to choose a smaller furnace. The more you emphasize wood heat, the more you can lower the capacity of your boiler or space heater. However, I think it is a good idea to have a capacity big enough to keep the house reasonably warm (perhaps 40°) when you are away and the wood fires are out, at least in those parts of the house where there are pipes to freeze.

All the calculations assume your house is designed to take good advantage of its heating system. If you have very high ceilings and have provided no way to prevent the warmer air from staying in a puddle up at the roof peak, you will need much more than the calculated amount of fuel. With a wood heat system, you might need extra fuel to heat spaces remote from the stove, unless these rooms can be used for activities that can be done comfortably at a lower temperature.

The next step is to extend the calculations to find out what your approximate yearly heat needs will be. You do this by comparing the building heat loss with local weather data to find the Btu needed for the heating season. Then you can find the cost with different fuels. You first need to know the number of degree-days in the area where you live. Degree-days is a measure of the average difference between the outside temperature and 65° on a given day. For example, if on January 27 the average temperature is 35° F., that is 30 degree-days for that day, because 65°–35° is 30°. Weather bureaus keep records of the average temperatures from year to year and use this information to figure an average number of degree-days for the entire heating season. Figure 357 shows the average number of degree-days in different regions. The more degree-days there are, the more severe the weather and the more Btu needed.

Here is the procedure for finding your annual fuel consumption:

1. Take the total heat loss figure and redivide it by the degree difference you originally used to figure it. This takes us back one step, to convert your heat loss total into a form you can use for this computation. In the above example, we divide 26,945 Btu/hr. by 50° to get 539, because the figure 26,945 assumed a degree difference of 50°. This number (539) represents the total Btu loss per *hour*, per degree of temperature difference.

2. Then multiply this figure by 24 (hrs). In the example, 539 × 24 = 12,936. This is the Btu lost per *day*, per degree of temperature difference.

3. If you multiplied this second result times the degree days for any given day, you would get the total heat loss in Btu for that day. For a 30 degree-day day, our heat loss would be 12,936 Btu × 30 = 388,080 Btu. Similarly, if you multiply the figure times the total degree-days in your region you get the Btu needed for the entire heating season. For example, if the figures we have been using above were for a house in Southern New Hampshire, we would multiply 12,936 Btu × 8000 degree-days to get the 103,488,000 Btu needed for the whole heating season.

4. Before figuring the approximate fuel costs, you can subtract from your Btu total the free solar heat you get through the south windows of the house. In most parts of the continental United States, a south window will contribute about 100,000 Btu per heating system, per square foot of unshaded glass area. If your climate has very clear, hot weather, the figure might be more like 120,000, and in more overcast climates, such as Portland, Oregon, around 80,000 Btu/sq.ft. of unshaded south window.

When you figure your south glass area, subtract for any shading due to trees, other buildings, hills, curtains, overhang, or shades. This rule of thumb assumes that your house is designed with the sun in mind. If the heat from south windows really only gets to 1 or 2 rooms, or

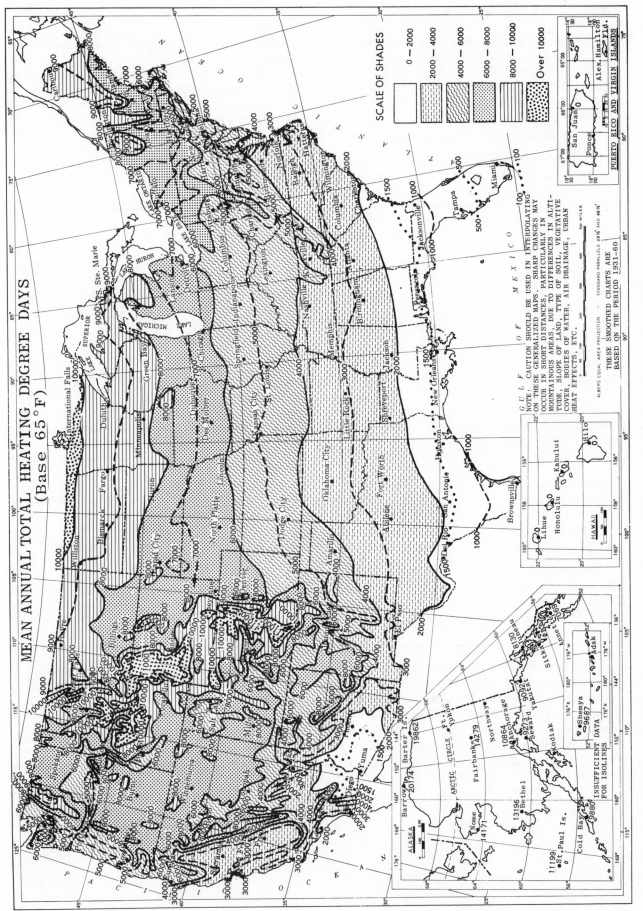

Fig. 357 Source: *Climates of the United States*, by John L. Baldwin. Washington, D.C.: U.S. Department of Commerce, 1973.

cannot circulate to the colder parts of the house, the usable heat gain will be proportionally less.

In the example I have been using, if the south glass area were about 150 square feet, solar heat gain through south windows would contribute about 15,000,000 Btu per heating season:

$$150 \times 100,000 = 15,000,000 \text{ Btu/yr.}$$

This represents about 15 percent of the total heat needed. This leaves 85,000,000 Btu (in round figures) to be supplied by the heating system. The percentage con-tribution from the sun may be more or less in your design.

5. To find the cost of the remaining Btu needed for any fuel, compare the Btu output of the fuel with its cost in your locale. Make sure the price figures you obtain are expressed in the same unit as are the outputs for the fuel. With all fuels except electricity, a lot of the heat goes up the chimney, so the outputs for each fuel must be adjusted for the degree of efficiency of the burner used. The table below gives the figures for the most common fuels.

EFFICIENCY OF FUELS

Fuel	Btu per unit	Assumed efficiency of burner	Btu/unit adjusted for burner efficiency
Oil	140,000/gal.	75–80%	105,000/gal.
Natural gas	1000/cu.ft.	80%	800/cu.ft.
Manufactured gas	525/cu.ft.	80%	420/cu.ft.
LP gas	92,000/gal. or 21,700/lb.	80%	73,600/gal. or 17,360/lb.
Electricity	3412/kwh	100	3412/kwh
Hickory, oak, sugar maple	27–30 million/cord	50%	13.5–15 million/cord
Birch, ash, elm, red maple, paper birch, cherry, Douglas fir	21–27 million/cord	50%	10.5–13.5 million/cord
Eastern white pine	15.8 million/cord	50%	8 million/cord

(Note: Btu output of wood is primarily proportional to the weight of the wood when dry, about 7000 Btu/lb. Data on wood heat output is from Larry Gay, *Heating with Wood* (Charlotte, Vt.: Garden Way Publishing Company, 1974), pp. 38ff. Other data is from the 1975 pamphlet *Styrofoam Brand Insulation Can Improve the Thermal Efficiency of a Wall of Almost Any Design*, Amspec Inc., 1880 Mackensie Drive, Columbus, Ohio 43220.

To find the cost of a particular fuel for the heating system, divide the adjusted Btu output per unit of the fuel into the total Btu needed (Step 4 above). Then multiply the product times the price per unit in your area. In our example, 85,000,000 Btu are needed per heating season. Elm wood puts out about 24,000,000 Btu per cord (a cord is a pile 4′ × 4′ × 8′) but since half of this heat goes up the chimney, the usable product is about 12,000,000 Btu. The annual need divided by the output per cord is

$$\frac{85,000,000}{12,000,000} = 7.1 \text{ cords needed/yr.}$$

At $50 a cord, the annual heating bill would be $355.00.

TABLE 1
R Values for Common Building Materials

Material	r(R/1″)	R
Fiberglass	3.3	
3″		11
6″		19
Foam boards (see ch. 17 for further description)		
Beadboard (expanded styrene, molded beads, 1-lb. density, white color	4.17	
Dow Styrofoam (blue color) 2-lb. density	5.4	
Urethane foam (2 lb. density, greenish yellow color)	6.25– (7.1)	
Plywood		
3/8″		.47
1/2″		.62
3/4″		.93
Sheetrock		
3/8″		.32
1/2″		.45
Sidings		
Shingles (wood)		.87
bevel, drop		.79
vertical T & G boards		1.0
Wood		
Softwood, 3/4″	1.25	.94
Hardwood, 3/4″	.91	.68
Roofing		
Asphalt shingles		.44
Wood shingles		.94
Roll roofing		.15
Insulation board, i.e., Homasote, Bracewall, sound deadening board, etc., ½″ thickness	2.3	1.14
Particle Board		
Low density	1.85	
Medium density	1.06	
High density	.85	
Finish Flooring		
Carpet and fibrous pad		2.08
Carpet and rubber pad		1.23
Cork tile		.28
Vinyl tile, linoleum, etc.		.05
Masonry Materials		
Sand & gravel concrete block		
4″		.71
8″		1.11
12″		1.28
Lightweight block		
4″		1.5
8″		2.0
12″		2.27
Face brick		.44
Common brick		.8
Concrete, oven-dried aggregate		.11
Concrete, aggregate not oven-dried	.08	
Stucco	.20	
Papers		
Felt		.06
Plastic film, used as window		.89
Plastic film, inside wall, roof, or floor		.00
Windows		
Single glass		
Insulating glass, 3/16″ space		1.44
Insulating glass, 1/4″ space		1.55
Insulating glass, 1/2″ space		1.72
Triple pane insulating glass		
Triple 1/4″ space		2.13
Triple 1/2″ space		2.78
Storm window		1.79

Sources of Data: R values differ from source to source. Usually these discrepancies are small. Also it is not always clear what building material a source is referring to, since the technical names of materials are often very different from the names by which materials are generally known. This confusion is particularly true with foam insulations. In each case I have taken ratings from the least ambiguous source. In a few cases I have substituted the common name of the material when the technical name is obscure. Also in a few cases I have combined similar materials under one heading when their ratings vary only slightly (insulation board, for example). The standard source is the *ASHRAE Handbook of Fundamentals* (1972 edition). Some entries are taken from an Amspec, Incorporated, pamphlet (see note, page 234). These entries are often more clear, being intended for people in the trade. Ratings for windows are from *Architectural Graphic Standards* by Ramsey and Sleeper (New York: John Wiley and Sons, 1970 edition), the standard architectural reference work.

The worst confusion concerns the R values of foams, which are sold and listed under a profusion of inconsistent and confusing names and rated with a profusion of different R values. The names listed in my chart are different from those given in technical sources, but they are those used in the insulation business. I have given the R values that are most widely agreed upon — and plausible. Two values are given for urethane foam board and I don't know which is more accurate.

TABLE 2
R Values for Air Spaces

The insulating value of an air space depends on its thickness, the reflectivity of the surfaces creating the air space, and on temperature conditions. The following R values reflect average conditions and are accurate plus or minus about 20 percent. For more precise figures see *ASHRAE Handbook of Fundamentals* (New York: American Society of Heating, Refrigerating, and Airconditioning Engineers, Inc., 1977), from which this table was computed by the author.

	Foil Both Sides of Air Space		Foil One Side of Air Space		No Reflective Surfaces	
	3/4″ Air Space	4″ Air Space	3/4″ Air Space	4″ Air Space	3/4″ Air Space	4″ Air Space
Flat roofs	1.8	2.2	1.6	1.9	.9	1.0
Floors	3.4	.8.1	2.6	4.6	1.2	1.4
45° Sloping roofs	2.2	2.5	1.9	2.1	1.0	1.0
Walls	3.0	2.8	2.4	2.3	1.1	1.1

APPENDIX F
SOUND ISOLATION

Sound can pass through a wall or floor in three ways. First, it can leak under doors or through holes or cracks. Second, sound waves in one room can cause the wall itself to vibrate like a drum, which will generate other sound waves in the next room. This is called *airborne noise*. Third, one side of the wall or floor can be struck directly — as by a footfall — again causing the wall to vibrate and create more sound waves on the other side. This is called *impact noise*.

You can control unwanted sound in your house several ways. The really noisy places can be separated from the quiet places by other rooms. The noise level within a room can be reduced by sound-absorbing surfaces in the room. A tile shower is good for singing in because all the surfaces are hard and smooth, which allows the sound waves to keep bouncing around and reverberating. Soft, uneven, textured surfaces limit reverberation by absorbing sound waves. Rugs, pictures on the wall, furniture, hangings, and textured surfaces all help keep noise down.

Sound can be controlled by eliminating air leaks between rooms. The most soundproof wall construction will be ineffective if doors don't fit right or if sound can find its way through small cracks at the edges of walls. One common leak is back-to-back electrical outlets.

When all these factors have been taken into account, you still may want to make some of the walls or floors in your house more soundproof. The most straightforward way to do this is simply to make the wall or floor heavier so that they are harder to vibrate and therefore less able to transmit sound. You can do this by building masonry walls or floors, but this is expensive. Some of the same results can be achieved by simply locating heavy masses between rooms. In many old houses 2 bedroom walls will often be separated by a space about 2 feet thick. This space will contain a chimney and 2 closets, one opening into each room. This makes good sense, because it increases the mass of the wall without any extra cost, since the closets and chimney are needed anyway. The closets are particularly good if they have good doors and are full of nice, soft, sound-absorbing clothing. The mass of a wall can also be increased by locating bookcases or other heavy objects on or next to it.

When this approach is inappropriate, you can build a regular-size wall or floor to minimize sound transmission without making it very massive. The idea is to construct the wall or floor so that it makes an ineffective drum. A conventional 2 × 4 wall, consisting of studs with sheetrock on either side, is a drum that transmits sound from one side to the other very efficiently. The sheetrock itself is hard and smooth, making a good sounding board, and the studs transfer the sound very well from one side to the other.

A common way to improve this situation is to build a stagger-stud wall, as shown in Figure 358, which eliminates the sound transmission through the studs themselves. This does not solve the problem completely, however, because the air inside the wall can itself transmit the sound between the two layers of sheetrock. One solution is to weave fiberglass insulation between the studs to impede this transfer. This stuffing acts much like clothing in a closet.

With a single row of studs some of the same effect as staggering the studs can be achieved by hanging the sheetrock on resilient clips or channels (Figure 359). These are springy fasteners that hold the sheetrock off the stud slightly, preventing the studs from conducting the sound directly through the wall.

The wall surface itself can be designed to vibrate less. It can be done by increasing its mass or by using thicker sheetrock or more than one layer of sheetrock. But for a similar cost you can get better results by backing the sheetrock with ½-inch sound-deadening board, a soft, light material similar in texture to Homasote, which cushions the connection between the sheetrock and the studs and impedes the sound transmission between the studs. The sheetrock is glued to the sound-deadening board, and the sound-deadening board is nailed to the studs. Otherwise the nails through the sheetrock into the studs will transmit the sound to the stud.

Floors over inhabited rooms have to resist impact noises as well as airborne noise. Here again, massiveness, soft materials, and resilient clips will reduce impact noise considerably, but the most effective protection against impact is to have a rug with a pad under it.

Resistance to airborne noise is indicated by the Sound Transmission Class or STC of a wall or floor:

STC Number	Effectiveness
25	Normal speech can be understood quite easily
35	Loud speech audible but not intelligible
45	Must strain to hear loud speech

STC Number	Effectiveness
48	Some loud speech barely audible
50	Loud speech not audible

Impact noise is indicated by the Impact Noise Rating or INR of a floor (Figure 360). The charts below show STCs and INRs for various constructions. Both the charts and the effectiveness ratings above are from the excellent U.S. government book *Woodframe House Construction*, by L. O. Anderson, a government engineer who has written much of the best material for owner-builders.

Fig. 358   **Sound Transmission Class (STC) for Wall Materials**

WALL DETAIL	DESCRIPTION	STC RATING
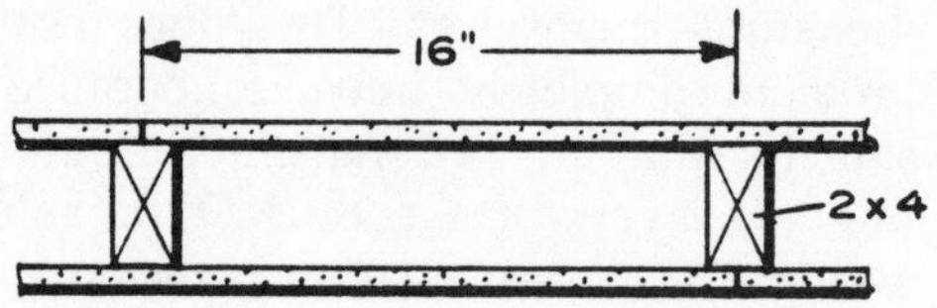 A	½" GYPSUM WALLBOARD	32
	⅝" GYPSUM WALLBOARD	37
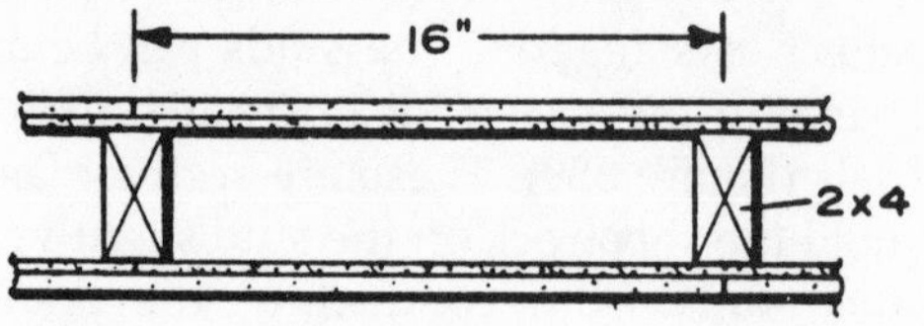 B	⅜" GYPSUM LATH (NAILED) PLUS ½" GYPSUM PLASTER WITH WHITECOAT FINISH (EACH SIDE)	39
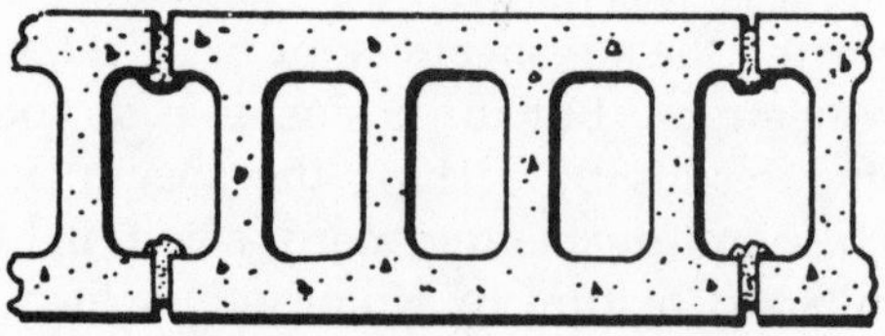 C	8" CONCRETE BLOCK	45
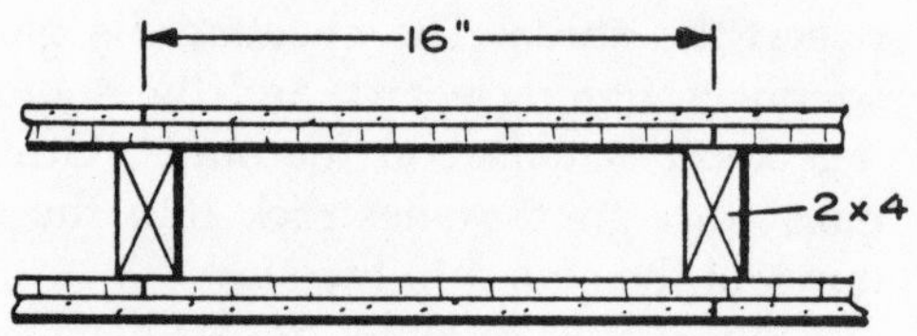 D	½" SOUND DEADENING BOARD (NAILED) ½" GYPSUM WALLBOARD (LAMINATED) (EACH SIDE)	46
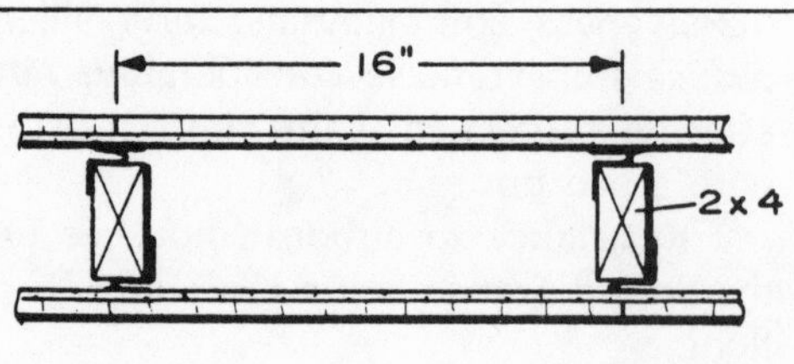 E	RESILIENT CLIPS TO ⅜" GYPSUM BACKER BOARD ½" FIBERBOARD (LAMINATED) (EACH SIDE)	52

Fig. 359   Sound Transmission Class (STC) for Wall Materials

WALL DETAIL	DESCRIPTION	STC RATING
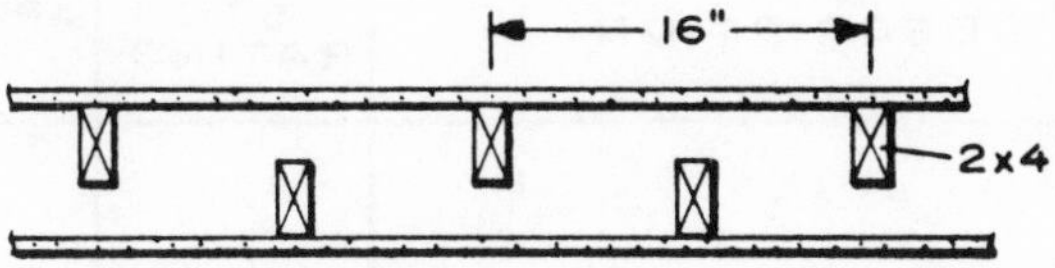 A	½" GYPSUM WALLBOARD	45
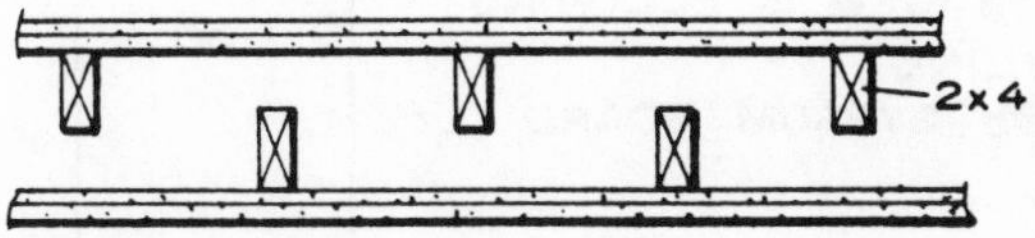 B	⅝" GYPSUM WALLBOARD (DOUBLE LAYER EACH SIDE)	45
 C	½" GYPSUM WALLBOARD 1½" FIBROUS INSULATION	49
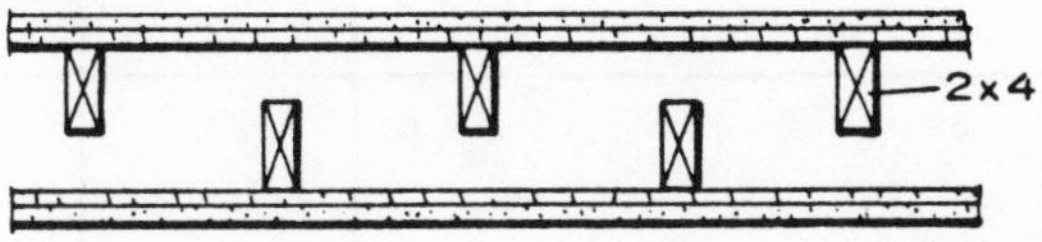 D	½" SOUND DEADENING BOARD (NAILED) ½" GYPSUM WALLBOARD (LAMINATED)	50

Sound Transmission Class (STC) and Impact Noise Rating (INR) for Floor and Ceiling Materials

Fig. 360

DETAIL	DESCRIPTION	ESTIMATED VALUES	
		STC RATING	APPROX. INR

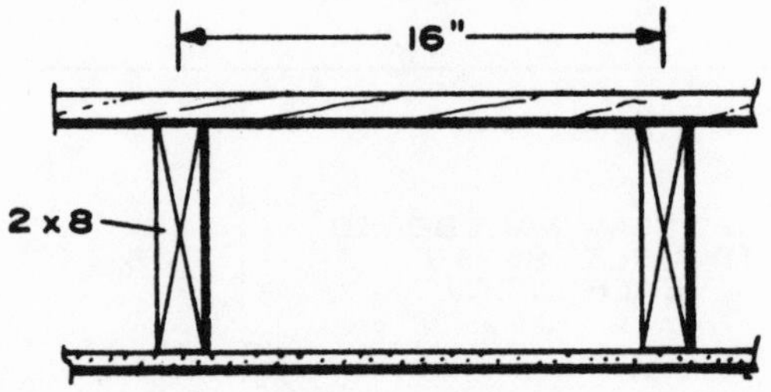 A 16" 2 x 8	FLOOR
	  7/8" T. & G. FLOORING
	CEILING
	  3/8" GYPSUM BOARD
		30	-18

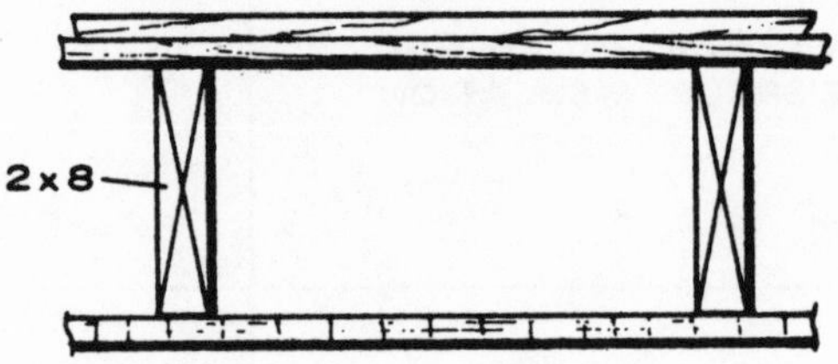 B 2 x 8	FLOOR
	  3/4" SUBFLOOR
	  3/4" FINISH FLOOR
	CEILING
	  3/4" FIBERBOARD
		42	-12

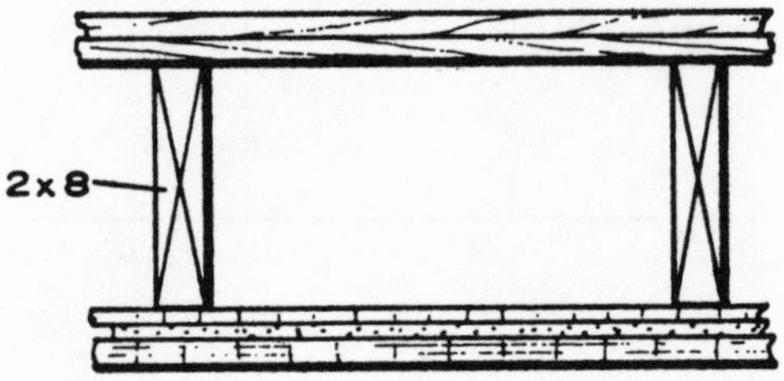 C 2 x 8	FLOOR
	  3/4" SUBFLOOR
	  3/4" FINISH FLOOR
	CEILING
	  1/2" FIBERBOARD LATH
	  1/2" GYPSUM PLASTER
	  3/4" FIBERBOARD
		45	-4

APPENDIX G
WOOD PRESERVING

The microorganisms that make wood rot need continuous moisture and air to thrive. Most of the wood in your house stays dry and will never rot. Wood that gets rained on and then dries thoroughly will not rot either, because it does not stay damp. A log under water will not rot because there is not enough oxygen under water. Similarly, the part of a fencepost or wood foundation post that is underground will only rot very slowly because there is little oxygen even a foot underground.

A post, however, will tend to rot where it enters the ground. Here there will be continuous moisture from the earth, so the post will be unable to dry out thoroughly. There will also be plenty of oxygen because the wood is near the air.

Similar conditions occur commonly in several parts of a building. Unheated or unventilated cellars or crawlspaces often pick up moisture from the earth, and if there is no way for it to escape, the house framing there will eventually rot. Window and door sills tend to rot eventually because, being nearly level, they don't shed water well. Typically, water will leak into cracks around a knothole or into cracks where the sill meets the adjacent frame. Such accumulations will often dry out before rotting starts. But as a building ages, joints inevitably widen, knots loosen in their holes, and, perhaps in a wet season, some rotting will start.

When wood rots, microorganisms actually eat parts of the wood. The wood they don't eat often becomes spongy, and, like a sponge, absorbs and retains water longer than does dry wood. The wood then becomes an ideal home for rot, which gradually spreads.

When a windowsill rots this way, eventually it will be eaten through. Water will leak into the inside of the walls, and the wall framing will start to rot too. This process can be delayed almost indefinitely with good building and maintenance techniques, but it can also happen in a few short years.

Porches and decks — or any framework exposed to rain — will eventually start to rot at the joints in the same way. Old porches will often appear on the outside to be in good shape. A jackknife stuck in the wood may fail to locate any amount of rot. But when the porch is dismantled, the inside of the boards and framework will be totally rotten, particularly where wood has touched wood. Usually by the time a porch (or anything) looks rotten on the outside, there will be almost nothing left of the structure underneath.

When you build a house, you avoid most rot problems by using good building practices — which I have tried to enumerate in this book. These practices reduce to two strategies. First, make the building shed water effectively, make it very easy for the water to flow away. Try to avoid water traps. Second, protect the building where potential traps occur. These will be located particularly where framing is exposed — as in decks — and where materials change. Where windowsills or trim meet siding, or where a roof butts into a wall above it, for example, water can leak in. Where the danger is severe, such as above a window or where a chimney comes through a roof, there will usually be some sort of metal flashing, which laps under the higher surface and over the lower surface to guide water away. Where the potential leak is less, such as between the side trim of a window and the siding, the usual solution is to fit everything carefully to keep water out of the joint, or to caulk the joint, or both.

Decks present a special problem because they provide such an ideal home for rot. Covered porches usually have a tightly fitted floor of tongue and groove boards, pitched away from the house so the rain that blows in flows out again. Open decks should have spaces between the floor planks, so that water can drip between the boards down onto the ground. Still, water can be trapped between the flooring and the supporting joists below. A good protection is to cap each joist before putting in the flooring with a strip of 15-pound felt paper slightly wider than the top of the joist. This acts as a little roof to shed water. Generally, design the deck as much as possible to keep the water out of joists and to help it drip away. This is particularly important where the deck meets the house, because when the deck does rot (as all decks eventually do) you don't want it to take the house with it. Usually the deck can be carefully separated from the house with a flashing.

Even with careful building, some parts of your house should be protected with wood preservative. The house sills, window and door sills, all deck lumber, wood gutters, and all lumber touching or within perhaps a foot of the ground, will need protection. The simplest approach is to use species of lumber containing oils that make them inherently rot resistant. Resistant woods include cedar, redwood, locust, and wetland cypress. In any resistant wood, it is the darker heartwood that is resistant, not the outer sapwood.

You can also buy lumber that has been commercially pressure-treated with wood preservatives. Such lumber is expensive and often hard to get, but pressure treating is very effective and may be worth the money for important members that are highly subject to rot, such as wooden foundation columns.

Usually it is sufficient to treat lumber yourself with commercially available preservatives such as creosote, pentachlorophenol, or copper arsenite (Cuprinol). The usual procedure is to put on rubber gloves and your oldest clothing and simply paint the lumber with several generous coats of preservative, with a few hours between coats. Put on as many coats as you have patience for. Let the lumber dry thoroughly before you handle it to reduce the amount of preservative you get on your skin. Don't get any in your eyes. Always coat lumber after it has been notched, cut, and drilled, but before any pieces are assembled. Give extra coats to the end-grain, notches, and surfaces that will touch other pieces.

Sometimes you can contrive a way to submerge all or part of the wood for a more effective treatment. Do this by sticking one end of the piece at a time in some sort of bucket. For large pieces, make a giant soaking tray by nailing large rectangles of 2 × 4s to your subfloor. Drape some 4 mil plastic over this frame to create a shallow pool. Fill this pool 1 or 2 inches deep with a few gallons of preservative. Soak each piece in this pool for several hours or more, rotating it periodically so that each surface is submerged part of the time. When a group of pieces is done, let them drip for a few minutes above the pool so excess preservative can be recovered and used again. If you do this several days before you actually need the wood, the pieces will be nice and dry when you have to handle them.

These methods will be fine for most purposes. If you are building a pole house or otherwise need to treat a large amount of wood, you can find instructions for making and using an effective homemade preservative in *Low-Cost Pole Building Construction*, by Merrilees and Loveday (see bibliography).

APPENDIX H
BEARING CAPACITY OF SOILS AND BEDROCK

A snowshoe keeps you from sinking into soft snow by distributing your weight over a broad area. Similarly, your foundation must be broad enough to prevent serious settling in the earth. Most foundations widen into footings at the bottom to provide the needed area. Usually the footing size is chosen by rule of thumb. For masonry wall foundations the footing is generally twice as wide as the wall is thick. An 8-inch wall will have a footing 16 inches wide. Usually a one-story house on a column foundation can have 20- or 24-inch-diameter footings under each column, and a two-story house can have 30- to 36-inch diameter footings.

If you want to compute approximately how big in area the footings should be, you can divide the presumed bearing capacity of the soil into the presumed total weight of the building to get the total area of the footings in square feet. If your soil will bear 1000 pounds per square foot, and the house weighs 50,000 pounds, you will need 50 square feet of footing in total. If there are 10 columns supporting the house, each needs a bottom surface area of 5 square feet.

A wooden house with a column foundation weighs about 100 pounds per square foot of living space, including live loads. If you have large masonry masses, such as a fireplace or concrete walls, their weights should be added to the total. Masonry weighs about 150 pounds per cubic foot.

You can find the weight of your house more accurately by adding up its live and dead loads according to the load assumptions in Appendix A. Divide live loads (except heavy storage) by 2, because the maximum live load will never occur throughout an entire house even during a dance.

Building codes have established standards for the bearing capacity of various bedrocks, clays, sands, and gravels. The chart below provides the values in tons/sq.ft. given in the Massachusetts code. Even the poorest bedrock base will support a lot of weight. Usually on bedrock a footing is needed not to provide surface area but simply to make a connection between the foundation column and the rock.

Sands, gravels, and clays (or mixtures of them) also provide good support. For example, a 1000-square-foot house on stiff clay (2 tons capacity per square foot) would need a total footing area of about 25 square feet. If there were 10 columns, each could have footings about 20 inches in diameter.

Building codes do not commit themselves on the bearing capacity of topsoils or soils containing organic material. They leave the question in particular cases up to engineers or building inspectors. However, if a soil is well drained, that is, if it doesn't turn to mud part of the year, you can safely presume its capacity to be 1/2 ton or 1000 pounds per square foot. With a significant proportion of gravel or rock in the soil, the capacity will be higher. You can tell a lot by looking inside the foundation holes you dig. If the soil is dry — and you think it will stay that way — and seems solid at the bottom of the hole, it will provide a good base for your house. If it looks strong, it probably is.

On a site with more than a gentle slope, the footings rigidify the foundation as well as carry the vertical load. On a sloping site the footings should therefore not be too small, even if the ground has a high bearing capacity. If in doubt, get some experienced advice.

Bearing Capacity of Soils and Bedrock

Class of Material	Tons per Square Foot
1. Massive crystalline bedrock, including granite, diorite, gneiss, trap rock, and dolomite (hard limestone)	60
2. Foliated rock, including limestone, schist, and slate in sound condition	40
3. Sedimentary rock, including hard shales, sandstones, and thoroughly cemented conglomerates	20
4. Soft or broken bedrock (excluding shale) and soft limestone	20
5. Compacted, partially cemented gravels, and sand and hardpan overlaying rock	10
6. Gravel, well-graded sand, and gravel mixtures	6
7. Loose gravel, compact coarse sand	4
8. Loose coarse sand and sand and gravel mixtures and compact fine sand (confined)	2
9. Loose medium sand (confined)	1
10. Hard clay	4
11. Medium stiff clay	2
12. Soft clay, soft broken shale	1
13. Compacted granular fill	2–5

Source: Massachusetts Building Code.

APPENDIX I
FROST LINES

The frost line is the depth to which the water in the ground freezes. When water freezes, it expands with tremendous power. Water freezing below your foundation can lift it up or sideways, throwing the whole house out of shape. Therefore, the bottom of your foundation should be below the frost line.

The chart below gives frost lines for different locations. It is taken from *Foundations for Farm Buildings*, Farmers' Bulletin No. 1869, U.S. Dept. of Agriculture, an excellent pamphlet on building foundations correctly. Frost lines may also be specified in local building codes, but there will also be a rule of thumb agreed upon by farmers and builders that may differ from the official one. In Massachusetts the official frost line in the building code is 4 feet, but most builders and many building inspectors use a figure of 3 feet.

These standards are really just rules of thumb or averages. Actual frost penetration will vary greatly. Uncompacted snow is good insulation, so snow-covered ground will often stay completely unfrozen. Where paths have compacted the snow or where it has been plowed away, the frost will penetrate much deeper. In cold climates you can see the evidence of this in summer, because plants that can't take extreme cold — like alfalfa — will be killed off within a few feet of any well-traveled winter path. Wet soil will freeze below the nominal frost line because the water helps conduct the warmth up out of the soil. The drier the soil is, the better it will insulate.

Sometimes a gravelly or sandy soil will drain so effectively that even when freezing temperatures go deep frost heaves will not occur because almost no water remains in the soil to freeze. In general, however, dig below the frost line and choose a well-drained soil.

Suggested depths for placing bottoms of footings
[Figures in column A apply to milder areas; those in B to colder areas]

State	Light buildings		Farmhouse[1]		Heavy permanent barns and storage		Local considerations
	A	B	A	B	A	B	
	Inches	Inches	Inches	Inches	Inches	Inches	
Alabama	12	12	18	18	18	18	Reinforce footings and floor, and use piles in Blackbelt area.
Alaska	48 to 60	60 to 72	48 to 60	60 to 72	48 to 60	60 to 72	In nonpermafrost areas place polystyrene on outside of the foundation walls.
Arizona	12	20	18	36	18	36	Closeness of irrigation a factor.
Arkansas	12	12	16	16	18 to 24	18 to 24	Continuous foundations preferred.
California	6	12 to 18	8 to 12	18 to 24	12	24 to 30	
Colorado	12	18	18	24	18	24	Protect from roof water.
Connecticut	—	(²) 24	—	30 to 48	—	30 to 48	
Delaware	18	24	24	30	30	30	Consult county building code.
Florida	surf	surf	surf	6 to 12	surf	6 to 12	Wide footings near surface; sandy soil.
Georgia	6	12	12 to 18	18	12 to 18	18	Conditions variable; seek local advice.
Idaho	12	18	24	36	36	48	Reinforce in wet cold locations.
Illinois	12	18	24	36	36	48	Reinforcement advised.

State							Notes
Indiana	18 to 24	18 to 24	24 to 36	24 to 36	36	36	
Iowa	18	20	36	42	36	42	
Kansas	24	24	60	60	48	48	Reinforce; heavy footings needed on swelling and shrinking soils.
Kentucky	18 to 24	18 to 24	18 to 24	30	30	30	
Louisiana	2 to 12	2 to 12	2 to 12	2 to 12	2 to 12	2 to 12	Wide footings on alluvial soils.
Maine[3]	48 to 60	60 to 72	48 to 60	60 to 72	48 to 60	60 to 72	
Maryland[4]	—	—	—	—	—	—	Conditions variable; seek local advice.
Massachusetts	24 to 48	24 to 48	24 to 48	24 to 48	24 to 48	24 to 48	Soil conditions fairly uniform.
Michigan	(4) 18	24	36	36	36	36	
Minnesota	12	18	60	60	(5) 18	(6) 36	
Mississippi	9	9	(7)	(7)	(7)	(7)	
Missouri	12	18	18	24	24	30	
Montana	18	18	44	44	30	40	Seek local advice.
Nebraska	12	18	18	24	18	24	Guard against roof water and rooting animals.
Nevada	0 to 6	18	0 to 6	18	12	24	
New Hampshire	36	48	72 to 96	72 to 96	48	72	Greater depth is for masonry.
New Jersey	6 to 8	24 to 30	16	36	(8) 16	(8) 36	
New Mexico	12	(4)	15 to 18	20 to 24	18 to 20	24 to 30	
North Carolina	12	12	12	18 to 24	12	18 to 24	
North Dakota	18	18	—	—	—	—	Reinforce.
Ohio	18	24	36	42	36	42	Do.
Oklahoma	12	18	18	24	24	24	Reinforce masonry for swelling, shrinking and heaving soil.
Oregon[11]	—	—	—	—	—	—	
Pennsylvania	36	—	48 to 72	48 to 72	48	48	
South Carolina	10 to 12	12	14	18	14	18	
South Dakota	18	18	54	54	24	24	For frame buildings use continuous foundations.
Do	42	42	60	60	48	48	For masonry buildings use continuous foundations.
Tennessee	12	12	24	24	24	24	Guard against termites.
Texas	12	20	20	30	30	34	
Vermont	12	12	60	60	60	60	Conditions vary widely; carry to firm soil.
Virginia	24	24	24	24	24	24	
Washington	—	—	—	—	—	—	Conditions variable; seek local advice.
West Virginia	18 to 24	24 to 30	18 to 24	24 to 30	24	30	
Wisconsin	30	42	36	48	(9) 36	(10) 42	
Wyoming	24	30	36	42	36	42.	

[1] Where depth is 48 inches and over, basements are generally used.
[2] For temporary buildings.
[3] Use buttress on outside face of wall or use a footing; less depth is required in gravelly soils:
[4] For snow-protected ground.
[5] Wooden barns.
[6] Masonry barns.
[7] Depth to uniform soil.
[8] Footings for storage structures reinforced.
[9] 48 inches if building is unheated.
[10] 54 inches if building is unheated.
[11] Conditions vary (climate, elevation, soil and soil moisture) seek local advice.

APPENDIX J
SNOW LOADS

Below is a map showing approximate maximum snow loads. Reprinted from *Time-Saver Standards for Architectural Design Data* by John H. Callender. Copyright © 1974 by McGraw-Hill Inc. Used with permission of McGraw-Hill Book Company.

Fig. 361

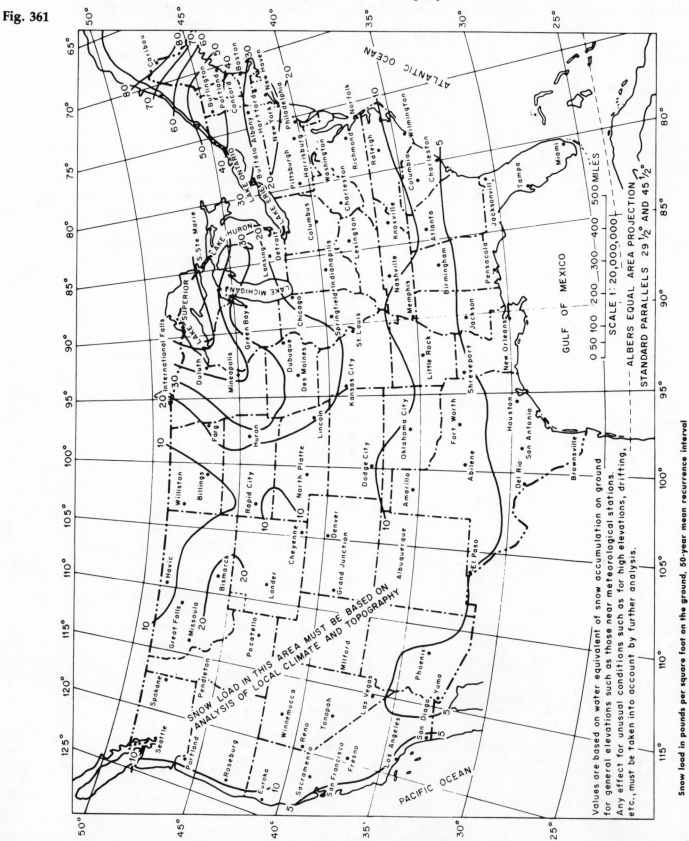

Values are based on water equivalent of snow accumulation on ground for general elevations such as those near meteorological stations. Any effect for unusual conditions such as for high elevations, drifting, etc., must be taken into account by further analysis.

Snow load in pounds per square foot on the ground, 50-year mean recurrence interval

APPENDIX K
WEIGHTS OF VARIOUS MATERIALS

Material	Lbs./cu.ft.
Glass	160
Seasoned Timbers	
Ash	41
Cedar	22
Douglas fir	34
Eastern fir	26
Hemlock	28
Maple	42
Red oak	44
White oak	46
Norway pine	32
Ponderosa pine	28
White pine	25
Yellow pine (long-leaf)	41
Yellow pine (short-leaf)	35
Poplar	30
Redwood	28
Spruce	28
Walnut	38
Liquids	
Water	62.4
Ice	57.2

Material	Lbs./cu.ft.
Snow (fresh)	8
Earths	
Earth	76–115
Sand/gravel	90–120
Concrete	144

Building Materials	Lbs./sq. ft.
Sheetrock, $1/2''$	2
Boards, $3/4''$	2
Boards, $1''$	$2^{1}/_{2}$
Plaster	5–8
Plywood, $3/4''$	2.2
Particle board, $3/4''$	2–3
Asphalt shingles	2
Wood shingles	3
Slate roofing, $3/_{16}''$	7
Slate roofing, $1/4''$	10
Tin roofing	1

Source: *Time-Saver Standards for Architectural Design Data* by John Hancock Callender (New York, McGraw-Hill Book Company, 1974).

APPENDIX L
NAILS AND SCREWS

NAIL LENGTHS

Nail length is indicated by penny size, summarized in the chart below. A 2½-inch nail is an 8 penny nail, abbreviated 8d.

Penny Size	Length	Number of common nails per pound
4d	1½"	316
5d	1¾"	271
6d	2"	181
7d	2¼"	161
8d	2½"	106
10d	3"	69
12d	3¼"	63
16d	3½"	49
20d	4"	31
30d	4½"	24
40d	5"	18

(Source: American Plywood Association Information Sheet X473-873).

NAILS   **Fig. 362**

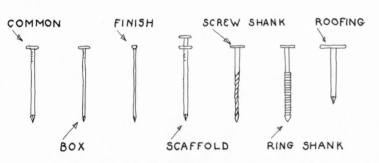

COMMON   FINISH   SCREW SHANK   ROOFING

BOX   SCAFFOLD   RING SHANK

KINDS OF NAILS

The ordinary nail (Figure 362) used for framing and many other tasks is called a *common nail*. Common nails come in all the above sizes. Like most nail types, they are also available galvanized, which means they are coated to prevent rust.

Box nails are like common nails, but with a more slender shank, which is less likely to split the wood but more likely to bend during pounding.

Finish nails are even more slender and have a very small head. They are used primarily on interior finish work where you don't want the head of the nail to show. Often the head will be driven about ⅛ of an inch below the surface with a nail set to make the nail unobtrusive. The ⅛-inch hole can be filled with wood putty to completely cover the nail.

Scaffold nails, also known as duplex nails, are used for scaffolding and other structures you want to be able to dismantle. The second head enables you to extract the nail with minimum damage to the wood.

Threaded nails and ring nails have better holding power than common nails and are often used for flooring, sheathing, and siding. Threaded nails are designed for nailing down boards, and ring nails are designed for nailing down plywood. Sheetrock nails are special ring nails with a blue rust-resistant coating.

Roofing nails are made of copper, aluminum, or galvanized steel, and have extra-large heads.

SCREWS

Figure 363 shows the most common types of screws. Flathead screws are intended to be countersunk flush with the board they hold down. Roundhead screws usually are used with a washer. Both types are available in many thicknesses and lengths, and with both the regular slotted head or the X-shaped Phillips head.

Lag screws are large screws used to carry heavy loads. They are driven with a wrench instead of a screwdriver. I like the hex-head type, which you can turn with an automotive socket wrench.

It is usually necessary to drill a pilot hole for a wood screw, particularly for the larger sizes or

SCREWS

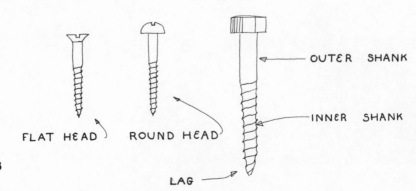

FLAT HEAD   ROUND HEAD

OUTER SHANK

INNER SHANK

LAG

Fig. 363

in harder woods. Regardless of the type of screw, the hole in the first piece the screw goes through should be the size of the outer shank of the screw — so the screw slides right through. The hole in the second piece should be approximately the size of the inner shank, the shank inside the threaded portion of the screw. If you plan to use many screws of the same size, you can buy special pilot bits in corresponding sizes that drill both pilot holes at once. Lubricate the screw with soap or wax before screwing it in.

SHEETROCK SCREWS

Sheetrock, especially on ceilings, is now often screwed rather than nailed in place with special thin-shanked, rust-resistant, self-tapping, Phillips head screws. Self-tapping screws need no pilot holes because the thin shank keeps the wood from splitting. They can be driven with an ordinary Phillips head screwdriver or a spiral ratchet Yankee screwdriver, but the best tool is a $3/8$-inch variable speed, reversing drill with a magnetic screw-driving bit.

Sheetrock screws come in sizes up to 3 inches and can be used to attach wood as well as Sheetrock where nailing is awkward or inconvenient. With a $3/8$-inch drill you can drive a 3-inch screw into a stud in 2 or 3 seconds.

BIBLIOG-RAPHY

SOURCES OF BOOKS AND PAMPHLETS

A U.S. Government Bookstore, if you live near one, is an excellent source of information on all building subjects. A good mail-order source of building and homesteading books is Mother's Bookshelf, P.O. Box 70, Hendersonville, N.C. 28739.

DESIGN

Cole, John N., and Wing, Charles. *From the Ground Up.* New York: Atlantic Monthly Press, 1976. A good book on simple design, influenced by Rex Roberts.

Kern, Ken. *The Owner-Built Home.* New York: Charles Scribner's Sons, 1975. Another classic, with introductory information on a large variety of economical building systems.

Roberts, Rex. *Your Engineered House.* New York: M. Evans and Company, 1964. A classic book on efficient house design, but I don't recommend his system of insulation or ventilation.

ENERGY AND SOLAR HEAT

Anderson, Bruce. *The Solar House Book.* Harrisville, N.H.: Cheshire Books, 1976. Currently the best solar heat book.

Eccli, Eugene, ed.: *Low-Cost, Energy-Efficient Shelter for the Owner and Builder.* Emmaus, Pa.: Rodale Press, Inc., 1976. Excellent overview of energy efficiency.

Leckie, Jim, et al. *Other Homes and Garbage.* San Francisco: Sierra Club Books, 1975. Detailed technical information on solar heating and other energy subjects, but not an easy book to use.

Watson, Donald. *Designing and Building a Solar House.* Charlotte, Vt.: Garden Way Publishing Company, 1977. Also an excellent book.

MAIL-ORDER TOOL COMPANIES

Brookstone Co., 121 Vose Farm Road, Peterborough, N.H. 03458.

Peck Clamp Tool Company, 1170 Broadway, New York, N.Y. 10001.

U.S. General Supply Corporation, 100 General Place, Jericho, N.Y. 11753.

Woodcraft Supply Corp., 313 Montvale Avenue, Woburn, Mass. 01801.

MASONRY AND STONEWORK

Dezettel, Louis M. *Mason's and Builders' Library: Concrete, Block, Tile, Terazzo (Audel's guides).* Indianapolis, Ind.: Howard W. Sams and Co., 1972.

Love, T. W. *Concrete and Masonry.* Craftsman Book Co. of America. The best general masonry book.

Northeastern Region Agricultural Research Service, U.S. Dept. of Agriculture. *Foundations for Farm Buildings (Farmer's Bulletin #1869).* Washington, D.C., 1970. An excellent pamphlet.

Orton, Vrest. *The Forgotten Art of Building a Good Fireplace.* Dublin, N.H.: Yankee, Inc., 1969.

Schewenke, Karl and Sue. *Building Your Own Stone House Using the Easy Slipform Method.* Charlotte, Vt.: Garden Way Publishing Company, 1975. Another good book on the slipform method.

Sunset Books. *How to Plan and Build Fireplaces.* Menlo Park, Cal.: Lane Books, 1975.

Vivian, John. *Building Stone Walls.* Charlotte, Vt.: Garden Way Publishing Company, 1976.

Watson, Lewis and Sharon. *How to Build a Low-Cost House of Stone.* Sweet, Idaho: Stonehouse Publications, 1975. On the slipform or Nearing method of stonework.

MISCELLANEOUS TECHNICAL MATERIAL

American Plywood Association. *Here's the All-Weather Wood Foundation System.* Free from A.P.A., 1119 A St., Tacoma, Washington 98401.

———. *Nailed Plywood and Lumber Beams for Roofs and Garage Door Headers.* Free from A.P.A., 1119 A St., Tacoma, Washington 98401.

Construction with Surface Bonding (Agriculture Information Bulletin #374). U.S. Dept. of Agriculture, Washington, D.C., 1974.

Soil Conservation Service, U.S.D.A. *Soils and Septic Tanks (Agriculture Information Bulletin #349).* Washington, D.C., 1971.

United States Dept. of Agriculture. *Water Supply Sources for the Farmstead and Rural Home (Farmer's Bulletin #2237).* Washington, D.C., 1971.

U.S.D.A. Forest Products Laboratory. *Wood Handbook: Wood as an Engineering Material (Agriculture Handbook #72).* Washington, D.C., 1974.

POST AND BEAM

Ellicott, Stewart, and Walles, Eugenie. *The Timber Framing Book.* York, Me.: Housesmiths Press, 1977. An excellent book on old-time mortise and tenon framing.

Garvey, Helen. *I Built Myself a House.* San Francisco: Shire Press, 1975. A wonderful book.

Merrilees, Doug, and Loveday, Evelyn. *Pole Building Construction.* Charlotte, Vt.: Garden Way Publishing Company, 1975. The basic source on pole buildings.

U.S. Dept. of Agriculture. *Low Cost Homes for Rural America (U.S.D.A. Handbook #364).* Washington, D.C.

THREE GOOD CARPENTRY MANUALS

Anderson, L. O. *Woodframe House Construction (Agriculture Handbook #73)*. U.S. Dept. of Agriculture, Washington, D.C., 1970.

Blackburn, Graham. *Illustrated Housebuilding*. Woodstock, N.Y.: Overlook Press, 1974.

Brown, Dan. *The Housebuilding Book*. New York: McGraw-Hill, 1974.

WIRING

Richter, H. P. *Wiring Simplified*. St. Paul, Minn.: Park Publishing, Inc., 1974. The best on the subject.

WOOD HEAT

Gay, Larry. *The Complete Book of Heating with Wood*. Charlotte, Vt.: Garden Way Publishing Company, 1974.

Vivian, John. *Wood Heat*. Emmaus, Pa.: Rodale Press, Inc., 1976. A very complete book.

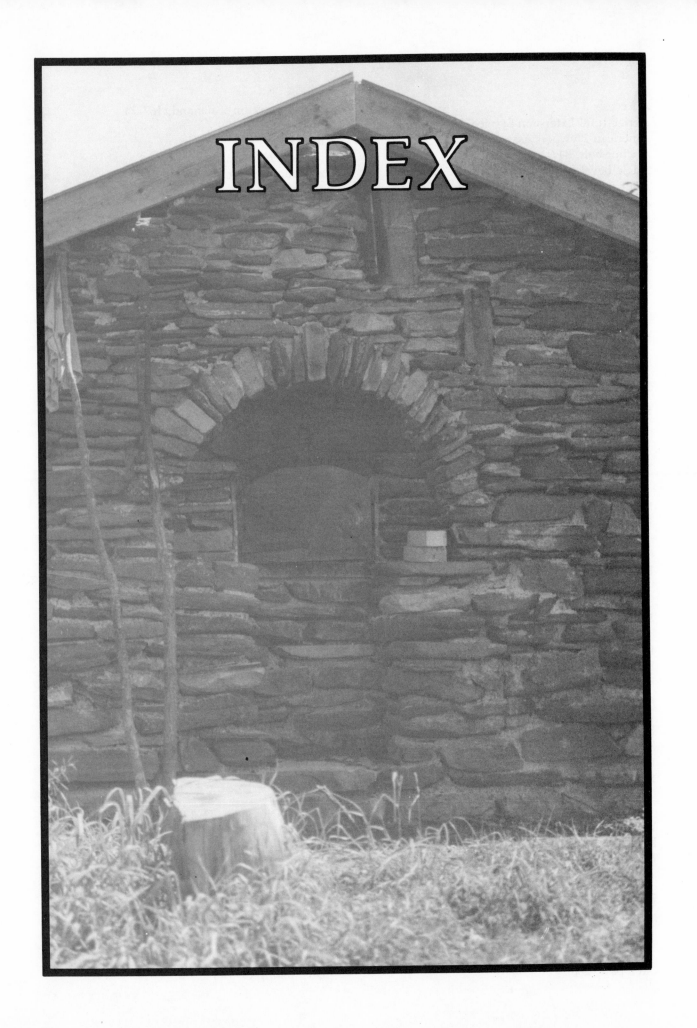

INDEX

Access, 3
Agricultural Extension Service, 5
American Plywood Association, 90
Anchor bolt, 84
Angle bevel, *see* Bevel gauge
Appearance, house, analyzing elevations for, 29
Architect's scale, 15, 22
Architectural Graphic Standards (Ramsey and Sleeper), 235
Ashrae Handbook of Fundamentals, 235
Asphalt shingles, 129, 132–33
Attic
   floor joists, 41
   insulation of, 162
   roof, 115

Bars, 200
Baseboards, finish work on, 177
Basement foundation, 76–78
   block, 87–88
   building of, 86–90
   poured concrete, 87
   stone, 88–89
   treated wood, 90
Battening, defined, 172
Batts, 98
   friction, 98
Beadboard (expanded polystyrene), 163
Beams
   cantilevered, 36–37
   strength of, 210–15
Bearing surface, 42
   defined, 38
Bearing wall or beam, 41, 42
Belt sander, 201
Bevel gauge, 198
Bids, 192
Bird's mouth, 42, 116
Blocking, 94, 98
Bolts, 38
Bracewall, 163
Bracing
   diagonal, 40–41, 107
   exterior, 41
Bricks, strength of, 33
Butt-nail joints, 39
Buttress, 41

Cantilevered beams, 36–37
Carriage
   defined, 182
   dropping, 184–85
Cat's paw, 200

Ceilings
   finish work on walls and, 167–74
   materials for, 179
Chalk line, 199
Chisels, 199
Circulation (traffic patterns), 10–11
   kitchen, 23
   vertical, 28
Clapboard siding, 154
   how to apply, 157–58
Clivus Multrum, 65
Closet location, 22
Collar ties, 39–40
   installation of, between roof rafters, 41, 42, 115
Colonial houses, 67, 70
Column foundation, 76
   building of, 81–86
Columns, 214–15
   safe loads on solid wood, 226
Combination
   square, 198
   stone, 199
Compression, tension and, 32–34
Concrete
   columns, pouring, 85
   foundation walls, poured, 87
   materials, figuring, 91–93
   mixing, 83–84
   pouring, 84
   slab foundation, reinforced, 76, 78
   strength of, 33
Condensation, 163–64
Conventional roof, 122–23
   how to cover, 123–25
Cooling, site conditions for, 55–56
Corner posts, 106
Cost(s)
   design and planning, 190
   estimates, 13, 190–92
   labor, 13, 192–94
   materials, 13, 190–92
   of plumbing, wiring, and heating, 192
   of subcontractors and hired help, 192
   tool, 192
Cross sections
   making schematic, 11–12
   making trial, 24
   See also Elevations

Dado, 200–201
Dead-air spaces, 162
Decks, rot in, 241
Deflection, 213–14
Design
   goals, listing of, 7–8

revision of, 19–21
strategies, 12
testing of, on site, 21
Digging, 82–83
Door(s), 22
  flush, 150
  hanging of, 150–52
    on butt hinges, 152–53
  panel, 150
  trim, finish work on, 174–76
  when to install, 137
Dovetails, 39
Dow Chemical Company, 163, 235
Dowels, 38, 39
Drainage, 3–5
  fields, 64, 65

Elasticity, modulus of (E value), 214, 216
Electric drill, 200
Electricity, 3
Elevations
  analyzing, 28–29
  and cross sections, making schematic, 11–12
  making trial, 24–27
Estimating, estimate, 190
  cost, 190–92
  labor, 192–94
  making preliminary, 12–13
  sample schedule, 194
  See also Cost(s)
Exposed beam roof, 122–23
  how to cover, 125–27

Fastening devices, kinds of, 38–39
Fiberglass, used for insulation, 53, 162–63
  installing, 165
Fiber stress rating (F value), 210, 214, 215, 216
Finish carpentry techniques, 177–79
Finish work, 166–67
  on baseboards, 177
  on flooring, 176–77
  materials list for, 179
  on walls and ceilings, 167–74
  on window and door trim, 174–76
Flashing, 135–36
Floor(s)
  blocking, 94, 98
  building second, 100–103
  finish, 95
  finish work on, 176–77
  headers, 94, 96–97
  how to build, 95–100
  insulation of, 94–95
  joists, 94, 95, 96–97

materials list for, 104, 179
parts of, 94–95
rain cover for, 100
reinforcing blocks, 94
soffit, 95, 98
subfloor, 95, 98–99
vapor barrier, 95, 98
working drawings of, 103
Floor plans
  detailed, making, 21–22
    revising, 22
  schematic, making, 8–11
  trial, making, 18
    evaluating, 18–19
Foam insulation, rigid, 163
Footings, 83
  building, 86–87
Foundations
  basement, *see* Basement foundation
  block, 87–88
  choosing type of, 76–78
  column, *see* Column foundation
  crawlspace, 76
  and drainage, 90
  figuring concrete materials for, 91–93
  how to lay out, 78–81
  poured concrete, 87
  reinforced concrete slab, 76, 78
  stone, 88–89
  treated wood, 90
  types of, 76
  wood versus masonry, 78
  working drawings for, 90–91
Foundations for Farm Buildings (U.S. Dept. of Agriculture), 244
Framing methods, post and beam, 69–72
Frost lines, 244–45
Fuels, efficiency of, 234
  See also Heat

Gable roof, 25, 26, 41, 114–16
  how to lay out steep rafters for, 118–19
  installing rafters for, using ridge board, 121
Gauge
  bevel, 198
  miter, 199
Girder, defined, 95
Glue, 38, 147
Gussets, strengthening joints with, 39, 40

Hammers, 199
Header(s), 105
  cutting of, 96
  installation of, 96–97

Header(s) (cont'd.)
  sizes, 106, 225
Heat
  central, 51
  costs of, 13, 192
  efficiency, 53-54
  electric, 52
  loss, computing, 230-36
    minimizing, 53-54
  solar, 52-53, 54
  space, 51-52
Homasote, 163, 167, 172
Hotbox, 62
How to Use the Stanley Steel Square (L. Perth), 117, 198
Hydraulic ram, 59

Impact Noise Rating (INR) of floors, 238
Infiltration, 53-54, 55, 230
Insulation
  board, 163
  fiberglass, 53, 162-63
    installing, 165
  of floors, 94-95
  importance of, for summer
    cooling, 55
  materials list for, 165
  rigid foam, 163
    installing, 126
  R-values, 235
  thickness of, 162
  and vapor barrier, 95, 98, 163-64
  and venting, 163-64
  window placement and, 53

Jig, plywood cutting, 202-3
Joints
  butt-nail, 39
  strength of, 37-40
Joist(s)
  cutting of, 96
  hangers, 96
  installation of, 96-97
  maximum spans for, 221, 223

Kitchen layout, 23
Kneewall design, studwalls for houses with, 111

Labor estimates, 13, 192-94
Level
  twenty-eight inch, 198
  water, 202

Level cut, 116
Load(s)
  actual, and load assumptions, 211-13
  computations, examples of, 212
  concentrated, 36, 37, 212
  dead, 34, 35, 41-42, 211
  live, 34, 35, 41-42, 211
  safe, on solid wood columns, 226
  snow, 246
  supporting inside, on posts and beams, 111
  uniformly distributed, 36, 37
Low Cost Energy Efficient Shelter (Eugene Eccli, ed.), 56
Low-Cost Pole Building Construction (Merrilees and Loveday), 242
Lumber
  buying native, 47-48
  drying of, 45, 48-50
  framing, 48-49
  grades, 217-18
  planing, 45
  planning and ordering, 48
  pricing of, 45-46
  processing of, 45
  sawing of own, 50
  sources of, 46-47, 50
  used, 50
  yard wood, 46
    sawmill versus, 46-47
  See also Wood

Masonry
  strength of, 33
  versus wood foundation, 78
Materials
  estimates, 13, 190-92
  weights of various, 247
Miter gauge, 199
Moisture vapor, 164
Molding and battens, 172
Mortise and tenon, 38

Nails, 38
  kinds of, 39, 248
  lengths of, 248
Nearing method of stonework, 89
Noise
  airborne, 237
  impact, 237, 238
Notches, how to make, 205-6

Outhouses, 65

Paneling, wood, 172-74
Partition, interior, 110-11
Passageways, measurement of, 22
Pegs, 38
Percolation (perc) tests, 4-5, 65
Planes, 199
Planing, 206-7
Plastic, used for supply and waste lines, 62
Plates, 105
Plumb cut, 116
Plumbing, 65-66
    compactness, 19
    costs, 13, 192
    house, 62-64
    See also Pumps; Sewer system; Waste disposal
        systems; Water system
Plywood, for sheathing and siding, 106-7
    textured, 154, 159-60
Plywood cutting jig, 202
Pole house construction, 72
Porches, rot in, 241
Posts, *see* Columns
Post and beam construction, 67-69, 111
    framing methods, 69-72
Privacy, 9-10
    evaluation of, 18
Pumps
    electric, 60
    jet, 60
    location of, 59
    protection of, 59
    submersible, 60
    sump, 90
    types of, 59-61

Rabbet, defined, 148
Rafter(s)
    installing, 120-21
    laying out and cutting, 116-20
    maximum spans for, 221, 223
    sizes for heavy timber, 222
    square, 117, 198
    units, 115, 120-21
Rake, defined, 124
Reinforced concrete slab foundation, 76, 78
Rife Hydraulic Engine Manufacturing Company,
    59
Rigidity, structural, 40-41
Roof(s)
    angle of, 116
    attic, 115
    conventional, 122-23
        how to cover, 123-25
    design decisions for, 116

drawings for, 127
exposed beam, 122-23
    how to cover, 125-27
frame, covering, 122-27
lines, 24-25
materials list for, 128
pitch of, 116
structure, rigidity of, 41, 42
    types of, 25-26, 114-16
See also Gable roof; Roofing; Shed roof
Roofing
    asphalt shingles, 129, 132-33
    double coverage roll, 129, 131-32
    how to put up, 130-35
    materials list for, 136
    metal, 129, 133-35
    number 1 wood shingles, 129, 135, 136
    roll, 129, 130-31
    types of, 129-30
Rough opening, 105
    sizes, determining, 107
Router, 201

Sander, belt, 201
Saw(s)
    circular, 200
    hand, 198
    how to, 204-5
    radial arm, 201
    saber, 200
    skill, 200
    table, 200-201
Sawhorses, 201-2
Scaffold, how to build, 196-97
Scale drawings
    how to make, 14-17
    of stairs, 181-83
Schedule, sample, 194
Screens, how to build, 147-48
Screws, 38
    sheetrock, 169, 249
    types of, 248-49
Scribes, 199
Scribing, 207
Sears, Roebuck and Co., 192
Septic system, 4-5, 65
Septic tank, 64-65
Sewer system, 64-65
Shading, devices for, 55-56
Shear, 214
    joint in double, 40
    strength of nail joints in, 39
Sheathing, 106, 154
    -siding combinations, 106-7

Shed roof, 25, 114, 115–16
  how to lay out moderate pitch rafters for, 117–18
  how to lay out steep rafters for, 118–19
  installing rafters for, 120
Sheetrock, 167–72
  compound, 167
  screws, 169, 249
Shingle(s)
  asphalt, 129, 132–33
  number 1 wood, 129, 135, 136
  siding, 154, 158–59
Shutters, how to build insulated, 148
Siding, 106, 154
  clapboard, 154, 157–58
  finishing wood, 160
  horizontal board, 156–57
  materials list for, 160–61
  -sheathing combination, 106–7
  shingle, 154, 158–59
  textured plywood, 154, 159–60
  vertical board, 154–56
Sill(s), 82, 85–86
  defined, 76
  location, framing to correct errors in, 97–98
  sizes, 82, 225
Site
  plans, making, 6–7
  qualities to look for in potential house, 2–5
  testing design on, 21
Size, evaluation of, 18
Soffit, floor, 95, 98
Soils and bedrock, bearing capacity of, 243
Solar heat
  collector, 52–53
  passive, 52, 54
Sound isolation, 237–38
Sound Transmission Class (STC) of walls or floors, 237, 238
Springs, development of, as water system, 57
Stair(s), 28, 180
  how to build, 183–86
  landings, 185
  layout of, 181
  location of, 180–81
  materials list for, 187
  scale drawings of, 181–83
  winding, 185–86
Steel square, *see* Rafter square
Stickbuilt construction, 67
Storage, 19
Stories
  number of, 10
  two-story plans, 22–23
Storm windows, *see under* Windows
Strategies, design, 12
Stretcher, defined, 88

Stringer, defined, 182
Structural soundness, evaluating, 41–42
Structure
  rigidity of, 40–41
  strength of joints for, 37–40
  strength of timbers for, 34–37
  and tension and compression, 32–34
  three criteria for strength of, 34
Studs, 105
  jack, 106
Studwall(s)
  building of, 108–10
  constructed in place, 111
  construction, 67, 68, 104
  for houses with kneewall design, 111
  parts of, 105–6
Styrofoam, 163
Subcontractors, bids from, 192
Sump, 90
  pump, 90
Sunlight, 3, 9, 11–12
  evaluation of, 18–19
  gauging elevation of, 28–29
  paths of, 227–28
  and windows, 22
Surface bonding, 88

Tape measure, 199
Tension
  and compression, 32–34
  member, 35
Thermopane, 53
Timber(s)
  calculations, F and E values for, 216–20
  maximum spans for heavy, 224–25
  size calculations, examples of, 213
  strength of, 34–37, 210–15
Time-Saver Standards for Architectural Design Data (John H. Callender), 246
Toe-nailing, 39, 40
Tool(s)
  cost of, 192
  drafting, 14–15
  edge, 199
  hammers, 199
  hand, 198–200
  hand saws, 198
  to make, 201–3
  measuring, 198–99
  miscellaneous, 200
  power, 200–201
  safety, 204
  sharpening, 203–4
  using, 203–7
  See also individual names

Tracing paper, 15, 17
Traffic patterns (circulation), 10-11
    evaluation of, 18
Triangle, 15, 16
Triangulation, 40-41, 115
Trim, window and door, finish work on, 174-76
    materials list for, 179
Truss roof, 115, 116
T-square, 15, 16
Two-story plans, 22-23

Urethane, 123, 163

Vapor barrier
    installing plastic, 165
    insulation and, 95, 98, 163-64
    and venting, 163-64
Ventilation, venting, 55
    vapor barriers and, 163-64
Ventridge, 123-24
Vents, 62, 148
Views, 10
    evaluation of, 19

Wall(s), 42, 105-6
    designing, 106-8
    finish work on ceilings and, 167-74
    framing, variations on, for special situations, 110-11
    materials list for, 113, 179
    working drawings for, 113
Waste disposal systems, alternative, 65
Water, availability of, essential to choice of house site, 2
Water level, 202
Water system
    constant flow and runback, 61
    four parts to, 57
    moving water to the house, 58-61
    sources of, 57-58
    See also Plumbing; Pumps; Sewer system; Waste disposal systems
Weatherstripping, 148-50
Wells, dug and driven, 57
Western Wood Products Association (WWPA), 216, 217-18
    Span Computer of, 214
Wind, 3
Window(s), 137
    casement, 137, 143-45
    double glazing, 137, 147

heat loss and, 137
    hinged, 137, 143-46
    homemade, 137
        materials list for, 153
    hopper, 137, 145-46
    how to make fixed, between studs, 138-41
    placement and insulation, 53
    ready-made, 137
    sash, how to mount, 143-47
    screens, how to build, 147-48
    shutters, how to build insulated, 148
    sliding, 137, 146-47
    south, 55
    storm, 53
        how to build, 148
    sunlight and, 22
    trim, finish work on, 174-76
    types of, 137
    units, how to make, 141-43
    used, 137, 150
    vents in, 148
    weatherstripping of, 148
    when to install, 137
Wiring
    costs, 13, 192
    in floors, 98
Withdrawal, strength of nail joints in, 39
Wood
    air-drying, 49-50
    flooring, finish work on, 176-77
    grain of, 44
    hardwoods, 45
    knots in, 44
    lumber yard, 46
    versus masonry foundation, 78
    paneling, 172-74
    preserving, 241-42
    sawmill, 46
        versus lumber yard wood, 46-47
    shingles, number 1, 129, 135, 136
    shrinkage of, 43-44
    siding, finishing, 160
    softwoods, 45
    strength of, 33-34
    structural defects in, 44-45
    warping of, 44-45
    wavy or angular grain of, 44
    See also Lumber
Woodframe House Construction (L. O. Anderson), 238

Zoning, 3